AMERICAN MOJO:
LOST AND FOUND

AMERICAN MOJO:

LOST AND FOUND

RESTORING OUR MIDDLE CLASS
Before the World Blows By

PETER D. KIERNAN

TURNER

Turner Publishing Company

424 Church Street • Suite 2240
Nashville, Tennessee 37219

445 Park Avenue • 9th Floor
New York, New York 10022

www.turnerpublishing.com

AMERICAN MOJO: LOST AND FOUND
RESTORING OUR MIDDLE CLASS BEFORE THE WORLD BLOWS BY

Book design: Kym Whitley
Cover design: Maddie Cothren
Front Cover Image: © Thinkstock/Stockbyte/Getty Images

Library of Congress Cataloging-in-Publication Data

Kiernan, Peter D.
 American mojo, lost and found : restoring our middle class before the world blows by / Peter D. Kiernan.
pages cm
 ISBN 978-1-63026-923-4 (hardcover : alk. paper)
 1. Middle class--United States. 2. United States--History--1945-
3. United States--Social conditions--1945- 4. United States--Economic conditions--1945- 5. United States--Civilization--1945- I. Title.
HT690.U6K54 2015
305.5'50973--dc23

2015000339

Printed in the United States of America

15 16 17 18 19 0 9 8 7 6 5 4 3 2 1

To Eaddo and our adults Eaddy, Mareill, Lacy, and Peter

We're a chain!

Contents

PART II: FOUND

Acknowledgments

To Eaddo, my warm southern sunshine: Your loving, generous spirit creates the center of gravity of our lives. You are the soul of our family and my reason for being. Your sparkling sense of humor has kept us all laughing through every turn—here's to thirty four more years of laughter, love, and joy.

To our spectacular Eaddy, Mareill, Lacy, and Peter: If our goal was to have our young adults be more interesting than we are, we have succeeded. But our hearts glow warmer at what giving, dear, and decent people you have become. You bring us joy in ways I cannot describe.

To my beloved parents—you are still with me in countless ways, and I miss you so.

To my oh-so-Irish siblings: John, Casey, Greg, Michael, Stephen, and Amy, our annual reunions with spouses, in-laws, outlaws, and children of every variety sustain me like an elixir.

To in-laws Jean, Boo, Garrett, and Ross, and to beautiful C.J., Hayes, and Neely: your love is redolent with the charms of the low country. And to dearly departed Lawson, Eaddy, and Lawson III, we carry on in your name.

For all those twenty-one nieces and nephews and an in-law too—joy in life is being your uncle Pete.

Singling out one of the dedicated faculty who nudged me forward, Ray O'Brien, Mark Ryan, Jim Shea, Jules Viau, John Coffin, Fred Rudolph, C. Ray Smith, Bill Sihler, John Colley, Jack Weber, Alan Beckenstein, Les Grayson, Ralph Biggadike, Sarah Gage, Sam Bodily, and so many more who undertook the task of polishing my rough cuts, should be impossible. But for all their greatness, it isn't. Sheafe Satterthwaite changed the life of a gangly Williams sophomore with the simple question ,"Are you Kiernan—do you know you wrote me a great paper?" My reply, "Really, I didn't mean to," pretty much says it all.

That moment forever altered the direction of my life.

To Ray Kennedy: a gallant newspaper publisher who gave me my first reporting jobs, and Paul Zindell, who taught me the ropes of newspapering.

To T. Lincoln Morison, Thomas Murphy, and Hank Paulson for giving me a shot.

To Ian Jackman: a dedicated and unflinching editor who invested so much energy in pushing me to sharpen and improve this story. I admire your passion for the American middle class and for making me get things right.

To Todd Bottorff, Katherine Rowley, Kelsey Reiman, Caroline Davidson, Lisa Grimenstein and the good people at Turner Publishing for joining in the cause of this powerful story and in getting it told. It's great to be with you again.

To Steve Ross of Abrams Artists Agency, who has been more than an agent: How many would tell a writer to tear up an insufficient draft and start over? Your passion was for telling this important story with grace and authority; your guidance, tough minded and superb.

And a huge thanks to Sandi Mendelson and David Kass of Hilsinger, Mendelson East. You are the definition of a class act and it is a privilege to work with you both.

To Patty Sardinas, Roger Souto, and Charles Petti, and to so many others who keep my life sane.

Thank you from the bottom of my heart. You all contributed to this marathon effort.

INTRODUCTION

"*THE GENIUS OF YOU AMERICANS,*" *Egyptian president Nasser reportedly observed, "is that you never make clear-cut stupid moves, only complicated stupid moves, which makes us wonder at the possibility that there may be something to them we are missing."*

I FIRST BEGAN TO SEE dead people as they truly are when I toiled as a young obituary writer for the *Hudson Register Star,* a daily afternoon broadsheet in upstate New York.

While more experienced reporters chased Watergate stories and their own tunes of glory, I compiled these small daily histories and in the process came to a basic conclusion about life that formed the premise for this book.

Even the grandest sweep of history turns on the role of individuals and their contribution to events of their day. Some folks serve as the point of a spear, others are a structural pivot in a narrative arc, and a sad number are steamrolled by circumstance.

Each person forms a shard of a mosaic, and their individual contributions give a clearer indication of what drives society than a pundit's observation or a plank in a party platform.

In the story you are about to read, individual histories play a vital role in one of the greatest forces ever conceived—the American middle class. Each chapter commences with just such a framing vignette—a story of individual consequence.

This is a chronicle of triumph and achievement, sickness and struggle. It is a tale of a shared quest where high peaks were scaled, momentum faded, and direction was lost.

It is also the story of rebirth and an exciting journey we are about to share. It's your rendezvous with reality—the brilliant prospects we face, together with fresh challenges the world will bring to our door.

It all began long ago, as the biggest conflagration mankind ever imagined was drawing to a close, millions were coming home, and songs of victory rang in our ears.

AMERICANS WAX NOSTALGIC ABOUT THE period after World War II when the matchless engine of economic power—the middle class—was at the zenith of its influence. Settled between the Korean War and Vietnam, the fifties and sixties are recalled as a time of peace and prosperity—an era of picket fences and Thunderbirds, when happy, well-scrubbed families could aspire to and realize the elements of the American dream: a house, a car, health care and education for the family, a comfortable retirement, and the satisfaction of knowing your kids were set up to do even better.

No matter how authentically American it might appear, this modern middle class did not spring organically from the country's soul. It was induced by our collective actions and government interventions when 16 million GIs returned home and the rest of the world's manufacturing facilities were smoldering.

In the days of postwar victory, the United States was more than just a superpower—it was *the* superpower. While the rest of the civilized world foundered in some stage of ruination and despair, all of our mainland cities stood unblemished and our manufacturing might was unscathed. More than that, pushed by the demands of war, U.S. technology was evolving at an incredible pace.

The energized middle class was fed by a harmonic convergence of world events and a nationwide unity of vision. It burst into prominence as veterans returned to a nation where government, bankers, businesses, regulators, and every citizen singularly focused on "Welcome home!" and "How can we lend a hand?"

No one can deny that our citizens rose to the occasion.

But what truly empowered the middle class was the driving force of its ambition and aspiration, an individual refusal to accept the status quo. Americans who had the moxie to beat their personal sword into a plowshare found the world receptive and rewarding. You could tell the men and women who had fought at a hundred paces. And millions of them seized opportunities they found or made for themselves back home. This was American Mojo, and it was manifested in the birth of a new mass middle class.

It was still hard work—the GI Bill was no handout, and the returnees' story of struggle is a stark reminder that a strong middle class is neither a God-given right nor American absolute. It needs to be protected and nourished to prosper, even to survive.

Today's middle class bears little resemblance to the glorious group that grew to prominence in those postwar years. Many Americans still lose themselves in sweet reverie about those days, with very good reason. We can endlessly recall them, but we cannot repeat them. Too much has changed about our nation, our populace, and the world. America has altered in profound ways, yet we haven't made shrewd course corrections. This has been our mojo lost.

FACING THE WORLD

IN TWENTY YEARS THE GLOBAL middle class will be unrecognizable. Why? Because outside our border lies 80 percent of the world's purchasing power, 92 percent of the world's economic growth, and 95 percent of the world's consumers. And they are hungry for change in a way that should be familiar.

Today, dozens of nations have explicit plans to create their own middle-class miracle. A billion more middle-class members should emerge in the next decade. What does that surge mean for the restoration and livelihood of the American middle class?

As we did in the fifties, these countries are short-cutting their way to a dynamic middle class by providing it with conditions to prosper. Meanwhile, we drift along, vaguely concerned that our middle class is shrinking, that wages are sideways at best, and that our population is changing right before our eyes. Together we will explore just how seismic these changes have been.

If we have no plan at all, what does that mean for our prospects?

We still look at middle-class problems myopically—as purely domestic affairs. The year 1955 is dead and gone. This book assumes the missing global perspective ignored by domestic policy ostriches who so often dominate discussion. When it comes to the middle class, all the world's a stage.

Today, we remain an economic behemoth, but the nations of the world are creating their own vision of modernity. The United States has played a major role in building these countries, for both altruistic and economic reasons. They want what we have. Now we face an entirely transformed chessboard, yet our moves haven't changed.

Which raises a central question for policy makers speeding to save the day with their eyes glued to the rearview mirror: Is a vibrant global middle class an endless shining sea of opportunity, or is it an infinity pool where water flows over the edge to be distributed to other parts of the pool?

To answer, we have to examine how the middle class was created, who was swept along by its momentum, and who was left behind. Otherwise, imperfect recollections will prejudice our ability to embrace the enormous change that is coming. We have to peer into the crystal ball of international growth and make tough choices. There simply isn't enough growth at home to sustain our middle class. There is no case for a strong American middle class that does not involve powerful interaction with international trading partners. Yet the exploding markets in the developing world are uncharted and changing very quickly.

Look at a most basic metric—population growth—where the playing field is changing profoundly. Today, the United States ranks third at 320 million people, far behind China and India, who each handily exceed a billion. (China boasts a billion more people than the United States.) That much is common knowledge. But in the last few years, change on the leaderboard has been dramatic and less well known. The next five nations in size are Indonesia, Brazil, Pakistan, Nigeria, and Bangladesh, which range from 250 to 165 million souls with population growth rates exceeding our own—and all with economies growing quickly (most of their GDPs are growing faster than 5 percent, or roughly double ours).

By comparison, France, the United Kingdom, and Italy are all around 60 million and aging. Germany is at 80 million and Russia is at 140 million and shrinking, unless you count annexed countries. Japan's government predicts its population of 127 million will shrink by a third over the next fifty years. These countries face a very different future.

But there is one thing that all these nations have in common—a serious interest in maintaining or growing a strong middle class. What does that mean for us?

The "next five's" metamorphosis gets less spotlight than the massive growth in the top two. India expects to grow by nearly half a billion people by 2050 and their average age is already well below China's and our own. Even more surprising, Pakistan and Nigeria combined are expected to add more people over the same period than currently live in the United States. Bangladesh is tricky; it has the GDP of Utah and a population in extreme poverty that has been only too happy to lead the manufacturing race to the bottom. Even if the country survives the rising oceans, where will it be in twenty years? Brazil and Nigeria are blessed with exceptional mineral wealth and also cursed by extreme poverty. Yet, combined, they approach $3 trillion in GDP. Brazil is already the seventh-largest economy in the world, not long ago surging past the United Kingdom. Are they a competing interest, a collaborator, or both? There is no major American middle class possible without a powerful relationship with these rising tigers.

The psychology of each developing country is in many ways more important than whether they can succeed in creating a vibrant middle class. They are fighting for an articulated national goal—while we blithely drift along. We should expect billions of new members of the world's middle class, with trillions in spending capacity, in a generation, perhaps two. What is our response to so many passionate strategies from so many different countries? Do we even have a plan? Because rest assured, they do.

Facing Ourselves

FOR ANY WHO RECALL THE glory days, it is agony to watch the American middle class battle to keep pace. The American middle is not shrinking because so many are moving upward but rather steadily moving downward. Sideways has become triumph.

There are 45 million poor in America. But just above them are another 50 million who are the hovering poor, just one bit of bad luck or a lost paycheck away from a stint below the poverty line. Perhaps a long stint. Along that seam is where the action is today: real-life chutes that send an astonishing 40 percent of American kids into poverty for some period of their lives with fewer, harder-to-find ladders to make the trip back. Big changes in poverty, the steady entering and leaving of it, represent a new order of social mobility, yet we are using policy and social service weapons that are half a century old.

The middle class is beset by tribulations. Its members have endured a decades-long dry spell of no wage growth. Great jobs they once enjoyed have been replaced by millions of low-paying, entry-level jobs. People are falling out of the middle class, not ascending into it.

Folks are angry because our middle class is running out of options. Washington, state governments, and political parties offer pantomime solutions without results or relief.

Where did we go wrong?

After a couple of decades of expansion, worldwide harmonic alignment and domestic unity that birthed the middle class evaporated. Aspirations that characterized the middle class gradually became unattainable. Too many Americans were never invited to the party, and cracks in the façade began to form. So did our inability to adapt to global developments affecting the middle class.

Comprehending how the middle first blossomed and its undulating path over the last fifty years is a prerequisite for rebuilding the fortunes for people located somewhere between the vast poor and few rich. We also need to understand how different the rich and poor are today from that half century. Both have changed dramatically, and yet we still use tired old saws from generations ago. We need a fresh look at our social compact and new tools with teeth to rejuvenate the middle class.

The business story of our time is only half told, with little focus on what can be done to resolve the disparity. The rich/poor divide is a dish warmed over. It's time for solutions. Facing global middle-class opportunities is the title bout and the rich/poor divide the undercard. The divide is the symptom; a robust and growing middle class is the cure.

It's far too simple to call the United States unequal—we are, and worsening. Take the global view—the world's richest 85 individuals are worth more than the bottom 3.5 billion who inhabit the planet: the top 85 versus half of everybody else. The only way out is found in the middle.

Here's the dilemma.

We have created a $16 trillion colossus—an economy of majesty and of dangerous flaws. We do not manage it to build a broader, more powerful middle class that encompasses the majority. Imagine spending a trillion and a quarter every single month and yet job creation remains anemic; hunger and homelessness achieve all-time highs in lock-step with the record Dow; and the quality of the jobs we are creating steadily declines.

Here is a single great truth of our society:

Capitalism left unchecked is the greatest peacetime concentrator of wealth ever devised. Having a supermajority of wealth held by a tiny few, a vast and diverse poor populace, and dwindling membership in between dooms us to the wrong side of history.

Bringing more people into the middle is the best way to restore American momentum. Inclusion, not exclusion, will propel our nation forward, and this book points to concrete solutions.

So How Did We Get Here?

WE HAVE CONSISTENTLY MADE WRONG choices as we wrestled with the great forces of economics.

As an adolescent, we transformed our economy from tending our flocks and our harvest toward the Machine Age. With painful grinding gears, Industrial Society staggered to prominence bearing the first stirrings of the new middle class.

That fledgling middle class grew up in a very different nation. Once there were but thirty millionaires in the entire country, and most came from a single city. Surely it must have been New York, Boston, Chicago, Philadelphia, or Richmond?

Try the seat of King Cotton: Natchez, Mississippi, a city where Midas might have felt at home, and today they barely have cable. What knocked Natchez from its perch was the crushing of a system deemed unacceptable to the rest of society. Greater good for our citizens trumped individual economics; and an equitable society banished slavery as an economic imperative—even if slaves constituted the bulk of plantation owners' wealth.

A lot of blood was spilled and treasure expended searching for national fairness.

This parable that economic power is fleeting is a theme we will return to again. Few companies survive as long as the people who work there. Today's powers are tomorrow's second-class citizens. How do we as a nation manage that life cycle?

What must last is a strong middle and a system that encourages and supports upward mobility—and a path to meeting those aspirations held by so many. That is the truest measure of a just society—the provision of a genuine chance.

After Reconstruction, the exodus to manufacturing hubs created industrial laborers fanning the flames of middle-class expansion. Brilliant business leaders seized the opportunity.

Henry Ford did the unthinkable. In a single day—January 6, 1914—he doubled the pay of 25,000 employees to $5 a day and cut their workday to eight hours from nine. He was derided as a socialist and a fool who would bankrupt Ford Motors. Instead, 10,000 job applicants surged to his Model T plant outside Detroit. Nicknamed the "Tin Lizzie," the $800 automobile helped crank-start the American middle class.

Where is that vision today?

In the days before income tax we saw the birth of our own working aristocracy. A hundred years of income taxation has funded massive government programs, but it has lost pace with wealth creation. Coping with the growth of today's working aristocracy is another theme we will face often in the coming pages.

The 1950s brought the golden age of the middle class followed by a challenging aftermath. During the 1960s societal upheaval in race relations and the loss of innocence in Vietnam, young Americans lost trust in their parents' middle-class aspirations. Hordes of them dropped out.

Profound changes were sparked at American laboratories where integrated circuits led a third revolution and later a fourth. Each innovation wave brought another surge for the middle, particularly for those willing to develop new skills. But many got left behind.

The 1970s brought inflation and petroleum instability. Filling your tank was a victory. Loss of faith in the dollar by global partners brought a second commodity crisis as gold glittered greater than the greenback.

By the 1980s, the middle class was surfing a sine wave of ups and economic downs—notably the three double-digit uglies of inflation, unemployment, and interest rates. Harsh medicine prescribed by President Reagan and administered by Paul Volcker broke the fever of stagflation, but like any chemotherapy, there were side effects that brought frightening volatility to the financial markets and even greater wealth to the highest earners. Reagan did not seem to mind.

In coming years, each catastrophic loss was followed by a predictable (in hindsight) and often speedy rebound. The well-off watched their holdings reflate while the middle class and the poor sat glumly on the sidelines counting pennies.

The knowledge worker revolution brought new opportunities for the middle. But technological progress always carves out winners and losers. Advances in software, mobility, and access created even more opportunity for skilled workers to prosper. Innovation is a crop we harvested unevenly, leaving some even further behind.

At the same time, industrial America drifted toward balmier weather and regulation. The journey south was prelude. Manufacturing jobs raced toward emerging economies, leaving many American workers in the dust.

Enter the Japanese dragon; then, later, two dynamos, India and China. With accommodating currency strategies, China created 10 million manufacturing jobs as we watched 6 million evaporate, most never to return.

We are signally failing to create the right kind of new jobs—people in authority simply do not know how. Worse still, over 3 million skilled jobs go unfilled. We don't have people trained for them, though at least 15 million Americans want work.

Jobs data has devolved into a weather report . . . with similar predictive accuracy. Worse, the key ingredient—the market value of a job, i.e. what it is worth—is entirely left out. (Can you imagine the New York Stock Exchange reporting only the number of shares that traded every day without saying whether the value of the stocks went up or down?) Meanwhile, business and government circle each other warily like a couple of caged cats.

When the pressures first began to build, home economics forced the middle class to adjust. Out went the traditional one-breadwinner (male) household and in came the dual-income family.

And while no one was watching, America became a matriarchy.

Women flooded the workforce in droves, shattering glass ceilings and fighting for pay parity. Family dynamics changed so that a style, but not necessarily a quality, of life could be maintained. Families changed too. Over 40 percent of U.S. households count a woman as prime provider. Think of it: The time is coming soon when most households will be led by a woman who is sole or lead provider. Where is that development in our policy formulations? Women are poised to drive the next surge in the middle class. We'll explore how.

As these changes were consolidating, we hit the millennium. By 2000, overall inflation was low, but *relevant inflation*—the actual cost of a 1950s-style middle-class life—was climbing. Energy, health care, housing, food, education, automobiles, prescription drugs, old-age care—all saw explosive lift in prices.

Middle-class workers agitated for more wages and benefits and often met with success. But the cost spiral was unrelenting. Despite setbacks, spending continued.

What could these people do?

Suddenly, the miraculous answer appeared. The explosion in housing values created a bridge to fill the gap between zero wage growth and spiking relevant inflation.

Just borrow! Middle-class borrowing on credit cards, home mortgages, home-equity lines, auto and student loans, and life insurance soared. Hocking every asset and monetizing every cash flow led to the land of milk and honey.

In 1957, few Americans had a credit card. By 1967, there were 100 million of them, and by 2007 nearly a billion. Consumer indebtedness peaked in 2008 at $12.68 trillion—that's twelve point six eight thousand billion in old money.

This worked out to $45,000 for every American—which means we were each spending $8,000 a year for interest alone.

Debt fed off relevant inflation like an addict. Soaring housing prices meant leverage could create more leverage. Public servants demanded that home ownership dreams become a wider reality. Mortgage magic worked like a charm. Until it didn't.

Dual-income households became dual-benefit-holder households. Until they weren't.

Companies promised to stay in communities and provide jobs and pensions. Until companies couldn't.

Two raging rivers flowed side by side, intertwining and separating cause from effect.

One, the flow of American genius from agrarian to industrial to information to digital economies; the other, the single-paycheck, GI Bill–benefited middle-class family, to the dual-income family, to the marginally employed/financially crushed household, to the undertrained forty-something male and the working single mom.

Worst of all, forward leaps in social integration were being matched by increasing economic segregation. But once the bottom fell out in 2008, most Americans were too busy bailing their own boat to countenance the diminishing middle class. Everybody groaned at the agonizingly slow recovery.

So Are You or Aren't You?

You've heard the politicians' war cries.

"I will spare no effort to protect the middle class" or, my personal favorite, "My opponent is a traitor to the middle class."

There's just one problem. No one really knows what they are talking about. Or even who. We know there is a worsening middle-class crisis, but we can't agree on who that means—which puts a crimp in anybody's rush to the rescue.

Ask around.

The Census Bureau seems like a place to start, but there's no definition there. Probe the halls of Congress and answers bounce around. Same for economists. Most pick an income range—from as low as $27,000 to over $100,000 for a working couple. Others define it by education—"college grad and above" employed workers. Still others figure by what people spend—as a percentage of income or an absolute amount.

In its best attempt at definition the Census Bureau suggests the following—divide the population into quintiles and lose the bottom and top fifths. (The average earnings in this group in 2010 ranged from just under $29,000 to just under $80,000.)

Census folks also point out that U.S. median income is about $50,000 a year, which begs the question: Just how far does the middle really stretch? (One New York State study holds the indoor record at $300,000 of income for Manhattan residents.)

After exhaustive study the Heritage Foundation found a middle class in the middle 60 percent of earners, and the top 20 percent and bottom 20 percent become the well-to-do and the poor, respectively. Did such a breakthrough really require an exhaustive study?

The top 20 percent in the Heritage model started at $97,000 in 2008 but has drifted down since. On the lower end, the pain of recent years means the spread between high and low quintile is wider than ever. That drift worked out pretty well for the richest Americans. Incomes of the top one percent increased 19.6 percent in 2012 alone, accounting for 19.3 percent of total household income, breaking a 1927 record—while for the bottom 99 percent, incomes grew only one percent.

So the middle got a lot wider and the poor got a lot more company.

MOLECULAR MIDDLE

THIS BOOK WILL PUT A finer point on how today's middle class bears little resemblance to Ozzie and Harriet families in our sepia-tinted rearview mirrors.

Fact is, statisticians and politicians are trying to define a group that really isn't one group at all. Its main characteristic is its fluidity. Individuals and families—the poor and the hovering poor—are constantly falling out of the middle class and trying to claw back in. Things are no less stable at the higher reaches. Many people check in and out of the 5 percent, and even the one percent sees comings and goings. Twenty percent of Americans will be wealthy on some measure in their lifetimes, if only temporarily.

Dynamic swirling means the middle class is not a monolithic chunk of granite that we can slice and dice to make a political point. It's a molecule with a small core and millions of orbiting elements that look different every time we take a snapshot.

It's a mapmaker's nightmare—always shifting shape. To understand the middle, study changes in the poor—the bottom 50 million—as well as the increasing concentration of wealth by the top 3 million, and then the top 3,000. Add to the demographer's brew the fact that Americans over-identify themselves with the middle even when circumstances disqualify them—the middle class is where most Americans want to be.

Just don't look back for your definition.

Today, millions more women attend college than men. One in four children in the United States is Hispanic (by 2019 most American children will be of color), and for a decade, most of our population growth was Latino. (The 2008 economic collapse caused subsequent birth-rate and immigration slowdowns.) Retracing a generation's struggle, the African-American middle class has been decimated to an average net worth in the single-digit thousands. And the white organic majority in America ended in 2013—more non-Hispanic whites died than were born. The new trends are speaking.

Some foreign economists use an interesting statistic: what people spend—which is not a bad idea. But credit's undulating availability adds noise, as does insecurity spending, where folks buy more as a way of keeping score.

Another answer came in January 2010 from an interesting source. At President Obama's insistence, Joe Biden chaired a cabinet-level "Middle-Class Task Force." Aspirational budgeting, where people lay out what they hope to be able to buy, is the truest key to finding the middle class, the Biden committee concluded.

They were on to something important.

In today's global context there simply is no more useful definition. It's an exceedingly complex world out there and what measures precisely at one rate in the United States will be of scant value in the emerging world.

With so many moving pieces, like availability of credit, inflation, wage expansion and contraction, job mobility and outsourcing, the growth of two-career families and single-parent households, immigration and technology and productivity enhancements—income levels are a pretty poor gauge over time.

Defining the middle class by what they aspire to own is more telling than what they earn. Dead center are fifties-style aspirations about a home and a car; a good job; higher education, including college and more; health care for one's family; and maybe the occasional vacation—even into retirement. But there are newer aspirations encompassing inclusion, digital literacy, access and training for the great new business opportunities we are creating.

Biden's group got one more thing right. Relevant inflation was inescapable. Inflation for every single key middle-class aspiration was climbing dramatically higher and faster than the rise of wages. Striving harder and longer would not keep pace. More incomes in the household helped temporarily, but the disparity between aspirational budgets and the real increases in expenses could not be bridged by earnings.

But our middle class is not a construct of Thorstein Veblen or C. Wright Mills or any of the myriad sociologists, economists, and cultural anthropologists who devote endless chapters to trying to define exactly what the middle class is.

The middle class is not a collection of statistics. It is your mother, your brother, or your uncle Joe. It is the gay couple down the street or your kid's gym teacher. It's the guy you say "Hey Marty" to when he insures your car, or the nurse giving you a booster shot where it really hurts. It's a taxi driver or the store manager or the soldier with a stripe or two. It's the salesperson fetching shoes in your size, or a wonderfully skilled technical worker in your IT department.

It may well be you.

Virtually every person who reads this book will at some time have been a member of the middle class, since it comprises the large majority of our citizenry. For others it remains an aspiration. The middle class is as core to our national being as our DNA—it courses through so many family histories like the blood in our veins.

Just as our society, our economy, and our lives have changed, our middle class has changed too. But it needs to disarrange, not simply adjust course. Change will be hard, because we are five decades into this behavior pattern. And the world outside our borders is changing even faster than we are. They want what we've got. What worked in the industrial age—4 percent unemployment and one-career households—is a charming relic that we can endlessly appreciate but we cannot endlessly repeat.

We need greater justice in the treatment of working men and women and their families. The middle class, as our majority, does more of the bill paying and the sleepless tossing over job worry and mortgage payments than anyone else. The middle class are law abiders and community builders, and no one is more central to keeping things balanced.

We need the kind of just society where aristocracy of merit and hard work trumps birth and entitlement. It is high time the one percent became a bigger part of the solution beyond tax avoidance and carried interest. It's time for the arrogance of wealth to be replaced by greater common concern. There is a leadership role that everyone in the point one percent and the one percent must exhibit with far greater vigor. Disproportionate gain brings similarly lopsided responsibility to improve the lot of those less fortunate and to level the playing field. We must also ask sacrifice of the next wealthiest—the 5 percent, the 10 percent, the 15 percent.

The solution will not be found solely in confiscatory taxation, but in redistribution of opportunity; not affirmative action for one race or another, but in affirmative action for the poor. Any thoughtful approach requires elevating the poor in all of their extraordinary number into the class of working families that can pay their own way.

You can't make a powerful middle class without the key ingredient of inclusion.

There have been rich and poor since time immemorial. Few rich and many poor are history's absolutes. Not so the middle class. The middle class is a modern creation that brings balance, stability, and reliability to all that is great in our culture.

The story of the middle class is a journey spanning many generations. In ways I hope to show you here, we have all traveled it together.

The decline of the middle class cannot be stopped by the right or left alone. Neither has sufficient dogma or determination. Neither possesses the perfect crystal ball to predict how the nations of the world will respond. Their self-determination will be bound up in our own. Yet Washington cannot seem to develop a trade and relationship strategy for these nations. The United States is no longer the only game in town. Countries can build a robust middle class with little help from the USA.

In a very real way, our middle class needs them more than their middle class needs us. Which leaves us with a fundamental choice.

Either we redistribute opportunity or we will redistribute poverty.

This book is an unabashed love story about struggle, triumph, and moments of despair. It venerates the middle class in a way very different from what has been done before. It traces history through the consequential actions and experiences of real individuals, not demographers' digits. And it points the way forward through the risks and opportunities in the juiced-up world of global middle-class effervescence. It also uncovers the essential ingredient for making things great again. We possess every virtue necessary to rejuvenate and create the middle class our society needs. The point of this book is that American Mojo has already been found . . . and all that remains is for you to harness its power.

WE OPEN THE STORY NOT at the beginning, when all was backlit with momentum and joy, but instead at the beginning of the end, when we were looking the other way, overconfident and unaware, when all of the trouble really started and our newfound fears were given a face.

Like so many stories close to home, it begins far away in a place you'd least expect.

AMERICAN MOJO:
LOST AND FOUND

PART ONE

Lost

CHAPTER ONE

———— Paradise Lost ————

Misplacing America's middle class—the beginning

The group leader bit his lower *lip in a nervous tell. At twenty-six his look was lean and cocky, intense but unworried. He was coiled like an athlete, and ready.*

Yuletide in old Vienna swirled. On every corner Christmas markets charmed visitors with warm gingerbread, roasted almonds, sweet chestnuts, and liters of Gluhwein. On this Sunday morning the spirit of the holidays flurried on the growing crowds, and Christmas melodies filled the air.

Vienna has always been an elegant city, ruled for centuries by the mighty Hapsburgs from not one but two palaces. The Schonbrunn on the edge of town was their summer escape. Even busy Hapsburgs need a getaway. And the glorious Hofburg dominates the town center. No place on earth looks more delightful in snow.

The tempo of the season ruled so much of the energy in Vienna that morning; almost everybody was dreaming of a place where they would be in just a few days. It was the best part of Christmas: anticipation.

Anton Tichler had recently turned sixty, and he was starting his last shift on duty before vacation and, shortly thereafter, retirement. He spent the morning chatting amiably with folks in the office and found his mind wandering to the trip to Switzerland that he and his wife had planned.

Tichler was a security guard in a charmless seven-story office building that housed tenants like Texaco, the Canadian Embassy, and the Organization of Petroleum Exporting Countries—better known as OPEC—which was holding a three-day price and production conference. This was the final session.

It was Sunday, December 21, 1975, and as was OPEC custom, it was an hour past the scheduled start of the meeting when order was finally called. Eleven of the thirteen OPEC oil ministers were present, plus some staffers, aides, and bodyguards. Inside the crowded room there was near-complete indifference to the surrounding holiday cheer.

Among those assembled were leaders like the Saudi oil minister Ahmed Zaki Yamana and the Iranian minister Jamshid Amuzgar, who was also reportedly head of the Iranian secret police. In the last two years this group had been dictating terms to some sovereign oil-importing countries that were pretty unaccustomed to taking orders. Most smarted at the impertinence of the new rules. The whole world pecking order was shifting like the desert sands.

Tichler was joined in the lobby by Josef Janda, another plainclothes police officer. Both wore holstered Walther automatics, but they gave little thought to their weaponry. Anchoring the small ante-room was a twenty-something receptionist named Edith Heller, who may have been dragging a bit from a night of holiday cheer.

Snow had fallen and was melting into a wet slush. A damp chill blew in the first-floor entry when the leader, four men, and one woman breezed into the main lobby. The leader paused briefly to chat at the front desk while the rest of the team, carrying sport bags, made a beeline for the stairway door.

Unusually, the door was unlocked, and without a word the team quickly took to the stairs. It was just after 11:30 a.m. and a whole new season had just begun.

Tichler's shift was less than an hour from conclusion. As was his routine, he went to the hallway to check the elevator. The delegates had just sent a staffer for more coffee.

In the narrow passageway, a scuffle ensued and the woman, a dark-haired beauty, posed a single question to Tichler: "Are you a policeman?"

As quickly as he responded "Yes," Gabriele Tiedemann pumped two rounds into his skull.

Then she posed the dying man in a spread-eagle position in the elevator and sent it to the ground floor. Tichler would not live to make the short trip to the lobby, much less to a holiday drive with his wife.

Terrified, the groggy young receptionist, Heller, dialed the wrong number trying to reach police to sound the alarm. Hans Joachim Klein aimed his gun at her head but instead shot the phone as she lamely begged into the deceased receiver for help.

Suddenly, a lone Iraqi bodyguard gallantly took Tiedemann by surprise, wresting the machine gun from her in a writhing death match. He lost the struggle when she drew a handgun from her belt and fired a shot that ricocheted into his brain. The woman's nom de guerre was Nada and she had already killed two that morning. Bafflingly, an undrawn handgun was holstered at the Iraqi bodyguard's side. Why hadn't he used it when he jumped her from behind? His chivalry died with him.

Only moments before the terrorist leader had killed too, gunning down the chief Libyan statistician in cold blood, an interesting statistic in itself because it was Libya that reportedly supplied the group with its weapons cache.

Grabbing the remaining security guard, Janda, by the neck with one arm, the terrorist leader proceeded down the hall toward the conference room, spraying bullets at the ceiling from his semi-automatic, leaving the passage shrouded in dusty darkness. Everything he did was designed to terrify the oil ministers.

He was succeeding.

The terrorist leader then dumped Janda in another office, fully expecting him to sound an alarm; he entered the conference room with a swagger and coolly introduced himself to his captives. "I am Carlos. Perhaps you have heard of me."

As Carlos had expected, Janda phoned the Einsatz Commando unit of the Austrian police. The clock read 11:44. It had taken just fourteen minutes for Carlos the Jackal and a cohort of Baader Meinhoff terrorists to capture eleven OPEC oil ministers and as many as sixty other hostages. Three lay dead, and one captor was seriously wounded in an exchange of fire with Austrian policemen.

Yuletide instantly vanished.

Carlos, of course, had a list of demands. The Austrian prime minister,

Bruno Kreisky, was summoned to Vienna by helicopter, the Federal Cabinet
called an emergency session, and five hundred Austrian police surrounded
the perimeter.

Carlos demanded a plane to Algiers and safe passage to the airport
at 7 a.m. sharp the following day, and further, that Austrian broadcast-
ers read a statement about the Palestinian plight every two hours. If his
bidding was not done, a hostage would be killed every fifteen minutes. He
picked out the most comely assistant and dictated his rant to be broadcast
as she nervously typed.

Then he settled in for a long night.

Everything was going according to plan.

NEVER BEFORE OR SINCE HAD so many powerful politicians
from so many countries fallen into the hands of a terrorist commando.
Imagine the tributaries flowing together into the Danube that day. It was
like hell's runoff: German and Arab terrorists—militants like the Popular
Front for the Liberation of Palestine (PFLP) and Baader Meinhoff . . . and
a publicity-seeking antagonist with severe delusions of grandeur.

Into this strange amalgamation one might insert a couple of questions:

Why were these guerrillas attacking OPEC? And were they intending
with the expected worldwide reaction to send a message somewhere else
entirely? Think for a moment about how it is possible that the River Danube might flow all the way to American shores.

Because if you take a moment to peel the onion and look inside the
actions of that holiday attack, they lead directly to our door.

Middle-class America had been thriving, surging since the Second
World War, and prospering because the rest of the world's manufacturing
capacity had been reduced to rubble. These were heady times for American strivers in the middle. It was oil that changed the growth dynamic. In
a generation, the United States went from energy independence to rely-
ing ever more on offshore oil sources, requiring more than a third of the
world's oil production to slake our thirst.

For all our strengths as a nation, we have never spent enough time assessing the consequences of our actions overseas, or the grievances we may have caused, especially when it comes to the economic behavior of our government and major corporations. We tend to see ourselves as how we hope to be: the world's policeman and superpower good guy.

But our actions, covert and otherwise, can have a very long tail.

In 1953, the CIA and the British SIS helped overthrow the democratically elected prime minister of Iran, Mohammad Mosaddegh, who had nationalized the Anglo-American Oil Company (AIOC). Thus did Iran fall under the direct rule of the Shah Mohammad Reza Pahlavi and his secret police force, Savak, until the 1979 Iranian Revolution a generation later. The Iranian people's reaction to the United States many years afterward needs to be seen in the light of the events of 1953. So, too, for this Sunday-morning attack.

A search for perfection in American foreign policy will yield few results in the oil-rich Middle East. Foreign-policy moves like those in Iran and Israel, and geo-economic maneuvering by major oil companies with their Middle Eastern counterparties, had lasting effects and sometimes elicited undesirable responses and unintended consequences.

It's never easy being the keeper of world order. Playing the role of economic and military superpower involves making tough choices and forging relationships that may not cast us in the same light in which we see ourselves. These choices have lasting impact on our nation and our economy . . . and, yes, on our middle class.

Consider the array of forces beneath the surface as we follow the action of this erstwhile super-terrorist. In the story that unfolds are some of the keys to middle-class decline in the United States.

Let's start with the terrorists themselves, and then move to OPEC. If we watch closely how they maneuvered, and make the connection to anxieties we faced at home, the importance of this awful Sunday morning to America's middle class will become clear.

The PFLP is the second-largest group of the Palestine Liberation Organization (PLO) after the much more widely known Fatah. Founded in 1967, the PFLP has been an increasingly hard-line defender of Palestinian nationalism. After merging with the PLO in the late sixties, the group's venomous and balding leader, Wadi Haddad, and his henchmen fired their opening salvo in international terror—the successful hijacking in 1968 of El Al Flight 426 from Rome to Tel Aviv.

Haddad demanded release of imprisoned Palestinians. After a month of negotiations, uncharacteristically, the Israelis blinked.

Subsequently, the PFLP found alignment with Baader Meinhoff and funding from the KGB.

Baader Meinhoff began as an urban guerrilla gang not long after the Second World War and evolved by 1970 into the Red Army Faction. One of Nazism's haunting legacies was the wedge it hammered between generations. Post-war German youth were naturally suspicious of any authoritarian rule and many anti-establishment organisms flourished.

Andreas Baader and his girlfriend, Gudrun Ensslin, the daughter of an evangelical pastor and a former Girl Scout, firebombed a Frankfurt department store in 1968 in a vague Vietnam War protest that only managed to maim a few mannequins. It is interesting to note that Germany played no role in our Vietnam War. But the bombers hoped their message would travel.

Thus began a life on the run with left turns through numerous European havens leading to an ultimate furtive return to West Germany. Picked up for speeding by a traffic cop, Baader was sent to prison for his crimes against store fixtures.

But a flame had been set to a fuse.

Ulrike Meinhoff was a German journalist who found ignominy and fame both by her writing and by helping Andreas Baader plan and execute a prison escape in 1970. Baader had a penchant for stealing sports cars and was arrested again in a sleek little number that landed him in Stuttgart's Stammheim Prison in 1972. But the gang's dirty work continued.

As the snow fell that Sunday evening in Vienna, questions flowed: How had these German and Arab groups found one another in the worldwide winter of discontent? Who funded the operation? What was their true mission? And who was Carlos? Why was security so lax? Was this part of an OPEC snit between members, or something much broader? Could this have been a backhanded swipe at the United States? How could five people possibly have pulled this off?

As is so often the case in matters of global terror, we now know 100 percent of half the answers.

Carlos is a reasonable place to begin the inquiry—he'd like that. He was the first son of a wealthy Venezuelan lawyer who named his three boys for his idol, Vladimir Ilich Lenin. Ilich Ramirez Sanchez was schooled by his father in Communist doctrine and "Carlos" was baptized in secret by his mother in her Catholic faith. As a boy he embraced the Venezuelan Communist Youth, preferring their unique and violent demonstrations to his mother's ministrations. Sanchez was mentored by Cubans at an early age, and later the KGB sent him to the Middle East for terrorist training.

This "millionaire Marxist" was driven to be something more—to be the modern age's first super-terrorist, who cultivated with undisguised elation the nom de guerre "Carlos the Jackal," taken from the Frederick Forsyth novel found in a police search of his lair.

He languished at Moscow's Patrice Lumumba University, where he bonded with Palestinian students who spoke glowingly of the PFLP and its rebel leader Wadi Haddad. Their singular mission was to commit acts of violence against the Israelis, their allies, and anyone who thwarted the return of Palestine to its people.

Later, the new recruit Carlos was stationed in London. There he quickly reverted to his playboy mode, favoring ladies and fine wine. He prepared for the assault on OPEC headquarters from a villa in Beirut; then, shortly before the big event, he billeted at the tony Vienna Hilton, where plans were refined over equally refined meals at Vienna's finest nighteries. This terrorist had champagne tastes.

Events in the ensuing days did little to clarify who was behind the abduction. Many speculated that Libyans provided weaponry for the assault and managed the inside of the process (such as ensuring somehow that a perennially locked door was kept open at precisely the convenient moment). But how did that square with the assassination of an unarmed Libyan statistician?

Others claimed the attack was caused by Saddam Hussein agitating for higher oil production for Iraq. Debate would rage for years, because little about this effort was as it seemed. Even the Israeli Mossad was later blamed—by no less an authority than Carlos himself.

The drama continued to unfold in Vienna . . .

Carlos's demeanor swerved between controlling and magnanimous. At dawn, a curtained yellow bus arrived at the office building, and Carlos was suddenly inspired to free most of the Austrian hostages. Carlos stood at the bus door like a prom chaperone and made a great show of shaking hands with and embracing those to be left behind. The charismatic terrorist fawned for the cameras. Some thirty-five hostages remained in his clutches, including his two crown jewels, the Saudi and Iranian ministers.

A fueled DC 9 was waiting, just as was demanded. Chancellor Bruno Kreisky said, "More proof of his will to kill was not necessary for me." Many second-guessed the Austrian leader.

Soon after takeoff, Carlos paraded the aisles like a conquering hero, offering autographs to his captives. The Jackal directed the volunteer pilots to land first at Algiers Airport. Algeria was an OPEC nation, yet when the plane taxied to the terminal bearing captive OPEC ministers, Carlos was warmly greeted by the Algerian foreign minister. Not exactly a pledge of allegiance to the cartel.

After a brief sojourn in the airport VIP lounge, Carlos agreed to release all non-Arab delegates and officials. With both his airplane and his ego refueled, Carlos and his remaining OPEC hostages winged their way to Tripoli, the capital city of another OPEC nation, Libya.

Nothing in Tripoli went as expected.

Perhaps it was the cold-blooded murder of the Libyan attaché back in Vienna, perhaps Libya preferred to remain clandestine on the world stage even if they supplied weapons and support, maybe all Libya really wanted was an end to the dominance of Saudi Arabia and Iran over OPEC proceedings, or maybe Khadafy needed to be the biggest, baddest terrorist on the planet and didn't like to be upstaged.

It is hard to gauge precisely why, but the Libyans had a simple requirement for the young terrorist—release your Libyan hostages or prepare to meet your virgins.

There was no VIP reception for the Jackal.

Carlos had other plans than a trip to the hereafter, so the Libyans and some others were released. Carlos and the remaining hostages, including his crown jewels, were asked to leave. Refueled and chagrined,

Carlos limped toward Tunisia longing for a better reception. This was shaping up to be the victory tour from hell.

Things got worse. As they approached in the gloom of desert night, Tunisian authorities refused to acknowledge the plane, denying it access. When Carlos insisted on commencing his landing process, the runway lights were extinguished. It was simply too dark to risk it. Scratch Tunisia from the itinerary. Some hostages are just too hot.

There was nothing to do but seek asylum.

Back in Algiers in the wee hours, Carlos had an epiphany—he would trade his crown jewels for dollars and beat a hasty retreat. In days the Iranian and Saudi leaders were freed and Carlos made his escape in a peloton of limousines. Speculation was that Carlos was set for life in the transaction, but his terrorist accomplices were outraged.

His task had been to kill his crown jewels, not to ransom them.

In short order, Carlos would be expelled from the PFLP. Wadi Haddad, his mentor and sponsor, reportedly handled the dismissal himself.

OPEC wins again.

Or did it?

From the Outside Looking In

"ONE MAN IN HIS TIME plays many parts," Shakespeare suggests in *As You Like It*. Carlos's dark play made the bard guilty of understatement.

OPEC members played every imaginable role in this sad caper: victims, captives, harborers, planners, supporters, armorers, protectors, rejecters, financiers, negotiators, ransom payers, and ultimately the world's whipping boy.

Never has the world stage seen such a one-man performance. OPEC's ministers were themselves so stunned and ultimately mistrustful that they would not all gather in the same place for another twenty-five years. Worst of all, the world had little compassion. OPEC was hardly a sympathetic defendant.

OPEC was a virtual unknown when, just two years before, in October 1973, they launched the oil embargo. Back then, everyone was convinced that OPEC was not just the sworn enemy of America, and especially of its middle class, but the cause of all our problems. The United States had many responses to the arching of OPEC, but chief among them was paying them whatever they asked.

The image of the oil sheikhs throwing a magic lever in the middle of the desert, shutting the spigot, played out amid Western outrage. But the truth is we missed the whole point. We have never been self-aware enough to sense the ache of historical grievance in others.

Many Americans still believe the OPEC embargo was the moment that the hammer hit: The end of cheap oil meant the beginning of the end of the golden age of our middle class. The trouble, of course, with branding OPEC as the whipping boy is that the lamely constructed consortium gets a lot more credit than it deserves. Cartels rarely hold their form for long even if oil and money are the chief attractions. Inevitably someone always calls the other guys ugly, and the glue evaporates.

But OPEC was convenient in one respect.

We were and are so quick to point the finger at someone else. But history suggests we should look inward at choices we made in the face of not one but two commodity crises. Middle America had spent the prior twenty-five years growing and spending exponentially. Everything was straining to the breaking point.

If we explore the nature of things in American society at the very same time, we might well conclude that OPEC was certainly at fault, but also that blame lies elsewhere. It always did. OPEC was more than a mirage, but in a great many ways we set our middle class up to fail. Frankly, all of the above played a part—but the victim in the case was the American middle class. It's time you knew the whole story.

It began in earnest when millions of American men and women put down their arms and began the long trip home to our collective warm embrace.

CHAPTER TWO

The Invasion

A postwar middle-class miracle

HIGH BLEACHED GRASSES TUMBLED EVERYWHERE *on the sixty-thousand-acre Long Island prairie—the largest east of Kansas. Three powerful air masses battled for climatic control of the vast expanse. They still do.*

Frequent planetary atmospherics send cold, dry air from the continental interior down from the Arctic and Hudson Bay. Prevailing southern winds transport warm, humid air up from the subtropical Mexican gulf. The third cameo player, a subordinate maritime influence, struggles for importance and colors the climate with inland North Atlantic flows, producing cloudy and bone-chillingly damp conditions. Cold in the winter, beastly hot in the summer.

Nearly every major storm system along the Eastern Seaboard and every frontal system moving eastward across the continent passes through the landscape.

It is a rugged Yankee ecosystem that has held itself intact no matter the onslaught. Whatever survives there is tenacious.

For generations, hardy German immigrants bent low to the task of clearing the chest-high brush of the eastern prairie to carve out sustenance growing cucumbers and cabbage, at least until a blight turned their eyes to the horizon and to dreams of another cash crop—potatoes.

For another twenty-five years farmers produced potatoes with little or no rotation until one cropper noticed his vines had become discolored and their production timid. Still, it's no surprise his country farm bureau took no particular notice despite repeated requests—the prairie was bountiful.

But with the passage of another five years the farmer's production had slumped 70 percent and examination was more than overdue.

The investigation uncovered a haunting discovery to anyone of German, Irish, or Scottish descent—all agronomies with potatoes as a major source of food energy. Affixed to the roots throughout his forty-acre field were swollen golden nematodes—a resourceful and resilient insect with a penchant for destroying entire crops. It protects its eggs in pinhead-sized cysts holding 500 larvae.

Since many renters on the prairie reused burlap bags and shared farm equipment, the die was cast, and continued testing found thirty more farms so afflicted. In time new nematode-resistant potato varieties would be developed—but the pesky insect cast a very long shadow.

By 1946, potato production peaked on Long Island at over 62,000 acres. It would drop by over a thousand acres per annum in each of the next twenty-five years.

It was at this turning point that two brothers stood at the edge of the vast expanse with an entirely new vision. They borrowed heavily and purchased 4,000 acres from all-too-willing, soon-to-be-former, potato farmers.

AT THE VERY MOMENT WHEN nematodes gorged and potato farmers raced for economic exit, the entire axis of the earth was shifting: 16 million GIs were wending their way home from theaters of war in the Pacific, victorious from campaigns in Europe, and from Navy and Army and Air Force and Marine bases all across their home continent.

It was a convergence of epic proportions, with a single overriding problem—America went from having nobody home to having no home for anybody to return to.

Although mobilization and Rosie the Riveter production had boosted our economy into sustained recovery from the insecurity of the Depression, redirected commodity and materials rationing had crippled the housing industry.

Concern about a postwar economic relapse was everywhere. But the surge of returning veterans and the rescinding of restrictive rations caused an explosion. Amplified by the GI Bill, which supported both housing and education loans, and by the pent-up desire for family and hearth, the American housing industry was ripe for revolution.

During the postwar years, America became the Fertile Crescent. After so many years of worry and restraint, Americans became fruitful and multiplied. In the five years after the war, more than 12 million Americans were born. The GDP grew from $200 billion in 1940 to $300 billion in 1950 to over $500 billion in 1960.

Until that time, American home builders were often jack-of-many-trades craftsmen and the average home builder completed about one dwelling per business quarter.

Watching this Greatest Generation tidal wave, two brothers conceived a whole new way to make a house a home—and in doing so they channeled Henry Ford.

Once they had purchased Long Island potato farmland at dramatically reduced rates, Bill and Alfred Levitt brought an entirely different sensibility to home building. On one level they became the GM of suburban sprawl. Alfred had studied architecture as an intern for Frank Lloyd Wright, and Bill became the master salesman, visionary, and operations chief.

The perfect storm of economic prosperity, pent-up demand, and mass production techniques developed by the Levitts was joined by another mighty wind—massive government intervention.

The Federal Housing Administration (FHA) and the Veterans Administration (VA), created by the Servicemen's Readjustment Act (GI Bill), guaranteed long-term mortgages. Federal insurance programs shrunk both interest rates and down payments.

Returning servicemen had little desire for sustained bunking-in at family apartments. One couple was so desperate that they famously resided in a department-store display window to publicize what Americans were just figuring out and what the Levitts foretold.

The *Saturday Evening Post* conducted a famous survey that found only 14 percent of the population was willing to live in apartment buildings or used homes. Every American deserved a new home for their tribulations, and they fully expected to get one. Between 1946 and 1953, FHA- and VA-backed financial institutions loaned enough to build more than 10 million homes.

The potato fields just twenty-five miles east of Manhattan on Long Island were rechristened Levittown, and the brothers began to build what would become the largest single development by a sole builder, ultimately commanding more than 17,000 homes and 82,000 people.

Bill Levitt is often credited with the manufacturing and production genius that broke home building down into twenty-seven discrete steps. He had served as a Seabee in the Navy, and his father, Abe, won a contract to build 2,350 housing units for defense workers in Norfolk, Virginia, in the early 1940s.

Just forty at the time, Bill Levitt created separate special teams to execute each of the twenty-seven steps at every home site. Mass production and total vertical integration (even the appliances were bought direct from manufacturers) meant that he could build a house and sell it profitably at $7,900 retail. In the beginning they built the homes to rent, fearing the weight of a mortgage might be a deterrent, but demand was so brisk the brothers quickly changed course, adding a cousin to the standard cape they were already producing—the American ranch. And they said, "Sell!"

With all the subsidies of construction and the buyer's loan, down payments were as little as $90. Throwing in free appliances when you signed on the dotted line was like moving in for free. And low-cost mortgages with payments of $58 a month meant living in Levittown was cheaper than renting.

Even at these low prices the Levitts cleared about a thousand dollars a home. By July 1948 the brothers were turning out thirty houses a day.

There was more besides the numbering of lumber boards and the manufacture of their own nails that marked the Levitts as innovators.

The Levitts had devised an image of home and community that would be repeated often. Their idea had an element that distinguished it from all other suburban housing concepts: scalability. Houses were placed at sixty-foot intervals along curved streets, not in straight-sided city quadrangles. Picture windows looked over wide-open, fence-prohibited backyards and patios. The vista, like the dream, was shared. And Abe made sure that every house came with at least one tree. Space and openness were matched with the comfort of backyard intimacy. In the earliest years, Bill would cruise the alphabetically ordered curved streets gauging who had sufficiently manicured their front lawns. Offending homeowners would be visited by Levittown employees to tidy up the yard, and then later by a bill for services rendered.

Never have the pent-up needs of the middle class and the hopes and dreams of its government been more in tune. The American marriage rate surged to a new high, and the age at which Americans married found an all-time low. In 1940, the median age for marriage was 24.3 for a man; 21.5 for a woman. In 1950, it was 22.8 and 20.3, respectively, and these numbers were unchanged in 1960. (By way of comparison, the figures for 2010 were 28.2 and 26.1, respectively.)

Soldiers returning from every sort of front turned their attention to baby making. As women during this period had more babies and in tighter succession, a boom such as the nation had never experienced commenced.

National publications called Levittown "Fertility Valley" and "The Rabbit Hutch." And while there was certainly conformity for this white American explosion, there was a deeply held joy in it too.

Had the Levitts created the ultimate chicken-or-egg situation? Did purchasing a house like theirs make you middle class, or were they shrewd enough to provide the place where a nascent middle class chose to live?

Both statements have an element of truth, and however you slice it, Americans who had a job and a house like this increasingly described themselves and their families as members in good standing of the middle class.

President Eisenhower brought his own mark to the American landscape. In 1956, a decade after the cessation of hostilities, Ike launched a second D-Day in the form of the 41,000-mile Interstate Highway Bill. Not since the great rail race had the nation sought to link the previously unlinked in a massive government infrastructure spend.

The Levitts expanded beyond Long Island, constructing their next development in Bucks County, Pennsylvania, and yet another in Burlington County, New Jersey, where they purchased almost the entirety of a single township. New roads and infrastructure placed both these Levittowns within easy reach of Philadelphia and Trenton.

Ike had more than suburb spawning on his mind. Wherever he went, the military-industrial complex and the Cold War construct was lurking. During his planning to cope with "atomic attack on our key cities, the road net must permit quick evacuation of target areas."

Had Levitt created a Communist buster?

Whatever his intention, whenever you bring society and the banking system and the government into alignment, amazing things can happen. As the babies boomed and the housing miracle blossomed, by the end of the 1950s studies began to show that most Americans considered themselves middle class. Imagine that—a nation with nearly 60 percent of its number fitting into that amorphous definition: middle class.

America was literally on a roll. We had mass-produced autos, we had cheap gasoline, we had the open road, and we had one more thing that seemed so reassuring.

The comfort of conformity.

But for all the coziness of living and working with people just like you, there were clouds on the horizon. And in another of the era's great ironies, much of what we were doing about it helped the middle class.

A Constant Gardener

No sooner did VE and VJ Days pass in a hail of kisses and streamers than the stomachs of the vast military machine began to grumble. Postwar settlements were going poorly, and in due course the Iron Curtain descended across the face of Europe. The United States, spent and war-weary from global conflagration, found itself increasingly polarized against an intractable and expansionist Soviet Union.

While no open hostilities broke out between the two powers, proxy wars took place all over the globe—in Africa, in Central America, and in Southeast Asia. Little about the Cold War appeared cold. Everywhere in the world of armament manufacture the advice was the same.

And tragic as its implications were, the case they made was sound.

Any immediate cessation of military spending would inhibit the good times that were being felt by all. But there was a far more Malthusian calculus at work. If you asked Winston Churchill at the time, as many did, how the Allies bested their enemies and won the war, he would look you squarely in the eye and growl, "American mass production."

He would also have told you something that Ike and the Defense establishment had already surmised. An arms race once commenced demands perpetual motion.

For generations we prepared ourselves for war by redirecting our manufacture and inventory stockpiles for the conflagration already in progress. The requirements necessary to mount a victorious campaign during World War II and afterward meant changing the face of modern warfare. Gone were the episodic fits and starts that accompanied the call to arms and the turning of swords into plowshares as the last notes of the bugle faded into history.

During the Second World War, the federal government spent $350 billion, nearly double the government expenditures in our history as a nation.

Roosevelt wanted to avoid re-creating the command economy of World War I, brimming with excessive windfall profits for manufacturers and profiteers. He identified dozens of superb business executives to steward government commissions for the princely compensation of a dollar a year. The result was a government that spoke with business fluency when ordering new plants and equipment to be built.

Reasonable profits were tolerated, and Roosevelt cheered on supplier competitions in private and in his fireside radio chats. With CEOs in the government mix, many productivity initiatives flourished. From a slumbering start, the United States had created world-class engineering, manufacturing systems, and products by war's end. In retrospect it was the greatest industrial restart in history.

A month following the Pearl Harbor attack Roosevelt spoke before Congress with an intense focus and an urgency of mission that would carry on for generations:

"Powerful enemies must be outfought and outproduced . . . . It is not enough to turn out just a few more planes, a few more tanks, a few more guns, a few more ships . . . We must outproduce them overwhelmingly so that there can be no question of our ability to provide a crushing superiority of equipment in any theater of the world."

FDR's military experts had advised him that American entry into World War I in April 1918 was stymied because the United States was woefully unprepared for conflict. After hasty attempts to rearm, the American forces had instead been forced to rely on Allies for most of its heavy equipment and tanks.

By 1939 America's army had slipped further, ranking thirty-ninth in the world in size and capability. Incredibly, our cavalry still used horses to pull the artillery. We did, however, possess exceptional production capability. In 1941, more than 3 million cars were produced in the United States. Roosevelt and his leadership realized that a complete transformation was required for wartime. Autos would have to take a backseat. In the following four years, fewer than 150 American cars rolled off the assembly line.

Pressures on Roosevelt were enormous. Just fourteen days after the attack on Pearl Harbor, Winston Churchill arrived at the White House for what has to be a record length of stay for a visiting chief of state. For the better part of three weeks the British leader lived at the White House, night after night drawing FDR into the wee hours for debate, smoking and drinking in the private quarters. Long after Roosevelt had at last retired Churchill would wander the halls, often unaccompanied. He was on a singular mission. Sleep was irrelevant.

The First Lady considered Churchill a somewhat less than ideal influence on her husband. "The thing that bothered me most," Eleanor Roosevelt later wrote, "was the unconscionable hours the Prime Minister could work through the night."

But Churchill had American manufacturing might on his mind. He was keen to bind closer with his potent ally, and he was terrified that America's attention would be diverted to the Pacific and Japan at the expense of Britain and the Allies.

While the German bombardment haunted the nights of Britain, Churchill had pleaded with FDR, "Give us the tools and we'll finish the job." Roosevelt developed a plan to "lend-lease or otherwise dispose of arms" to any nation whose security was vital to American interests. Long before America entered the war, we were supplying it.

A line had been crossed and America had become then and forever "the great arsenal of democracy." Central to serving that role was America's middle class.

Roosevelt bent the auto manufacturers to his will, including the mass hiring of women and blacks. America was on a transformational mission, and he led like a man possessed of a supreme vision. In something of a vertical take-off, American aircraft manufacture soared from a standing start. Under FDR's unceasing pressure, by 1944, more than 96,000 airplanes a year were produced in American factories.

Leading-edge technology in metallurgy and electronics gave American defense manufacturers a competitive advantage. But even more powerful were the quantum leaps in productivity achieved. One example is the production time of the "Ugly Ducklings" in Henry Kaiser's shipyards at Permanente Metals.

Liberty ships, regarded by history as the workhorses of World War II, were ultimately constructed in thirteen states by fifteen companies in eighteen different shipyards. Nearly three thousand of these ducklings were constructed during the war effort at an average expense of just under $2 million.

The first, the SS *Patrick Henry*, was launched after a galling 150 days of construction. That agonizingly slow start can in part be blamed on the fact that the shipyard itself had to be designed and constructed at the very same time they were building the ship.

FDR furiously demanded faster turnaround—maritime losses were mounting.

In the first two years of the war, German U-boats and surface raiders sank almost three thousand Allied ships, while the United States fabricated more than 850 vessels to replace them. As workers gained experience, production timetables shrank considerably. Eventually, the shipyards created a competition to see who could build a Liberty fastest.

Kaiser's No. 2 Yard in Richmond, California, won the race. The SS *Robert E. Peary* took just four and a half days from the laying of the keel to her launch. In all, the *Peary* required about 250,000 parts weighing about 14,000,000 pounds . . . and a significant dash of public relations. But the hastily assembled ship served the nation with distinction until 1963.

FDR and his team fought harder to keep the nation vigilant.

In 1942, after dithering by the auto manufacturers and the government, FDR finally had to force the companies to convert their plants to the manufacture of planes. Massive disruption ensued—more than 400,000 autoworkers were immediately furloughed. Nearly every auto dealership and salesperson was redundant.

Imagine the complexity. The average Ford car used about 15,000 parts. The B-52 Liberator bomber suddenly being produced at Ford's Ypsilanti, Michigan, plant boasted more than 1.5 million parts. But America was nothing if not focused on its new war mission. At the peak of production efficiency Ford was churning out a Liberator every hour.

Considering the virtual nonexistence of a peacetime armaments industry, the United States had become the industrial warrior to rival its strongest adversaries. But the industrial adjustment had come at tremendous sacrifice and disruption.

In 1948, President Harry Truman proposed his own arsenal of democracy with America's second-largest peacetime budget of just under $40 billion. His principal justification for the enormous request was that the $18 billion earmarked for military and international affairs was both vital and necessary to meet the continuing threat of totalitarianism in the world.

Like FDR's World War II mobilization policies, there were armaments companies that were entirely supported by the federal government, especially the Defense Department. But Truman's budget broke new ground.

Unlike the Second World War appropriations, this time there was no end in sight.

World without armistice, amen.

Domestic business interests and foreign-policy concerns formed a tidy consistency. It made good business sense, the manufacturers and their supporters argued, not to shutter these war machinery initiatives.

During the Second World War, nearly 10 percent of all war dollars were spent in California. Aerospace companies grew and flourished there, especially after the Soviet Union tested its first nuclear weapon in 1949.

As companies like Douglas, Lockheed, and North American developed missile technologies to maintain American superiority in the new technology and war machinery, they were abetted by nearby research labs and universities. California Institute of Technology, Lawrence Livermore Laboratory, and Stanford University were magnets for the leading scientists in defense weaponry.

The true economics of the Cold War and keeping ahead of the Soviet jackboot and their desperate sense of expansionism meant we had to sustain, rather than eliminate, major defense spending initiatives, even in peacetime. And the forces behind the growing defense electronics/aerospace industries flew in very tight wing formation.

Military and the aerospace, defense, and electronics leaders could complete one another's sentences before congressional committees. And often did.

In a membranous way, generals and military leaders found they could retire comfortably only to have their brass folded into the alloy of the newest Wall Street darling: the Aerospace Defense Electronics Industry, or as Ike ominously foretold it in his farewell address, the military-industrial complex.

IT'S OFF TO WORK WE GO

THE WORK THAT PEOPLE DID also changed dramatically. When Bill Levitt built his first home, the majority of American workers made things for a living. Their livelihood and their craft were tied directly to producing products. Manufacturing in mass capacities was a true distinctive competence, and as the world markets tentatively reopened after World War II there was acknowledgment everywhere that American-made goods stood for quality without peer.

Alongside the American manufacturing juggernaut grew a collection of businesses whose sole function was to provide services to those workers engaged in manufacturing.

Companies mass-producing products needed a battery of lawyers and accountants, and increasingly computer and other services. The complexity of manufacturing brought with it greater needs to sell, persuade, keep track, and insure. Banks played a vital role in postwar expansion, and the robust capital markets brought more companies to the public market.

The year 1950 proved a tipping point for the American economy. Two crucial developments occurred during those glory days with permanent impact on the American middle class. During the 1950s, the number of American workers providing services grew with vigor until they equaled and then surpassed those who produced goods for a living. We became once and forever a service economy.

For many economists the explanation is that the rise of the service economy meant white-collar service jobs had replaced quality industrial jobs, leaving a residue of low-skilled, low-paying service jobs and lower-quality manufacturing.

Unfortunately, the reality is far more complicated, with much greater impact on the middle class.

The explosion of service jobs directly resulted from several important trends. First, the demand for skill-intensive output and for ever-higher quality came as middle-class Americans themselves earned more money. The proportion of American service-sector work as measured by value added grew from 60 percent in the 1950s to over 80 percent in the 1980s, according to the National Bureau of Economic Research. Service work was expanding way beyond clerical and administration jobs.

Our economy was fundamentally shifting right under our feet. The great sweep from agriculture to manufacturing was continuing as America became a service economy.

What historians have grappled with less successfully is that America was at the same moment the largest manufacturing power in the world and the largest agricultural producer of important crops on the globe.

Excellence was required—and realized—in all fields of endeavor, even as the basic power of our economy was facing seismic shifts.

If you look beyond American consumption of services brought on by increased economic well-being, something powerful emerges. The pattern of growth for skill-intensive services and the relative quality of this high-skilled labor created something extremely important but often overlooked—a skill premium.

And nothing had higher impact on the burgeoning middle class than this skill premium.

Higher-skilled jobs produced relatively greater output—greater value added. It was natural that those jobs would require more intensive preparation and education, a more demanding work ethic, and higher compensation. High-skill worker output increased during this period, even as low-skilled industrial output declined. Textiles and small machinery manufacture moved south within the country, then offshore in a steady retreat.

How did that skill premium influence take-home pay? From the 1950s to the '80s, the wages of college-educated service workers rose from 125 percent of high school workers' pay to more than double high school grads' compensation. And the proportion of college-educated workers rose during that same period from 15 percent to more than 60 percent.

Students poured into classrooms as higher education swelled with returning GIs and war workers. In California in 1960, University of California president Clark Kerr and other education leaders created the "Master Plan For Higher Education." It established that the University of California schools must admit undergraduates from the top 12.5 percent of the state's graduating high school seniors; another cohort would attend California state schools, and still more would attend California community colleges.

The model involved low-to-no tuition.

Hailed as a stroke of collective genius, Kerr and his master plan were a *Time* magazine cover story. Enrollment in California higher education institutions tripled from 1930 to 1960, and state funding kept pace. Marshaling all these schools caused trouble almost immediately. Some were new postwar creations and others had been around for generations. Every school, it seemed, longed to become a major world-class research university, while few had the urge to be a back-bencher. But everywhere higher education surged.

Though warning signs were on the horizon, the music really stopped at the end of the school year in 1978 when Proposition 13, a ballot measure that limited property tax appraisals, was approved by California voters. It was only the first of many taxpayer revolt measures that began to choke the steady flow of state funding.

But during its heyday, higher education was exploding. Progressives everywhere saw college education as the key to the middle class. UC president Kerr wrote: "The campus is no longer on the hill with the aristocracy, but in the valley with the people."

Other states and other schools followed suit. American leadership had collectively come to the progressive conclusion that education was the key to creating a vibrant economy and educated citizenry.

For any who doubted what education might do, the brio and the power of the emerging American middle class was the proof of concept.

ALL OARS PULLING

HERE IS THE ECONOMIC MIRACLE that began in the 1950s: The middle class had choices to specialize, to gain skills, and to increase their own personal productivity on a relative basis. Hard work over many years, together with personal investment of money and time for education and training, was required. High-skill jobs often required apprenticeship. And they were synonymous with higher education.

The industrious American middle class responded with such vigorous energy that a virtuous circle was created.

As labor productivity grew, income grew at a disproportionate rate, and with that increase, the consumption of ever-broader and more-complex services ensued. The middle class was feeding its own climb up the rungs, and demand kept shifting toward services for which high-skilled workers hold an ever-larger productivity advantage.

The government played its part by pump-priming the economy with massive defense spending. High-skilled middle-class manufacturing jobs abounded, and the peacetime benefit of the war-sized arms manufacture included skill acquisition for some (a route to the middle class) and, at the very least, a stint off the welfare rolls for others.

So how did the economic men and increasingly women of the middle class respond? They aimed higher.

Faced with better relative pay and output, and the general sense that each step someone else took propelled you further, industrious Americans did what they needed to do to be ever higher skilled, and during this period we created an upward-sloping supply of higher-skilled workers.

By 1956, a majority of U.S. workers held white-collar jobs rather than blue-collar jobs. We were striving, and that energy created more opportunities for more strivers.

The middle class was well and truly made in America.

Measuring and defining the middle class was difficult in this period of momentum and upward mobility because so many American workers were swept along by this tide.

But whenever there are winners of this magnitude, there are always losers. Things were pretty strained down on the farm.

The mechanization of agribusiness led to enormous productivity gains, with the result of many farms expanding to produce more than ever before. Overproduction and economies of scale squeezed out small farmers and raised the stakes necessary to compete.

After generations as a cottage industry, farming became big business. Productivity crushed small farmers and also reduced the number of employees per acre planted. The land that had bridged so many generations of American farmers became a curse if you chose not to consolidate. Even as agricultural output mushroomed, employment disintegrated. Postwar farm employment was nearly 8 million. By the millennium it was closer to 3.4 million.

The self-made middle class created a prosperous and upwardly mobile urban and, increasingly, suburban American success story. The children of these skilled service-sector workers aspired for more than their parents had, and in most cases, they had the opportunities to make that dream a reality.

But America had no God-given right to a prosperous middle class. The government had played a hand in creating it by keeping the country on a war footing after the hostilities ended and by freeing up educational and housing opportunities. As we will see, they could just as easily make it more difficult for the middle class. And the great sweeps of global economic shifts, which governments have little sway over, can wreak havoc. It was inevitable that agriculture would mechanize and jobs would be lost, and that American manufacturing would see its jobs move east in huge numbers. What was not inevitable was our response to threats to the middle class. We spent more energy trying to protect it than grow it.

The middle class that we are nostalgic about is, then, a relatively recent phenomenon and in many ways an artificial product. There was certainly authenticity surrounding the way our nation thrilled when so many returned home.

And it is impossible to argue how effectively we build things when there is alignment between government, business, regulators, bankers, and the American consumer. It seemed at the time that everyone believed in the promise of the American worker, in the power of our mass production, and in the intellect of our white-collar service corps. The voters and their government facilitated the re-entry for 16 million men and women in the armed forces and for the nearly 700,000 Purple Heart wearers out of a sense of duty —a standard of care and appreciation, not of entitlement.

So why the label of artificial? The middle class we are sentimental about was formed by the pressures and the enthusiasms of a moment. We stood at the manufacturing apex even as we spent heavily to rebuild the industry of Europe and Japan. If you are ever to lose a war to someone, pray that you are defeated by American forces. Our penchant for reconstruction has been the salvation of these economies (and you might even get baseball too).

As the decade of the 1960s commenced, America had achieved the highest mass standard of living in the history of man. From 1940 to 1960, the United States' gross national product more than doubled. War-curtailed consumer demand burst in a wave of fresh spending in peacetime, followed by a baby boom that equated to even more demand. Add to that surge the move to near-perpetual building of our collective armory and you have the perfect conditions for growing a vibrant middle class.

But for all of the momentum behind the creation of the middle class, it was formed as much by our intense commitment as by government mandate. Outside forces lined up like a chorus.

It was not a natural occurrence of nature.

It was crafted with pride by hand in America. And as a bespoke creation it was also extremely vulnerable.

There is a powerful historical message in all of this:

As we had such an important hand in making the middle class, and then endangering it, we must understand that only by acting decisively can we get it back.

It will not get there on its own.

THE UNINVITED

LEVITTOWN, NEW JERSEY, EMERGED AS yet another white middle-class planned community. That vision as much as his mass-production techniques got Bill Levitt the cover of *Time* magazine.

Their New Jersey development grew to nearly 12,000 homes spread over ten neighborhoods. The suburban planner in Levitt is reflected on closer examination of the community. Each of Levitt's neighborhoods there came with a pool, an elementary school, and a playground. A single high school served the entire community, fed by all the neighborhood grade schools.

Levittown had other central services—a library, a small shopping center for sundries, and what served as a town hall. But underneath this infrastructure were all kinds of mini networks—kids' football teams, parents' associations, reading groups, newsletters, and even newspapers. Central postings for parties and fundraisers were common.

Any visitor to a Levittown community would naturally get the feeling that "we are all in this together."

At least, most any visitor.

CHAPTER THREE

_____ CHOCOLATE MILK _____

First cracks in the façade

A WHISPER OF MOVING AIR BRUSHED *against the open window. The ping-ping-ping bug dance against the screen on a steamy August night was the only discernible action outside. Daisy hummed a tired tune as she tried to put her two excited young children to bed. It was a timeless parental dance made more tiresome by the oppressive heat. Daisy cooed, cajoled, insisted. Her husband, William, an electrical engineer and World War II veteran, was tending to matters at work. So much the better, because it was his norm to generate more energy just at the very point Daisy was trying to wind things down.*

Raised "proper" in Richmond, the studious church-going girl had grown to a professional woman with master's degrees in education and guidance counseling. She was both maternally and professionally skilled to deal with the energies of her two rambunctious boys, Barry and William Junior. Tonight both skill sets would be fully taxed.

What could be more exciting than moving into a new house? The boys bubbled at the concept of an as-yet-undiscovered backyard. William Senior was thrilled to find a unique home with a double bay garage—one for the family car and the other for a workbench and an endlessly exciting array of projects. The young family had purchased the pretty house on the corner with the enchanting address of 43 Deepgreen Lane in the Dog Hollow sec-

tion of Bristol Township, New Jersey—the second of Bill Levitt's handcrafted communities. There were trees and, more important right now, there was more space. Daisy Myers rested her hands comfortably on her swelling stomach. The impending birth of their third child meant that the Myers' old two-bedroom home just a few miles away would never suffice.

Daisy smiled at the prospect—she felt certain her boys were getting a baby sister, but she kept her convictions to herself. It was a happy, purposeful time.

Finally, with everyone in bed, Daisy Myers stood in the stillness and surveyed the scene. She and Bill had spent two solid days cleaning every inch of the place before moving in. She thought to herself that August 13, 1957, would be one of the happiest days of their lives. There was joy in everything that night.

Daisy turned when she heard the footfalls outside—William was home from work!

But there were more footfalls, then more . . . then even more.

Whispers near the windows made her ears perk up—Daisy strained to hear the word, the word, the word. Bill and Daisy Myers were living the American Levittown Dream. Like thousands of families before them, they had moved into another pretty house in another pretty neighborhood that Levitt mass-produced.

Only, Daisy and Bill Myers were the first blacks of all those thousands to ever buy a Levitt house—and their sweet reverie was about to explode into a nightmare.

Suddenly, the phone rang, piercing the night, and Daisy jumped. "You want to die in that house, you goddamn—?" the voice belched from the receiver. The pregnant woman ran silently to the door, and what she saw made her freeze with fear.

IN THE FOLLOWING HOURS, HUNDREDS of angry Levittowners and others from far away hovered on the boundaries of the Myers' yard, banging on the mailbox; screaming the word, the word, the word; throwing lit cigarettes at the house. Quarter sticks of dynamite landed in the driveway. A long nightmare had just begun. Years later, Daisy swore she never expected the overwhelming revulsion. In the neverland of middle-class white America, Daisy and her family had just entered something darker than they could have dreamed.

Police were summoned that night . . . and every night for months thereafter. Crowds as big as a thousand surrounded the house. Flaming crosses burned on lawns, Confederate flags were planted in yards like evil weeds. Housewives gathered and spat on their lawn during the day. One irate woman yelled at Daisy, "I will not let my children drink chocolate milk as long as I live!" Rocks were thrown through their windows. Threats of violence were daily occurrences.

Local police were simply undermanned to cope with the large and agitated crowds that gathered as night closed in. Terrifying threats to burn them out like "black ants" were matched with more generally obnoxious antics, like the neighbor who purchased a black dog and named him a racial epithet that was bellowed endlessly through the neighborhood: "Here____ . . . Here ____" . . . over and over like the endlessly repeated punch line of a tasteless joke.

At least twice, death's proximity forced the Myers' to flee their home. The pregnant lady, her hardworking husband, and the two traumatized boys refused to cow to the madness, returning to Deepgreen as the mob slipped into a torpor—and the world took notice of all of it.

Not everyone was opposed to the desegregation of Levittown. Many bristled at the form required of all Levittown buyers, but sign it they did.

The statement, in all caps, required that they would "NOT PERMIT THE PREMISES TO BE USED OR OCCUPIED BY ANY PERSON OTHER THAN MEMBERS OF THE CAUCASIAN RACE." Two local families, one Jewish and the other Quaker, were particularly supportive, but each in its own way brought their own diversity concerns. Suddenly, the whole country was confronting an undeniable fact—that the very soul of the suburban dream was at stake.

Even in the tortured black/white racial politics of the moment, there was nuance. A friend of the Myers', Lewis Wechsler, who was Jewish and white, had alerted them about the availability of the Deepgreen house. He and his wife, Bea, were accused of being labor and tenant organizers, and worse, were described as members of the Communist Party. Suddenly, red peril was poured into the racial soup.

In the beginning the Myers' and the Wechsler's were targeted, but prejudice and fear are contagious. The Bristol police sergeant assigned to guard the Myers' home was stoned by concerned citizens. And a local car salesman thought to have sold Daisy a car found a burning cross on his lawn.

When we choose to be ugly we are without peer.

Local police were powerless to stop the venomous racism that clutched at the throat of the suburban enclave. Newspapers called Levittown "a disgrace to America."

Still Bill Levitt was unbowed: "If I sold to Negroes, 90 percent of the white people now buying homes would not buy."

He was not alone in his views. In agonizing slowness a tide was beginning to turn . . . or was it?

Racial segregation in the military wasn't officially ended until 1954, though President Harry Truman had ordered the integration of the armed services during the summer of 1948. But any soldier in the service knew as late as the mid-1950s that structural segregation in the military was everywhere.

In late 1955, Rosa Parks refused to give up her seat for a white passenger on a city bus. Martin Luther King, Jr., had only recently been elected president of the Montgomery Improvement Association. He led a boycott of Montgomery city buses, which meant poor blacks had to find other ways to get around. A year later, just months before Bill and Daisy Myers created a national furor by behaving like the middle-class family they had become, the town fathers of Montgomery, Alabama, relented and desegregated their bus lines.

At the very same time that mobs surrounded Daisy's house, nine black teenage students bravely led desegregation of Little Rock High School. Just three years after *Brown v. Board of Education* upheld such actions, President Eisenhower was forced to call in National Guard troops so that nine high schoolers could attend classes over violent protest.

Racial victimization had moved front and center, though the pressures had been evident for a very long time. In 1955, a Northern black teenager, Emmett Till, on a visit to the South, either looked at or whistled at a white woman—the truth may never be known. What is most certainly known, however, is that the young man was killed and then mutilated for his supposed actions, and the story spread like a national wildfire.

American racial violence was not unknown at the time. When the Civil War ended, six Confederate veterans from Pulaski, Tennessee, formed the Ku Klux Klan as an immediate postwar insurgency against the black claim on civil rights. Ninety years later, the calendar days may have turned but the fever had not subsided.

In the midst of this social agony and upheaval, black sociologist E. Franklin Frazier ignited another blaze with his book *The Black Bourgeoisie*, which scalded contemporary blacks who saw themselves as an emerging middle class. Almost no one reacted passively to the treatise. In subsequent editions, Frazier prefaced his findings by citing "a false consciousness which led to a cultural elitism and material existence based solely on acquisitiveness."

Frazier went on to say that the emerging black middle class was living "in a world of make-believe."

What Professor Frazier did in harsh terms was shed light on a brewing division underneath the racial tension. His frontal treatise asserted: "The total assets of all Negro banks in the United States are less than those in a single small bank in a small town in the state of New York."

Members of the emerging black middle class regarded the book as a threat to both their race and their economic interests. Frazier was unbowed: He argued that these blacks and powerful whites had "helped to perpetuate the myth of vast purchasing power of the Negroes which had become their justification for large corporations to employ Negro salesmen so as to exploit the Negro market."

What was seminal about Frazier's work was less his hard-edged economic and social views than that he had introduced another variable into the discussion of civil rights—the existence of tension between race and class in the burgeoning civil rights movement.

Despite the wrangling over the relative importance of the black middle class, most historians argue that in the mid-1950s and early 1960s the apogee of black unity was a vital ingredient of creating the civil rights movement. A hundred years since the South fell, African Americans had grown tired of the endless daily indignities they had to suffer. Elevated by the worldwide obsession with the plight of the Myers family, the naiveté and innocence of Emmett Till, and by the ennobling invective of Martin Luther King, Jr., African Americans were ultimately joined by an important minority of the white majority.

Brown v. Board of Education of Topeka formed one side of the parenthesis in 1954 and the Civil Rights Act formed the other a decade later. Historians may focus on the first phase of the civil rights movement as a moment for fighting for truth, but a careful review of the writings of the civil rights leaders reveals that the movement was as much about jobs as justice.

In the Civil Rights Act and the 1965 Voting Rights Act, African Americans came to enjoy rights of citizenry. In his landmark book *The New Black Middle Class*, Bart Landry points out that more blacks became affluent in the late 1960s than had done so in the prior fifty years. But in a chilling tale he picks up on Frazier by describing the widening economic gap between the white and the black middle classes.

Despite the gains, as University of Illinois professor Clarence Lang says, the civil rights movement was never as unified as it has been portrayed, especially after the twin passage of laws in the mid-1960s. "That's because class is often a key missing element of the story."

The class-versus-race nuance was too fine a line during those horrible months for Daisy Myers and her family. There were supporters, friends from local churches who brought food and flowers. But many more were afraid—a local druggist refused to drop a prescription for fear of being targeted. The Myers' fire insurance was summarily canceled. Someday somebody was going to burn that house down.

A "Levittown Betterment Committee" circulated door-to-door with a petition "protesting the mixing of Negroes in our previously all white community." Such are the passions that raged around "betterment."

Pages of their petition were dirty with signatures, but a tide was beginning to turn.

Decent people could no longer watch the agonies of this family and remain silent. A "Citizens Committee for Levittown" deplored the violence, appealing instead to the better angels of people's nature.

With slow and steady consistency these signatures of reason began to pile up.

But ugly won't be deterred. Behind the Deepgreen house was an empty bungalow. Someone moved in, hung a Confederate stars and bars, and proceeded to blast music day and night. "Stupid is as stupid does," said the poet Forrest Gump.

Pressure on public officials was building. "We were completely surprised by the riot," explained a town commissioner, Hal Lefcourt. "We met that afternoon . . . and there were several thousand people on the lawn outside, screaming at us to get them out of Levittown."

Even the town officials saw it was a time for backbone. "I said Myers had a right to live anywhere he wanted," asserted Lefcourt.

All across the nation, Americans started questioning what kind of postwar suburban enclaves they were creating.

As the pressure built, it was clear intervention was required. The Myers' had no intention of moving, and violence was a gathering storm. At long last, the governor's office got involved. With the state attorney general at the helm, a court injunction came. And, as so often happens when courage of conviction confronts them, the mob of dissenters vanished into the mist.

Some years later, the Myers' did move on. Then their story simmered for a long time.

Shortly before her death at eighty-six, Daisy mused: "I never forgot what happened in Levittown. I describe it as a wound that never really healed. You can stay angry and bitter, or you move along. It's not like you can accept an apology and it's over. You have to work at it, sometimes a long time, maybe the rest of your life."

Daisy returned to Levittown, sometimes accompanied by her two grown sons and the daughter, Lynda Patricia, she carried during the trauma. The town Christmas tree was named in her honor, and she would light it against the dark night sky as a symbol of love and tolerance. For many years, people would react to the energy of the Yuletide cheer and apologize for what had happened. She acknowledged each with what became her stock answer right up until she went to her final reward: "Let's be friends, okay?"

No matter where historians stand on the matter, certain things are clear. The lives of Daisy Myers and Emmett Till spanned the glorious and the profane. Each was the designee of fate in a twisted and painful period when we all faced the issue of race and alternatively disgraced and perhaps redeemed ourselves as a nation.

What cannot be contested is that states and municipalities with a penchant for mistreating racial minorities were brought to task or at least to intense scrutiny.

Opportunities, though far from robust, were improved. The white flight that Levitt and others foretold never came to pass.

Doors long sealed shut began to open, and programs and services of the government slowly welcomed those shunned for so long.

But for all our enthusiasms of the age and the indisputable gains by the emerging black middle class, a fundamental truth would emerge:

The more successful we became at ending racial segregation in society, the more economically segregated we became.

CHAPTER FOUR

———— DREAM STEALER ————

The uninvited demand their rights

THE AROMA OF WARM BAKED BREAD *wafted through a steady thrumming fan into the courtyard. But in the din of the close kitchen all oleofactored joy just evaporated.*

He was sick of that smell, and tired to his bones of the same four walls.

Straightening his crooked back, he stared at a four-foot-by-five-foot box shoved unceremoniously into the corner and daydreamed.

Life had gone from simple days with nothing to show but time served, to sudden sour notes, screw-ups, and inevitable punishments consisting of . . . more time served. No proficiency, no feats, no realizations. After a spell, indolence would settle back on his life like a pall and the pattern would repeat—like some inept pendulum that could never manage to swing free.

The only remarkable thing about his life was that absolutely nothing remarkable had ever happened to him. With seven siblings he was likeable but lost in the sauce. By tenth grade he had had enough. At the tender age of fourteen he did odd jobs for a local whorehouse until he was apprehended stealing a patron's trousers. Not long after, he was arrested for attempting to sell newspapers he had just stolen.

He was a fixture with the police in the local towns—like a colorful character, except lacking both color and character.

When millions of Johnnies came marching home in 1946, he joined the army, drawing an easy tour in postwar Germany. But he quickly found himself in the brig for intoxication and sentenced to atoning labor, until one day the axe just fell. His Uncle Sam declared him incompetent, inept, and in need of a discharge. He barely made two years in uniform.

Stateside, he tried honest employment but found the tug of petty crime irresistible. At that, too, he was painfully incompetent—dropping his ID accommodatingly at one crime scene and later at another, falling out of his not-so-true-to-its-label getaway car.

Putting loser in the three-time-loser sobriquet, his bungling earned him a procession of new homes. Following an armed robbery conviction he drew two years in a Chicago hoosegow, and then soon after earned a four-year promotion to federal incarceration at the mighty Leavenworth.

It's not nice to rob a U.S. Post Office.

By the yardstick of common criminality he was moving up in the world. By every other measure his life was a big sideways, destination nowhere.

By 1960 he had drawn his first serious time—twenty years in the Missouri State Penitentiary. After a year in the maximum-security enclave, rabbit got into his blood and he attempted escape. Less than one percent even try at the Jefferson City facility, and no one ever seemed to succeed.

Two punishments resulted—one that felt like an eternity and another that, in fact, was. First came solitary in the E-Hall—a century-old hellhole. The second was the unending enmity of his jailors. Nothing deprecates correction officers like successful escape—and failed attempts are only a margin better. Of the thousands of men at Jeff City, only a score were marked by the warden as flight risks—he was now one of them, his first true distinction.

From that moment he chose two paths: He would learn to bake in the prison kitchen, and he would escape again. Predictably, he succeeded at only the first. His dough punching was commendable, but his flight was interrupted—he was discovered hiding in the ceiling, having never made it off the premises.

Left with opportunity to leaven the daily bread, and another round in solitary, he fell naturally into the role of quiet, invisible, more or less model prisoner.

Every morning the prison bakery produced an abundance of fresh loaves, enough to feed thousands of men and workers at the penitentiary and also the local honor farmers charged with growing organic food for the inmates.

For years he watched platters get loaded in the box for delivery to these satellite farms. The only barrier between the kitchen and freedom was a sole truck tunnel where deliveries and garbage were hauled under intense scrutiny. Other inmates dreaming of a bread run presumed that the loaded box would be thoroughly checked at the exit the way garbage and other hauls were.

But men can live by bread alone.

Into the box he climbed, underneath trays of loaves. The box was picked up one April day in 1967 and for reasons no one can explain was never checked. So began his run for the northern border. For once his lifelong ineptitude helped. . . he was capable of being underestimated.

Certain he had hidden on the premises, his jailers mounted a several-day search across the fifty-acre prison complex before determining that he had indeed escaped. When the alarm was raised, somehow the wrong fingerprints were sent far and wide to law-enforcement authorities. His competency was contagious.

So great was the angst about his escape that the reward was set at $50.

Thus began an odyssey to Chicago, where he bussed tables, and then to Canada. There he allegedly tried to book passage overseas, but instead he returned to the United States, visiting Alabama long enough to obtain a driver's license and a year-old 1966 Mustang.

Life was good. He piloted his sporty Mustang down Mexico way to visit Acapulco and Puerto Vallarta. Armed with dark glasses and mail-order film-making equipment, he shot his first porn movies, though trouble erupted when a local prostitute proved a hard sell. Stymied as a director, he shifted his sights to Los Angeles, where bartending school and dance lessons beckoned. He also squeezed in time to work on the George Wallace campaign as a matter of racial preference and civic duty. For all the self-help, the year passed aimlessly on the fringe.

And like any escapee living the dream in L.A., the time came for a nose job—which was sculpted in March 1968. Shortly after, the Mustang was mobile again, this time with a bit more purpose. Stopping in Birmingham,

Alabama, he purchased a Gamemaster 30 aut 6 and a box of 20 shells. He paid extra to have a sight mounted on the rifle.

Two days later, he drove to Memphis and checked into the $6.24-a-night New Rebel Motel. Early the next evening, he stood in the tub of a shared bathroom, resting his rifle on the window ledge.

Without fanfare or warning, he took aim across the parking lot. His single shot slammed through the face and neck of Martin Luther King, Jr., who stood on a second-floor balcony of the Lorraine Motel surrounded by friends and supporters as they gathered for dinner.

In an instant the voice was gone . . . and in that permanent silence his whisper became a roar.

STUNNED MEMBERS OF KING'S COTERIE raced to staunch the bleeding. The projectile had slammed into his right jaw—they could see that much. But the bullet had severed the civil rights leader's spinal cord and the poor man's fate was sealed. An hour later, at 7:05 that evening, he was declared dead at St. Joseph's Hospital. He was just thirty-nine years old.

On that balcony, brave associates stood in plain sight and pointed in the direction of the single shot in a photo that is burned like a daguerreotype into our memory— an essay in black and white.

Police quickly uncovered an orgy of evidence.

Next to the New Rebel Motel was an amusements company belonging to Guy Canipe. Guy and two customers claimed to witness a well-dressed white man drop a package before speeding off in a white Mustang.

Police recovered a satchel and bedspread containing the Remington 30.06 rifle, its sight, and plenty of fingerprints.

Two guests at the rooming house recalled seeing a suspect bounding down the stairs just after the shot was fired. A search of room 5B, belonging to a "John Willard," turned up another trove of clues—pliers from a Los Angeles hardware store, and a laundry mark that helped identify the rogue's address as the Saint Francis Hotel in L.A.

The name on the cleaner's list was Eric Starve Gait, but when visiting the hotel in California the FBI was directed to his bartending school and the dancing classes. There all aliases melted away to reveal the true object of their attention: a forty-year-old three-time loser whose given name was James Earl Ray.

What followed was the largest and most expansive manhunt in the history of the FBI. As the word spread, the man's father, James Gerald Ray, shared his unending confidence in his son. "He couldn't have planned it alone. He wasn't smart enough for that."

Across the nation, cities burned. The depths of hopelessness for millions of Americans of all races became a silent scream. It was an American Guernica. Black Americans had lost a beacon.

Racial tensions were ferocious, despite Dr. King's lifelong pledge of satyagraha—Gandhi's insistence on nonviolent protest. Riots raged in a hundred cities. Robert F. Kennedy is credited with calming Indianapolis with a speech that openly stated, "I had a member of my family killed . . . by a white man."

The massive FBI manhunt could not prevent Ray's escape to Canada. His smoothly executed bolt to the border still raises questions. Little is known about how he financed his flight to Toronto and then later on to England. But the nation's outrage forced an even wider dragnet. Eleven days into the manhunt Ray made his life's only top ten list—the FBI's Most Wanted.

Two months later, Ray was apprehended at London's Heathrow Airport, bound for Brussels and apparently en route to Rhodesia; just three days before his capture, RFK too was killed by another "lone gunman."

Each of these three murders (JFK/MLK/RFK), all "conclusively" committed by single warriors, each intrigue examined by a blue-ribbon review panel as credentialed as it was suspicious, was a turning point where America lost a part of its soul. Conspiracy theories abounded for each assassination, but long before those doubts emerged, a lasting anxiety blossomed like a black dahlia.

Glumness settled on the American psyche.

Any fair reading of middle class aspirations would be dishonest if it ignored the gloom pervading these three murders. Deep in the American spirit, many living at the time saw a seam of igneous coal running through these tragedies. It was a requiem for the purity of the American dream writ large by national TV.

For Americans it was a time of despair and concern. Where had their postwar enthusiasms gone? Had a new sense of fairness shifted the playing field? Whither the middle-class dreams if so many were cast aside?

For Ray the inveterate bumbler, there were only questions upon questions.

In the custody of Scotland Yard, Ray admitted to the killing. Later, in U.S. custody, he pleaded guilty to avoid a jury trial, which his lawyer, Percy Foreman, advised would result in the death penalty. Assessed with a ninety-nine-year incarceration at Brushy Mountain State Prison, Ray recanted his confession and begged for a new trial with a jury.

Ray pulled the usual tricks. He claimed he was paid a half a million to murder King; he asserted his confession was to protect his father and brother, who police threatened would be charged; and then he claimed a murky figure named Raul orchestrated everything.

New lawyers, new claims, new conspiracy theories did nothing to soften the position of his jailors.

At the same time, it's hard to imagine the world's most inept criminal pulling off the assassination—knowing the precise moment to shoot Dr. King; escaping across the American landscape into Canada with the FBI in full pursuit; fleeing to the U.K. and Europe; staying at hotel after hotel, including a five-day sojourn at the famed Hotel Portugal; discerning that Rhodesia had the most accommodating laws for fugitives from justice, even finding Rhodesia on a map; evading the FBI and Scotland Yard for months; and funding the whole experience on his own.

Questions aside, Ray never got that trial before his peers. The case was closed, and Ray rotted in prison till his last breath, in 1998.

The Measure of a Man

NO SINGLE TREATISE COULD CAPTURE the full impact Dr. King had on American society, much less on the growth of the middle class. As with all our heroes today, there are books written highlighting human tendencies that might dilute the legacy of a Nobel Peace Prize winner. There are others describing the schisms of the civil rights movement, and still more that trace the role of the media in the unfolding story of race in America.

Few accountings of Dr. King spend much attention on his role in the development of the American middle class. But some sophisticated historians believe King's legacy was as much about economic justice as social justice, and that his battles were as much about the dignity of holding a job as the dignity of the individual.

After all, Dr. King was in Memphis on behalf of the sanitation workers on strike for fairness. The segregated jobs carved out for black workers paid a whisker above minimum wage, brought zero vacation days, and offered no pension or retirement benefits.

For that precise moment the civil rights movement was the labor movement. These were sometimes strange bedfellows: The sanitation workers' union strike had not gone smoothly for King. Previous attempts to march and protest had deteriorated into vandalism and violence. He was derided at some appearances.

But the civil rights movement was about far more than Martin Luther King, Jr. Even its best-known spokesman acknowledged the importance of other more militant leaders.

An economic reading of Dr. King and his compatriots, even those less prone to peaceful solutions, is both a greater inclusion of black Americans in the economic promise of his native land, and also a lifting of all boats. King's impact went far beyond just elevating his African American brothers and sisters. He was, to borrow the words of a Jackie Robinson eulogist, "a credit to his race . . . the human race."

But Dr. King would never cross the River Jordan.

In 1968 as King lay dying, only about one in eight black households could have been even remotely characterized as middle class. Ten years later, a blink on the calendar of shifting economic fortunes, that number approached one out of four.

Martin Luther King's economic legacy can succinctly be tallied by the notion that more blacks found economic well-being in the late 1960s than in the previous five decades combined. Economic opportunity was still elusive for most black Americans, but it was a start.

At the end of his life, Dr. King lamented the role competition was playing in attracting the news media. He complained to newsmen like Daniel Schorr that television was beguiled by the violent and outrageous. Certainly King, Stokely Carmichael, and other civil rights leaders had become skilled at the sound bite and the telegenic moment particularly as the use of videotape and live satellite feeds drove a greater sense of the instant.

But King was prompted to inquire of the media: "When Negroes are incited to violence, will you think of your responsibility in helping to produce it?"

The narrative of the civil rights movement was changing. Certainly, the bravery of the Freedom Riders helping blacks register to vote in places like Mississippi was center stage. Many Northern liberals could watch with disdain as obstructionists in Southern regulatory regimes blocked the rights of the disaffected African Americans. But their stiff collars tightened as the rhetoric turned from Southern civil rights to themes like open housing in Northern cities, to jobs, to a huge march of the poor (both black and white together) in Washington, D.C., which Dr. King was planning . . . and most potently of all, to staunch opposition to the Vietnam War.

The final refrain should have been predictable; blacks at the time made up just 11 percent of the overall population but comprised over 23 percent of the combat soldiers in Vietnam. The well-to-do deferred while the black and poor served.

Things came to a boil for King during President Lyndon Johnson's January 1968 State of the Union address. Johnson was highly aware of the impossible war on two fronts he had joined. The centerpiece of his domestic policy—the "Great Society"—was hugely expensive, as was the increasingly frustrating war in Vietnam. Just six months earlier, racial tensions had boiled over in many American cities, which hardly unleashed party unity to continue supporting the costly social programs.

In the speech, the Great Society was mentioned just once, crowded out by Johnson's obvious frustration with the progress of the war. His defiance in the face of Vietcong duplicity—they had violated the New

Year's truce even as they called now for a halt to the bombings and a cease-fire for Tet—was interpreted as hawkish and defensive. Worst of all, Johnson appeared to actually believe in his war plan, and the once-leonine persuader in the Senate was simply unable to convince Americans of the wisdom of his strategy.

Dr. King could hold out no longer. Virtually every other major civil rights leader had long ago denounced the war and saw Vietnam as a way to unite their movement with the antiwar effort.

King called for a massive, inclusive antiwar March on Washington: "We will no longer vote for men who continue to see the killings of Vietnamese and Americans as the best way of advancing the goals of freedom and self-determination"—in Vietnam, and by extension, anywhere else.

Johnson was on the run. His party was divided not just by hawks and doves. His signature Civil Rights Act of 1964 gained passage despite opposition from every member of the congressional delegations of Alabama, Arkansas, Georgia, Louisiana, Mississippi, North and South Carolina, and Virginia.

Eight weeks after his State of the Union, Johnson eked out the New Hampshire primary by an embarrassing 230 votes against one-issue candidate Gene McCarthy. Flustered by his inability to win the hearts and minds of the American people, or to win Vietnam, or to fight the spiraling costs of his twin programs, Johnson sunk deep into his own reverie. Maybe it was Bobby Kennedy parading back and forth like Hamlet that drove him to drop his own bomb on the election proceedings on March 31.

"Fifty-two months and ten days ago, in a moment of tragedy and trauma, the duties of this office fell upon me." He continued, "There is division in the American house now . . . Accordingly, I shall not seek and I will not accept the nomination of my party for another term as your president."

Imagine the whirlwind.

Just five days later, Martin Luther King would be mercilessly murdered, and in sixty more so would LBJ's nemesis, RFK.

Johnson's reaction to civil unrest in American cities in the summer of 1967 had been to ask Illinois governor Otto Kerner to lead an eleven-member commission to understand the dynamics of these racial disorders.

In the same month of LBJ's "I will not seek" speech, the commission released its findings. It concluded, "We are moving towards two societies, one white and one black, separate and unequal." It went on to criticize the media for its willingness to exaggerate the violence and to underreport the real story of growing and entrenched poverty, particularly among inner-city blacks.

That commission delineated some of the difficult choices we had to make as a nation—specifically, that the $30-billion-a-year cost of prosecuting the Vietnam War was prohibiting us from meeting pressing and urgent social challenges at home.

And presaging what would happen after King's assassination, the commission warned of a sea change in the inner city, a shift of mood that was feral, powerful, and yet was not spoken of in such stark terms. The Kerner Commission cited: "A new mood has sprung up among Negroes, particularly among the young, in which self-esteem and enhanced racial pride are replacing apathy and submission to 'the system.'"

Even as King, Carmichael, and others were earning greater social rights for black Americans, the seeds for structural economic inequality were being planted, some as distant as the Mekong Delta. We had created a pathway to middle-class opportunity for increasing numbers of black Americans. But benefits came to a tiny percentage.

For the first time, civil rights leaders and the commission were pointing to the same split—the racial gap might be narrowing, but the class gap could not be ignored. Yet it was unspoken that black America would have to cope with its own class divide.

There are statistics to support the absolute numbers of lives economically improved by the civil rights movement. In 1967, there were about 266,000 black American households that earned an inflation-adjusted $50,000 or more. That number reflected some of the early momentum of the civil rights movement. On a percentage basis, the number marks a huge move in just a decade, even if the absolute numbers were still very small.

Twenty-two years later, in 1989, that number had surged to over a million households earning an inflation-adjusted $50,000. Sure, it was progress, but still a pittance in the overall scheme of the poor in the United States.

In the early 1950s, more than 55 percent of black families lived below the poverty line. By the late 1980s, that number was closer to a third—an improvement, but still miles to go.

Sadly, these numbers fail to paint the whole picture, even as they are cited as proof of the robust black middle class. In the late 1980s, sociologists began to focus more thoughtfully on the class divisions within the African American community.

Unsurprisingly, they came to varying conclusions, but no analysis is complete without delving into the two main issues that the numbers miss: the role of race versus class in African American life, and the overall vulnerability of the black middle class.

Shelby Steele provides an extremely lucid explanation of the dynamic tension and incompatibilities blacks encountered as the civil rights momentum lost steam in the late 1980s.

Middle-class blacks, Steele maintains, were caught in a double bind that kept two powerful elements of their identity at loggerheads. American middle-class values were certainly shared by black Americans—like work ethic and striving for a great education, economic and family stability, property ownership, and civic responsibility are race-less—he called them assimilationist. These values serve as a tributary that flows naturally into the mainstream toward integration of shared values independent of ethnic background. It is an American recipe for success, for joining, and toward a strong identification with overall society.

But, for Steele, the patterns of racial identification that first emerged in the 1960s pushed middle-class African Americans and perhaps all blacks in another direction too—choosing to don the armor of an embattled minority, of ethnic identity, of separatism and racial unity seeking justice for all.

Could progress in one come without sacrificing a part of the other? This double bind is not a zero-sum game, but it is a complexity often overlooked by many policy makers and social economists. And if you have not lived it, you cannot fully appreciate how difficult it has been for black Americans to balance.

Managing these adjacent boundaries was an acute challenge in the 1960s. Many have glossed over the decade, calling it the apogee of African American unity. Careful reading of black historians paints a very different picture of schism and divides, even among the icons of the movement. Dr. King's ability to communicate and capture the limelight so effectively caused great frustration among more-radicalized splinter groups—especially those that considered violence and strong rhetoric more effective than balance.

Many civil rights activists, including those in the SNCC (Students Nonviolent Coordinating Committee), were openly critical and even booed King during his speeches. His rejoinder was classic MLK: "Whenever Pharaoh wanted to keep the slaves in slavery, he kept them fighting amongst themselves."

But violence and more outrageous language was a magnet for the media, and it brought more confrontation with police, which begat even more media.

Stokely Carmichael, the leader of the SNCC, had lost patience with King's nonviolence, embraced Black Power, and seeded the Black Panther Party, which was founded in California with Huey Newton and Bobby Seale. In late 1966, Carmichael banished all whites from the SNCC.

On hearing of MLK's death, Carmichael's epigraph was, "Now that they have taken Dr. King off, it's time to end this nonviolence bullshit."

But the Black Panther Party was in the process of fizzling out. Huey Newton's three trials for the 1966 murder of one Oakland police officer and wounding of another ended in a triumvirate of mistrials. By the late 1980s, much of the violence and intensity had abated, even if the racism and lack of equal opportunity had not.

For all the improved statistics, the momentum of the black middle class was clearly lost, and relative growth was still seriously lacking for black families. The numbers in the late 1980s were daunting.

Most black children in the nation were still living in poverty. Over a third of the black population was poor. These figures are starker when you realize that from 1975 to 1987 and the great stock market crash that October, more than 2 million black Americans became poor. Unemployment among blacks hit new highs—12 percent of black workers were unemployed versus 4.8 percent for white workers.

Black America was firmly established on an economic roller coaster —they enjoy disproportionately lower improvement in the good times and fare disproportionately worse in the bad.

It's a prescription for pain that was never filled more fully than in 2008. The black middle class was hammered to such an extent that by 2009 the median net worth of a black household was $2,000, only 2 percent that of the white median. From such a position, personal recovery is extremely difficult to achieve.

While Dr. King was alive there was neither time nor opportunity to affect the kind of structural changes necessary to address the vulnerabilities of the black middle class. His life was cut short just as he was about to bring his influence to bear on inequities affecting all Americans. If he had tackled the continued prosecution of the Vietnam War, Dr. King would have found allies in some unexpected places.

CHAPTER FIVE

Love/Haight

Youth in revolt

WITHIN DAYS OF THE FIRST AMERICAN *bomber raid on Nazi Germany, the Japanese withdrawal from Guadalcanal, and the dedication of the Pentagon, a young girl screamed into existence in Port Arthur, Texas.*

It was an even match.

Her daddy toiled as an engineer for the company that would become Texaco, and this bundle of joy dropped in just as the world drifted deeper into cataclysmic war. Before long, she was wrapped in the loving embrace of a brother and sister, and the impressionable bairn turned to painting to fill her childhood reverie. Refined by Port Arthur, she wrote, and from time to time drifted off into song . . . and trouble.

Port Arthur cradles the Gulf Intercostal River and lies along the western edge of Lake Sabine. The town owes its current existence to the Spindletop boom that burst in a black-gold gusher from the famed Lucas well in 1901.

The Texas Company and partners would build the largest refinery network in the world there, a lakeside petrochemical colossus. Civilization in the form of Houston was a two-hour drive, and closer in, a 3,500-acre local atoll called Paradise Island featured ballrooms and other amusements. Across the shimmering lake sat the wilds and the temptations of Louisiana.

Into Port Arthur's ecosystem flowed every imaginable combination of skill, background, and pollutant.

Paris it wasn't.

She was a colorful, sensitive girl with a broad wing-span that helped her cover a lot of ground—from venerating her family, to joining glee club, to playing the offbeat girl hanging out with a posse of ne'er-do-well boys. She talked trashy and tough . . . but the truth was in her eyes. Anyone really looking might have doubted her hard exterior, but it was a good front—and at times her best defense.

With these dueling sensitivities she floated into adolescence. Those years brought trying physical changes to everything but her sparkling eyes. For the rest of her days she would veer between a tough Mae West exterior and a vulnerable girl, never really finding the answer at either pole, always searching.

That quest took her far from Texas and State College in Beaumont—far from the hot-rodders and Titan footballers of Port Arthur. She joined other young wanderers lighting out from home and family like Huck Finns, floating on a changing tide, as if drawn on an invisible river.

Pilgrims to San Francisco found like-minded settlers in North Beach and Haight-Ashbury who sprang up like magic mushrooms on the lawn.

Go ask Alice . . .

Instinctively, they found one another. She discovered camaraderie and inspiration, and brought back home dress and manner that only set her further apart.

Before long that underground river wound through Texas, and scarce as they might be, she found kindred souls in Lone Star territory. She sang at open-mike nights, pick-up style with guitar buddies in local saloons, and basked in homegrown and genuine applause. But she had changed too much, and a few like-minded souls couldn't prevent the inevitable.

In the heart of all of us lurks a dark animus, a fear of the new and the outrageous, a lust for similitude. A need to be the same. And that spirit, when unleashed, can be downright mean.

She was an idiosyncrasy of the worst kind, a disparity, a challenge, and a foil. The way to stop her was to crush her vulnerable spirit. With marksman's accuracy their arrows hit her most fragile point of entry.

Trying college for the second time in Texas, a fraternity named her the

Ugliest Man on Campus. The motion carried and the moniker stuck.

In an aching letter to her parents she lamented her prodigal return. Her father, with whom she shared a deep intellectual connection, urged her to defect to the faraway place that welcomed her.

With that blessing, Texas became a biographer's entry—a waypoint of no return.

Back in Haight-Ashbury she found her voice.

She drifted down to Monterey for the 1966 Pop Festival with a local band that had befriended her first, then gamely brought her on to sing lead vocals. It was a variation on a Texan theme—make friends, play nice, and when they let you sing . . . get it while you can. Watching her edge toward the mike in Monterey in frilly peasant top and matching pants, perched on some half-heels, she barely looked her twenty-four years. There was sweetness and a timorous, almost coy, start to her performance. That would quickly change.

Bearing no resemblance to the band playing just inches from where she stood, she was suspended in time and in midair. No one could have predicted what happened next.

After a shrill riff by the lead guitar, the band dialed it down to a bluesy unadorned pulse—a solid bass guitar backbeat and a soft rhythm. She quivered at the threshold. Softly she purred.

"Sittin' down by my window looking out in the rain . . ." A murmured phrase laced with smoky, got-nobody-in-this-world despair. She repeated the same, this time more plaintive and achy.

Then all of a sudden it happened . . .

What emerged at that moment is still visible when you watch it today. Like a volcano she came, wailing, thrilling, and leaving every shred of herself on the stage. The simple blues melody was shed like a chrysalis, revealing an unearthly magical talent.

Anyone who had ever sniped about her was silenced by the raw superiority of her musical presence and the sheer power and unvarnished beauty of her interpretation of the old canticle "Ball and Chain."

Her stunning performance changed the shape of things and launched a career of enormous continuing impact. This girlish toughie fairly skipped with glee off the stage—as if every East Texas debutante and Friday Night Lights hero was at long last beguiled. She was finally home.

More than victory over insecurity, she willed herself into completeness by renting every garment, shearing every appendage, shedding every skin.

The pure joy of the experience launched a journey with stunning highs and shattering consequences. Her Kozmic aura so eclipsed her psychedelic band, it was transformed through fan response into background music. Big Brother was ample and popular on their own . . . but they had just caught lightning in a bottle. There was nothing that could be done.

With so much sudden and meteoric success, tragedy was the only possible counterpoint.

In just three years her narrative arc would span explosive ingénue on the stage in Monterey to a lonely hotel room, a lost Saturday afternoon, and a missed recording session to cover the instrumental "Buried Alive in the Blues."

It would be the last song she would never record.

But her sheer emotional force could not be contained. Her song would not be silenced. And the true addiction was less to the poisons that overcame her heart than to the intoxicants that freed her soul.

Richard Goldstein described her commanding connection to her audience in Vogue magazine.

Janis Joplin would inhabit each song, he said . . .

". . . clutching the knees of a final stanza, begging it not to leave."

Watching a river of youth wash through Haight-Ashbury, San Francisco, in 1967, no one could have predicted the transformation that was about to surge through middle-class society—but wandering minstrels like Janis and other disaffected young people did. So did Grace Slick, and later Jimi Hendrix. They saw things through a purple haze.

They called for cultural revolution . . . and yet there was something highly irregular.

History has long heard disaffected voices rise from the depths clamoring for change. Hunger and revolution always inhabit the same room. This time rebellion came from somewhere unexpected.

The middle.

Michael Joplin calls his sister a "middle-class white chick singing the blues . . . and that in itself was odd . . ."

Certainly Janis had her blues influences: Lead Belly, Bessie Smith, even Big Mama Thornton caught Janis's attention in her teens. But what captured the nation on college campuses and in coffee houses, at the Bitter End and Fillmore East, at Yasgur's farm and "Hashbury," was the rejection of middle-class acquiescence by equally middle-class youth.

The revolution actually was televised.

The Summer of Love in 1967 was not the end of the middle class, just the beginning of the end of the middle class as we knew it. So much of what happened in the late sixties and early seventies was calculated to make middle-class parents gasp. And gasp they did.

Youth became a separate class. In less than two years, the hippies emerged like a middle-class permutation—they were predominately white, middle class, educated young people lodged between ages seventeen and twenty-five. And like a massive on-switch, their ranks of supporters and emulators exploded into the imagination of American youth.

Straight society was swept up in the feeling.

The issues that arose in a gathering cry from young people in the late 1960s formed a prospectus of lost values and a crisis of alienation. It was a time when baby boomers were coming of age, and, some cynics wrote, these students had more time and money than their parents had to indulge in protest and activism.

Like some vast consortium the tributaries flowed together—the new left, the black nationalists, the civil rights activists, the anti-war movement, the women's rights movement, the gay rights movement, and the brown berets of the Latino rights movement.

Their rage was powered by a teeming brew of runaway inflation, blacklists and McCarthyism, and the unending insecurity created by the Cold War, Vietnam, and the nuclear age.

This collision was expressed by bumper-sticker battles ("Make Love Not War" versus "Peace with Honor"), changes in clothing, music, and lifestyle. But nowhere was this revolt by the young middle class more pronounced than in campus unrest.

The Students for a Democratic Society (SDS) was a loosely aligned organization boasting 35,000 members in 250 campus chapters—though less than 20 percent paid national dues. Focusing naturally on civil rights in its early days, the SDS found the siren of the Vietnam War irresistible, and by 1966 it had changed tactics from working through the political system to something tougher and sometimes darker—to becoming a radicalized and independent force for change.

Gathered in Port Huron, Michigan, in 1962, the SDS identified the war, minority rights, and the broken democracy of the American political system as its principal targets. Tom Hayden and his group were opposed to imperialism, racism, and oppression—and in their improbable assessment American universities were guilty of all three.

There's Something Happening Here

WHAT WAS IT ABOUT THE 1960s that drew so many young Americans into political activism? What had changed so profoundly since the 1950s to turn youth into a reform movement?

It was certainly a bit about chocolate milk. The nagging sense that the promise of the American Dream was foreclosed to so many black Americans may well have been a catalyst.

But there was a larger issue at stake, and it drove right into the heart of the middle class. For so long the abundance and well-being of the 1950s left Americans with the sense that the only agitators were Communist sympathizers bent on wrecking the American Dream. But by the 1960s, Americans from every point of the compass began to find contradictions in the Great Society.

Middle-class affluence was still largely a white experience. The bitter and sometimes deadly racial divide, the race in nuclear arms, an increasingly aggressive Communist Party apparatus, and the nagging sense that middle-class opportunity was simply not the commodity we had hoped for.

For a great many, the fires were stoked by John F. Kennedy's inaugural exhortation about the torch being passed to a new generation.

He closed that impassioned speech with the now catechistic "Ask not . . ." On the wings of his youth and inexperience flew such exotic and unlikely species as blacks, students, women, and any American driven to ask instead what they could do for their country.

The Port Huron effort fairly blared against the complacency of the 1950s, and railed against lives spent progressing through the predictable patterns of the middle class.

According to the scribes and Pharisees of the time, the great American irony was that the very tactics we so deplored in the Communists were increasingly characteristic of our own government.

No less an intellect than Daniel Patrick Moynihan warned that "when fascism finally comes, it will be disguised as anti-fascism."

Generations later, there is ample evidence that the FBI had targeted civil rights leaders, including Dr. King, and that the agency ran a counterintelligence effort with a goal of dismantling the student apparatus. FBI papers describe a twelve-point plan to discredit the movement.

This flawed approach to protecting democracy planted two seeds that continued to blossom in opposition to one another for the next fifty years: the coalescence of the student movement with Great Society liberalism, and the greening of the conservative Republican.

The glue that bound all these liberal causes would not hold for the decade. But at the time there were centripetal forces that kept driving the strangest bedfellows back to the same home base.

The student protest movement gathered steam, and the nation's reaction in some measure helped Nixon win the White House in 1968 with the promise of a speedy and honorable end to the Vietnam War. Just twenty-six months later, when Nixon ordered the invasion of Cambodia, he poured napalm on student unrest and activism exploded.

The tributaries conjoined in a collective wail.

Up till that time fewer than 24 campuses of the nation's 2,500 were the object of truly obstructionist demonstrations. The 6,700,000 collegians across our nation in those days were aware, tuned in, but nowhere close to dropping out.

The spring of 1970 was a point where even school leadership had begun to despair.

American universities suddenly were transformed into the political arena.

As far back as 1968 certain Ivy's had led the way. While Harlem slumbered that May a thousand of New York City's finest, armed with both weapons and warrants signed by Columbia University's board of trustees, marched on the snoozing students to take back by force five buildings that had been occupied by dissidents for nearly six days.

Student organization, if you will excuse the expression, found collective voice, as did faculty and administration in the face of the police brutality. But as happens, the pale version fought in the first act often turns scarlet after the intermezzo.

Two years later, on May 4, 1970, National Guard troops finally snapped. Tensions had been so acute after the Cambodian invasion that billy clubs were bound to be trumped by sterner stuff. The tide turned at Kent State. Four students lay dead and twenty more wounded—all on national television.

Shortly thereafter, policemen at Jackson State, with far less notoriety, opened fire on students, raining hundreds of shots on a women's dormitory, killing two students.

At schools all across the nation recess was called early. The punishment for insubordination had become too great—and Nixon lost even the parents. Schools had become the war zone in part because America's middle-class youth had lost faith in any other institution's ability to confront the major issues of their time. Congress failed the Port Huron test of addressing war, race, and poverty. Bizarrely at that time, these young people could fight in Vietnam, be conscripted into service, demonstrate, and campaign . . . but they could not vote.

American middle-class youth had lost faith and the universities had lost neutrality—dangerous positions for both.

The unbridled enthusiasms of the Summer of Love lay dead by the dog days of 1970.

The American middle class by this time was hopelessly confused.

And from these ashes came the first green shoots of the Conservative majority in the Republican Party. During the early 1960s, the conservatives found little sustenance. Calvin Trillin wrote, "in the United States at this time liberalism is not only the dominant but even the sole intellectual tradition . . . It is a plain fact [that] there are no conservative or reactionary ideas in general circulation . . . ," just a handful of "irritable mental gestures that seem to resemble ideas."

That the menacing uprisings of students and anti-war activists stoked the fires of Republicanism cannot be disputed. Nor can the racial tensions and the white backlash against civil rights incursions be discounted.

Economics played a role too. The robust growth of the 1950s and early '60s brought a new generation of middle-class haves who became allergic to paying taxes—especially for the numerous social programs they financed.

The middle class was the "go to" tax base for elevating more Americans from poverty into the center. A progressive tax rate had been employed, with stratospheric proportions due on the high end—but loopholes were most accommodating and few if any paid the higher rates.

The silent majority that reacted to urban riots, student unrest, and anti-war protests in the streets and the rise in violent crime brought Nixon to power. But this group also planted another seed—the slow-building resentment of the over-exertion of federal government power.

The 1960s saw the culmination of many movements—civil rights, the women's rights, and youth power, for example—but often overlooked is the split it created in the middle class into those who looked to the government to resolve all social ills and those who sought a conservative revival because big government no longer served their interests.

The middle class, flawed and exclusionary from the beginning, was being fractured from within and pressured from without. While African Americans wanted in and were denied, the values that allowed for this kind of social exclusion were being undermined by the progressive politics of middle-class youth. At the same time, it was becoming clear that the political will for the government to permanently underwrite the massive expense of multiple social and economic programs was fading.

By 1970, the spring was gone from our step.

CHAPTER SIX

The Three Uglies

Nixon's hydra of economic woes

1971 OPENED BADLY.

Richard Nixon inherited two very expensive crusades from Lyndon Johnson: the war in Vietnam and the War on Poverty. Rather than raise taxes or retreat from either, Nixon soldiered on into the breach. To fund these twin vexations, both Johnson and Nixon borrowed and then spent billions back in the days when that was considered a lot of money.

Deeper into the first term things got even trickier for Nixon. While both programs languished in failure, a ghost hovered on the horizon: the looming election of 1972. And voters were getting restive.

The middle class and the poor were being crushed in an economic vise of our own creation. They faced the ugly and unprecedented trifecta of high unemployment, low growth, and surging inflation, a combination of simultaneous forces so baffling that economists had to devise a whole new way to describe it.

Whenever economists come up with an entirely new term of art they also create a leading indicator with near-perfect predictive value. If they have to invent a name for it, then they have no idea how to cure it and bad policy inevitably results. The economic miscreant in this example was the garbled mouthful "stagflation."

We were headed nowhere economically, and yet wages and prices were surging. How had the middle-class postwar miracle devolved into the three uglies?

For the first time in the twentieth century, the United States was running a triple deficit. All of the following were running red: our trade, our balance of payments, and our federal budget.

The first simply meant we were importing far more than we were exporting. The second was more troubling, because it meant that our incoming sources of funds (export goods and bonds sold and loans obtained from abroad) were far below our outgoing uses of funds (paying for imported goods and repaying foreign loans or bonds). Nixon and his advisors knew this was bad, and worse, they had no obvious way to stop it.

The final river of red ink, the federal budget deficit, seems a matter of little anguish today, but at $23 billion, it felt crippling at the time.

Without making serious war cuts or raising taxes, both anathema to middle-class voters, there were just three ways to "cover" foreign balance-of-payments shortfalls: (1) By earning money on foreign investments (as they were saying in Britain, "Not bloody likely"); (2) By receiving more loans from other countries (one look at our allies' economic woes made that a long shot); or (3) By running down our central bank reserves.

Since balance-of-payments deficits meant more and more dollars were being held outside the United States, the third alternative was initially attractive because it was inconspicuous—who really monitors reserve levels? But as events unfolded, this reserve action became by far the most troubling choice for the simple reason that things quickly got outside our control. Reserve depletion became ugly and obvious.

In the first six months of 1971 more than $22 billion in assets left our shores.

Nixon had to slam the door, and quickly. The elites and the middle class demanded action—they just didn't know what. Something, anything, was better than standing still. The president would not get many chances. He had to select the tide that would lift all boats, even as he was counseled he might be unleashing the mother of all unintended consequences.

With an international meltdown swirling offshore, Nixon took aim at the one thing that was closest to an eternal verity, the closest thing to the center of the earth. It was Nixon Agonistes . . . he had to be heroic.

There were no good options, only less bad ones. Raising taxes on a strapped middle class, cutting social programs, or retreat from the black hole of Vietnam—none of those would lift him into a second term.

Nixon and his team did something that would change our economic profile forever. It would lift the national spirits for the briefest of highs before crashing to earth and bringing even more woe to the middle class.

Nixon called together a small group of advisors, and in that closed circle he weighed his dwindling options. And on a Sunday evening, without telling an ally or trading partner, he made his far-reaching decision.

He dropped the gold standard.

SOMETIMES HISTORY IS AN ECHO.

In his job as Master of the Royal Mint, Sir Isaac Newton persuaded England to convert from the silver standard to gold long before an independent America was a gleam in anyone's eye. In the run-up to our Civil War, Britain began issuing paper money that was legal tender instead of precious-metal coins that bore value in proportion to the metal in the coin itself.

Back in Henry the VIII's reign, the combination of foreign wars, recession, price inflation, and numerous ex-wives led to the debasement of his coinage. So much copper was secreted into the minting process that the silver rubbed off raised surfaces of his coin. Throughout the realm and history Henry was known as "Old Coppernose."

Nixon studied the oft-married monarch's plight and drew a dark conclusion—debasement might be the way out.

The age-old gold standard policy whereby a currency is backed by a physical store of gold was used by most Western nations. In the United States, the Gold Act of 1900 made the gold standard law.

Gold was solid in most circumstances but strained in times of economic upheaval and war. During the First World War, most countries, including the United States, suspended the gold standard so they could print enough money to pay for their costly involvement in the conflict. While their military was supported, printing excess money promoted hyperinflation. Prices skyrocketed throughout the West. Once hostilities ceased, most Western nations returned to the safety and sobriety of the gold standard.

Then 1929's economic firestorm hit with such force that the world once again abandoned the discipline of tying currency to gold. But during depressions, gold is sometimes the only true value. Americans sought all that glittered.

As the price of gold rose, people behaved in their self-interest and traded their dollars for bullion. The U.S. Federal Reserve was caught in an upward spiral, trying to raise interest rates quickly enough that the greenback could compete with the rising price of gold.

Sadly, higher interest rates can rarely beat a more basic measure—confidence. But raise rates we did. And higher borrowing costs worsened the Depression obliterating many companies' ability to meet their obligations. Thousands of bankruptcies and record-breaking unemployment ensued. The middle class got crushed.

In 1933, Franklin Roosevelt ended Americans' right to surrender paper dollars for gold and even to own gold bullion. Roosevelt was essentially nationalizing gold to gain a greater control over the money supply.

Within a year, the U.S. government owned most of the gold in the country, and Roosevelt used the authority given to him by Congress to raise the price of gold to $35 an ounce (by early 2015, gold was $1,300 after falling from a record $1,889 in 2012).

During the Second World War, most countries, including the United States, adopted the Bretton Woods system, which set exchange values for all currencies in terms of gold. With that agreement the world shifted away from the gold standard to the gold *exchange* standard.

Under the gold exchange standard, governments could hold U.S. dollars and British sterling as reserves because those currencies were exchangeable into gold. Since America held most of the gold in the globe, the dollar became a de facto world currency.

How we managed, stored, and monitored our gold became a matter of keen worldwide interest, because under a gold standard the government is limited in the amount of paper money it can print. During the Johnson years, the United States could print only four times the value of its gold reserves.

In May of 1971, concern about the growing number of foreign dollar holders exchanging into gold drove West Germany to withdraw from the Bretton Woods system. The combination of excess printed dollars and the continuing negative trade balance led other nations to demand redemption of their dollars in gold. (These foreign governments behaved no differently than many Americans did during the Depression—they fled to gold—only now the rules were different at home.) What Americans were forbidden from doing was now accepted practice for foreign governments.

The privilege of serving as a world currency had become a curse. And Nixon's advisors were getting very nervous.

Confidence in the dollar was sinking. Switzerland demanded $50 million of gold for its paper that July. And France developed a keen appetite for gold, redeeming $191 million of the precious metal from American reserves.

It was beginning to feel like a run on the bank. And that bank ... was us.

In early August of 1971, Switzerland withdrew from Bretton Woods altogether. They were no longer economically neutral.

Nixon had to move boldly and swiftly. Countries were motivated to swap greenbacks for gold. Reserves were dwindling. It was time to rule by fiat.

He made his move on August 15, 1971. It was a Sunday night, and he acted ahead of the world markets opening the next morning. With great reluctance, he broke into the beloved TV staple *Bonanza* with a plan that might have baffled Hoss and Little Joe.

Nixon imposed a ninety-day freeze on wages and prices, a 10 percent import surcharge, and, most profoundly, he "closed the gold window," ending "temporarily" the convertibility of dollars into gold. (That temporary closure is now forty-four years old.)

People involved in the discussion recounted that more time was spent assessing the impact of breaking in on the Cartwrights on TV than on the long-term implications of the plan. In historical context, Nixon was making one of the seminal decisions in modern finance. Imagine you were hearing an interruption to your regular programming for this special report from the president:

"If you want to buy a foreign car or take a trip abroad, market conditions may cause your dollar to buy slightly less."

But . . .

"If you are among the overwhelming majority of Americans who buy American-made products in America, your dollar will be worth just as much tomorrow as it is today."

Let's face it, the logic was clear. A devalued dollar married to a 10 percent import tax made America more "competitive" on the international markets, while freezing wages and prices would contain inflation at home.

Logic often looks fine on paper. And that alone bought Nixon some time as well as his re-election (at least until the tapes were erased). But he and about a dozen advisors made these decisions without consulting members of the international monetary system. Those nations' affectionate reference to this plan was the *"Nixon Shock."*

What does Nixon's decision have to do with the middle class? His medicine was cynically and practically short-lived. And the result was that he inadvertently painted a target on the backs of middle-class earners, borrowers, and small businesses. The calm his shock created acted more like the eye of a hurricane, a pause in the hostilities. After an interlude, we entered one of the most painful periods in our history.

The dollar became a fiat currency—its only value is in exchange for goods and for other currency. But more important, our money supply was no longer determined by our store of gold. The power to print money now vested firmly in the hands of the Federal Reserve. It could print as much money as it deemed appropriate.

In the thirty-four years before Nixon closed the gold window, the money supply in the U.S. did not even double. In the thirty-four years after the *Nixon Shock,* the money supply expanded by thirteen times. And after 2008, we printed dollars like confetti at a wedding. We have moved a long way from the gold standard.

Nixon had hoped to improve our nagging trade balance, and there was some improvement for a year or so in the mid-1970s, but America has not run a trade surplus since 1975. Not even we believed we could run a trade deficit for this long.

Nixon trounced McGovern in '72; the Democratic challenger mustered a total of seventeen electoral votes, winning just Massachusetts and the District of Columbia.

But as 1973 opened, Nixon's moves to contain inflation had failed. Both the leading currencies' home markets were a mess. The U.K. attempted a rent freeze with no more success than freezing in the United States—by 1975, U.K. inflation hit 25 percent. By 1974, our Consumer Price Index hit 11 percent, a record peacetime surge in American history.

The stock markets and bourses of the world swooned. The United States' major indexes wouldn't return to the same level again until 1993, twenty years later.

Since the *Nixon Shock,* the American middle class has declined in every conceivable measure, with one sole exception—debt. Our money supply, trade deficits, education missteps, and energy dependence have all expanded beyond our wildest expectations. Nixon's decisions that day changed the course of our economic history, especially for our middle class.

In fairness, middle-class Americans in the 1970s were overwhelmed by the three doubles. They were facing double-digit inflation, unemployment, and interest rates. Just getting by took all their energy.

Slamming shut the gold window had another immediate and far-reaching impact as well. But few middle-class Americans could sense the wave that was heading right for them.

OIL SLICK

OPEC WAS SEETHING. THE DEFLATED dollar gave them a concussion. Since oil trading then, as now, was conducted in dollars, a weak dollar diminished every asset they possessed above and below ground. Once again, the West had out-maneuvered them.

As they say in Hollywood, these two had history.

In 1960, seven Arab countries had joined six other major producing nations to form OPEC in order to push back on demands of the Seven Sisters, major oil companies with U.S., U.K., and Dutch heritage. OPEC's ambition was to create a common front against the Sisters.

Western oil had huge influence over pricing and production, but even more galling to OPEC was that over 65 percent of the revenues generated by the oil underneath their feet went instead to "the majors." For a dozen years, OPEC suffered in ineffective silence.

Western insult and indifference kept piling higher, like an ever-growing mountain of tinder. It was like American colonialism in reverse, with the United States claiming some sort of dominion over the world's natural resources. American energy dependence on Middle Eastern resources gave the producing nations growing confidence in their own ability and in the critical strategic value of their assets. It was just a matter of time before something blew.

Why had Americans turned to foreign resources when they possessed so much oil on their continent?

This is an important irony to bear in mind. By protecting the middle class and businesses large and small from rising energy prices, the economic leadership sowed the seeds for even more painful and intrusive energy reaction.

Though postwar controls over petroleum prices were finally removed, there was plenty of jawboning by the U.S. government. Whatever inflation America suffered, oil prices were not keeping pace. In 1961, the Federal Power Commission imposed a price ceiling on well-head natural gas. The impact was unsurprising but pronounced. The number of U.S. natural gas producers fell from 18,000 in 1956 to under 4,000 by 1973.

Mandatory oil price controls in 1971 drove down domestic production. Increasingly America turned to exports, which exceeded 35 percent. In the twenty prior years before 1973, U.S. rig counts were down nearly 50 percent. Foreign oil was cheap and available. Price was the chief determinant, and supply from abroad seemed unlimited. But even foreign sources drowning in oil weren't immune to inflation.

Nixon's price controls prevented oil companies from passing the full cost of imported crude to consumers. So Big Oil did what it does best— it made efficiencies happen. It stopped selling to independent service stations, instead focusing on its wholly owned stations. By May 1973, long before the embargo, more than a thousand independent service stations had closed or curtailed fuel sales.

Nixon was facing his second global commodity crisis in as many years.

By June, selective rationing of ten gallons per gas stop was implemented. But middle-class operators of small stations everywhere prevailed, after a fashion. Congress passed the Emergency Petroleum Allocation Act in September, mandating that supply allocations be shared between the independents and the branded and wholly owned stations. Critically affected states were given a governor's kitty for the state to ration.

The law was a classic example of two things: too little and too late. And it showed we had fundamentally missed the shifting sands of world oil markets. The shape of the beast was completely altered, and we never saw the whole picture.

It also showed that protecting the middle class meant understanding its position, its consumption pattern, and its needs in a global context. Our growing thirst for petroleum was casting a shadow far across the sea. Our trade policies were placing us in the path of a freight train, but we were still blissfully unaware. Pressure was building and dark forces were slowly coming into alignment.

For most Americans, life was a battle of higher prices and fewer jobs. Most middle-class Americans followed their leaders and remained dulled to the events of the world and their impact on the United States.

Something profound was about to break. Whether we knew it or not, we had set ourselves up for a massive payback. The only missing ingredient was the triggering international incident. Once again the middle class was about to be affected by developments a long way from home, but this time from a place very close to our nation's heart. All nations live and prosper alongside allies. But some nations mean even more to us than a mere pledge of allegiance. When such relations are threatened, we must choose to stand beside them or question what indeed we stand for.

America had always been closely tied to the fortunes of Israel, and our kinship to that country is a given. Israel has often asked for our help, and when such entreaties came our way the Arab and oil-producing world took notice with little menacing. For decades the oil powers sat by and let us pursue our path of friendship with the Promised Land. But 1973 was different.

Atonement

Israel's neighbors were determined to redress the crushing defeat they suffered in the Six-Day War in 1967, a conflict euphemistically called *an-Naksah*—the setback—in the Arab world. In a single day, the air forces of Egypt, Jordan, and Syria were nearly destroyed. Two days later, Israeli fighters left Egyptian tanks strewn all over the Sinai desert. Israeli forces stood at the Suez Canal and every Jordanian soldier was swept from the West Bank of their storied river. It was victory swift and sure.

But no victory is ever absolute.

The '67 Israeli triumph more badly damaged the Arab psyche than the near-dismantling of the Egyptian Air Force. Tiny Israel had vanquished all foes. But war is patient.

Six years later, at precisely 1:55 p.m. on Yom Kippur, Israel's holiest of holy days, Egypt and Syria struck.

Praying at their temples and their homes, Israelis were caught uncharacteristically off guard. Troops from Damascus poured over the Golan Heights and Russian-armed Egyptians flooded across the Suez. Their mission was to wrest back control of territory Israel took six years before in the Sinai, West Bank, and Golan Heights. As the superpowers lined up behind their respective allies, Israel rebuffed the attacks, but with less forceful momentum than in 1967. America was heavily preoccupied with the twin fiascoes of Watergate and Vietnam at the time. Nevertheless, the United States engaged in "resupplying" Israel during the conflict.

And a new weapon made its way onto the battleground: oil.

For years, blame for the world oil crisis has been laid at the feet of OPEC. But it was U.S. consumption, economic policies, and foreign affairs that drew the Arab states into the fray.

American middle-class energy consumption was a key factor. With just 6 percent of the world's population, Americans consumed over a third of the oil. Stymied by price restraints that Nixon imposed, American oil producers paused and sought foreign oil to quench the growing need. Energy self-sufficient in 1950, the United States grew its imports to over 35 percent in the following decades, despite ample North American proved reserves.

Marry the arrogance and power of the Seven Sisters Big Oil companies and their insistence on making production and pricing demands, and OPEC was spoiling for a fight.

Ten days after the start of the Yom Kippur War, the Organization of Arab Petroleum Exporting Countries (OAPEC) met in Kuwait. The organization had been created after the Six-Day War because there had been such a halfhearted attempt to curtail exports in 1967. That anemic embargo had ended after just nine and a half days, and Saudi production concluded the year up 9 percent. Hardly the "oil weapon" that was intended.

But this time the OAPEC members had lost all patience with the West, and particularly with the United States.

OAPEC resolved to cut oil production 5 percent a month, "until the Israeli forces are completely evacuated from all the Arab territories occupied in the June 1967 war." On October 16, the broader OPEC members announced their decision to raise the posted price of oil by 70 percent to $5 a barrel. (Imagine, oil was running at $3 a barrel—that barely gets you a gallon of premium gas today. A barrel of oil is 42 gallons.)

Nixon's response was immediate and unmistakable, loyal and, in the end, all that OPEC needed to hear. Two days later, he directed Congress to appropriate $2 billion in emergency aid to Israel. The die was cast.

OPEC in their boycott meetings designated the United States a "principal hostile country," and Arab state and non–Arab state alike all joined in the embargo.

The effects of embargo were immediate. Gasoline, which had been under 30 cents a gallon that summer, spiked to 60 cents and then to over $1.

By 1974, oil zoomed to $12 a barrel.

These numbers seem almost laughable compared to today's oil costs, but in 1973 they brought us to our knees. In the next 45 days, the New York Stock Exchange lost nearly $100 billion of value—staggering in

1973 terms.

U.S. imports from Arab countries dropped from 1.2 million barrels a day to 19,000. The embargo came at a time when 85 percent of Americans drove to work every day.

Everywhere Americans carried the haunting image of the oil sheikhs in the desert yanking back the lever. No one seemed to have a clue what we had done to deserve such hostility.

It was only when our greatest friend in the region and the number-two exporter behind the Saudis, the Shah of Iran, described what he was seeing to the *New York Times* that things began to fall into place. When asked if the price of oil would rise, he said:

"Of course [it] is going to rise. Certainly! You increased the price of wheat you sell to us by 300 percent, and the same for sugar and cement . . . You buy our crude and sell it back to us, redefined as petrochemicals at a hundred times the price you paid to us . . . It's only fair that from now on you should pay more for oil. Let's say 10 times more."

In another interview the Shah waxed about "the mystical power of the oil companies." The Shah had keen insights into American commerce. For years he had been a key ally in the region, and he acquired squadrons of fighter aircraft to defend his nation. Reviewing declassified notes from meetings between the Shah, Secretary of State Henry Kissinger, and former CIA director and ambassador to Iran Richard Helms, a fascinating portrait emerges.

First, the Shah had an extraordinary understanding of the capabilities of different U.S. fighter aircraft, with a particular penchant for the F-14. What was emerging was a cozy arrangement where we bought Iranian oil and they bought missiles and fighter jets.

Ultimately, President Ford would tire of the Shah's ever-increasing demands for higher prices, and against advice he cut a deal with the Saudi Kingdom for defense armaments in exchange for more modest oil price demands. The loss of U.S. support would ultimately sink the Shah and his economy.

But global petro-politics were far from the minds of average Americans that autumn of '73. For the first time since their parents were young, Americans had to cope with a drought of an essential commodity.

Middle-class Americans had a target painted on their backs and they never had a clue.

It was becoming a bit of a habit.

A NATION RESPONDS

FACED WITH OUR FIRST FUEL shortage since World War II, all Americans responded.

Congress, which is better than anyone in the world at slowing things down, dropped the speed limit to 55.

In November, President Nixon proposed an extension of daylight savings time and a complete ban on the sale of gasoline on Sundays. But he also took the opportunity to push Congress to approve the Trans-Alaskan Oil Pipeline, capable of transporting over two million barrels a day.

Congressional approval came in less than a month, and the project was completed in four years. Amazing what a focused nation can do, isn't it? Fear is a great motivator and a pretty decent legislator too.

More rationing ensued. Americans turned down their thermostats, gas stations were asked to limit sales to ten-gallon increments, and the White House Christmas tree went with no lights that year.

The non-Communist world of oil importers all suffered recessions, and in the United States the spirit of camaraderie faded as long lines snaked out from filling stations like tentacles in a neighborhood. At its peak, gasoline soared to $1.20 a gallon. That would be like $24 a gallon in California today.

OPEC made its own structural moves against the Seven Sisters. Producer nations would eventually form major state-run corporations to absorb many of the functions that the oil companies had once performed, particularly relating to production. The goal was to end forever the days when two-thirds of the revenues from their assets went to the benefit of the Big Oil companies.

Nixon appointed William E. Simon the first energy czar. In March of 1974 the embargo ended. Israel and Syria negotiated a settlement and gasoline found its way into all those middle-class gas tanks once again.

Americans had learned the difference between a critical commodity and a mere commodity. But many other important lessons went unheeded. Many middle-class families looked to American manufacturers for fuel-efficient vehicles but found the offerings sadly limited. The Ford Pinto, the Chevy Vega, and the ignoble AMC Gremlin were all Detroit had to offer. Especially on the coasts, imported cars from Toyota and Datsun captured much of the attention.

Something profound had happened—the Detroit disconnect.

Suddenly, for many Americans there was a tug-of-war between the American cars that filled the showrooms and the peppy imports. For the nation's midsection the changeover was slower. Too many families depended on Detroit for their daily bread. But the farther you got from Dearborn, the more tenuous the chivalry.

American manufacturers had a moment—an opportunity—to redirect their efforts to more fuel-efficient vehicles. It was a marketer's dream: a whole new armada of vehicles under the extraordinary brands of Ford and General Motors and Chrysler—a replacement fleet if you will, the world's largest automotive mulligan.

Considered at a distance, it was the greatest single new-product opportunity in the history of the automobile. Here was one of those rare tectonic plates of economics where American might had been challenged, and yet we had once again survived.

And what was Detroit's decision?

OIL BUST

As THE TANKS BEGAN TO fill, Americans returned to the full-size cars they had grown to love. When the crisis hit, the average fuel efficiency for the American fleet was 13 miles per gallon. A dozen years later, the fleet average had picked up just 4 mpg.

More to the point, by 1975 those full-size beasts, the Olds Delta 88, Cadillac Deville, Lincoln Mark V, and Buick Electra, were back in style, all boasting fuel efficiency well under 10 mpg. By 1976, the U.S. market had bifurcated, with Cadillac (at 5,000-plus pounds) and Toyota (at around a ton) each selling more than 300,000 autos.

By the end of the decade, all of the big bears had been forever downsized. But the disintermediation of Detroit was well under way and the stigma surrounding the imported car had disappeared.

What was good for General Motors was no longer automatically good for the nation. And across the land, men and women who earned their living by virtue of the auto industry saw the ice melt underneath their feet. Slow-to-change auto manufacturers catered to American taste and denial even as oil prices were kept deliberately low.

The missed opportunity to reimagine that industry was another element in the decline of the middle class. The exportation of manufacturing jobs was already long under way before the "outsourcing" label was dreamed up by some tall-building consultants.

No one was more dramatically affected than the middle class.

The federal government continued to regulate oil prices for the remainder of the 1970s. President Carter announced a phased-in deregulation in April 1979—oil traded at $15 a barrel.

In just a year, freely traded oil surged to $39.50. (By June 2008 West Texas Intermediate crude hit $145 a barrel before collapsing in a free-fall to $44 in January 2015.)

Naturally, the producers both here and abroad chased the opportunity. In a tale as old as time, the cartel lost its unity; producing nations like Mexico and Venezuela overbuilt just as the excess capacity drove oil prices into a multiyear swoon.

The Saudis moved increasingly like the big engine of oil.

After the Yom Kippur War, the Saudis commenced the creeping nationalization of their oil production. Forty years earlier, Standard Oil of California had been granted the concession to explore for oil in the Kingdom. Amazingly, they found nothing for four years, and Texaco was brought in as SoCal's partner.

Now the Saudis wanted to own their production. First at 25 percent in 1973, then at 60 percent a year later, Oil Minister Ahmed Zaki Yamani, former Carlos crown jewel, ultimately brought Aramco under complete Saudi control by 1980.

Through this nationalization the Saudis controlled the most valuable company on earth. And it was paying off. Between 1973 and early 1979, Saudi Arabia's annual oil revenue surged from $4 billion to $36 billion.

OPEC lost its ability to ever again seize the world markets in a single motion. Infighting and relative power prevented the cartel from creating the third world resource axis we all feared in the 1970s. OPEC still controlled just 40 percent of the production, but it boasted 70 percent of the reserves. That meant they were a minority that nevertheless had staying power.

Over the decades Saudi wealth and influence expanded in ways that are hard to fathom. Just one indication is the expansion of the Saudi royal family. Today there are more than 22,000 Saudi royals, with about 7,000 princes among them, making the population ration about one royal for every thousand Saudis. About 70 percent of the government's revenue relies on oil. That buys a lot of peace even during the Arab Spring.

The day that Egyptian president Hosni Mubarak stepped down in 2011, Saudi King Abdullah announced an economic benefits package totaling more than $130 billion, including massive unemployment benefits, salary increases, housing loans, and even a cost-of-living adjustment for inflation.

Through it all, Americans have kept on burning that oil at a rate of about 20 million barrels a day. Since the darkest days of the embargo we have gone from 35 percent of our oil imported to a peak in 2008 of 57 percent. And since those dark days of '73, every U.S. president has called for achieving energy independence on his watch.

We have remained in a state of denial, using defense dollars and foreign relations to protect our supply of oil. Years after the embargo, Saudi oil minister Yamani did concede that their actions were far more effective than they had estimated. He had not concluded that "we could reduce imports to the United States . . . the world is really just one market. So the embargo was really more symbolic than anything else."

Symbolic or not, the OPEC embargo was the beginning of the end. Americans longed for the old days, when cars were big and fast, life was uncomplicated, and we made all our own energy and most of our own clothes.

Those were the golden days for our middle class and, by extension, the country as a whole. It seemed in those moments like everyone was young, industrious, and glowing with opportunity. We were the agents of our own destiny. We had all been engaged in a global battle against evil; we were victorious; we were the global good guys. And more than anything else, we had belief in the kind of world a middle class could create. But before long, profound divisions and economic pressures shattered that belief.

What so many Americans were searching for was another voice and another direction. But the howling winds of recession drowned out the chorus.

CHAPTER SEVEN

FLYING THE HUMP

Surviving the Republican wreck

SCREAMING ENGINES GASPED FOR AIR.

Thermals bounced the cargo ship like a kite stuck on a telephone wire. The radio beacon stuttered and atmospherics sent gauges dancing and tumbling. Cloud cover was constant, thunderstorms frequent, and hail hath no fury like what pounded the fuselage.

Pilots called this kind of navigation "heading hoping," but they had little cause for concern.

In their tank was enough fuel for the mission plus at least twenty minutes.

Once past the halfway mark, they were committed. At 20,000 feet there were no emergency landing sites, just the shark-toothed jaws of the Himalayas.

Some days the clouds would lift and pilots were guided through the mountains by the glint of aluminum wrecks that dotted the peaks. But when the fog descended they were flying blind, typically unaccompanied by fighter support, and loaded like an aerial trucker with jeeps, gasoline, bombs, and all the necessary implements of war.

The math was inescapable. The C-46s and C-47s they flew struggled above 10,000 feet, and the mountains they had to pilot over ran to 35,000. The air-stream and the prop wash made formation flying herculean. Many days the pilot would be soaked in sweat even as his crew and airmen fought frostbite.

Flying 500 miles of hell from Chabua, India, to Kunming, China, seeking a passage through the triangle of India, Burma, and China, was the only option afforded the American troops. All other routes to China were closed. It was a damnable strategy born of no other options.

The Empire of Japan clutched the entire China coast and dominated much of the interior railway.

Flying the hump was the kind of supply-line strategy that can only be born in wartime, guaranteed to create heroes and angels in plentiful measure. Supplies traveled overland 800 miles on rail through India to the Tibetan border. There boxcars were broken down and trucked to numerous hump terminals. Then, deep in the interior, far from the well-machined loading docks, transfer to cargo planes was done by hand, turbaned barefoot workers rolling bomb after bomb up steep ramps to the hold—one at a time for hours and days on end.

In these outer reaches the past clung desperately to modern warfare.

The airlift began humbly enough. After a year of operation, in 1943 the 10th Air Force had grown from a squadron of ten borrowed transports to more than 140 aircraft. Under General Edward Alexander, airmen would deliver more than a million tons of supplies and a million soldiers over the Himalayas into China.

Never was a riskier or more costly necessity of supply created. Every four tons of gasoline delivered required expending three and a half tons just to get it there. At the airlift's peak the 46s flew continuously—some days ships taking off every two minutes. During the twenty months of principal operations, 250 transport planes were lost—250 cargoes and more than 800 airmen.

Often they crashed in plain sight of fellow flyers or over the shared crackling radio. Chances for survival even when ejecting were remote—many froze to death on the side of an unreachable and uncharted peak, their grave marker a shattered hulk of fuselage on a mountain with no name.

Piloting over the hump tended to boil things down to the essential: survival, God, and country. Pick your own order.

Like most ferry commanders, this pilot had hoped for combat missions. But every hump airman knew that saw-toothed mountains were far deadlier than the errant Japanese fighter plane that might cross their path.

Hump flying was deadly, draining, and reserved for a rare breed of pilot. There were no tall walking aces or top guns. The hump was the work of quiet dependables who took obscene risk as a matter of course in the name of getting the matériel through no matter what.

It was their sheer force of will that stemmed the tide for China and turned out the Japanese marauders. And for such pilots came the deep, if unheralded, knowledge that they were truly the backbone of the war effort.

Combat indeed. The greatest of heroes are unsung.

This pilot's character had been hammered delivering on some of the toughest sorties imaginable. The Hump was just another résumé entry. He was chief pilot of the Fireball Route from Miami to Brazil, South Africa into India. He was also chief pilot of the Crescent Route through the Azores to North Africa.

While a Fireballer he took to filling his empty planes on the deadhead leg back with war-weary soldiers due to ship out and who otherwise would wait months for a formal sortie home. Undaunted, he kept filling his planes with these soldiers despite direct orders not to do so. Deadheading empty while homesick soldiers pined for a way home was wrong . . . to hell with his superiors.

In a daring bit of piloting that won him a reputation and the coveted Air Medal, he and a few cargo jockeys loaded P-47 Thunderbolts with extra fuel tanks and flew the spritely fighters across the North Sea route to Greenland, then to Iceland and into the European theater, against all odds. As with the Himalayas, the frigid stretch of North Sea provides no place for emergency landings. Bailing out meant certain death.

He was a dedicated pilot and a patriot. By his career's end he was reported to have piloted more than 165 different types of aircraft. As with many self-taught pilots, his aviation beginnings were humble.

During the Depression, while a teenage store clerk, he had snuck out after work for flying lessons. When war broke out in Europe in his twenties, he was already a first lieutenant in the Army Reserves. He had also risen to be president of the family business—a downtown department store.

Reporting at last for an active tour, he was quickly frustrated, because the combination of poor eyesight and being over thirty meant pilot training was out of the question. He was assigned to work in public relations. To him, it seemed like the gulag.

But something was driving him to serve his country, and the wild blue yonder, not PR, was going to be his ticket. He would not be deterred.

Such was the resolve of young department store manager and hump flyer Barry Goldwater.

———————

TOO MANY OF US REGARD Goldwater through the blurred lens of the 1960s, when his party's conservatism was still driven by an eastern elite and youth culture had chased Republicans deeper into the fringes.

Historian Richard Hofstadter argued that the "right was not a serious long-term political movement but rather a transitory phenomenon led by irrational paranoid people who were angry at the changes taking place in America."

One expositor wondered in *Commonweal* whether a right-wing student group was "merely a new political organization out to repeal the twentieth century?"

Tough-talking, independent, and too quotable, Goldwater was the definition of irony. He was a reporter's candy store, and glaring overstatements obscured what the man meant to the nation and the middle class. He was bitter-tasting medicine with healing powers for his party. But to most Americans he was the mighty Casey.

As a rejoinder to his slogan de guerre, "In your heart you know he's right," came the wet-witted but memorable "In your guts you know he's nuts."

It sure didn't start that way.

He began his political career as a nonpartisan, landing a seat on the Phoenix City Council. That first assignment eclipsed the family business, and he never worked in the department store again. But it was surprising that this erstwhile retail maven never comfortably wore the cloak of retail politics.

By 1952, he found succor in the Arizona Republican Party. His dogged pursuit of a U.S. Senate seat held by no less than the august body's majority leader, Democrat Ernest McFarland, led to an upset and his first foray onto the national stage.

In a replay six years downstream, Goldwater again prevailed. He stepped down from the Senate in 1964 to seek the presidency and a shot at the heavyweight crown.

In 1960, he compiled his seminal *The Conscience of a Conservative*, drawn from his syndicated newspaper columns, and abetted by William F. Buckley's brother-in-law, L. Brent Bozell, Jr. The book became the conservative alpha text, selling more than 3.5 million copies in an endless number of printings.

Goldwater's opinions set the stage for an elephant's dance in the 1964 nomination. At stake was control of the party—a title bout pitting the eastern Rockefeller Republicans against the western conservative upstarts.

A Red State Winner-Take-All

Arizona comrade Senator John McCain saw glory in the ignominious party skirmishes and defeat that followed; Goldwater "transformed the Republican Party from an Eastern elitist organization to a breeding ground for the election of Ronald Reagan."

Picture the American landscape at the time. The nation's axis was listing to the left. Even moderate Republicans appeared hopelessly out of touch. The nation was still mourning the fresh wounds of JFK's assassination, followed too closely by King and Kennedy's brother. It was an age of martyrdom, and the nation's heart was aching.

Joseph McCarthy's anti-communist rhetoric was dimming in the memories of American voters. But Goldwater's refusal to censure his Senate colleague was indelibly etched in voter recollections. (Seventy-eight senators had voted to censure.) Goldwater's staunch opposition to the spread of communism was well delineated in *Conscience*, but at least he had the good sense not to name any names.

Yet another irony plagued Goldwater. As a department store execu-tive he had hired the first blacks to work in a major Phoenix retailer. He was a public supporter of his home state's NAACP and was outspoken in leading the desegregation of the Arizona National Guard. (He would retire with the rank of Major General.)

Later in his career, he would be equally outspoken about gays in the military: "You don't need to be straight to fight and die for your country. You just have to shoot straight."

And later: "Quit discriminating against people just because they are gay. You don't have to agree with it, but they have a constitutional right to be gay."

He would be equally outspoken on abortion: "They think I've turned liberal because I believe a woman has a right to an abortion. That's a decision that's up to the pregnant woman, not up to the pope or some do-gooders on the religious right."

Yet for all of his instincts, none trumped his zeal for individual inde-pendence, even civil rights. And many Americans hated him for it.

As a senator he supported the Civil Rights Acts of 1957 and 1960. But when the much more expansive bill, which conferred even greater rights on those with diverse backgrounds, made its way to the Senate, Goldwater came to the proverbial fork in the road.

On one hand, for the first time, Americans of all races and creeds could share equal treatment and access to the promise of the American dream. But on the other, the expansion of the federal government into matters of commerce, business management, employee relations, and, even more to his frustration, a legislated morality seemed excessive to Goldwater.

He voted against the march of history and the Civil Rights Acts of 1964. His trade-off of two greater goods, civil rights versus individual liberty, was misunderstood. He was denounced as a racist, and his "no" vote provided his critics with a flag of convenience that waved for years to come.

But as was often the case with Goldwater, there was more to the story. Paraphrasing his central argument: "A government that is big enough to give you all you want is big enough to take it all away."

The path to the 1964 nomination was filled with blistering attacks, and Goldwater's penchant for speaking his mind provided fruitful opportunities to those who plotted his political demise.

He was so often tripped up by his comments that reporters in 1964 claimed that Goldwater staff would ask them to "Write what he means, not what he says."

He denounced foreign aid, high taxes, and budgets rife with red ink. He argued vigorously against the growing power of the federal government, and he targeted labor and communism for their increasing power.

Goldwater's *Conscience* was written to "awaken the American people to the realization of how far we had moved from the old constitutional concepts toward the new welfare state."

As chairman of the Republican Senatorial Campaign Committee in 1960, Goldwater had visited dozens of states and was a frequent spokesman at party functions. Long before the assassination, the erstwhile candidate eagerly anticipated facing John F. Kennedy in the '64 election.

Later, Goldwater spoke and wrote of the pall that had descended over him when Kennedy was shot in 1963. He gave serious thought to withdrawing from the race. He had respected Kennedy, even if he disagreed with him.

But reflecting on grassroots Republicans he had encountered in his pilgrimages supporting his party's Senate candidates, Goldwater sensed the gravitational pull. He was becoming a fulcrum separating his party from the grips of eastern moderates. Tooth extraction might have been easier—and less painful.

On the road, Goldwater did not have the makings of a champion. A write-in candidate, Henry Cabot Lodge, bested him in the New Hampshire primaries. And the moderate Nelson Rockefeller gained traction in Oregon and appeared to have an early lead in bellwether California.

But the gravitational pull away from the east could not be denied. Goldwater had shrewdly identified a young Ronald Reagan to co-chair California Republicans for Goldwater. Reagan delivered his stirring pro-Goldwater speech, "A Time for Choosing," many times, most famously on television on October 27, 1964.

Watching it was like witnessing a star rise in the firmament.

Goldwater had chosen wisely. Reagan had only been a Republican for two years, but "The Speech," as the address is also known, was his beginning. Beholding the crowd respond was like watching a great lever move. As Reagan warmed to his subject, you can see the audience turn their full attention to him, not on the shock value of a snarky comment or a "gotcha" sound bite. Reagan brought something profound and otherwise missing from all Republican rhetoric of the time—he was uplifting.

"Alexander Hamilton said, 'A nation which can prefer disgrace to danger is prepared for a master . . . and deserves one.'"

"The martyrs of history were not fools, and our honored dead who gave their lives to stop the advance of the Nazis did not die in vain."

"For three decades, we've sought to solve the problems of unemployment through government planning, and, the more the plans fail, the more the planners plan."

Rockefeller, the far-and-away favorite, succumbed to the Goldwater onslaught in California. Something Orphic was happening. Incredulous eastern Republicans mounted a last-ditch effort.

But it took just one turn of the wheel at the convention. Goldwater was his party's nominee in a single ballot.

It was a watershed moment for the party, a new beginning—yet everything about it spelled disaster.

Goldwater stoutly declared from the podium at San Francisco's Cow Palace that he had no plans to back down from his conservative stance, leading a reporter on the scene to gasp, "My God, he's going to run as Barry Goldwater!"

His message in the following months fell on many deaf ears, but for a few shrewd listeners Goldwater foretold something powerful in the Republican Party.

Change

To LBJ, Goldwater was the man that wasn't there. In the entire election, the two men never met for a single debate. The Texan's strategy was a shrewd one. It was hard to see how the still-grieving nation could be open to the notion of a third president in fourteen months. Johnson understood this instinctively and played to the nation's heartstrings.

After his defeat, Goldwater quipped, "We would have lost even if Abraham Lincoln had come back and campaigned with us."

By Election Day, the Republican Party looked like a farmer's burnt-out field.

The results were so one-sided and horrifying that almost every pundit missed what had actually happened.

Goldwater won his home state in a squeaker and took a confederacy of five states on the strength of his choice of private property rights over human civil rights. In a straight line across the South, Goldwater took Louisiana, Mississippi, Alabama, Georgia, and South Carolina—all states formerly Democratic strongholds, and all willing to vote against the march of history.

The bloodbath ran through the halls of the great domed Congress building. Republicans lost thirty-six seats in the House, giving the Democrats the biggest majority any party had enjoyed in the House since VJ Day in 1945. The GOP lost two Senate seats, pushing the Democratic majority to 68–32, enough to block any filibuster. The Senate lurched left like it hadn't in decades.

Goldwater delivered a Democratic majority so large it freed Johnson from dependence on conservative Southern Democrats. Turns out he needed that liberation: 68 percent of Senate Democrats supported the historic Civil Rights Act, while a stunning 81 percent of Senate Republicans did.

Even Republicans embraced the surge of liberal activism that swept across the nation. The newly minted 89th Congress elected in the Goldwater debacle passed in stunning sequence Medicare and Medicaid. Bilateral work across the aisle enacted one of the most sweeping immigration-reform bills in our history, opening the borders for more than 40 million new Americans, most from third world nations and most achingly poor.

Democratic gains in the Congress in 1958 and 1962 were exceeded in 1964. The liberal tsunami made the moment ripe for a rollback.

All Republicans had to do was fly the hump.

But the path would pitch and roll like a cargo plane bouncing on the thermals. Histories that describe the long Republican path back as an unbroken tradition miss the Himalayan peaks that had to be crossed.

In a true-life example of what-does-not-kill-us-makes-us-stronger, the Republican Party began to revive. Goldwater had won almost 39 percent of the popular vote despite his puny 52-electoral-vote tally. And by the '66 mid-terms Republicans had picked up 47 seats in the House of Representatives.

Almost no one grasped the implications of the Goldwater campaign on the real people . . . certainly not the cognoscenti. Goldwater drew twice as many volunteers as Johnson did. More than a million American citizens gave money to Goldwater in 1964, versus 66,000 to Nixon and Kennedy in their 1960 campaigns.

Goldwater brought the people something—and the pundits were too besotted with liberal victories and national heartache to appreciate what had just happened.

Like the Magi, the Goldwater campaign bore three gifts. The magazine *Human Events* bravely identified them: "The Republican Party is essentially Conservative; the South is developing into a major pivot of its power; and a candidate who possesses Goldwater's virtues but lacks some of his handicaps can win the presidency."

Something even more profound had happened in the landslide. Goldwater had captured the attention of thousands of young Americans who quietly reserved doubts about the turmoil of youthful protest.

Among them was a Yale dropout with a couple of sobering DWIs under his belt. The arrests caused a young Dick Cheney to reconsider his life. Married to Lynne Vincent in 1964, Cheney tried a bit of homeschooling at the University of Wyoming, where in rapid succession he turned his life around, earning a BA and a master's in political science by 1966.

Just ten years later, Cheney would be named President Gerald Ford's chief of staff.

The lure of the District was impossible to ignore, and Cheney, like other young conservatives, flocked to Washington to make a difference. Armed with "a powerful anti-charisma," Cheney won a fellowship to work for Republican congressman Bill Steiger. Cheney, like his wife, had been raised in a Democratic household, but the tenor of the times drove him in a fresh direction.

As Steiger's aide, Cheney displayed a canny sense for how things worked far beyond his years and pay grade. Sensing opportunity, Cheney penned a memorandum for then-Congressman Donald Rumsfeld, thoughtfully outlining the best way to manage confirmation hearings in the legislator's bid for directorship of the Office of Economic Opportunity. Steiger showed the memo to Rumsfeld, who was so impressed he hired Cheney immediately.

For decades, every Republican administration would reflect the combined efforts of these two young conservatives.

Theirs is just one example of the legacy of the Goldwater landslide. Obituaries written for the conservative cause, in fact, had read things exactly wrong. It was the beginning of the American conservative movement, not the end.

But like so many beginnings, the first steps were painful.

The Republicans of 1964 were vilified even as they began to find their footing. The image of a young girl picking a daisy while nuclear catastrophe blossomed in the background haunted liberal and conservative middle-class Americans alike. The Daisy Girl commercial ran just once on NBC during a September 7, 1964, *Monday Night at the Movies*. The Johnson campaign, in a play for gallantry, pulled the offending footage immediately.

The damage was done. Goldwater had misspoken and indicated a greater willingness to use nuclear weapons than he meant. Middle America had recoiled at the combined message of cutting social programs and building military might.

Because it had seemed too extreme.

There are those who see an unbroken tradition from then to now of Republican Conservatism. Certainly, voices like William F. Buckley's, Milton Friedman's, and Russell Kirk's still echo through the party. But pragmatism flourished . . . and the electability longed for by *Commonweal* meant that Republicans went from making a point to trying to win elections.

The middle class was their chief target.

Twenty-four months after the Goldwater debacle, Ronald Reagan, who had never run for public office, found his voice in the nation's most populous state, slamming the incumbent Democratic governor of California, Edmund "Pat" Brown, by a million votes.

Reagan might have won the governor's mansion without the Goldwater endorsement and his campaign cameo in "A Time for Choosing," but few would deny the enormous middle-class momentum that carried him into office.

It is fascinating to study how measured Reagan was in office in contrast to his tough-minded campaign rhetoric. The result was less Reagan revolution and more center-right Republican. The cuts in the state budget were nowhere near draconian, and on the social side, a liberal abortion bill was passed on his watch.

California law at the time required that government income and outflow be kept in balance. Reagan used his network of business and logistical experts to make government hum more efficiently. Two standout programs that drew derision were in retrospect true indicators of his conservative view. The first was the highly controversial introduction of tuition for attending the state university system. The second was a welfare-reform program, the guts of which saw national adoption by the Clinton presidency a generation later.

After just six months in office, Reagan was whispered as a future fit for the chief executive role in Washington. He had given middle-class and aspiring Californians hope—and the nation was beginning to respond.

This post-Goldwater modification of conservatism did a few things. It allowed the American middle class to grow accustomed to a party that defended their small business interests. It got Nixon and many other center-right Republicans into office and ameliorated the liberal dominance they faced in Congress.

And it did one more telling thing. As conservatism regained traction, seeds were planted for the emergence of dormant strains—the neocons, the New Right, and the Religious Right—developments that would have telling consequences in the coming years for the middle class, because these new perspectives pulled so forcefully from the moderate view.

More to the point, the Republican turn toward the center did little to staunch the advance of the welfare state that grew under both Democratic and Republican administrations.

Care for our fellow Americans was a true growth business.

Some even point to continuities between the Carter and Reagan years—but let's not get carried away. The Gipper did little to reduce welfare or entitlements that were handed down from Jimmy Carter. George H. W. Bush adopted the Americans with Disabilities Act and a new Civil Rights Act.

Republicans were making the clear first steps at recovery, but something more profound than rehabilitation was simmering beneath the surface.

Whether you buy the moderation of the Republican Party at the time or not, there is a more central question worth posing:

How could conservatism be transformed from a fringe movement, regarded as demonic by liberals and unguided by the ruling eastern elite of the Republican Party, into one of the most powerful political and social forces in the country?

The answer in large measure can be found in conservatism's embrace of the middle class.

It was always an interpretive dance. That's why so many economists missed it entirely. No one provided more dynamic shifts than Richard Nixon, who lost often, but found that his penchant for swimming against the tide could be radically more effective when he instead swam with it.

Nixon could see middle- and lower-class Americans beguiled by elements of the conservative cause in the 1960s. Then, as now, grassroots activism played a role in the change. Goldwater had unleashed a wave of energy for volunteers to contribute time and treasure.

Nixon seized the opportunity in his own dark and effective way.

Through the lens of history we can identify what Nixon and his advisors so clearly saw happening—and, more important, we can see why. Cynics point to white backlash to the civil rights juggernaut. Nixon's unctuous Southern Strategy, aimed at drawing disaffected white voters into the Republican embrace, acknowledged the impact of Johnson's push and the South's gravitational pull.

Surely that strategy was effective, but conservatism gained wider appeal to middle-class members well beyond the Mason-Dixon. Conservatism flowered because of a convergence of complex forces beyond just race. No explanation is that convenient.

During the fifties and sixties, middle-class Americans enjoyed prosperity far beyond their parents' experience. Robust home economics meant that many newly minted middle-class Americans grew hostile to the notion of high taxes on their recent gains, especially since greater amounts of it were going to finance social programs and to a futile war effort that seemed to yield death and embarrassment in equal measure.

Violent student protests and the flames of urban riots acted like repellents, driving unsure citizens and those who had tired of disruption into the arms of Nixonistas.

But Nixon was far from a natural charmer.

Nixon lost an agonizingly close presidential race in 1960, and then, in insult-to-injury fashion, fell short in the subsequent gubernatorial run in California. Many counseled him that his role as Eisenhower's vice president was legacy enough.

ABC News graciously summed up his career in a program provocatively called *The Political Obituary of Richard Nixon*. As Twain himself might have intoned: "Rumors of my death . . ."

Ever wary of the emerging Reagan and channeling Goldwater's exhilarating effect on conservatives across the country, Nixon dedicated himself to his ailing party in the 1966 midterms. Stepping forward as a champion of the middle class—later called the "Silent Majority"—Nixon bared his long-held distrust of the elites and stood out for his vicious anticommunist views.

During the eighty-six days preceding the midterms, Nixon campaigned for a different Republican senator, governor, and representative almost every single day. Nixon's was an unparalleled homage to fellow party members, and he threw everything he had at the challenge. When the polls closed, fifty-nine had gained office.

It was by any measure a political grand slam—but for Nixon Agonistes, it spelled deliverance.

That's how Nixon created gratitude. Just a few Novembers earlier, after ignominious defeat in the '62 gubernatorial race and still smarting from the JFK loss, he launched into a desultory and sadly fitting phrase: "You won't have Nixon to kick around anymore . . ."

On election night just four years later, over a spaghetti supper, as

Nixon munched on a meatball, a flood of well-wishers confirmed two things he may have already suspected—one overt, the other spiritual, deeper inside the man. They confirmed that his exhaustive campaigning had christened him the engine of the Republican recovery.

What they didn't say, but everyone could feel, was that Nixon had also engineered his own revival.

Nixon had learned a thing or two about campaigning as well. Never at ease among people, and prone to telling stories that featured himself prominently, Nixon at last found the retail link: an emotional connection to the silent majority of hardworking Americans.

He played to their longing for national pride and love of country even as he cast doubt on Johnson's vision of the Great Society. He was shrewd and sedulous in courting the middle class. Unions that had often spurned him for Democratic candidates heard his sympathy for the working classes, for their pro–God-and-country rhetoric, and for their disdain for the spoiled elite and the liberal intelligentsia.

Nixon had never been truly popular before. But occasionally the river bends a candidate's way. When that happens, best to swim with the current, and Nixon was paddling with all his might, happy at last to have the American worker and the middle class pulling with him.

Though the 1968 Republican presidential field drew familiar names— Reagan, Rockefeller, George Romney, and Charles Percy—Nixon was nominated on the first ballot.

But once the cheering subsided, Nixon's alienating style campaigned beside him on the trail.

It was a surprise when he chose Maryland governor Spiro Agnew, but the running mate's pugnacity was seen to be a real asset. Isn't it striking how often a candidate's perceived strengths contain the very essence of their ultimate weakness?

Because Nixon was leading in the polls, and chastened by his TV shellacking by a youthful JFK, he refused to debate Democrat Hubert Humphrey. His margins narrowed.

Hoping to deflect criticism on Vietman, Nixon claimed to have worked out a "secret plan" to bring the conflict to an honorable conclusion. The strategy worked to a point, but it confused people.

Things turned topsy-turvy: The Democrat was urging a continuation of the war, while the Republican had a secret mission to bring it to a speedy end.

THE PARTY BREAKS UP

THE DEMOCRATS WERE SLICED AND DICED.

They were split by opposers and supporters of the Vietnam War; split geographically over civil rights; and split again when their sitting president performed limply against Senator Eugene McCarthy in the New Hampshire primary. The party split further when RFK-as-Hamlet, smelling blood in the water, finally plunged into the race just four days after the New Hampshire debacle. The party's disarray carried on when their chief executive decided to withdraw from contention altogether in his "I shall not seek" moment soon afterward. It seemed as if things were spinning out of the spinmeisters' control.

But nothing could have dispirited them the way the campaign was tipped on end by the RFK assassination after he narrowly won the important California primary.

Democrats were further disheartened that it was their convention in Chicago, where in fact the whole world was watching, which further split the party between those who favored order and those who favored the protesters.

Nixon continued on message, even if he was an imperfect candidate. George Wallace enjoyed an early surge, peaking at 21 percent favorability, particularly with southern Democrats. But Nixon was dogged and determined.

Even a last-minute Halloween Peace announced by LBJ could not thwart Nixon. Later, documents suggest that Nixonistas, eager to discredit and neutralize LBJ, had urged the Vietnamese to wait to come to the bargaining table until after the election. Such accusations are impossible to prove. No matter, Johnson was unable to deliver the hoped-for bump to his vice president. He and Humphrey believed to their dying day that Nixon had stolen peace from their grasp.

History might have turned on the failed cease-fire. But war raged on and Nixon eked out a one percent victory in the popular vote, faring only a bit better in the electoral college.

But much, much more occurred on that November night.

Though historians consider Reagan's morning in America the breakthrough in the conservative narrative, it was Nixon's narrow victory that truly realigned American politics. That Election Day, Nixon and George Wallace took home more than 57 percent of the popular vote—an antiliberal watershed moment impossible to have contemplated during the Goldwater election.

Consider the tipping point for a moment:

From the elections in '32, when the backdrop of the Depression proved ruinous to the aspirations of incumbent Republican Herbert Hoover, when Franklin Delano Roosevelt swept glamorously into office on the promise of a New Deal for the American people, all the way to Nixon's narrow victory in 1968, the Democratic Party had enjoyed both momentum and majority.

During those thirty-six years, the Democrats won seven of nine presidential elections, and their mission weighed heavily on the only Republican who managed to win the White House in all those years, Dwight D. Eisenhower.

But from 1968 to 2008 Republicans won seven of ten presidential bids, a near-complete reversal of fortune. Nixon and Reagan would each achieve the extraordinary—winning forty-nine states in their second-term elections. Republican policies also were major factors in the lives of the two Democrats who achieved the highest office during this forty-year stretch, Presidents Carter and Clinton. Carter resisted the urge to meet in the middle, but Clinton wisely shifted into the center, especially during his second term.

Jimmy Carter rose to power after the Nixon ignominy and Ford's sideways presidency. These "pilot errors" broke the Republican streak. But Carter's unique ability to alienate the middle class opened the door for Reagan's morning in America.

During this period of chaos when President Ford signaled a return to Republican moderation by selecting Nelson Rockefeller as his vice president, new factions maneuvered to gain strength in the Republican Party: the New Right and the neoconservatives. They were far from natural bedfellows, and a strong voice would be needed to bring them into the embrace of alliance.

Reagan was a natural to create that coalition.

The Gipper had already tried twice to win the highest office by the time he swept the nomination and later the general election in 1980.

Winning with an 8-million-vote margin, Reagan immediately recrafted his own version of the New Deal. No one could have predicted how wonderful and ultimately how raw it would turn out to be.

He was such a highly effective communicator he could steal thunder's thunder. And America needed someone who could both lead them and communicate with them, even if his avuncular style was writing the harshest of prescriptions.

As morning in America broke on inauguration day 1981, the nation faced economic travail that rivaled the Great Depression . . . only in some ways worse. According to Keynesian doctrines that had permeated economic policy since FDR, the state of affairs faced by the economy was deemed impossible to occur. But the nightmare fantasy was all-too-real. Massive unemployment, economic stagnation, limited borrowing, yet runaway inflation of prices and wages, spiking interest rates, and energy insecurity all swirled in our new reality—they could indeed co-exist.

Economics had become the art of the impossible.

And if something is impossible, that makes it pretty tough for the experts to combat it. Incrementalism was not going to fix the problem.

The nation searched for something new . . .

CHAPTER EIGHT

———— TALL PAUL AND THE TAMERS ————
Reagan reconsidered

A DAMP TROPICAL DAWN EMBRACED THE *Keys, and the giant frame of a man eased himself into the flatboat. He was as still as the waters and every bit as big. His guide was friendly and taciturn. No point in rushing things; they had all day together.*

He turned her over.

As the motor cranked quietly to life, the guide took the big man's instruments, two delicate fly rods, and stacked them neatly in cradles along the gunnel. The contrast was inescapable. In those large, steady hands the lightweight rods looked so slight. The guide had seen all kinds of styles. For all the technique and coaching, casting was still a dance of idiosyncratic bad habits with a single goal—put the fly in front of the fish. And with today's quarry, one of South Florida's big three, it meant casting in the right place, presenting so as not to spook, then strip, strip, strip like your daddy told you.

The guide kept a steady gaze on the horizon as the flatboat exploded into life, always so much faster, cleaner in the water that you expect. The big man beside him in the stern regarded the rippled water tickling the underside of the wakeless boat, pushed his glasses against his face, and looked forward across the bow toward the markerless frontier heading back toward the Everglade flats.

The guide never once consulted a chart or GPS. These boundary waters were his vast primeval playground. He had his own list of favorites, as most all guides do: a cut here, marked by sunken beer bottles, that was favored by tarpon when they rolled, a giant pool there amid the mangroves preferred by elusive snook, as fine an eater as swims.

And besides these special spots, the guide plied the open waters, vast expanses of flats, marked here and there by waving grasses, a swooping ray, or the errant hammerhead. That open water was the morning's destination. Their quarry was the shiny, flashing, silver swimmer that promised a unique fishing excursion—the bonefish. The whining motors threaded the odd poles and channel markers. Long white scars crossed flats on either side of them, marking a corner cut by another angler who may have sped to catch a coming tide.

The big man certainly had perspective. Growing up in New Jersey, he had learned fly-fishing theocracy the way everyone in his generation had, at the generally patient urging of his dad. It was small-mouth bass that "the boys," as his mother referred to them, were after as they ventured off purposefully together all those years. They had none of the pretensions of the trouters. His father, after all, was a municipal man. His lanky son was a basketball back-bencher and bright as hell. There was no need to be putting on trout-fishing airs.

Still, as the days passed on the water, it was the stories and the shared daydreams, one to another, that flooded the big man's recollections. Father and son would swap aspirations to one day try for the most regal of all game fish, the North Atlantic salmon, though both knew that cast was out of reach.

As the boy's quiet genius directed him upstream to Princeton, Harvard, and the London School of Economics, and, later, to the service of many presidents, the call of the salmon run was something close to instinctual.

As his success permitted, he parted from the pod of his deceased dad and found special joy fishing for salmon in the frigid rushing rivers of Quebec and New Brunswick. But the gentle chiding of the older man was never far from his ears. They fished these rivers together still.

His reveries drifted back to the present as the wailing of the engine changed pitch. The tiny rooster tail looped back toward the stern as the flat-boat assumed a sharp angle against the water, as if coming in for a landing, *and finally pushed to a slow putter plane-off. The hushed engine permitted renewed conversation. After a forty-minute honk to reach the Everglades, the guide squinted, cut the motor, and let the shallow craft drift in the slow current.*

Silence.

There were so many things to consider and take into account. The tides were running with little difference between high and low, even here in way back country; the moon was a sliver, suggesting neap tides were on them; the wind had been cold and from the north last night; and though calm now, foam still laced through the mangroves. A storm blew through yesterday, a good one, and the weather change would be brief. Another warm front with more storms was due tomorrow. After all the action and reaction, the fish might just be settling in. The sun was up, but still low in the sky. It was peaceful, somber . . . possibly feeding time.

The big man liked weighing all the factors, looking for stress or anomaly. Folks are always quick to draw parallels, he mused. Sometimes fishing is just fishing. But the complementarity of how he spent his workday and how he spent his holiday crossed his mind on occasion.

He had a calling perhaps, but he was no fisher of men. He was like his father, a patient and humble public servant. Years of battles had made him gruff and resolute. His life was filled with the ministrations of money men. Sometimes cocky, inattentive to risk, they could be frighteningly and maddeningly unaware of what the rest of the world was doing, especially at feeding time.

His whole life, it seemed, was spent surveying the waterfront. And keeping an eye on them.

Slow and steady, he too scanned the horizon for a misplaced variable, or a clue. Finding nothing obvious, the next order of business was to try to feel all the rhythms, consider what the bonefish reaction had been to all the stirring of the pot in the last twenty-four hours and find them where they feed.

Bonefishing is more like hunting. They are stalked, found, and sight-fished in various ways depending on . . . everything. One way to find them is to stand the caster on the bow like a sharpshooter while the guide perches on a platform astern just above the outboard motor. Gently, rhythmically, the guide then takes a twenty-foot pointed pole and eases it into the sand and pushes forward like a silent gondolier.

Another way is to have the rod holder leave the boat entirely, gently slip into the two-to-three-foot water, and slowly walk the vast flat underwater plains. Everything requires such delicacy because few fish are more skittish and less forgiving than bonefish. Catching one requires patience, determination, a steady hand, and cool-headedness at the moment of execution. You simply cannot get flustered when you spot them.

There will be no second chance.

The big man spots a dozen or more bonefish tailing. As they feed in the shallows, bonefish dip their heads down, reaching toward the sandy bottom. On the surface, the observant angler may glimpse the slightest suggestion of a swishing tail.

Let's join him in that moment—like spirit of his father, present, focused, far from the ministrations of money, alert with the priority of now . . .

At the guide's prompting, six-foot-seven-inch Paul Volcker adjusts his glasses and slips wordlessly into the water. He slides his feet ever so carefully one in front of the other, taking great pains not to create as much as a ripple. Everything depends on accurate assessment. How close to get? He notes the wind, the angle of the sun, the current, and the small waves. He is now fifty yards from the boat, and less than half that from the bonefish. A school of bait fish darts by. He stands frozen, assessing everything.

There is no sound but for the breeze and the gentle lapping around his calfskin. His shirt ruffles against his chest. He closes the distance by half— forty feet away. No closer. Holding the fly in one hand and the rod in the other, he lets the excess line he drew out in anticipation drop silently into the brine. He is a giant clutching a slender reed. Considered at a distance, Tall Paul dominates the flats. Nothing taller is within miles. He stands hovering like an oversized heron in the Everglades wilderness.

He needs a precise cast to plink the fly down oh-so-delicately just beyond where they are eating. A foot too close and they will spring in all directions, never to return; a foot too far to either side and he will never be able to pull the fly through them in a credible presentation. He needs these things all at once: Delicacy. Precision and the humility to remain invisible as his exacting execution draws them to the fly. There is no room for misunderstanding. Ego is an enemy. All the forces of nature today and tomorrow swirl around this exact instant in time. It can never be duplicated. Every factor is uniquely positioned.

Sensing the moment, he flings his fly in a fluid motion, hoping against hope it will do nothing until he intends it to.

HOW TO MAKE A STAGFLATION COCKTAIL:

Take the emergence of manufacturing prowess around the globe, add to it the exhausting financial and other demands of Vietnam and Johnson's Great Society, stir in the loss of pricing control and availability of oil, watch interest rates rise and deficit spending jump, and sprinkle liberally the appearance of foreign autos, steel, and other products and you have the expected result:

High unemployment, higher inflation, and low to no growth.

Worst of all, the middle class, like most Americans, had become demoralized—it was a moment that begged for a new leader with a fresh vision.

A parade of presidents failed to calm the beast.

Any fair reflection on Reagan's legacy must account for where things stood as he was sworn into office. Whatever long-term questions arise, let's start with that base case.

When it was his turn at the controls, Reagan's plan was to get government off our backs.

He promised to do three things to free up the "free" markets: He promised to slash the bloated bureaucracy through spending cuts and streamlining government; he pledged to cut endless regulations at all levels of government; and he promised to cut taxes across the board to return those funds to taxpayers.

He promised to do one more thing that a lot of his predecessors promised yet failed to do: He vowed to tame the beast of inflation.

For that final miserable task he turned to "Tall Paul" Volcker, the six-foot-seven-inch head of the Federal Reserve who had served in the Nixon treasury on the suspension of gold convertibility and as Jimmy Carter's Fed chief.

As Volcker described it in prior interviews, "Gradualism . . . had been developing and it gave you this feeling that we could deal with this problem gently and that is we go about it in this sophisticated way we can do it with relatively little pain. [This approach] never seemed realistic to me."

To his credit, Reagan stood by his newly reappointed Fed leader even though the medicine was harsh—particularly for the building trades and the middle class. Imagine hiking the federal funds rate (at which banks lend to one another) up to 20 percent. (It already averaged an atmospheric 11 percent the year before Reagan was elected.)

Volcker recalled, "If you had told me at the time when I became chairman . . . that the prime rate would get to 21.5 percent, I probably would have crawled into a hole and cried, I suppose. But then we lived through it."

Carefully, Volcker slipped over the side of the boat. Inflation was feeding everywhere. He had to present his fly in just the right way to draw the markets . . . then strip, strip, strip. There would be no second chance.

What Reagan and Volcker had to do was shatter the momentum of expectations—the ultimate propulsion for inflation. In an interview, Volcker explained: "Inflation is a good part of expectations. You begin expecting it, and you get it, because wage earners will want more wages, and businessmen will put the prices up because they think they can sustain it, and that whole thing sustains the process."

The political pressure against the Reagan antidote was enormous. But to slay the dragon of inflation a near-death experience was required. And he got it.

Every class howled, and the middle class felt singled out. The economy went quickly from being overheated to a full-blown recession crushing the middle and lower classes. A little juice to the money supply might make for a soft landing, they countered. A gentler measured way to let the air out of the balloon was widely counseled.

Reagan courageously did not vary.

Auto sales sank to a twenty-year low as middle-class Americans realized that purchases like homes and cars were impossible under the regime of double-digit interest rates and double-digit unemployment. Midwest manufacturing ground to a halt creating a Steinbeckian rust belt.

Americans of every station blamed Reagan and his Fed czar for their misery. The recession took a huge toll and unemployment skyrocketed to levels not seen since the Depression.

Surely, there were moments of doubt. It was an unevenly shared agony guaranteed to create distrust and hatred. Everyone looked at the other guy's wallet for their solution, but it was a collective chemotherapy and the strain was ubiquitous.

Farmers drowning in debt drove their tractors through the streets of the capital in protest, blockading the Fed chairman's building.

But by 1983 the smoke began to clear, and amid the wreckage were signs of better times to come. Inflation, which had ravaged the economy at 13.5 percent in 1980, was remarkably just 3.2 percent in 1983. And the green shoots of economic growth were unmistakable.

Markets began to anticipate more good news—and began their scramble out of a long, deep valley.

From the mid-1960s to 1982 the stock market had lost nearly a quarter of its value, and in real terms given the runaway inflation, more than two-thirds of the market's real asset value was wiped out. From the year of Reagan's inauguration to the end of the decade the stock market would triple (except for a brief and terrifying respite for six months after "Black Monday" in October 1987).

From late 1982, the economy began sixty consecutive months of growth, the longest uninterrupted period since the government started keeping such records in 1854. During this five-year period almost 15 million jobs were created, and nearly $20 trillion of goods and services were produced.

Whatever the debate about distribution and sharing of these benefits, no fair reading can dispute that a raging fire had been extinguished. As with many forest fires, however, there were embers in the root system smoldering beneath the surface, patient, potent, and waiting for their moment to reignite.

As for Reagan's other three pledges—cutting government spending, taxes, and deregulation—he began earnestly trying all three. But his resolve wavered almost immediately.

If there was a crown jewel of Reagan's plan, it was cutting taxes to spur investment, savings, job creation, and economic activity. Reagan had enormous faith in economist Arthur Laffer, who believed that lower tax rates would encourage people all along the earnings spectrum to further stimulate the economy by spending, hiring, and investing.

Reagan's tax-reform bill, passed at the dawn of his presidency, had cut everyone's tax rates by 25 percent over a three-year period.

A corollary component of this program was cutting the marginal capital gains tax rate to 20 percent from 28 percent. But there was a hero in the piece that preceded Reagan.

Just three years prior, President Carter had been angling to move the capital gains rate from 49 percent to the marginal income tax rate of 70 percent. Bill Steiger, a baby-faced Republican congressman who first won his seat at the tender age of 28, fought back with his own measure, passionately advocating with empirical evidence rather than conservative ideology. He proved that more high-technology companies had been formed when capital gains taxes were low and that the higher rates had starved new start-up creation to near zero.

His earnest and straightforward style astonishingly swung the Congress, including many democrats. Carter signed the young man's amendment into law in November 1978, cutting the capital gains rate almost in half. It was a middle-class tour de force despite carping by some that Steiger was lining the pockets of the rich. Sadly, within thirty days of his legislative victory, Steiger died of a massive heart attack at age forty.

Among many things that resulted, top earners searched for ways to create cheap long-term capital gains, and investment vehicles like venture capital and private equity flourished, with thousands of firms blossoming everywhere. For the best-heeled Americans, this long-term appreciation was the engine of wealth.

A key element of Reagan's plan was the notion of trickle-down economics. But it did not take long for evidence to pile up that there was little intersection between the Dow Jones Industrial Average and the cycle of poverty.

Reagan's remaining two pillars deserve study.

As for slashing government overhead and cutting back spending, the record is unambiguous.

Under Reagan, the federal budget deficit almost tripled to just under

$3 trillion. And the number of government employees at all levels approached 18 million and crossed the 7-percent-of-the-population mark (a proportion that continued for the next thirty years).

Truth be told, Reagan was stymied and determined to borrow his way out of the dilemma. Cutting defense was simply not in the lexicon of the conservative leader, and the entitlements of Social Security and Medicare constituted then and now a political third rail—no matter what your political beliefs. Putting a ringed fence around those three activities crushed any ability for meaningful cost containment. But intractable budget items were hardly the problem.

Rather than cut spending Reagan increased it meaningfully, transforming the United States from the world's largest international creditor to the largest debtor nation.

All of which demanded that our tax activist pursue another course after his first year in office. Change taxes. Fully a dozen times in six of his eight years in office, Reagan brought enormous new tax initiatives to the legislature to enact.

And they did so with brio.

Being equally fair in hindsight, the bill for the gap had to be sent to someone. And while much is made of the continuing large absolute taxes paid by the rich, few could argue that the tab would be paid in many ways over many years by the middle class.

Under Reagan, the capital concentration and formation to the wealthiest was taxed at reduced rates, while the income and payroll taxes of the middle class and lower classes increased. The Reagan revolution created many good things. His confidence in America's prosperity was infectious and the economy was humming—with a major shortcoming as a result: On his watch, a pattern of income inequality launched and would gain momentum for the next thirty years.

Nothing would split the nation's economic experience like the income disparity that commenced under Reagan's tutelage.

Much is made of the gap between rich and poor, with good reason. But peering deeper, a far more lasting covenant was broken with the middle, its continuing impact barely noticeable in the context of the stock market's euphoria.

The shaving of middle-class opportunity was masked too by the surging job numbers—month after month at more than 250,000 jobs—many decent middle-class jobs among them.

For all the joy, the middle class was commencing a multi-decade journey into a narrower and narrower canyon. But the changes were so subtle at first that the middle class cheered them on.

Taxer in Chief

In 1982, Reagan signed not one but two major tax increases: the Tax Equity and Fiscal Responsibility Act (TEFRA) and the Highway Revenue Act. TEFRA was so mammoth that it increased taxes by almost one percent of GDP, making it the largest peacetime tax increase in our history. The following year brought his Social Security tax increase, which had the special feature of automatic increases in the taxable wage base— so this levy is a gift that keeps on giving. Many middle-class workers still see their payroll taxes increase annually today.

Still stymied by spending in 1984, Reagan signed the Deficit Reduction Act, which brought in another $18 billion a year, though it was designed to be "revenue neutral."

(By the way, there is no such thing.)

In 1985, '86, and '87, Reagan also raised taxes for a combined two-term total of 2.6 percent of our GDP.

According to Paul Krugman and other economists, these tax increases more than offset Reagan's tax cuts for the middle and working classes. According to Congressional Budget Office estimates, the average middle-class income taxes combined were up, not down, during the period of the Reagan presidency.

Structural Redistribution

What was happening structurally was redistribution—whether or not you believe that was the insidious intent all along, or the commencement of a trend that should have been addressed. A subtle but profound shift had occurred.

By cutting income and capital gains taxes paid at a higher rate by the wealthy, and substituting and increasing payroll taxes, which are mostly paid by the middle class and the working poor, the income-tax burden was redistributed down the income scale.

The tide was rising, to be sure. But absorbing the increased spending was the plight of the middle class. And it wasn't many years before the income disparities began to reflect this structural imperative.

As tax rates and regulations evolved, the top one percent came to pay a higher and higher proportion of the total tax pool. But that is only part of the story.

Middle-class earners are still flush with Social Security, Medicare, Obamacare, state, municipal, sales, real estate, sewer, asset taxes (for cars, boats, trucks, RVs), and a litany of whatever else can be squeezed out of the wallet by government authorities, including the perplexing "medical device" tax.

Despite this increasing tax burden on earnings, income disparities carry on. The concentration of wealth in just a few hands grows faster than the tax friction can manage, proving clearly that you can reduce to near zero the taxes on many in the lower middle class and those who aspire to be middle class—and they still never catch up.

The key to concentration is to not get opiated by the tax rate. It's a simple yet ineffective tool for balancing economic return. Yet it is the hammer that keeps getting pulled out of the tool kit, even when there is no nail.

The first rule of fairness: Follow the money closely and understand how it appreciates before shooting the tax pistol.

Here's how things started with the Reagan revolution:

The share of total income enjoyed by the richest 5 percent of Americans grew from 16.5 percent the year before Reagan took office to 18.3 percent as he departed 1600 Pennsylvania Avenue. During that same period, the share of income that went to the poorest 20 percent of households fell from 4.2 to 3.8 percent.

The middle-income category went from 55 percent of all households in 1980 to 51.1 percent by 1989, so the middle class did indeed shrink—just not all to the down side. The middle class did "shrink upward" during the period as some earned their way out.

The incomes of the richest one percent increased by more than half during the Reagan years, while those of the bottom 90 percent decreased and middle-class incomes were barely higher than they had been a decade before.

But nowhere was the impact of the Reagan revolution more joyously experienced than in the stock market, which tripled in value. As this explosive growth enriched the wealthiest Americans, ever more middle-class investors were drawn into the opportunity. Nearly 30 percent of Americans owned stock either directly or through mutual funds that their retirement accounts purchased.

In 1988, George H. W. Bush ran to succeed Reagan, asking all of America to read his lips: No new taxes. In retrospect, having inherited a spending habit that caused nearly a quarter-of-a-trillion-dollar deficit in 1990, it was a foolhardy claim. But presidential politics and reputations can turn on the adoption of a signature phrase.

Of course, when Bush relented there was little forgiveness in the Republican ranks, even if the man basically had no choice. Nevertheless, Bush launched the first Gulf War deep into his presidency and emerged a conquering hero, though some at the time wished he had not stopped at the Iraqi border.

THE SURE THING

THERE WERE FEW SIGNS OF any particular trouble for Bush as he basked in postwar esteem. His poll numbers were nearly insurmountable, and the nation seemed poised to bring him back for a second term with the kind of encore electoral dominance that Reagan and Nixon enjoyed.

But over Philadelphia on a spring morning in 1991, a helicopter and a small plane collided, spilling wreckage on a schoolyard as children played during noon recess. It was a tragic moment, and yet nobody figured it sealed the president's fate as well.

Aboard was Senator John Heinz, a moderate Republican whose firm grip on his U.S. Senate seat could only have been interrupted by an act of God. He was one of those men whom everyone mourned regardless of station or persuasion.

Governor Robert P. Casey named Democrat Harris Wofford, a former college president and aide to JFK and MLK who had never held elective office, to fill the respected man's shoes.

The runoff election that resulted in Wofford facing Richard Thornburgh, a former two-term Republican governor and the sitting U.S. Attorney General, seemed quixotic from the start. In early polling, the Democrat lagged by a staggering forty-seven points. Thornburgh did his best to label Wofford as another tax-and-spend liberal.

But Wofford had been watching the slow disconnect of the Republican Party from the middle and working classes. At his opening press conference he began by staking out unusual ground: His first order of business would be a middle-class tax cut—a surprising twist for a tax-and-spend Democrat.

He then went on to pound the table for much broader health-care coverage, especially for the poor and the middle. His indelible advertising served a simple message: Treat the middle class differently and provide health care: "If criminals are entitled to a lawyer, then all Americans are entitled to a doctor."

In perhaps the greatest political come-from-behind win in the annals of congressional politics, Wofford bested the much-better-known Thornburgh by ten points. The morning after his victory, Wofford took a call from Little Rock, Arkansas. The caller was an endlessly curious young governor with equally quixotic designs on the White House.

Bill Clinton quizzed the senator-elect on everything from his stance on middle-class taxes, to the economy, to his plans for broadly offered health care. He was dying to know who had advised the campaign. Wofford shared his thoughts freely, including the names of the two aggressive and "inexperienced" managers who had steered his campaign. They were Paul Begala and James Carville—and Clinton thought they had promise.

Clinton went on to form a close bond with the new senator (Wofford would be a finalist in the VP sweepstakes that ultimately settled on Al Gore), and Begala and Carville would propel the young governor into the White House.

Bush, of course, enjoyed the same early lead as Thornburgh had. Yet Clinton won back the presidency for the Democratic Party by pounding heavily on how out of touch the Republicans had gotten from the middle class.

What is striking even today is how both parties lay claim to the middle class though both have watched a steady erosion of the very group they purport to save.

Clinton rode the wave all the way to the White House and kept his campaign promise to increase taxes on the rich, placing the marginal rate just under 40 percent. Markets generally soared and Clinton did manage to balance the budget, leaving office with a unified surplus of $236 billion, the highest in our history.

Supersized Government, Always a Bigger Serving

Many of these advances were quickly undone in the George W. Bush presidency, when Reaganomics became Bushonomics. But the music had changed and the old dance no longer fit the tempo. Bush accumulated more debt than all previous presidents combined. And the thirty-year march of income inequality carried on unabated.

It strikes me that the Reagan revolution, reimagined by Bush 43, deserves a bit of reconsideration. Certainly there was a pro-private-sector tilt that drove, and still drives, economic growth. No one should take that away from either president.

Fresh issues arise every time our economy expands.

Despite what advisors may claim, a surging $14 trillion economy cannot be contained—it might not be possible to even *influence* it—but it is a gilt-edged certitude that it cannot be controlled. And with global players whose strengths are a match for our own, every surge is different, characterized by its own set of unintended consequences.

In later chapters we will engage with major geo-stratagems that play heavily into the uncontrollable growth issue: free trade with partners who don't embrace the concept, the financialization of the American economy (40 percent of profits earned in the United States come from financial institutions), the surge in technology and productivity and how it is shared today, the worldwide blend of deregulation and consolidation of business, and how wealth and poverty are created and dealt with.

These tectonic forces trump income taxation in creating the demise of the middle class. Forget for a moment that both Democrats and Republicans, conservatives and liberals, lay claim to the care and feeding of the middle class.

Is there anyone who seriously believes that adding a few points to a marginal tax rate will staunch a forty-year bloodletting and dissolution of the middle class? Or that putting a few percentage points more on the highest tax rate will stave off the continuing concentration of wealth?

These so-called remedies are glancing blows—momentarily painful but not determinative of the outcome. It's time to move beyond palliative care.

There are more exasperating questions that should be posed.

We have created an unattractive reality that middle-class wages have not risen in real terms for more than thirty years. Is it time to address that reality by asking the basic question: Will American middle-class wages ever go up again? And have the expectations that drive inflation created a problem where our middle-class expectations are themselves inflated?

The average size of a single-family home has increased 150 percent from the days of Levittown five decades ago. Most households in the country have a minimum of three TVs and at least two cars, and one out of five households is coping with student debt to finance college—a doubling since 1990.

Is it reasonable for the political parties to step back and ask whether they have met their own targets and expectations?

Taking a moment to review the Conservative movement may be illustrative, but things have not fared much better under Democratic administration.

A primary objective of conservatism is to limit the size and influence of government.

Most Democratic candidates echo the same bromides.

George Washington Meets Jenny Craig

Our federal government has only a spare number of enumerated powers, if one really reads the Constitution. At the dawn of the republic there were only four federal cabinet-level departments: Treasury, State, War, and Justice. When George Washington was indeed the father of our country there was one federal employee for every 4,000 (or so) citizens. Today there is one such employee for every 150 of us. And if you count all employees of government at all levels, there is one for every 13 of us. We are very well governed . . . or at least very thoroughly.

Is it any wonder that the emerging Tea Party activism has focused on the growth of government and its involvement in our lives?

The quarrel develops when we admit to ourselves that we are increasingly looking to what government can provide—which explains in part why the dividing line between us has become so absolute.

Since Reagan took the reins in early 1981, federal government outlays have more than doubled in constant dollars, and Congress, armed with enough of both parties to share blame, has created a $15 trillion debt for the nation.

While campaigning and in office, Reagan advocated closing the Energy and the Education departments. When Newt Gingrich was Speaker and held in his hands a Contract with America, he proposed shuttering those two plus a couple more.

In the past twenty-five years, these departments have not only not been shuttered but have expanded meaningfully, and two more, Homeland Security and Veterans Affairs, have been created.

The number of government employees at all levels grew from 17 million under Reagan to 22 million under Bush and Obama. As a percent of the population, the total has hovered at about 7 percent, though it faded slightly during the beginning of the Obama presidency.

But with an expanding federal bureaucracy and a meaningful 7 percent of the population represented by all government work, any claims to have staunched the growth of big government fail the test of Republican and Democratic leaders alike.

Entitlement programs have expanded under both parties as well, with the advance of some veterans programs, Medicare Part D, and SCHIP health insurance for poor kids. Not to mention Obamacare.

Some of these have been enacted with the complicity and help of the conservatives in government.

There have been innumerable studies about the proportion of Americans who depend on some form of government assistance and subsidy. The simple summary is that most of us do, either individually or through broad support of universities and other institutions.

A staggering one in five Americans rely on the federal government for food assistance, income, student aid, housing, health care, college tuition, and more—some 67 million individuals have come to count on federal help. Almost 70 percent of the nation's budget goes to individual assistance programs. Particularly in the years since Lehman fell, dependence is a growth business in the country under every type of administration.

A reasonable question is whether most of us truly need those benefits. It's the kind of query that lures resentment out of the shadows and yet begs to be studied.

In my view, these should be personal decisions. We are the best determiners of our own degree of need. Personal responsibility is the ultimate arbiter of the right decision.

At the same time, there are broader issues creating middle-class erosion apart from our culture of dependence. Rather than point the finger of judgment, let's focus instead on changes in manufacturing cycle and the transition of our economy; global trade and the nature of our partners; on technology and productivity; and how workforce needs and requirements have changed. Our entire being has tolerated a diminishment of the middle class through acts of omission and commission.

WE NEED GREATER COMMAND OF what is happening today with the rich and poor, the new leadership role of women in our society, the expansion of Latino influence in the nation, and the explosion of middle-class ranks around the globe.

Understanding these forces will do far more than accusing others of leaning on government largesse. So let's ask the bigger questions.

Because the keys to the middle-class murder mystery can be found by investigating those issues first and by blaming others as a matter of last resort.

Let's turn to finding that mojo in the pages to come.

PART TWO

Found

CHAPTER NINE

——— THE ONE PERCENT PROBLEM ———

Not the invisible hand, but the invisible handshake

ALL IDAHO WAS BUZZING: SOME KNUCKLEHEAD *stole the dead man's hat. The missing curved-brim relic from long-defunct Purcell's Western Wear served as centerpiece for his memorial service floral arrangement. And it, like its wearer, had slipped out of Boise in the still of the night.*

Off-white with green and orange feathers, the faux Stetson served as signature headpiece for a generation—both owner and the topper had become cultural icons. Nine months after the pilferage following a blistering column in the Statesman, *a sheepish caller returned the hat with the proviso of protected anonymity. "Stupidity" was the reason the caller gave for the theft.*

All this fuss over a centenarian's hat would have been impossible to predict eighty-five years earlier, but that is when the trouble really started. High school basketball fever was the trigger. Predictable ingredients provided drama—a controlling father, a big game, and a dairyman's fourteen-year-old boy who cared more for hoops than milking cows. Forbidding his son to go should have been the end of it—but for this mulish teen it was simply the last straw.

The youngster wheeled on his heels, let the screen door slam, and never went back. Paying a buck a day for a room and a meal at Declo, Idaho's sole hotel, he frugally survived on four twenty-dollar gold coins his mother had slipped into his pocket. During meals he encountered fellow boarders, a group of teachers who were equally parsimonious because they were paid on scrip in the form of interest-bearing notes.

The teenager bought the paper for fifty cents on the dollar, using most of his liquidity to cash the teachers out. The next day he went down to the local bank and pledged the scrip as collateral to buy 600 young underfed hogs at a dollar apiece. The bank was paying ninety cents on scrip.

Next, the teen had to fatten his passel of pigs.

He built a massive cooking apparatus that could hold thirty bags of potatoes and the meat of two horses. In the nearby desert, hundreds of wild broncos thundered through the hills. The teenager shot and skinned the horses, selling the hides for a few dollars and cooking virtually everything else to fatten his slender hogs. In between, he labored in potato-sorting workhouses.

By spring his swine were the fattest at market and he sold some of his one-dollar hogs for prices up to $7,500 apiece, netting a cool hundred thousand dollars. He had just reached the ripe age of fifteen. That seed capital got him into the potato business.

In 1924, he rented 160 acres from a man he called "an alcoholic" and he and his wobbly partner split the cost of a new electric potato sorter. His renter taught him how to grow great potatoes, planting certified seed rather than the more typical cull potatoes. The headstrong fifteen-year-old and the old man quarreled, leading to the decision, in one particularly testy exchange, to flip a coin for ownership of the machine. Kowtowing to authority was not his thing. Winning the toss, an expansion-minded young entrepreneur became sole owner of the potato business.

It was the last time he would have a boss.

In less than ten years, the then twenty-six-year-old had become a millionaire and the largest shipper of potatoes in the West, with thirty-three warehouses in Oregon and Idaho along the mighty Snake River.

A fortunate brush with a Chicago executive taught him the opportunities in drying onions and later potatoes. Using an old prune dryer, he parlayed his first-year profit of half a million dollars into building the largest potato-dehydrating plant in the world. During World War II, the high school dropout supplied about a third of the dried potatoes and onions consumed by our troops.

Restless visions took him to new horizons. Facing mounting expenses for fertilizer, he purchased phosphate reserves and created a fertilizer-production facility that for decades was among his most profitable ventures. Living frugally and plowing his profits back into his businesses, he waged a campaign of buying timber tracts, ranches, and cattle.

The postwar boom brought new opportunities as frozen foods found their way into restaurants and households. But frozen potatoes turned mushy when defrosted. And the most flavorful variety, the Idaho Russet, was not available during the summer months. When one of his scientists developed a way to keep a defrosted French fry firm, a huge new world awakened.

In 1967, he and McDonald's founder and master franchiser Ray Kroc agreed by handshake that his frozen fries could circumvent the laborious local process of hand-cutting fresh potatoes. Kroc knew that this technology also meant he could provide frozen Russet potatoes all year long—a true taste advantage. Within five years, all McDonald's French fries were frozen.

It was love at first bite. Americans bought billions upon billions of McDonald's French fries.

By 2005, the Idaho potato magnate was delivering most of them. But he could not be contained. Borrowing from his basic strategy of seizing opportunity with hard work and an appetite for risk and never selling out, he sought new adventures. Cattle ranching was a natural move, and he made it boldly. Among his dozen large cattle ranches is the nation's largest, the 137-mile by 64-mile ZX Ranch. He crossed business boundaries like they were small streams.

He expanded again, buying a large stake in Dallas-based Remington Oil, but few could argue that his biggest gamble was putting more than $20 million into semiconductor startup Micron Technology at age seventy-one, taking him from potato chips to microchips. For all the volatility in the component parts, he had struck gold again. In time Micron would be the largest private employer in Idaho.

Staying with his winners and reinvesting proceeds and dividends led him increasingly to land purchases. "I now own more deeded land than any man in America" (more than 3 million acres), he said toward the end of his life. His was an extraordinary run: feeding a crusading American army; selling French fries to flotillas of families streaming through those golden arches, not to mention Burger King, Wendy's, and the Colonel's Kentucky Fried. "That's what made me," J.R. "Jack" Simplot said as he reflected back on a lifetime of effort. "I got McDonald's to use my frozen French fries."

His would have been the perfect hand had he not tried to corner the potato market in 1976.

In a large trading scam, he and coconspirators were charged with trying to influence Maine potato prices by committing to huge futures contracts that they then refused to honor. The Simplot group was shorting Maine potato futures, hoping to drive the prices down, and some East Coast growers formed what the court would call the "long conspirators," hoping to do precisely the opposite.

Just about everyone was at fault; a lot of guilt got passed around, and Simplot received his full measure. He was banned from the commodities industry for six years, and he paid fines and restitutions.

Like an Idaho cowboy in a Russell or Remington painting, Simplot dusted off his hat, remounted his steed, and plowed ahead, finding ways to make money in heaps for at least thirty more years. When the wheels stopped spinning just short of the century mark, the headstrong teenager had become one of the richest men on the planet—and he kept true to his dictum: Be bold, take risks, work hard, and never sell a productive business.

His memorial service, held at Boise's Qwest Arena, felt like a state funeral, and the passing of an icon was marked with somber celebration. By life's end he had showered untold millions on his home state charities and educational institutions. In the daguerreotype of the Old West, Simplot was a larger-than-life force for the creation of wealth. People in the arena wanted to touch him, to feel his energy and tap into his soul. He had that Midas touch.

The caller returning the hat said "someone else" had stolen it in one of those swept-up moments: "It was one of those stupid impulsive acts and was almost instantly regretted." Kind of like trying to corner the potato market *when your license plate reads "MR SPUD." But the hat was returned, the French fries keep freezing, and the Simplot empire rolls on.*

You meet them in every walk of life, bold innovators and business drivers who see around corners, screening out risks. They plunge in and create successes where others see only peril. Genius drives their work, though intellect often takes a backseat to determination.

These steely-eyed entrepreneurs are like Old West heroes, pioneers on the business prairie, roaming the badlands, finding gold in barren and foreboding places.

Americans glamorize these working rich. The stirring combination of grit, luck, and refusal to back down creates a frontier fantasy that some call the American dream. The truth is often less glittering, the path to riches less straight, and many relish when they stumble, as these heroes often do.

Central to this romance is that anyone, even a grade-school-educated fourteen-year-old cow-poke, can make it big. Deep belief is sustained every time someone from nowhere creates Facebook or Dell or Microsoft in a dorm room or their folks' garage. These parables are a centerpiece of American business legend.

But they have little to do with the growing disparity between rich and poor.

It's not that these entrepreneurs don't create jobs—they do. They mint millionaires and middle-class members to boot. But the numbers of breakthrough billionaires are so spare, in the context of the millions of businesses that are created and fail, that you can't build your entire policy around them. At best they are an aspirational part of the solution, just as a snappy Corvette brings luster to all of Chevrolet.

Business has its own form of celebrity culture, creating stars that at their best pull us along. They deserve to be celebrated. No nation has provided the blank canvas for staggering success as consistently as the United States. We should maintain a business environment that encourages and supports these breakout players. The more we replicate these entrepreneurial triumphs, the better for our middle class.

But we can't rely on these prospectors to save the middle class for us.

Many laud Steven Jobs for his gloriously easy-to-use and beautiful everyday products. That was the public face of his genius. But he is unsung for an even greater flash of inspiration—the creation of whole new business ecosystems that grew up around his wonderful creations. Knowing little of the music business, Jobs repositioned a dying recorded album-based industry with a flaming, flashing digital version at 99 cents a song. Others built their empires on piracy, but Jobs saw an entirely new model that involved paying for content in portable, shuffleable form.

Today, paid music is more a part of our lives than ever before—just in an entirely different and disruptive form. Jobs saw opportunity swirling around a device, and an industry followed his lead.

This brilliant, often difficult, man is lauded for his enormous wealth and his avant-garde products. But we have buried the lead in his obituary. Jobs was perhaps one of the greatest middle-class job creators we have ever known.

But bold new ideas always come at a price.

Creative destruction is a hallmark of the American marketplace. We all enjoy epic tales of driven Davids conquering aging Goliaths—unless, of course, your job is in the crosshairs of a new technology or disruptive service.

On a micro level, change comes at a personally painful cost. Small towns everywhere show the wear that mom-and-pop retailing is feeling from category-killer big-box retailers and Internet players. Main Streets, once characterized by home-grown, family-owned emporiums occupying the same stores for generations, now all look like open-air shopping malls with national chains.

Somehow America has always found the right balance of bold new initiative and the status quo. But the path of business riches is littered with collateral damage, and today's innovation has left a lot of detritus for all the greater good it has done. Old jobs fade and new ones take their place.

Many of these off-shored, and robot-replaced, and disrupted jobs have come out of the hide of the middle class. And we have lost our commitment to reconnect the amputated tissue whenever a bold new wave washes through town. Capturing the opportunities that accompany brilliant innovation is the greatest gift we can share with the middle class.

As new riches are created, don't we owe some duty to those who were swept away on the wave of wealth aggregation?

A NEW BALANCE

THE CHALLENGE FOR OUR NATION is straightforward and yet tricky to execute. It requires thoughtful balance of liberty and justice.

We must preserve liberty to create fortunes and businesses without risking justice by also providing opportunity for the broadest array of our citizens as those fortunes and businesses are created.

Right now, liberty and justice are under severe strain, which is unusual for a country that promises both for all. And it leads to the central question: Can we reduce inequality in a meaningful way without harming the benefits of capitalism? Some say it can't be done.

Of course it can.

It bears repeating: Capitalism left unchecked is the greatest peacetime concentrator of wealth ever devised. But when managed with the right balance of freedom and justice, no system has greater power to create shared prosperity and broad opportunity.

Here's the important addendum: without killing the initiative to build wealth.

We cannot look to Washington alone for solutions. How can people incentivized primarily by reelection possibly make the tough trade-offs necessary to strike that balance? How can politicians create jobs and opportunities when they simply have no experience in doing so, even when their hearts are in the right place?

Here is the core of the middle-class dilemma: As massive wealth is being created, business and government maintain thinly disguised contempt for one another. The natural tension between regulated and regulator barely describes the problem—the enmity runs so much deeper.

The agonies since 2008 hold clues to the discomfiture: the achingly slow recovery traveling at one speed, the spirited reflation of the markets at another. Business profits are soaring; investments of the wealthy are more than recovered. Yet the middle class and the poor struggle.

These anomalies are impossible to bridge without concerted leadership on both sides, and agreement on how to split the spoils in a way that brings more Americans along.

A singular failure among the powerful in government and the wealthy today is their inability to create shared momentum. It is a rare tide that raises only a few boats.

Herein lies the central irony in America today. Until the one percent, and the 5, 10, and 15 percent, agree that change is needed, there will be none.

Everything turns on the willingness of the wealthiest and most powerful to bridge the divide. Many one percenters call for greater tax equity; others are generous in a way no nation has ever experienced. But power has been slow to react to the sea change of the last decade. Special interests block meaningful alterations in the disparity, and the greater angels among the one percenters are not carrying the day.

The irony is that until the rich can be persuaded that such potent changes are in their best interests, the gap between themselves and everybody else will only widen.

Until it won't.

Someone once asked Ernest Hemingway how he went bankrupt. He responded, "Very slowly . . . then very quickly."

The rich won't pick the moment when everyone else has had enough.

Even the best market timers will fail to pick the instant that the hammer hits. For decades, the gap between rich and poor has been increasing, as the economists say, increasingly. How far can the lines diverge?

Many are comforted by the near-complete disappearance of the Occupy movements. Others see Ferguson, Missouri, and other outbursts like a blemish that will pass in a week or more. They won't. Something is brewing far beneath the surface. It won't go away.

What is missing is an understanding, what we call the Grand Comprehension.

Many elite and the upper middle have been stubbornly slow to understand what the cleverest among them have long ago surmised.

A story is told of a burly young bully and a village sage who encountered one other along a pathway. The churlish boy had picked up a wounded bird and held it pressed between his meaty paws. He posed a question to the sage: "Tell me, wise one, is this bird I am holding alive or is it dead?" His plan, of course, was to squeeze the bird to death if the sage answered yes and to let the creature fly if he answered no. Sensing the contrarian in the bully's demeanor, the sage thought for a moment and made the following reply: "The answer is in your hands."

My sentiments exactly.

The answer for rebalancing opportunity and wealth disparity is firmly in the hands of those better off. We need a one percent solution—actually, a dozen or more of them. What falls to this chapter and to all of us is the task of persuading the rich that they have more to lose than anyone else if the rest of us decide instead to squeeze harder.

Call it a patriotic duty.

The Grand Comprehension is that one percent and more must act now, with force and vigor. They must lead in redistributing opportunity and in creating the broad-scale promise of those heady postwar days. The job will be much trickier this time. American demographics are far more vexing, and the ability to create social change will require more effort. But what must occupy Wall Street and Main Street and every thoroughfare is the comprehension that disparity can only be resolved by leadership among the wealthy and powerful—by a one percent solution.

FOR RICHER OR POORER

WHEN CONCEIVING PLANS FOR THE University of Virginia, Thomas Jefferson wrote to John Adams about promoting "a natural aristocracy of talent" to replace the "artificial aristocracy founded on wealth and birth." His was a recipe for a great nation as much as for a great university.

In bursts we have maintained the ability of the natural aristocracy of talent to flourish. But since those days when Tall Paul and the Gipper tamed the savage inflation beast we have seen an explosion of wealth.

Today, there is a millionaire on every block. In the last few years, the number has been growing at double-digits percent, so by 2015 there were

9 million or more households of them. That's one for every 16 households, up from one out of every 22 in 2007.

The raw numbers mean that we're talking about far more than just one percent of all Americans. No other nation comes close in minting millionaires. The United States boasts about 44 percent of the world's millionaire households, with China last year surging 82 percent past Japan for number two position with 2.4 million households.

Here is a dramatic example of the changes over time. Of all of the wealth created in America between 1983 and 2004, nearly 94 percent went to the top 20 percent. So for the bullish 1980s, 1990s, and pre-crash 2000s, the bottom 80 percent of Americans—both the poor and the middle class—shared just 6 percent of the new financial wealth generated.

That's Rich

THE BEST WAY TO SENSIBLY discuss wealth concentration is by setting aside the fury. Disliking the rich is an historical verity, but today's fierce feelings seem particularly ripe. There is no doubt that many got rich not by freezing the first French fry but by being bailed out at the right time. Or even being born in the right "super-Zip" code.

So many people are angry. We can return to that passion, but first let's explore things that angry people rarely take the time to learn.

Like the middle class, the wealthy are often displayed in one dimension, and in truth their position is a lot more complicated.

A more complete way to consider the rich is to focus not just on what they earn but, more important, on what they own, what they inherit, what they owe, how they invest, how they are taxed, what they give, and finally, what powers they protect.

The rich have a very wide range of skills and assets. Some make billions arbitraging a nickel gap between two securities. Some are extraordinary leaders of compassion and soul. Some get the biggest of the big things done. And some clip coupons in their endless free time.

Their relationships vary widely too. Some work in secret and cast a short shadow. Others have extraordinary influence, golden Rolodexes, and opinions that are widely sought and respected.

Even the most thoughtful treatises mix, match, and muddy these perspectives. And once folks go florid there is no reorienting the conversation. Breaking things down by these categories demystifies what is really going on in wealthy America.

The state of things may surprise you.

There is an orgy of evidence that the incomes of the wealthiest Americans have surged, even as middle-class wages have flat-lined. The one percent saw their incomes rise 275 percent between 1979 and pre-crash 2007. During the same period, the bottom fifth grew by less than 20 percent.

Let's look closer. According to the IRS, only about 199 Americans earned more than $50 million in wages last year. That leaves at least 350 million who did not. Clearly, life can't be so tragic at these levels. But how much do Americans need to earn to consider themselves rich?

Gallup polled Americans in 2011 and they shared that they would need to earn a median of $150,000 to consider themselves rich. Only 15 percent felt they would need earnings of a million dollars or more to be considered wealthy.

So how does that match reality?

The IRS ought to have a reasonable handle on what Americans earn. Their data suggests that about 1.5 million earn at least $350,000 a year. There are about 140,000 who earn more than $2 million a year. About five thousand earn over $10 million a year.

The Federal Reserve and the Tax Policy Center try to hit a moving target. Their cutoff for the top one percent is earnings of $521,000. For the top 5 percent, earnings are $209,000.

Many people interviewed during the writing of this book were surprised at how low that last figure was. Remember, 92 percent of Americans earn less than $100,000 a year. And 71 percent earn between zero and $50,000.

Here is how all this relates to the middle class. Fifty percent of American workers earned less than $26,000 in 2010, fewer jobs above that range were available, and overall pay was trending downward except for the people making a million or more—their pay rose 18 percent in that year.

It is always incendiary to talk about CEO pay, but the facts are relevant here. A CEO in 2014 made about 250 times the average worker's salary. In 2009, just after the crash, the multiple was 181 times. Part of the reason for the surge is flat compensation for workers—2013 pay for U.S. workers as a whole increased 1.3 percent.

Increases like these are not too shabby for the top 5 percent, but here's a key message about the wealthy: Earnings are an imperfect gauge of wealth in America.

The parable of the frozen French fry should tell you why.

The real determinant of wealth is what you own versus what you earn. IRS analysis of the richest income-tax returns clearly shows that the greatest growth came in the form of capital gains. Until 2008 rained down on all Americans, the richest 400 had been making huge gains in capital appreciation. From 1992 to 2007, the richest 400 saw their salaries barely double, but their capital gains increased by 1,200 percent.

NEW MONEY

AFTER 2008, THE WORLD OF wealth split. Economic turbulence led many wealthy people out of riskier and higher-returning (potentially) assets. Many reduced borrowings and sought comfort in gold and other "stable" investments. At the same time, many younger and bolder investors, by dint of company ownership and risk tolerance, saw huge gains from their shareholdings in the Internet, biotech, mobile, social media and digital space, and emerging markets investments. Others created and invested in vehicles like hedge funds, which pay enormous fees for outsized performance.

The risks of being rich changed in 2008. And those who played their cards cleverly are more than back to square one.

Those who doubled down in the depths of the crossfire, or held their ground in selected investments, enjoyed a rebound, and even those who sold the risky investments, deleveraged, and played it safe have all prospered and more than recovered. But others stayed leveraged or saw their wealth evaporate, which forced asset sales into a plunging market. Many of the rich survived the storm, but many more did not. Among the survivors is a new rich.

And the portrait that has emerged might surprise you.

The average millionaire in America now goes bankrupt at least three times. Drive . . . fail and get up; drive . . . fail and rebound. About 80 percent of today's millionaires are first-generation wealthy, and most are manager-owners of businesses. An intriguing study found that the longer the average members of an ancestry group have been in the United States, the less likely they are to become millionaires. Old money is not as old as it seems.

By any yardstick the richest are most certainly getting richer. But is it the same people year in and year out? During the span of the 1990s dramatic wealth expansion, 75 percent of the Fortunate 400 richest earners made the list only one year. Only a quarter were regulars.

At least 20 percent of American adults will enjoy the distinction of being rich for some part of their lives. With so many new players surging in and out, there are few permanent seats at the table.

The Associated Press and others have called this large and mobile in-and-out gang the New Rich. Temporary status in this club means that for at least a year the family earned $250,000. Sustaining that kind of earnings power for decades may be very hard for American families, but for a year or two or three, a surprising number can make it happen.

Recent research has nearly 21 percent of American adults making it into this group for at least one year before they reach the age of sixty. A large proportion visit and leave and revisit many times.

These new rich are untraditional because they have something rarely associated with the well-to-do: financial fragility.

Their purchasing behavior reflects their temporary stay. They buy mass-affluent products, they splurge, even if they know deep down they are just renters at the 2 percent lounge. They tend to invest so they will benefit when financial assets soar. But there is also a caution about them.

During those trying years of recession when American take-home pay cinched tighter and tighter, their paychecks held up and toward the end of 2009 edged upward. By 2012, the top 20 percent began to emulate the behavior of the top one percent. With a median income of $150,000 that year, the top 20 percent took home 51 percent of the nation's income.

We are learning more about this new hovering rich. Today, they are three times more likely to be white than any other race. But they are show-ing up in urban centers all across the nation.

We are finding them in industries and regions with special dividends and culture pockets. The explosion of well-being in the Bakken oil shale region centered in North Dakota; the social networking and Internet phenomenon in northern California and the Pacific Northwest; and im-ponderably the new tech players in New York City. And something very special is happening today in Texas; new wealth is being created there as quickly as it is in any part of our nation. And though some have seen their well-being diminish as oil plunged by a hundred dollars a barrel from its $145 peak, many other Texans are prospering just fine.

How Are Rich People Managing?

THE REAL GAINS HAVE COME from rebounds in asset values. The top one percent owns most of the country's stocks, bonds, and mu-tual funds. The Institute for Policy Studies says the bottom 50 percent of Americans own less than one percent of these assets.

The explosion of investment values since the dark days of 2008 means the 400 richest Americans have nearly doubled their net worth from a decade ago to more than $2 trillion—though they're certainly not all the same individuals. That means if you are worth a billion dollars today there are more than sixty people ahead of you waiting in line to get on the 400 richest list.

We've seen the way millionaires have multiplied since the dark days, but how are things in the middle? Those with $100,000 or more in net worth, not including their primary residence, climbed to 37.4 million households from 31.2 million in 2008.

The recession punished the middle class too. The median net worth of American households plunged 47 percent. And median family income in 2010 was 6 percent lower than at the millennium ten years earlier—hence the aptly termed "Lost Decade."

The recuperative power of the middle class is a decidedly mixed story. Almost all those who have recovered possessed at least one of the following attributes: They held on to their stocks and bonds, their house, or their job.

Rebounding has been hard. Wages have only just begun to provide a lift. Recapturing lost well-being has come from their asset-value increases and from hanging on to their jobs. Data is still pretty mixed on this front; suffice it to say a very significant percentage did sell their stocks (at precisely the wrong time), did lose their homes, and did lose their jobs.

How about everybody else?

It's pretty grim. If you have a net worth of a dime you are worth more than the bottom 25 percent of Americans. A huge proportion of our fellow citizens are actually in a negative-net-worth position. Many are upside down on their mortgage—even those trying to continue to pay when they have no equity left.

The Great Recession hit Latino and black households with a vengeance. By the time the smoke cleared, half of the net worth of the typical black household had vanished, leaving them with a median net worth smaller than a year's car payments.

Latinos fared even worse. Their median net worth collapsed by 86 percent to a mere $1,300.

That compares to a median white household net worth of slightly under $100,000.

What is particularly disheartening is that during the housing boom preceding the crash, black and Latino homeownership grew at record rates—in many cases by virtue of poorly constructed teaser rates and subprime loans. But getting assets to this cohort of our countrymen represented their first real shot at middle-class aspiration. Now the typical black family has no equity in their home. And Latinos report almost no financial assets.

So when home prices rebound and markets soar, these families are reduced to spectators.

All this opposite-direction momentum leads to antagonism for the wealthy and to some pointed questions. Among them: How much of this wealth was inherited?

The answer today is very different from not so long ago.

SILVER SPOONS

THERE ARE CERTAINLY STILL TRUST funders who were born on third base and think they hit a triple. But more and more of today's wealthy are making it on their own rather than inheriting it from their Auntie Walton.

In Forbes' 2013 listing of the world's richest people were a record 1,426 billionaires, with a combined net worth of $5.4 trillion. Astonishing. Of that group 961 were self-made, while 184 inherited their wealth and another 281 inherited part of it.

Inheritance is worth studying closely. Here are the two sides of the story. Only 1.6 percent of Americans ever inherit more than $100,000. Some obviously enjoy fabulous wealth transfers, but more than 91 percent of Americans never inherit anything with even modest monetary value.

For the top income quintile, gifts and inheritance amount to about 13 percent of household net worth, according to the Bureau of Labor Statistics.

The one percent inherits about 15 percent of its net worth. These numbers have decreased by almost half in recent decades for the wealthiest Americans.

What is worth noting is that inherited money makes up 31 percent of the second quintile's total wealth—so inheritance still plays a role in middle-class well-being. And policy makers should take note before acting abruptly.

As for the younger generation, a tsunami is approaching.

Between the moment you read these words and the year 2055, at least $30 to $40 trillion will go to new hands as Americans of all stations pass along the treasures of their life's work.

A huge proportion of those funds will go to the government in the form of taxation, or to charities designated in estate and trust documents. Many have no idea what good things are coming their way.

This massive transfer of wealth is coming as aging well-to-do learn firsthand that you can't take it with you. But because the middle ranks enjoy a larger proportion of their well-being from inheritance, the tsunami will have a bigger relative impact on the middle class—albeit at much lower absolute numbers.

The rich still search for clever ways to pass it on. Many generation-skipping plans that avoid paying 50 percent or more in inheritance taxes have been shut down, but an entire service economy exists to do just that.

In *Immortality and the Law,* macabrely subtitled *The Rising Power of the American Dead,* Boston College law professor Ray D. Madoff describes how certain states have enabled dynasty trusts, which can exist in perpetuity. Since they never die, inheritance taxes are avoided. At least $100 billion of these perpetual entities have been enabled—a pittance when the enormous transfer tally is considered.

For anyone keen on redistribution, trillions are heading to government coffers—it's just hard to predict exactly when. Tinkering around the margins of estate-tax law won't trim the coming flood of funds much. There will be massive rebalancing through inheritance taxation.

People may quarrel about double taxation of income (once to income tax and then later as inheritance). Or they may argue that long-term investments should step up at death. In the global context it does not matter. Too many loopholes have been closed. The one percent can't hide their massive gains forever. At least not a big proportion of them. And the biggest transfer of individual wealth to government hands in the history of mankind is coming in good time—if we can maintain the patience for it.

Neither a Borrower

ANOTHER WAY TO EVALUATE A family's economic power is to study what they owe. After six years of digging out from heavy debts assumed during boom times, Americans are finally seeing abatement. At the peak in 2007, Americans borrowed 135 percent of disposable income. By 2014 it had moderated to 108 percent. For those who mortgaged property, homeowners' equity is slowly rebuilding. But many of those same families are seeing their student debt surge. Student loan debt, which targets a large swath of the middle class, exceeds $1.2 trillion and shows no sign of easing. And, unlike mortgage debt, if you cannot afford the payments you cannot just toss the bank the keys.

Families are just beginning to realize how long-tailed and inescapable student loans can be. One study says that more than 6 million Americans are at serious risk of defaulting on their student loan payments; that's like every person in the state of Maryland.

Debt is a looking-glass opposite for the wealthy because it plays a small role in one percent finances. Their total borrowings are less than 5 percent of the nation's personal debt. In contrast, the bottom 90 percent has 73 percent of total debt.

By summer's end 2014, a disturbing trend not seen since 2007 resurfaced. Growth in credit-card debt once again exceeded wage growth in the United States. Did confidence boom in the middle, or instead was it that families could only maintain by using this expensive form of credit to make ends meet?

Borrowing plays a much smaller role when income and wealth are surging. Disallowing interest deductions for top earners has not kept them from consuming things that they can afford through other means. Policy makers should bear that in mind when disallowing deductions—there has been little solid proof that doing so has curbed their appetite.

Taxation With Representation

NOTHING ATTRACTS MORE HEAT THAN debates about taxing the rich. Reams of data supporting both sides of the argument do little to dull the anguish. People are rarely persuadable on the topic.

Let's put the pitchforks and placards to the side for a moment and see what the facts uncover.

It is true that the top 10 percent have paid a substantial majority of the federal income taxes, ranging from 55 percent in the mid-1980s to more than 70 percent now. With changes in tax law, that proportion is only going to increase. The top 10 percent pay so much for the rather obvious reason that they are earning so much more money.

What about the other 90 percent? They pay about 29 percent of the total. However, we all know thanks to Mitt Romney's tape that 47 percent of Americans pay little to no federal taxes.

Typically at this point the defense on both sides rests—"You pay nothing" versus "You should pay it all because you are making all the dough."

But don't call checkmate just yet. Neither claim is completely accurate.

Taxes have become political code. Some seize on increased taxes as an explosion of government intrusion in our lives. Others call the anti-tax/anti–big government rhetoric a front—that billionaires' and millionaires' sole objective is to protect their riches. The wealthy are accused of hiding behind the skirts of liberty when their true mission is to cling to every dime.

How does that square with Warren Buffet and other business leaders who are literally begging to be taxed?

So often the narrative boils down to a matter of economic justice. But the middle class seems to continually come out in the same place. The rich should be taxed heavily and should pay a "fair share," and those further down the line should pay far less proportionally.

How are we doing on the essential question of progressive fairness?

The Tax Policy Center says it breaks both ways. In a recent year, about 4,000 households with seven-figure incomes paid almost nothing at all in federal taxes—on the face of it, a misfire on fairness.

Perhaps history can lend a hand. Until the Tax Reform Act of 1986 there were really just two tax brackets: 15 percent and 28 percent. Since then, brackets have been on the move; currently there are seven, ranging from 10 percent to nearly 40 percent.

Special taxes have been added by the Obama administration and yet there have been trade-offs. If you pan the lens back and study capital gains, transfer and other benefits, and the behavior of state, local, and property taxes, the total picture comes into clearer focus.

Capital gains tax has been a mover and a shaker. It was reduced to 28 percent in the 1980s, to 20 percent in the latter half of the 1990s, and to 15 percent during the George W. Bush administration. Before leaping for the pitchforks on W, most people don't remember Bush's reduction of the capital gains rate to 5 percent for the lowest two income brackets.

True, the poor don't own many mutual funds, but capital gains does apply to homes, household furnishings, bonds, and inherited assets, so this clearly was an attempt at progressive rates.

Today, capital gains has morphed into something more complex—and somewhat more progressive. Short-term trading, as before, enjoys the ordinary tax rate. But capital gains on assets owned for longer periods is 20 percent for married couples earning more than $456,000.

And for the lowest two tax brackets, the capital gains rate has been cut to zero.

Under the banner of the Affordable Care Act, an additional 3.8 percent surcharge is placed on "investment income" for joint filers with more than $250,000 in income. What exactly is meant by investment income? The IRS explanation runs to more than a hundred pages.

They thought of everything.

Redistribution has become a loaded term, inviting debates about the effectiveness and waste in government. Cutting government cost is a target-rich opportunity. But so long as defense and entitlements are protected, then there are not enough other cuts that can be made. Taxation, like death, remains a certainty. And most Americans are prepared for the notion of higher tax rates. Even the one percent.

TOTAL TAXES

AS REASONABLE AS IT MAY seem, it is difficult to point at any group and determine what their total taxes are. There are so many different kinds of taxes today, so many schedules and assumptions, and so many people looking for a way around them that a true tally is tough. But a few organizations try to look at total taxation.

Here are some summary results cleansed of ideological bent. Factoring in all state and local income taxes, the top 10 percent of the earners pay about half the tab. On the progressive meter, this figure says that the top 10 percent pay about 30 percent of their income in total income taxes, versus about 25 percent for the middle class.

Other studies have looked at total taxes paid on everything, not just on income. They include sales tax, property, and so on. Citizens for Tax Justice says that the lowest 20 percent of earners paid 16 percent of their income (average wages of about $12.5 thousand a year); the next 20 percent paid 20.5 percent of income; the middle 20 percent about 25.3 percent; and the next about 28.5 percent.

By these measurements, 80 percent of the country is total tax progressive (the more you make, the higher proportion you pay)—but not by much.

How about the top 20 percent? The study concludes that segments up to the top one percent are modestly progressive—in the 30 percent range—and trail off after the top one percent.

They also fail to capture a massive category of untaxed appreciation—stealth wealth.

DOG CATCHES BUS

PROGRESSIVITY IS IN THE EYE of the beholder. Income tax really does not do the job on its own. Many super-rich never file anything as plebian as a W-2. But when asset-related taxes and investment taxes and inheritance taxes are folded in, we start to see something that would test some fairness.

The notion that you live your life choosing to spend, invest, and give money away freely until you and your spouse expire, and then some meaningful tax is due on what's left over, does not strike me as unfair. It's actually a pretty smart way to redistribute. Some carp about income taxed twice, but most investments are sold many times with gains due and losses applied all along the way. Where is it written that recognized gains should only be taxed one time?

But progressivity is all about definition, and most everybody misses stealth wealth.

How does this apparition work?

Back to the frozen French fry. If you hold an asset and it appreciates hugely in a year and you do not sell, does it matter economically?

Each year the Forbes 400 delineates Americans who enjoy a large position in a company's stock. They may well receive dividends, and earn wages or fees serving as officer or director. All those payments are obviously taxable.

If that stock doubles, a sizeable increase in on-paper wealth results. Without a value-creating event like a sale of that stock or of the company as a whole, stealth wealth accretes untouched.

Think of the value of 3 million acres purchased by Simplot over a lifetime. (For comparison, the state of Connecticut is about three and a half million acres.) Apart from property tax, there was no true reflection of how much wealth had accumulated. Imagine hundreds of square miles—all gaining in value as silently as falling snow.

All that compounding value, over all those years, and not a penny of capital gains taxes paid because Simplot's was a buy-and-hold strategy.

Stealth wealth is where big money is created. Even public company stockholders like Bill Gates and Larry Ellison can hide their gains in plain sight, as long as they do not sell. Massive steps up in wealth are made with significant bets and steady nerves.

It has long been said that behind every great fortune is a great crime. Today a more accurate comment would be "a great bet."

It is quite the opposite of what business academics recommend—portfolio diversification. Most of the great wealth can trace itself to a pure play or a heavy investment in a single stock, a specific asset, a business, or some alternative asset class.

This distinction is a seminal point in Thomas Piketty's lengthy analysis of wealth. While his sums have been criticized, and his assumptions maligned the work, *Capitalism in the Twenty-First Century* contains many powerful and thoughtful insights.

Piketty's prescription of a 10 percent asset tax follows his admonition that income taxes alone cannot offset the galloping concentration of wealth.

Take it as a given: Unequal ownership of assets, not unequal pay, is the primary driver of inequality and wealth.

His recommendation of a 10 percent or more asset tax on capital plus a 60 percent ordinary income tax rate starting at $200,000 that rises to 80 percent above $500,000 or a million in earnings, leads to the central question about wealth.

Are multimillion-dollar and billion-dollar estates—and similar high incomes—coming to be regarded as unacceptable?

Certainly a 10 percent global tax on capital starts to feel like expropriation. Take almost any 100-year period in American history and the prior century's investment performance did not generate a return of more than 4 percent compounded, especially when you factor in foreign wars, market crashes, civil wars, natural disasters, estate taxes, piracy, and other plundering.

Ten percent would represent an orderly liquidation.

Piketty has this valid point: When return on capital exceeds the rate of economic growth for long periods of time, the poor and the middle class can never catch up—even with a modestly progressive tax structure.

He tells only half of the story, because he is less interested in what should be done with the levied funds. You can't simply tax people into equality—providing better opportunity is the path to fairness. That is the business story of our time. We explore that concept in the remainder of this book.

There are endless quibbles we can make to make taxes more effective. Why should social security payroll taxes be capped? The rich should pay all the way up their earnings curve.

Does carried interest in hedge fund and private equity funds have to be classified as capital gains rates rather than ordinary income? These are small virtues that help fill the coffers—but they miss the bigger point.

If we are to truly use income taxes rather than some capital holding tax—the most likely course for the time being—then we need to pass a threshold understanding which is exceedingly unpopular.

"SOMETIMES THERE JUST AREN'T ENOUGH ROCKS"

SO SAID FORREST GUMP AS Jenny threw stone after stone at the family cottage where so many abuses had taken place.

The Buffett rule would have raised taxes on anyone making over a million dollars. President Obama said no family making $250,000 would see an increase in their taxes. Both were well-intentioned ways to keep tax increases away from the middle. Here's the rub: Neither plan will work.

Problem is, there just aren't enough rich people. It's a classic good news/bad news situation if you have redistribution on your mind. There is an elite one percent that is earning stupendous amounts of money. Some of that is from ordinary income. Most is not.

With median household income hovering at $50,000, creating any meaningful lift for folks below that level will require tax hikes on wages far below a million dollars.

Remember, Citizens for Tax Justice found that $240,000 puts you in the top 5 percent of earners in 2010, and an IRS study had over 90 percent of Americans making less than $100,000.

Here is the mathematical rub. Serious redistribution cannot be achieved solely with income-tax increases unless you begin to approach the median income as your cutoff. Even with super-high tax rates on the rich, the left tail of the distribution is simply too big.

There are not enough rocks: You cannot achieve serious redistribution if you exempt everyone making $250,000 or less in income. Using income tax alone, you would have to come much closer to the heart of the middle-class earnings range.

Suppose we gave the other 99 percent the total income of the one percent—how much would each household get once we had divided the spoils?

Less than $15,000.

So pick your own tax rate on the one percent and draw the same conclusion. Even with a massive tax increase, income taxes alone cannot make up the difference.

Better to Give

Through public policy Americans support education, food, housing, and health care. We spend vast sums, and more money is certainly required given the expanse of people who can't get the most basic needs. But the rich and the middle class ought to get invested in making sure these services are provided better and more effectively.

Because on many levels they aren't. We tolerate enormous failure rates in our public schools. Public housing has been an area of disinvestment.

Health care is still outlandishly expensive and Medicare frauds are costing us tens of billions.

Charities do a better job than government in some service areas. Still, from time to time, the notion arises that we should reduce the charitable-deduction tax levels available to families making over $200,000.

Frankly, limiting deductions for mortgage interest, sales tax, and state and local taxes makes sense on some intuitive level. So the rich have a little less income. They can handle it. But putting a cap on charitable giving at 28 percent so that the federal government can raise more taxes and support redistributing efforts is misguided.

Anything that limits the flow of charity is at its core a hollow proposition, because charity delivers when the government can't.

Nobody national tucks in your blanket.

BIGGER THAN YOU CAN IMAGINE

AMERICANS ARE A GIVING BUNCH. In fact, giving is our steadiest growth industry.

In 2014, Americans gave more than $335 billion to charity—over 2 percent of our GDP. No other nation comes close. Charitable giving has grown almost every year in the last fifty. It grows at about a third of the overall advance in the stock market for the individual year.

The breakdown is interesting too. Individuals are by far the biggest donors—more than 72 percent of the total; nearly a quarter of a trillion dollars—per annum. Surveys say 95 percent of American households give to charity— across all income ranges—so it is hardly the exclusive domain of the upper crust.

Foundations gave away another $50 billion and corporations almost $17 billion. These numbers, too, are steadily growing; foundations themselves grew by the thousands and should number over 100,000 within a couple of years.

The most profound growth in philanthropic giving comes from a source that is nearly invisible, unpredictably timed, and yet most certain—bequests. After-death generosity has surged to nearly $27 billion, and bequests are just getting warmed up.

A recent Bank of America study tried to do the impossible—guess how much charity would be bequeathed during the first half of this century. Even given the necessary assumptions, the range of outcomes is both wide and on one level unsettling. In the first fifty years of the 21st century, the expected range of bequests was $6 trillion to over $27 trillion.

Let's examine the changes in the world of family foundations. These are non-profit organizations created by families that serve as charitable entities. Many are set up to last forever.

In the last few years, family foundations have routinely given more than $20 billion annually. And before leaping to conclusions, consider that about half of the 39,000 family foundations were donors of less than $50,000. The rules typically require giving at least 5 percent of assets each year, which means most family foundations are smaller than a million dollars in total assets.

Nearly 40 percent of these family foundations have assets of more than a million. At least fifty family foundations have over a billion dollars in assets—and almost half of them exceed $2 billion. (Two billion means minimum donations of $100 million every year.) The rich have the capacity to be very generous.

Giving has blossomed along with the explosion of wealth. Fourteen thousand of these foundations have been formed since the millennium. And family foundations are steadily becoming the leading force among all foundations, accounting for 64 percent of such donations last year.

They must be encouraged to give more and give better.

The latter is tricky. Family foundations are many in number and largely unregulated. How are decisions made at these foundations?

Nobody can really say.

So what can you surmise about 14,000 organizations with little or no oversight, modest tax-reporting requirements, wide ranges of expertise, and few if any impediments to making bad decisions?

You know that, even accounting for excellence among the majority, that thousands of them are doing a sub-optimal job. We should watch foundations more carefully, because anything worth giving is worth giving well.

The same can be said for all philanthropy.

GOD'S WORK

PEOPLE SPECULATE THAT ALL THIS generosity is due to tax deductibility. They cite our massive participation rates in charitable giving compared to rates closer to 40 percent in more socialist nations like Germany and France.

Poppycock.

In recent years, at least 64 million American adults have volunteered more than 7 billion hours of service *per annum*—something that would cost over $175 billion. Socialism and tax codes cannot explain such massive goodwill.

The facts are in: Americans care, especially when there is trouble. It's in our DNA. Tax deductibility might help at the margin, but American volunteerism rates trounce those of nearly every developed country in the world. We give because we are giving.

How are we executing on our mission?

Consider the sheer enormity of the giving. Take $335 billion per annum and add to that at least another $250 billion from the government. If you examine the books of the thousand biggest nonprofits in America, you'll find that most of them get most of their money from the government.

That means that each year something like $600 billion will be spent supporting nonprofits in our nation. That's over $6 trillion in the next decade—more than any nation in history.

In 2013, there were more than 1.5 million charitable organizations in the United States, and in 2012, public charities reported over $1.65 trillion in total revenues.

They are minimally regulated, modestly supervised, highly duplicative, and intensely regional, many of them. In a major city like New York, there may be a dozen organizations pursuing the same mission or category of help, and yet they never talk, meet, or compare notes.

There is modest collaboration, and almost no sharing of best practices. Many have no articulated strategic plan. Most do not use independent outside observers to evaluate performance. Not enough have set metrics for managing their organization. Fundraising and administrative costs as a percent of total revenues are often not managed effectively, and many do not compare themselves to any industry or parallel standard.

Despite good intentions, poor performers have been able to carry on for decades without penalty. And here is the rub: Most donors do not check to see if their money has been spent at all. Fewer still scrutinize charities to see if their money has been well spent.

These concerns lead to a conclusion that many are uneasy saying aloud—that, of the 1.5 million nonprofits, hundreds of thousands are performing way below optimally—and too many are doing a very poor job.

Some are so blatantly ineffective that they should merge or cease operations.

Naturally, there is reluctance to punish well-meaning philanthropies. The passions of the director and team cover a multitude of shortcomings. But good intentions are not enough.

What we need are three things: much more aggressive and focused donors and board members, who ask for performance from the charities they are guiding; better regulation and oversight; and a true ranking system to promote best practices. Anyone who says charity cannot be focused on improving outcomes has a nineteenth-century worldview of a multi-hundred-billion-dollar enterprise.

We need an SEC for charity. Attorneys general across the nation have not added to their teams even as the number of charities skyrockets.

Consider that there are just 2,800 stocks on the New York Stock Exchange and about 3,800 companies that list on NASDAQ. With many regulatory regimes and oversight bodies, there are still Enron's and World Com's that manage to sneak by for years until they are unmasked as frauds.

Imagine that trillions of dollars, an important percentage of which is cash or checks, were flowing through corporate coffers. Imagine that these corporates were essentially self-reporting with no common market of measurability. Imagine that they were essentially self-regulating apart from occasional initiatives by their home-state attorney general. Further imagine that performance measurement and comparability were basically impossible to discern.

That is the *modus operandi* of hundreds of thousands of these nonprofit organizations.

There are few standards of excellence like Charity Navigator, which monitors charities. The Better Business Bureau has a list of standards that aren't bad either. But these are only the beginning. We need a greater sense of impatience and outrage. Hunger and homelessness are at all-time highs. Unemployment, incarceration, drug abuse, and troubled youth are present in numbers that command our immediate attention.

We spend trillions every decade. And two things we know for certain are that we will run out of money long before we run out of need, and as a result our charity must perform more effectively.

That call to arms for charity should echo down the canyons of Park Avenue and Rodeo Drive. We can either condemn the rich for what they have or guide them to their duty.

Charity is just one area where the one percent problem must yield to the one percent solution. There are many more.

CHAPTER TEN

The One Percent Solution

A time for wealth to lead the charge

FRUSTRATION WAS THICK IN THE BASEMENT *that night. For months a young engineer had been trying to do the simplest thing: heat and stretch a polymer to create an extremely mundane product—flexible plumber's tape. The polymer that was being so uncooperative night after night—PFTE—spent decades in the lab after its accidental discovery in 1930 and in small commercial use before it was finally branded as Teflon and landed in the frying pan. DuPont had worked the Teflon franchise hard and their interest was flagging, but the young engineer's father saw value where others didn't.*

At forty-five, his father departed the Delaware chemical colossus with a dream and a technology license. Neither seemed particularly valuable that 1958 afternoon. Few at headquarters expected more from Teflon than the great business they were already doing.

Choked for so long by innovation-killing bureaucracy, the newly liberated engineer imagined an entirely different kind of company. With his wife as business partner, they opened for business in the basement of their modest Delaware home.

They got off to a slow start, the very best kind. Poring over details of the polymer, he developed a ribbon cable of insulated wire—safe, flexible, and perfect for the innards of a new innovation called a computer. The husband-and-wife team wanted a company organized around a whole new principle. Everybody matters. Eschewing the term "employee," the early associates were paid in stock long before it became common practice to do so.

Then came the call—the city of Denver ordered 7.5 miles of their ribbon cabling.

Good-bye basement; hello more associates and more shares. Innovation was the cultural spark. But deep in the couple's heart was a more powerful idea of how business should be run—that strength should emanate from the middle and that rewards should be shared among all associates.

Captivated by the dream, his college-sophomore son suggested an innovation that earned the company's first patent and proved the apple didn't fall . . .

IBM and NASA were drawn to the cabling and to the lore surrounding the private enterprise—no longer just a company anymore but a culture. Their son signed on full time after years spent behind the scenes as he earned a chemical engineering PhD. This was no typical "son also rises" story.

Every person in the organization existed on the same level—imagine a lattice-work where everyone reports to everyone else. No hierarchy, no bosses, no vice presidents, no supervisors. The founders determined that the best way to manage was with no managers.

They further decided that the company would have no core businesses, only core competencies. With no layers of management, information would flow freely. Without job titles and specific areas of responsibility, and no organization chart, specific roles on the small teams had to be negotiated every time. Because associates served on many teams they were often asked to play a leadership role on one and a subordinate role on another. Every team, every project, every product was different.

Leadership was natural, organic. Team building occurred because an associate could draw talent to their project, not because someone was ordered. If nobody showed up, then the project didn't happen or someone else marshaled resources to pursue it. When a new CEO was required *the Board asked the associates to identify who the only titled person in the company should be. The family had no more say in the decision than anyone else.*

Premium was placed on collegiality, innovation, listening, and personal interaction. Anybody could speak to anybody else at any time on any project.

That night the young man struggled in his basement with a simple new product idea, and things weren't going well. He stretched the polymer carefully, but the Silly Putty consistency meant the warmed glop kept breaking. Night after night, he pulled more slowly and more carefully—always with the same result. His associates had great faith in his abilities, but no matter how slowly he stretched the material, it always broke.

So he tried something completely different.

On a lark, he stretched the material as fast as he could. Not only didn't it break, but it pulled and pulled and pulled. Eureka! . . . Or so he thought. The hoped-for plumber's tape was not to be. That product was a failure. But as he studied the little pores between the strands he found they possessed a surprising capability. They were so small that vapor could get out but water could not get in.

In his hands at that instant was a massive innovation disguised as a mistake—he just didn't know it yet.

His team spent seven years searching for the right commercial application. In 1976 they struck their claim. The Early Winters catalogue advertised Gore-Tex rainwear as "possibly the most versatile piece of clothing you'll ever wear." In weeks, hundreds of Gore-Tex items flew out the door. The catalogue purchased most of the ten thousand yards of fabric that W.L. Gore & Associates made that first year.

That was only the beginning—enough Gore-Tex has been manufactured to paper over several states. Their product revolutionized the outdoor wear market . . . and more.

Bob Gore and his father, Bill, continue to sustain the "everyone matters" philosophy, even as the private company has grown to revenues exceeding $3 billion and nearly 10,000 employees spread over 30 nations.

Today, Gore is one of the 200 largest private companies in the United States and has for more than a decade been listed in the enviable "100 Best Companies to Work For." And fifty-five years later there is just one title in the place that matters—Associate.

THE TIME HAS COME FOR something completely different—a declaration of interdependence.

Wilbur Lee Gore figured out early in life that the middle matters and that progress comes by celebrating and elevating people committed to team play. Hierarchies are the enemy of innovation. People produce and make commitments to a goal when they know that they matter. Gore's views were influenced by Douglas MacGregor in his book *The Human Side of Enterprise,* which became a business school staple in innovative organizational behavior.

The company's lattice concept requires a degree of dialogue and cooperation which seems impractical and un-scalable to broader, more complex organizations. But as the number of products from W.L. Gore & Associates blossomed to more than a thousand and the erstwhile cabling company diversified into leading "tech-styles" businesses and others—like guitar strings and synthetic blood vessels—a truth kept marching on.

Success came to those who harnessed the talent in the middle and brought their energies to the surface by the most simple and basic method —giving them the power to create their own opportunity.

That is the essence of our interdependence. Wealth well directed.

We are joined in a powerful ecosystem of reaction and counter reaction, punch and counterpunch. No group should stand alone. Rather than paint the one percent with a broad brush, let's harness all their gifts and talents.

Some members of the American elite have heard the clarion call. Some not even a generation from poverty give billions to better the lives of fellow citizens. But too many one percenters still pursue an island strategy. For every great sharer, there are legions who personify the division, whose possessions include a blazing sense of entitlement, and who resist helping those in the frustrating whirlpool of poverty and despair.

We must persuade these hold-outs to play a greater role—not only to propagate well-being but for self-preservation. Motivations may vary. But the mission to draw them into the fray must be unbending, because Americans live by the greatest single truth in the history of social economics.

Legitimacy is lost if a tiny elite enjoy all the benefits and they do not share them.

For too many Americans the Horatio Alger dream, where each generation surpasses the experience of the preceding one, has turned into an inescapable nightmare.

As we watch the middle class struggle to their knees like a prizefighter too many rounds into the bout, a question must hover for every one percenter, for every five percenter, or anyone else with the ability to lend a hand.

Are you a part of the solution or part of the problem?

It is time for wealth to lead and represent the change.

Unfortunately, we have come to rely on a basic prescription of increased welfare spending financed by higher taxation. That approach is as dated and flawed as using real-estate taxes to fund local education. Both are poor ways to redistribute, because the right zip code schools flourish while the less-endowed zips watch their schools and their opportunities wither.

We have been especially slow to recognize that we have made promises during good times that we may not be able to keep. The one percent must be drafted to help make those promises a reality.

SPLITTING THE POT

SO WHAT SHOULD WE DO about the huge divide and wealth?

Calling famillionaires in 9 million homes royalists will not yield results. Royals through history have a way of keeping their heads, at least until they can't. No one is better than the well-endowed at staving off the forces of history.

Okay, so American wealth is back from the brink, well ahead of the middle class and the poor. Now is their time.

We need a contagion to share winnings—in every form. If the one percent leads by example, the whole tide can turn. Because there is so much that needs to be done.

How are people doing today in America?

Tens of millions of our countrymen and -women are hungry. Homelessness is at an all-time high. Families in frigid climes must choose between eating dinner and heating their homes. For all those single mothers, is there relief they deserve because they served you French fries? Or is it because they are decent hardworking people stretching to feed and house their families?

Tonight 20,000 children will sleep in homeless shelters in New York City. As you sprint home to supper, do you pause to reflect on holding birthday parties, as many children do, in the warm embrace of a homeless shelter?

They say if much is given to you, then much will be asked. My question is by whom?

When was the last time a politician requested your help with homelessness or hunger? It doesn't matter what percent you are. Our leaders won't ask. They are afraid, or they would rather bully you in the media to gain points and harvest animus toward your good fortune.

But here is something that is true of virtually every rich person in America. They want to give back. Some are already generous beyond imagining. And some haven't got the hang of it yet.

One out of five of you will be in the top 5 percent for some stretch of time—many for decades.

So here is the bottom line. The top one percent should try to give 10 percent of their earnings to help the less fortunate. If you are in the top 20 percent, give half that much. And if you have the capacity to give anything, try to add 10 percent more next year.

Giving alone isn't enough. Keep track of how your charities are doing. A great number are basically well-meaning but mediocre. If you don't have time to learn the difference, use donor-advised funds, where expert evaluators help you give your money away more effectively.

Treat donations like investments. Measure and gauge outcomes. Switch to more effective charities if you are not satisfied. Charities sometimes dislike performance metrics, but the good ones welcome the challenge.

Go beyond donations. Serve on boards. Often the weakest link in a charity is the effectiveness of its leadership. The need for a fresh voice is often the only thing holding a charity back.

Be a local point of disruption and foment change. Harness your network of friends to the task—most everyone has an underutilized network of relationships that can help people in need. Monetize your network.

You don't need to be a one percenter to raise one percent money.

Many business leaders spend time and treasure advocating politically but do next to nothing advocating socially. What a missed opportunity.

These incursions can be time-consuming or slight. Your choice.

If you want to experience unremitting joy, find a kid in your community who is qualified and dying to attend college but can't afford it. Meet the parents and the child. Then make it happen. There are literally millions of households that could pay all or part of a tuition bill and transform a life forever. If you can't do it alone, form a syndicate.

Talk about making a difference.

Take a chance on hiring a veteran, especially one who needs a little training before fully engaging. Pay for a surgery, or braces, or a new car. Underwrite a funeral or a senior prom dress. Send someone to Disneyland with their family. Make a wish come true. There are organizations dying to help connect these dots.

FULL-TIME CITIZEN

FILLING THE COFFERS OF A think tank that tilts in a preferred direction is just one way to influence the outcome; instead, serve as an instrument of peace. Leadership from government has been lacking. Wealthy Americans who are powerfully activist in the corporate context turn to mush with social policy issues.

Politicians have figured this out. They get more short-term mileage by mocking you and talking about two Americas and the divisions and the thoughtlessness you represent. Don't personify the divide. Nothing should disturb you more. Defy it.

What can you do?

There are tens of millions of your fellow citizens who desperately need Social Security checks, which average about $1,100 a month. Yours will likely be higher, but just as likely it won't make the slightest difference in your life when you reach eligibility.

Why not just let it go?

That's right—give back your entitlement. Millions upon millions of Americans can use the money, just as there are millions of Americans who really don't need it.

Speeches I have given describing this Social Security Grant Back generate enormous hostility. Social Security is a paid-for entitlement they say. So what. If it is truly yours, then simply give it back.

Why give up an earned good?

Despite what reassuring bureaucrats tell you, Social Security is already straining to meet obligations that will explode in the next decades as boomers age in. Read the Trust Fund reports. They spell out dependency on current accounts. It's pay as you go.

Nothing about Social Security's burden will get easier unless a few million Americans opt out. Doing so now will do two things: lighten the load as the boomer bulge approaches, and, more important, demonstrate that you are willing to give up something to which you are entitled for the greater good. Others will follow.

Give Medicare a break too. If you must use the main corpus, at least drop from their drug plans and other elements where the government co-pays.

If you heart is not moved to help others, do it to preempt the means testing that becomes inevitable as the divide widens. "Non-insurance" benefits where there has been no payroll deduction will not survive in their current form.

If you don't preempt, you will certainly be preempted. Means testing is coming. Beat it to the punch.

Look through other benefits you are enjoying from the government that you don't really use or that you don't need. Cast a wide net. Check and see if your kids are among college students and young professionals using SNAP (Supplemental Nutritional Assistance Program) to bolster their food budgets. Really?

One percenters have influence in other areas. Are you sure you can't pay your hourly workers anything more? Forget what you can get away with. What can you afford?

Look for signs of weakness in government PR. Behind the headline lower unemployment rate and increasing job numbers, two things leap out: Hourly wages are going nowhere, and a huge proportion of the jobs are part time with little or no benefits.

Corporations are sitting on oceans of cash—to the tune of trillions. Earnings are up, as are margins because so much cost has been engineered out of the system. Most every company can afford to hire more people or to pay their employees just a little bit more.

The greatest threat to the middle class is not the lack of jobs but the lack of good jobs. And in the inner cities the rate of unemployment among black and Hispanic youth approaches 40 percent. Nothing about that picture portends a good economic outcome for them or for any of us.

A New Marshall Plan

WHY NOT PULL THE POLYMER as quickly as we can, approaching the one percent in a completely different way?

Castigation and confiscatory taxation is one approach. How about enlisting them as individuals instead, where they participate in a new Marshall Plan, using their influence and resources to rebuild the middle class?

The one percent is not one-dimensional. They are teeming with resources far beyond the funds in their accounts. Many possess leadership skills and experience managing complex organizations. They have global networks of business, government, and philanthropic relationships.

People owe them favors.

Many great leaders are winding down their life clock on the audit committee of some corporate board. Is that their highest and best use? By thinking through their skills, finding their passions, a lot of their spare energy, excess influence, untapped networks, and yes, financial resources could be pointed in a common direction.

They might even help the vast government bureaucracy run more efficiently.

A few examples:

Influencers should insist that government transform its role to asset allocator. Government takes ages to create a bureaucracy and then implements the closest thing to eternal life that you will see on this earth.

Medicare, Medicaid, Social Security, Head Start, Jobs Corp, and so on are ancient regimes creaking with tired habits that the world has long passed by. This notion that government must employ and control the entire delivery system is even more outdated than their programs.

It should farm out tasks, as the CDC has been doing for years. The Army, too, has hired independent operators. Government should be an asset allocator and deputize industry leaders the way FDR did in World War II. Inject some dynamism, shorten reaction times. Many one percenters today can well afford to take time to lead such projects.

Public–private linkages born of global conflagration transformed our economy in the middle of the last century. Today the middle class suffers from years of continuing attack. Why not offer your abilities?

The one percent is either an enemy or the centerpiece in getting back our mojo.

An engine of change is sitting right in front of us, underutilized and forlorn. And here's the best part: A great many of these leaders are more than eager to help.

They just have to be asked—because it has gotten awfully hard to volunteer. CEOs with astonishing records are still viewed as undesirables inside the Beltway. Great presidents from both political parties were once adroit at involving men and women of enormous commercial ability in the affairs of state and the nation.

Today, CEOs and political leaders hate to be photographed together. It's time for the one percent to become a photo bomber and get in the frame.

Understimulated

Fiscal policy has become an orgy of spending with little multiplier effect on the economy. Paying for new uniforms for the TSA so they looked a lot bluer, aiding libraries with few employees—these are a million miles from stimulus. They reek of pork and have done little to create good jobs.

Travel anywhere and our infrastructure is crumbling. One percenters should use their enormous influence to slash red tape to create true stimulus directed at rusting infrastructure. It will be hellishly expensive, but it will position the country for the remainder of the century and will truly create jobs.

Whether you are a one percenter or way down the scale, be a stimulator where government can't be.

Visit your community leaders or your local hospital or a congregation and ask what they need: A city by the sea has a need for rescue equipment for boaters but cannot afford it, a church knows of a park or a senior center that needs restoring, a community has no funding to help uniformed personnel who are injured or killed in the line of duty, a local hospital cannot provide outpatient services to veterans suffering from post-traumatic stress disorder, a public school library has almost no books.

These are all real examples. Why not ask your mayor what your community really needs and lead an effort to do something about it?

How much time does it take to send a kid to college or pay a hospital bill? Many citizens are the type of do-er's who get things done, while others get stymied by the first obstacle. What wise and positive thing can you do personally to improve the chances that someone in your community enjoys a middle-class life?

Stem-winders who see around corners in their business can do likewise with social causes. And you don't need a Rockefeller trust fund to make great things happen.

There are endless needs to help folks stay in the middle. Here are just a few where you can help:

- Childhood obesity is a major problem in the inner city. If a one percent mind and wallet can't tackle it, how about a delta force of others without the bulging billfold?
- Matt Taibi and others have researched and written persuasively that the justice system, particularly in jury trials, is both flawed and tilted toward the rich. The Innocence Project has found many irregularities and incompetency in the public defense of death-row criminals. Powerful arguments and persuasive data have been presented that indicate justice is not entirely blind to your W-2. How about funding a justice-for-all project?
- One of the leading causes of middle-class bankruptcy is cancer. Trouble is, one in three adults will get a cancer diagnosis in their lifetime. As toxic as the carcinogens may be to their body, there is equal toxicity financially. Leading cancer drugs can cost over $100,000 a year—with a required 20 percent or more Medicare co-pay.

Drug companies provide some modest relief for the poor, but the middle class is priced out. Some decide to take half doses to make the medicine last longer. These same drugs can cost 50 to 80 percent lower outside the United States.

Medicare is forbidden from negotiating with drug companies. Elsewhere in the world, such negotiations are commonplace. Prices are set, Big Pharma argues to cover the costs to develop the drugs, yet why are older drug prices increasing long after the development phase?

Where is the incentive to help the middle class crushed by these policies? Remember: The only drug that works is a drug the patient can afford.

Look around. There are middle-class-squeezing policies everywhere you turn. Education issues which prevent youth from building momentum into the middle class; working mothers who lose benefits simply because they have found employment; incarceration of teenagers at rates higher than those of any nation on earth; youth unemployment in the inner cities, setting up an annuity of disappointment for another generation. The list of threats to our middle class is endless.

Let's work with the one percent and engage them in solving our problems. Remember, they are waiting to be asked.

THE OTHER HALF LIVES

PEOPLE WHO CALL THE INCREASING dispersion of wealth the economic story of our time are wrong.

It is only half the story. The other part is to figure out how to balance wealth creation with the creation of opportunity. Redistribution will be a part of the solution—it always has been. But it is just one weapon, and we need an arsenal. Too much airtime is spent complaining about the increasing concentration of wealth, a bit less on how to get the money, and almost none on what should be done once we have it.

The time has come to encourage and ennoble, not scold—to explain clearly and to deliver results rather than paralysis. That will loosen the purse strings of the one percent.

We have stopped asking.

Because vision is a lot harder than division.

Thomas Piketty's solution of massive taxation comes after a thorough analysis of where the money came from. But his solutions are an academic's. Almost no thought was given to where the funds might be going. His animation comes from the need to liquidate and redistribute. His energy derives from the pure fact of the increased concentration of wealth.

And he is singularly detached from the other, less visible assets besides money that could be part of a one percent solution for the middle class.

The wealth divide is the symptom of broader ills. It is the undercard, not the main event.

As such, his orderly liquidation and economic moralizing won't fix things—only change them slightly. Haven't we learned how effectively the one percent can adapt?

Are there people who have more money than they can possibly need? Of course—and parting with some of it won't change their lives. They know that. So how best to enlist them in an honorable quest?

The problems of the middle class are so tricky that we cannot let simplistic ideas blind us. The challenge is to educate and lift our citizens. We must remove barriers to self-reliance. Every effort must be made to unleash the pride in learning a craft and completing a job well done. The middle class is the pivotal demographic here.

Place the fulcrum in the middle and we can tilt the earth. Duty falls to those who have to reach out and collaborate with those who have not.

The obligation of people in power is to govern in a way that enlists rather than divides, that taxes with a clear message of purpose and direction, and that moves unfortunates who are capable of doing more to a protected place where their skills are valued and their labors rewarded.

That is the soul of the one percent solution. We will tackle these in the pages to come: how to lift the poor; how to create jobs that enliven and inspire; how to rebuild our manufacturing; how to take advantage of the surge in women in the workforce and the emerging force of Latino culture and the black middle class. We also will examine how foreign countries count as both our greatest opportunity and threat, and what we should all do about them.

That is the one percent solution: The elevation of more Americans to the middle. Taking the Gore philosophy and scaling it large. Everyone matters. Pulling the polymer in innovative ways to rebuild our middle class. Making that happen is the economic story of our time.

CHAPTER ELEVEN

The Renaissance

Living a dream deferred

HER NAME IS SO EVOCATIVE IT'S *a noun, an adjective, and a verb.*

Restrained by rivers on three sides and sliced along the horizontal by a progression of east-west thoroughfares, she transcends that tidy geography, her reach extending beyond the city planners' metes and bounds.

Go anywhere in the world, say her name, and something adrenalizing happens.

Dutch masters took up quarters in the center of her wilderness and for centuries that farmland went largely undeveloped. Irish followed the Netherlanders, then Germans, Italians, and Jews. Harlem belonged to successive waves of settlers, yet it was middle-class and wealthy whites who superintended her transition from isolated country village to an affluent and upper middle-class suburb. By the mid-1800s the land's productivity waned and many of the farms and large estates were abandoned or sold. Irish squatters huddled in hastily arranged shantytowns.

Harlem fed the desperate . . . and waited.

By 1878, tentacles reached from the south of the island as elevated trains stretched ever higher along Eighth and Ninth Avenues sparking investment fever.

Speculators pounced, building fine row houses and multifamily gargan-tua. Genteel New Yorkers inhabited mansions among Irish and Italian im-migrants. With marshland along the waterways, the bottom classes could always find a lowland roost. In the last days of the dwindling nineteenth cen-tury, economic malaise haunted the nation. Appetites were curbed and de-velopers marked time in the agony of the over-extended. Glimmers of hope broke through in 1895 and, lessons forgotten, masons and artisans returned to their handiwork.

Applauding the northward reach of the Lenox Avenue IRT line, with targeted completion by 1904, developers built hundreds of anticipatory apartment buildings ready to receive the torrent of lower-Manhattan resi-dents anxious for a taste of the new Harlem.

It was crafted as a middle- and upper-class paradise within easy reach of midtown, and from across the river just a jump from the Bronx espla-nades. The early designs were noteworthy.

Though officially designated St. Nicholas District, the 138th Street neighborhood between Seventh and Eighth Avenues earned the sobriquet "Strivers Row," reflecting the social ambitions of its residents. America's best-known architects, like Stanford White, designed houses along the block— striking Georgians beside neo–Italian Renaissance mansions.

Just a few blocks south, twenty-eight row houses built by John Jacob Astor's grandson, William, were created for white middle- and upper-class owners, with the obligatory front yards and Charleston porches. They still call it Astor Row.

Harlem was a developer's daydream.

Compounding their folly, speculators built apartments by the tens of thousands. Harlem was a new frontier right on their own island, and dreamers were in hot pursuit. But the reverie had missed a telling reality. Throngs weren't moving.

The canyons were empty. Only a trickle was flowing north. Fear crept into developer conversations.

Sometimes, the simplest idea can alter the course of history. Phillip A. Payton had just such a concept. Payton, an African American janitor turned

real estate entrepreneur, approached a collection of panicked Harlem land-
lords with a galling but simple proposition. For many of them, his idea was
the solitary antidote to financial ruin. Through his company, Afro American
Realty, founded in 1904, he offered an unheard-of way to fill the landlords'
empty lease rolls.

Rent to blacks.

White landowners resisted, and many fled ahead of what the press
called a "Negro Invasion." Until that time Harlem had few black residents.

In an instant, Harlem found a fresh voice and a new place in the world.

PAYTON'S TIMING WAS IMPECCABLE.

Black families poured into Harlem from all over Manhattan Island, as well as from islands in the Caribbean and the West Indies and more distant ports of call. Already a Great Migration had commenced: a flood of humanity embracing over 6 million African Americans who left behind the rural South for the urban Northeast and Midwest and ultimately the West.

Their exodus came in two waves. The first was between 1910 and 1930, comprising more than 1.6 million migrants who sought employment opportunity in the industrial metropolises of the North. The second was bigger and broader. From 1940 to 1970, five million souls moved from the South to cities all across the nation. These pilgrims were joined by family members from all over the Caribbean and the world.

They wanted a new home.

Their journey was driven by much more than a paycheck. This was closer to an evacuation, a true expression of self-determination, a break for freedom by people long oppressed. The trip was painful, emotional, and wrenching. At stake was the very soul of their society.

And ours.

By the end of the second migration the African American population had relinquished roots in rural and agricultural America. King Cotton and the echoes of slavery were lost in the maze of history. Theirs was a new day in pursuit of a new life. By exodus's end more than 80 percent of blacks lived in cities, a near-total shift in less than a century—theirs had become an urbanized culture.

While most African Americans still lived in the South, at least 40 percent now toiled in the North—but they were now city people.

By the time the planned subway system and interior roadways finally reached Harlem, its black population had more than doubled. The end of World War I brought Americans and immigrants of all types to New York City seeking economic and artistic opportunities.

Harlem sizzled. Musicians, writers, and artists converged there. It was the blossoming of the Harlem Renaissance, one of the most robust and influential movements in American literary history.

Dramatic rises in black literacy inspired poets like Langston Hughes to congregate with other black authors in publishing *Fire!!*—a trailblazing effort to bring voice to African American experience and, as Hughes wrote in his autobiography, to "burn out a lot of the old, dead conventional Negro-white ideas of the past."

The Harlem Renaissance behaved in unique ways for an artistic movement.

The poetry of Hughes, Countee Cullen, Claude McKay, and Jean Toomer joined the massive public-building mural paintings of Aaron Douglas; the music of Duke Ellington, Cab Calloway, and Fletcher Henderson; and the acting of Paul Robeson and Josephine Baker to form a vast and powerful collective work. Together and individually, they declared an arrival of a true African American Voice—fresh and new, and yet evocative of the old.

It was the modern version of *The Education of Henry Adams*: a cultural recognition, or a line in the sand—call it what you will. Both white America and black America took notice.

What made the movement particularly profound was its direct linkage to social reform and the early stirrings of the civil rights movement. Any historian will tell you that respect and appreciation precede rights, even when grudgingly acknowledged. This Renaissance brought respect.

Reform organizations sprang up like the National Urban League and the National Association for the Advancement of Colored People. The

NAACP's in-house magazines, *Opportunity* and *The Crisis,* provided both gallery and bully pulpit for artists and writers of the Harlem movement.

The stirring cocktail of artistic expression reflecting African, Caribbean, and Southern plantation expression, shaken vigorously with the new black urban experience, brought forth works of striking vitality and impact.

The 135th Street Branch of the New York Public Library served as a salon for these artists to congregate, mingle, and yes, party. In those days, Harlem's tallest and most exclusive building was 409 Edgecombe Avenue, and living there were some of the most creative artists and thinkers in the country. The likes of Thurgood Marshall, W.E.B. DuBois, James Weldon Johnson, and Aaron Douglas entertained other agents of change—these were special days for a virtual black city within the borough of Manhattan.

The Renaissance began to manifest itself far beyond the streets of Harlem, though as its mecca the 4,000-acre "enclave" became a catalyst for new artistic expression and for the white elite's embrace of primitivism and experimentation. In cities like Chicago and other industrial centers, African Americans were labeled "The New Negro" by sociologist Alain LeRoy Locke.

The white literary establishment began publishing Harlem poets in large numbers. The dynamic period was originally called the "New Negro Movement" after Locke's descriptor, but the power of the poetry ultimately ushered in a more respectful and fitting allusion—the Renaissance.

Langston Hughes targeted his poetry to African Americans. Heavily influenced by jazz improvisation, his book-length poem *Montage of a Dream Deferred* bubbled from the cauldron of Harlem. Hughes read to crowds across the nation constantly, leading one biographer to wonder whether any American poet had recited his poems aloud to more people.

He opened his homage to Harlem with characteristic poignancy: "What happens to a dream deferred?"

His answer came when the Renaissance and the Roaring Twenties were chewed by the incisors of the Great Depression. It must have been agonizing for so many African Americans to see their dream deferred yet again after its realization appeared so close. Mass layoffs, homelessness, and, for the well-to-do blacks, foreclosure slammed the door on their American Dream.

Religious and community leaders lost their enthusiasm for the arts, turning instead to survival issues like hunger and shelter.

So devastated were the finances of the people of Harlem that they could not honor their debts to white shopkeepers who had prospered alongside them. For decades, vendor and customer peacefully cohabitated, but economic realities grew severe. Pressure kept building.

Neighborhood blacks took their tension to the street and enmity for white shop owners exploded in the Harlem Riots of 1935, possibly the nation's first inner-city race riot.

Angry voices composed the song of a Renaissance dying. Harlem lived on in ever-changing form.

Post-Renaissance Harlem

East Harlem became home to a large Italian community after 65,000 apartments were constructed when the IRT line was completed. Returning and resettling after both world wars, Puerto Rican immigrants also found a home base, drawing ever more Latinos into East Harlem's orbit. Thus was born El Barrio, or Spanish Harlem.

Commercial air travel took wing in the 1940s and '50s, and a one-way ticket from San Juan cost under $50. The steady migration meant the Italians were joined by an ever-larger cohort of Latinos. Increasingly, the two groups pressed on each other for housing and for neighborhood control of East Harlem.

The atmosphere became kinetic as young people allied themselves with gangs according to their heritage. Violent exchanges and simmering tensions among the black Dragons, the Italian Dukes, the Puerto Rican Viceroys, and the Italian Redwings became part of daily life.

Matters were only slightly less peaceful between adults. Jewish and Italian merchants watched their customers shift to Puerto Rican shops and eating establishments. With the introduction of large public housing projects into East Harlem, the fabric of the neighborhood was forever altered. Increasing numbers of blacks and Hispanics tightened the ring around the dwindling Italian neighborhoods.

During the Depression, unemployment in Harlem surged quickly past 20 percent and everywhere families were evicted from their homes. Infant mortality rates also surged—to 124 per thousand. By 1940 it had abated, but to levels still far outside national norms—to 1 out of 20. By the 1950s virtually all of the whites had left Central Harlem, and by the 1960s most of the black middle class was gone too.

A *Life* magazine special feature by the acclaimed African American photojournalist and musician Gordon Parks, published in March 1968, shared an intimate and searing look into the lives of Norman and Bessie Fontenelle and their eight children. Emigrating from the West Indies in the 1950s, Norman found part-time work as a railway section hand. For eleven years he toiled in the heat and bitter cold, barely making ends meet. In their grimy two-room apartment their dog and cat were occupied keeping persistent rats at bay.

Poignant images captured the days after Norman lost his job. The surrender in his eyes makes you feel like you are watching a man die. Parks never photographed the whole family at a meal, because there was never enough to feed the entire family at once. Instead, he captured four of the daughters sharing a supper comprised of a solitary apple.

Another series pairs an emergency room shot of Norman's scarred face with an image of Bessie, aged beyond her thirty-nine years, huddled with her youngest girl in the frigid apartment on the sole bed for the ten of them. Norman had started drinking to drown the shame of unemployment. Rage boiled within him. Beatings ensued. Bessie took a pot of boiling water, sugar, and honey and flung the scalding concoction into Norman's face.

Harlem had turned into an island filled with Parks's haunted faces.

In the mid-eighties a new pharmacological concoction was introduced, a darkly brilliant marketing idea, an enslaving notion first called freebasing, then called rock, then cooked, and ultimately crack.

Cocaine, an expensive but little-feared drug, was cooked to crystal form in a baking soda mix, then broken into little rocks that looked like they fell from the cracked plaster walls of a local walk-up.

The small rocks, sold in vials for just $10, were smoked and the high was instant, fleeting—and frighteningly addictive. In a phrase: it was cocaine for the masses. Start off people for a song and then wait for rampant addiction.

Three decades since twenty-eight-year-old graffiti muralist Keith Haring painted "Crack Is Wack" on a handball wall beside heavily commuted Harlem River Drive, we are still picking up after the madness.

And proving that the City gets it right sometimes, the space is called *Crack Is Wack Playground.*

Cocaine was purchased in expensive lots in a hierarchical distribution system involving a kingpin and layers of minions like the circles of hell. Crack was a different story.

Crack users smoked rather than snorted and found that a far higher percentage of the drug got to the brain essentially immediately.

This faster, more intense high delivered a double downside—feelings of paranoia and a fast-acting down where the overwhelming urge is for more.

Crack relied upon a free-style distribution system very different from that of the drug cartels. Certainly, the seed cocaine had to be purchased and processed. But mom-and-pop production facilities flourished. And most of the selling was grassroots.

When crack pushers were first arrested the typical question from police was, "Who does this lead us to in the Medellín cartel or the Dominican Republic or in Mexico?"

The answer was no one. Thousands of people sold crack hand to hand. Arrest a dealer and there is no one to offer up—there was simply no vast hierarchy to pursue.

Crack had one outcome for anyone hoping to escape the grip of poverty: to take away a dream and replace it with a nightmare. A dream permanently deferred.

As one user eloquently put it, "The problem is by the time you realize it's a problem . . . it's a problem."

For a time crack changed the face of Harlem. There were other epicenters in the City: Washington Heights, the Robert Wagner Houses in East Harlem, Alphabet City on the Lower East Side, and many sections of Queens and Brooklyn.

But Harlem faced changes that no other drug had ever lavished on an unsuspecting community. The "down" brought paranoia and with it violence, first on family and friends, and later on strangers. Another feature was the increased use of crack by women. In Harlem, where women run so many of the households, the matriarchy was threatened, and the social order was undermined by an avalanche of ten-dollar rocks.

Crack subsided in the 1990s, but prescription drugs and, more recently, cheap heroin replaced it. Overzealous drug prosecution, which never seems to bring victory in any drug war, sent more citizens to automatic arrest and incarceration than did any other nation on earth. In 1980, there were 500,000 Americans in jail; in 2008, the figure was 2.3 million, one million of them African Americans, who, according to the NAACP, are incarcerated at a rate six times that of whites. Fully one quarter of people in jail on the planet are in the United States. Incarceration has a dreadful set of consequences: more hunger, more homelessness and crime, and more disease.

Central Harlem had evolved into a community profoundly influenced by multigenerational poverty and a host of corresponding social ills, especially health related. As an example, for every incidence of tuberculosis reported in our nation in the early 1990s, Central Harlem had forty-nine cases—more than many third world countries.

Tuberculosis has moved on to other parts of the city, but as that problem faded fresh varieties sprung up to take its place.

Today, nearly three quarters of Harlem's children are born into poverty. Over 76 percent are born to single mothers. Almost a third of Harlem families have incomes of less than $15,000. Unemployment rates typically run at three times the national average. More than 25 percent of Harlem adults smoke cigarettes—much higher than the national average. HIV death rates are still double the already high New York City rates. Soon, half of the school children there will be obese.

Forget the War on Poverty, disremember the "I have a dream" speeches, dismiss the notions of trickle-down, forget blacks and Latinos finding their own path to the middle class. For most Americans the basic notion was to sympathize but let it go. Poverty and despair in Central Harlem were absolute and unremitting.

How could the people of this community ever hope for, much less aspire to, the middle class? Only a superhero could possibly step in and save the residents. Were they, as the movie title suggests, "Waiting for Superman"? Because superheroes never seem to find Harlem.

And then, suddenly, on a fine spring day . . . one did.

CHAPTER TWELVE

THE ZONE

Confronting dragons of poverty and winning

T HE MOST STRIKING THING ABOUT A *first encounter with Geoffrey Canada is not his lean welterweight frame, nor his arm-waving enthusiasms, nor even the shrewd truths that pour out of him. It is his voice.*

Sandy, like the rasp of an old blues singer, tough like a martial arts coach, caring and wise like your grandmother—these are the attributes that blend like a good wine when you first regard the man. He has the kind of voice you want to listen to again—like a hit record.

Geoff is at once the most likely and least likely hero you will ever encounter.

Raised in the South Bronx by a single mom who taught Geoff and his three brothers self-reliance, self-worth, and self-respect, he attended civil rights marches with his mother—his alcoholic father was no longer living in their home. He learned young about peaceful but profound change.

At fifteen, the promising and rambunctious teenager was sent to live with his mom's parents in Freeport, Long Island, where he continued to excel in his studies and won a scholarship to college at Bowdoin, far from the vicissitudes of poverty that marked his early life.

Steeling himself against the Brunswick, Maine, winters, Canada spent time studying psychology and sociology and raising his newborn son,

Jerry. Later he earned a master's degree at Harvard (in time so would Geoff's sainted mother) in education.

Geoff joined a high school for troubled youth in Boston and then returned to New York City—to Harlem, where he ran a truancy program for abused five- to twelve-year-olds. One of his secret weapons was Tae Kwon Do—using martial arts to connect with tough kids in an even tougher environment. Inside the arts discipline were two hidden attributes: a manner of resolving conflicts and a flash point to open dialogue with young people. The last word in Korean—Do—is by far the most important. It means "the correct way."

Geoff, it seems, had found one.

He went to work at Rheedlen Centers in Harlem with a notion of teaching his protégés to fight and be strong in the face of the dragons and monsters in their neighborhoods. Tae Kwon Do is the way of the fist and the foot—both for defense and offense. It is a language which leads to other kinds of fluency, and Geoff was the translator.

Acolytes visited the dingy basement of a local junior high school in droves. There his tutelage became a gateway to deeper conversations with his students. They examined the Do, the correct way, to address conflict resolution, and from there ascended to more aspirational themes, like courage and honor and values and excellence.

With these abused young men truancy was no longer the issue; they showed up for Geoff. Soon he was running Rheedlen—locating whenever possible in public schools. The centers offered homework help, recreational programs, and tutoring to thousands of Harlem young people.

Geoff was compelled to offer them something more—belief.

And it was there he began to hatch one of the most transformative ideas in Harlem's history. He named it the Beacon.

HOUSED IN A COMMUNITY CENTER named for poet Countee Cullen, the Beacon School took a different tack from traditional public schools. Long before charter schools were a glimmer in anyone's eye, Canada was seeing around the corner. Frustrated by the one-off nature of most after-school programs and shaped by the willingness of his martial arts students to share their life struggles, he designed Beacon to provide a multitude of support services to children and their families.

He brought his ideas to the Robin Hood Foundation, a New York City-based poverty fighting organization founded by the irrepressible Paul Tudor Jones, as outspoken and generous a soul as lives today. Robin Hood is notoriously possessed of a striking combination—a steady flow of funds and an attitude. They believed in heroes and knew they had found one in Geoff. Together the two organizations dared him to dream bigger and to take on more. Publishing his first work, *Fist Stick Knife Gun: A Personal History of Violence,* Geoff found a national audience.

It wouldn't be the last time.

Geoff had a big idea—to break the cycle of generational poverty in Central Harlem the only way he knew how: focusing on children, with the goal of changing the odds for the entire community.

Meeting with Robin Hood's trustees (I was present as a board member that day), the idea had been burning inside him for a very long time. The room fell dead silent when he finished speaking. His face had the satisfied look of a confessor—there, I said it.

Geoff's concept was to take a hundred blocks of Central Harlem and to provide every child in that community with a pipeline of services to support them from cradle to career. Doing so required engaging a community of grown-ups who had the vision and will to ensure that every child succeeded.

Talk about your extreme makeover.

As huge and provocative as Geoff's vision was—that's how humble were its beginnings. He started with the basic matter: All these subatomic particles swirled in a single city block in the dead center of Harlem.

The Harlem Children's Zone expanded over the next decade, step by step, stoop by stoop, block by block, until it encompassed 97 such blocks and more than 14,000 adults and children.

HCZ is one example of how a middle class can burst forth and flower in the most infertile soil, a dissertation on never accepting the status quo, and a brilliant and soul-searing poem promising his children's dreams were no longer deferred.

All that was required was gumption, vision, and something else.

Canada's relationship with Robin Hood would yield one more thing besides funding and strategic direction. It would launch one of the most unlikely and successful partnerships in the history of social intervention.

Stanley Druckenmiller is a long drink of water, and when he rears his head if you say something stupid he seems even taller. Few would have predicted that he and Geoff would become partners, but they should have.

You could say that their lives had been circling each other for years. Both men attended Bowdoin, though they could not have been more polar opposite. It's no surprise they didn't know each other.

In some respects, Stan is the ultimate white man. Stately, reserved, intellectually tough, and exceptionally bright, he is shy but seems even more distant in social whirl. Try not to be under-informed when you debate him—it will cost you. He is not so shy about being profanely direct. He is rarely misunderstood.

But he has a distinction few of us will ever enjoy. When he retired from managing other people's money at Duquesne Partners he had been for the better part of three decades the best in the world at his chosen craft. Without peer.

Think of it.

Druckenmiller managed money in large size, and in three decades he never had a single down year despite all of the crashes, asset bubbles, meltdowns, and a host of recessions ranging from the mildly annoying to the devastating. Through it all, Stan made money for his investors—a lot of it. He compounded at 30 percent a year for his investors.

Oh yes, and for himself—billions at last count.

Before you slip into the caricature of the hedge fund robber baron, consider this: He is one of the most generous men on the planet. In 2009 alone, he gave away $700 million to social causes. And anybody looking to find his name attached will have to expend an enormous amount of energy. He gives money the old-fashioned way—stealthily and highly effectively, with zero fanfare, just how he invests.

Ask him his investing secret, and he will share only a slice: Don't diversify. Pick a winner. Bet big. He is a finance professor's worst nightmare.

He eschewed their investment wisdom and compiled one of the greatest records in history.

Picking a winner means more than uncovering a big idea. It also means finding the iconoclast to make the big idea happen.

Knowing Stan's penchant for the big concept—for the winning idea—it's no surprise that despite their differences, he, Geoff Canada, and Harlem Children's Zone came together.

Their collaboration suited their competitive instincts, and HCZ's roll-out can best be described as controlled aggression. Beginning in 2000, the HCZ annual budget went from the philanthropically appropriate million dollars a year, to $4 million, to $7 million, inexorably toward Geoff's phase III budget of $64 million a year—then slicing through that target to $100 million or more a year. All-in, HCZ costs about $5,000 per young person per year.

They built buildings and created programs of every type—including charter schools under the Promise Academy banner. The nine public schools operating in the Zone became collaboration partners too. HCZ staffers work at all of the Zone's public schools full time.

HCZ uncovered significant incidences of teen pregnancy and single-mother households. It is harder to get a driver's license than to become a single mother in Harlem. Enlisting the aid of Harlem grandmothers and famed pediatrician T. Berry Brazelton, HCZ created the world's first "baby college."

Earnest grannies combed every inch of the neighborhood seeking out young girls and single moms in the earliest days of their pregnancies. As only grandmothers can, they got these expectant moms to baby college and on the path to decent prenatal care.

Treating prospective newborns with respect is emblematic of the HCZ approach.

Geoff readily admits that he looks to the middle class for guidance on the best ways to raise his "kids." His entire premise for the Zone is the provision of middle-class standards of care for these Harlem kids. He starts by providing resources and programs that middle-class communities take for granted, like working schools, useable playgrounds, and safe streets, plus preschool and after-school programs, arts, sports, health care, and mentoring. The goal is blending the same academic, community, and social supports that any middle-class family expects for their children.

Folks in that group have expectations—if your kids have a health issue, you address it. Geoff's design is merely a replication. When people push back and ask why the HCZ spends so much time, energy, and money on these poor children, he responds directly:

"But that is exactly what you are doing for your kids—this is not the ceiling but the floor of what these kids need. Middle-class parents don't say, 'Just because my kids have health care and sports and good teachers, that I don't have to do anything.' They are in there every day trying to make sure they get every advantage. We think we have got to do the exact same thing for poor kids here in America. People have argued that we can't afford it—about $5,000 per year per child."

Geoff explains that a failure to achieve his goals for Harlem kids inevitably ends in incarceration. The cost of jailing a young person in New York State averages $60,000 a year, and in New York City it's over $147,000.

And what do you get for that money and jail time?

People who can hold steady jobs? No.

People who can take care of their families? No.

Better citizens? No.

Yet everyone is resigned or on some level willing to pay that price. Few are yelling, as I did in my last book, about the absolute waste of $147,000. Why are we paying for a system of internment with huge recidivism? Because it is totally scalable and it temporarily removes the offenders from circulating in society. But it creates an annuity of pain, and wards of the state who return and return and return. And when they come back, it is most often for escalating terms at increasing cost.

Geoff and Stanley uncovered the true economics that had frustrated municipal, state, and federal leadership, the teachers union, and the parents of thousands of special young people. It all boils down to $5,000 a year per child, and to flawless execution.

How have Geoff's kids done?

Over a thousand Harlem young people have gone to college on their watch, at least 15 percent from Promise Academy. High school graduation rates are at unprecedented numbers. Nearly 83 percent of these young people raised in the meanest of streets are attending college. But more important, parents are supportive from the earliest age of their children's cognitive growth. Their four-year-olds are school-ready, willing, and able. As students they are improving their test scores and closing the racial achievement gap that some said could not be narrowed.

They have brought a second Harlem Renaissance.

Why should anyone really care about how these poor kids are doing?

There are two reasons; one will please you and the other is likely to upset you.

The first is that Geoff and Stanley are creating an army of adults in Harlem who are committed to creating a healthy, stable community . . . even as the streets fight back. On a deeper level, the Harlem Children's Zone is also growing a whole new cohort of members of the middle class. Just wait.

The second is that they are proving that you probably don't know much about how poverty really works in the United States today. It's not your fault. It has become far more diverting to speak or write or debate on just about anything else.

THE NEW FACE OF POVERTY

THE BEHAVIOR OF POVERTY IS nothing like what it used to be. And when your enemy changes, you have to revise your battle plan.

Once upon a time, poverty was experienced by a discrete and largely unmoving class of folks with many shared characteristics. For much of our history, the baton of the lowest rung was passed to successive waves of immigrants, who joined poor blacks and whites. The vast majority of the poor could be found in major cities.

These families were impoverished for years, if not generations. They were an entrenched layer of permafrost. Earnest and hardworking immigrants would slave at low-skilled jobs and save for the time when their children might aim higher. Subsequent generations expected to live better than their parents; many escaped poverty, but even those who couldn't were still better off.

Today's poverty is a whole new experience. Start with size. Analysts say 47 million Americans are poor—one out of every six. Still, you need to look deeper.

Since 2008, poverty has remained at about 16 percent of the population, the highest since the War on Poverty commenced in the mid-1960s. The record was 22.4 percent in the late 1950s. But today, the absolute numbers are so much larger.

The official poverty line of $23,492 for a family of four and $11,139 for an individual represents a wooden indicator—just another line in the sand. It does not include non-cash benefits like food stamps or tax credits, and it tells you nothing about the dynamics of poverty.

Here is the new reality.

Study the work of Mark Rank at Washington University, and of the Robin Hood Foundation and Columbia University, and you get a very different, very dynamic sense of what is occurring all around us.

One word captures the difference: velocity.

Rank estimates that nearly 40 percent of Americans between the ages of twenty-five and sixty will experience at least one year below the official poverty line, and 54 percent will spend at least a year at or near the poverty line.

If we add related experiences like welfare use, near poverty, and unemployment for some period of time, then four out of five Americans will encounter at least one of these poverty-related events in their lifetime.

Drilling deeper, Robin Hood/Columbia's *Poverty Tracker* follows two additional yardsticks—Material Hardship and Poor Health. In 2012, a majority of New York City residents faced these kinds of hardships.

The dispersion of poverty has increased meaningfully too. It has a home everywhere. Suburban poverty rates now exceed 12 percent. The image in your head may be inner-city nonwhite, but the reality, according to the latest Census Bureau numbers, is that two-thirds of those below the poverty line are white, and this number has been holding steady for nearly two decades.

On a grander scale, poverty has regained momentum. Child poverty will increase from its current 22 percent level. Half of American children will live in a house that uses food stamps for some period of time.

And the poorest of the poor—those at half or less of the poverty level, which is at an historical peak of 6.7 percent, are expected to remain there for years.

By any measure—income level, absolute numbers, and distribution— poverty is as high, or higher than it has ever been. And many of the poor are new to the experience.

Today's mobile poverty teaches us that the poverty line is an arbitrary number; that far too many Americans are going through poverty or something that feels very close to it; that they are or were working, not goofing off; that the dream of each successive generation prospering more than their parents is no longer a reality.

The best way to help the middle class is to minimize the likelihood that families are trapped in the vise of poverty and near poverty. The Harlem Children's Zone is ample, if expensive, demonstration that poverty for these kids is not a foregone conclusion.

We have to burn this candle at both ends. We must feed effective programs, like the HCZ, that guide young people to the next level. But we also need to protect the middle class so that fewer slip into new poverty.

The good news is that many of these new poor can expect to pull out of poverty or earn their way out—so their stay will not last for generations. What is vexing to policy makers is that besides record high unemployment there are increasing numbers of frustrated part-time or underemployed workers who may compile a forty-hour work-week but cannot afford to meet their family's basic needs.

Theory Plus Experience

Decades of working to fight poverty has taught me the ultimate irony of the poor.

At its core, poverty is not an economic problem. Sure, dollars that find the poor are like blood in the veins. But you cannot sprinkle dollars and expect outcomes. That's where most poverty fighting fails, throwing money at the problem without the right surrounding elements.

Walking into a high school class in the South Bronx, as generous patrons have done, and offering to pay all college costs for students does not equate to even a minority of them matriculating somewhere.

No matter how good-hearted, alms-paying carries with it a thousand years of disappointing outcomes. Charity without strings feeds the hungry and cures the sick—you cannot ignore survival—but in other circumstances it can soften the natural penalties and in some cases encourages self-destructive behaviors. So people have to give with both their hearts and their brains. And outcomes must be measured, though they rarely are.

You need theory and experience in social welfare. Poverty is not a social issue alone, nor purely an economic one. It is like a disease that shifts form and locus, develops resistance like a virus against antibiotics. Fighting requires vigilance and an unabashed frankness about causes and effects.

Concluding that the $20 trillion spent on the war on poverty was somehow wasted misses the point entirely. We have two gravitational forces at work in our society today with Newtonian certainty. These push a few people into a higher gilded realm and create poverty on a massive scale. Today, we expose not just the 50 million who are poor, but nearly another 50 more, to the likelihood that they will be poor during their lives.

So what have we done about poverty? The federal government sees the problem through the rearview mirror—a bad way to drive a car, let alone run a country. They conduct this war as if the responsibility falls on them for all execution. Let's adjust ourselves to a new reality of fighting poverty.

What does the federal government do well? There are issues of identification, tracking, compliance, uniform standards and application, legislation, regulation, and approval that play to government strengths. But personal uplift, motivation, customizing programs, nimble adaptability, and independent measurement do not.

"Nobody national tucks in your blanket" is a phrase you will hear from me often. It is hard for a national agency to supply the devotion and friendly relationship to address the deeply personal needs of the poor. It's not that their people are unfeeling or unprofessional. National programs are too uneasy with delegation and even less comfortable outside uniformity. People don't fit in neat boxes.

Instead, if the government worked more collaboratively with organizations, volunteer or otherwise, outcomes would improve.

In poverty, every client must be treated as an individual. Workers become involved on a close, personal basis. Measurement must be at arm's length and independent, because each case carries its own expectations and rewards.

Geoff Canada's genius is his ability to motivate the community and customize solutions for individuals and families. He teaches kids to sacrifice, make commitments, and defer present gratification for the future benefit. And he gets their family, friends, and neighbors to help.

Yes, his is a steeper climb than most service organizations demand of their participant families. Yes, it is a more expensive approach than government programs, and it is certainly harder to scale than prisons. But instead of focusing on costs per person, as policy makers and bureaucrats do, let's look elsewhere: at cost per outcome. The customized, expensive delivery of services through Harlem Children's Zone ($5,000 per kid) leads to outcome measures that trounce more general and cheaper approaches.

Isn't the most important number when they are counting the beans how many poor kids found a better life?

War Weary

PRESIDENT LYNDON JOHNSON LAUNCHED THE War on Poverty with aspirations that still hold up fifty years later. "Many Americans live on the outskirts of hope." He asserted, "Our task is to replace despair with opportunity." It was war. "The richest nation on earth can afford to win it. We cannot afford to lose it."

What can you say about a fifty-year campaign that cost $20 trillion? That's more than the market value of every company on the New York Stock Exchange and the NASDAQ combined. We could have given the poor every publicly traded company in America over the last fifty years.

Naysayers crow that the poverty rate is virtually the same as fifty years ago, signaling defeat; but look closer and you'll see a limited, costly victory.

The poverty rate established in 1963 by Millie Orshansky has not been aging gracefully. Poverty calculations miss some important things. Not included are some pretty key benefits, like the Supplemental Nutrition Assistance Program (SNAP) food stamps and the Earned Income Tax Credit (EITC).

(The Census Bureau created a supplemental poverty measure in 2011, sixteen years after the recommendations of a 1995 panel at the National Academy of Science. Why rush things? This measure sets the poverty line on the level of expenditure on essential items at the thirty-third percentile, meaning two-thirds of households spend more on such items. The gauge includes medical spending and makes regional adjustments. Poverty now stands at 16.1 percent, versus 15 percent the older way.)

Signs of Progress

It is true that, accounting for these elements of government subsidy, the poverty rate has only declined from 19 percent to 15 percent. But dare to dig a little deeper before declaring defeat.

Obvious positive impacts involve health, life expectancy, and poverty rates of the elderly. Three programs, one Johnson expanded (Social Security) and two he created (Medicare and Medicaid), have done significant good, even as they have gotten creaky.

The elderly poverty rate was almost 29 percent in 1966, says the Census Bureau, and for elderly women living alone a painful two-thirds were poor. Today, thanks largely to Social Security and Medicare, elderly single women are down to 20 percent in poverty and only 9 percent of the elderly are poor. Life expectancy was under seventy in 1960 and approaches eighty today.

In a very real way, we have shifted poverty from the eldest among us to the youngest. And increasingly, baby boomers are looking to the youth and the middle class to fund their dotage.

Any fair look at the War on Poverty breaks it down into three basic goals: First, to boost wages and opportunity through education and job training. Examples are Head Start and Pell grants. Second, to provide income support, especially to single mothers and the elderly. And finally, to bring a system of government health care to the poor and the elderly.

Innovations like the EITC, SNAP, and other working-poor benefits have clearly done two things: lifted millions out of poverty and helped keep many others from slipping deeper into the abyss. Lower-income Americans are healthier and better nourished as compared to the 1960s—amazing, since our population has nearly doubled.

And yet there has been an agonizing slippage since 2008.

Decades of economic growth that preceded the Great Recession have been far less successful in raising incomes for the working poor, prompting critics to declare anti-poverty programs a failure, especially in making the poor less dependent on government handouts.

A WIDE-SCREEN IN EVERY POT

THE NOTION THAT THE POOR are materially better off has a nagging ring of truth that has to be addressed.

Many have read the Heritage Foundation report by Robert Rector and Rachel Sheffield. It is groundbreaking and refreshingly unworried about political correctness—both assets in fighting any war.

The average American poor family has more living space than average poor Europeans and more than the average non–poor person in Sweden, France, and the United Kingdom.

Other comforts: 80 percent of the poor have air-conditioning; 75 percent have an automobile (nearly a third have two); 66 percent have cable TV; most have a computer; and nearly 42 percent own their own homes.

What accounts for the increase in material goods of the poor? Two things at once.

First is the absolute amount of federal assistance per low-income person. These increased benefits, many since 1996 changes in welfare reform, often encourage work, or even require it to earn the benefit. We have learned that for many in the hovering category, just one twist of life's knife away from poverty, and for the working poor, these benefits are what keep them at the margins of comfort.

A second trend is the Walmart effect. The price of virtually every consumer item capable of being manufactured offshore has plummeted. Flat-screen color TV prices are down tenfold since the 1980s, for example.

At the same time, the cost of crucial services like health care, education, and advanced-degree education are trending exactly the opposite.

Result: the differences in what the poor and middle-class families consume day to day are much smaller than what they earn.

These parallel universes swap throughout the lives of families on the margin. Once a life sentence, poverty has for many Americans become instead a predicament, perhaps a multiyear detour. And that is a dramatic difference.

And that change is resplendent with opportunity if we are willing to seize it.

Policy makers need to step back and consider the following issue. Many Americans who consume like the lower middle class, and possess things like the lower middle class, are subject to volatile swings that send them into poverty—often directly associated with market and economic swings and their aftershocks. Think of it, many millions of Americans are a surprise bill or a car accident or some unexpected event costing $500 or $1,000 away from slipping into poverty.

Risk and susceptibility must become part of our calculations.

The Demons of Deep Poverty

STILL, FAR BENEATH THESE FAMILIES are others who suffer in the anaerobic world of less than $6,000 a year, or $7,600 with children—families living at half the poverty index. In our country, more than 20 million adults and children get by on that much or less.

Think of every soul in New York City, Chicago, Los Angeles, Houston, Philadelphia, and Phoenix trying to live on less than $6,000 a year. That is the state of extreme poverty in our country today.

Mobility around this low threshold is common, but escaping from these ranks to anything approaching the middle class is not. Many millions cannot find escape.

Even as we weave new strands into the safety net, many benefits require employment before they can be obtained. EITC and Temporary Assistance for Needy Families (TANF), for example, have mandatory work requirements.

What options have we provided for the truly destitute? Housing assistance is often tied to some ability to pay. And even then it is scarce. Speaking with former HUD director and governor of New York Andrew Cuomo, he laments, "Housing for the poorest among us is extremely expensive and nearly impossible to find major funds to support."

Unlike school-related reforms, housing is going through the greatest retreat of any social program with little controversy, media punditry, or academic inquiry. MIT scholar Lawrence Vale comes closest in his well-researched *Purging the Poorest*.

For sixty years the U.S. government spent billions creating nearly a million and a half units of public housing, serving every major American city and plenty of smaller burgs and rural outposts in between.

Then we turned on a dime twenty years ago and demolished and decommissioned 25 percent of it. Cities like Atlanta and Chicago, which had nearly 60,000 units between them, have essentially torn them all down.

Renee Glover, who ran and then drove the dismantling of Atlanta's public housing, called it a "self-defeating system" that "virtually guaranteed chronic failure."

The new trend is for low-density, mixed-income, low-rise communities—many created by developers who must meet targets or quotas of public housing tenants. As with the Bible, many are called but few are chosen.

Where will the poorest among us go?

Other programs were slashed. The Center on Budget and Policy Priorities reviewed changes for low-income programs, besides entitlements that had automatic adjustments. Their findings were sobering: Subsidized housing was cut by 81 percent and job training and employment services by two-thirds.

What remains are piecemeal efforts. Food programs, health care at emergency rooms and in free clinics, and cash assistance are not designed to lift a family out of poverty. They are more focused on getting them through the next month, or even the next week.

"Food Stamp Nation"

SNAP (Supplemental Nutrition Assistance Program) has expanded to accommodate many more than the most hungry. SNAP expenditures quadrupled from under $20 billion a year in 2000 to $83 billion a year in 2012. The *Wall Street Journal* editorial page proclaimed, "Never has the program exploded like this. One reason is that the Obama administration has actively sought to turn food stamps into another middle-class entitlement."

The 1996 welfare-reform laws required nearly all employable recipients of cash welfare, including single moms, to work or get job training. President Obama eliminated a long-standing ninety-day limit for food stamps for employable adults. By 2011, only one in five food-stamp recipients was working. The number of employable adults on food stamps without children has gone up over 150 percent since the recession commenced. College students are receiving food stamps in record numbers.

The bad news: The allotment given to each household has been dropping by small amounts for the last few years. Small cuts in disbursements were more than offset by the expanding roster of people seeking assistance. In 2010, 40 million people were enrolled. Within two years the number had jumped 16 percent, and nearly half of those getting food stamps are children.

Not all of the 47.7 million food-stamp participants (one in seven Americans) were destitute. And the ethos of the 1996 welfare reform that focused on getting welfare recipients back to work is returning. The first target will be eligibility. It is only a matter of time before the SNAP benefits get trimmed again. But for all of the near poor and working poor who have found sustenance at the hands of the federal government, there are millions of parents and children who simply cannot survive without them.

Two major changes in welfare took place in the strong economies of 1964 and 1996. In the latter, a more conservative ideology was clearly at work, stemming from a belief that government programs were helping poor people but diluting their initiative.

Key assumptions behind these changes were that work was plentiful and that growth and prosperity would be shared. Trouble is, wages for the bottom 30 percent have fallen in every decade since the 1960s except for a few years after the 1996 rule changes. And job creation since 2007 has been barely keeping track with new entrants to the workforce.

The most stirring aspect can be observed by visiting any homeless shelter. An astonishing number there are children. An anguishing one out of six black children spend most of their childhoods in deep poverty.

For these deeply poor kids, safety-net programs are mostly about survival and do not prevent them from carrying their poverty into the next generation.

As for deeply poor adults, the vast majority have not worked for over a year. They face unstable housing, unreliable care for their children, lack of education, and mental and physical problems that are severe but not enough to earn disability benefits. Many have criminal records, which make them all but unemployable.

MODERN FAMILY

MARRIAGE AND FAMILY IN OUR society have been going through a seismic shift. Sitting in judgment is a poor strategy for helping folks on the margin, so let's just review the facts.

Out-of-wedlock birthrates have soared. Over 72 percent of black children are born to unmarried women, and for whites the figure is under 30 percent. These rates were both well under 15 percent at the end of World War II. Black marriage rates from 1890 to 1940 slightly exceeded white marriage rates.

It is so easy to jump to conclusions. Poverty rates among black married families, now at 8 percent, have been in the single digits for more than two decades. For married whites, the poverty rate is 5 percent. A child of married parents is 80 percent less likely to live in poverty than the child of unmarried parents. It is all well and good to decry the erosion of society, but the transformation has been too profound to ignore. The real work today starts by respecting all family structures. Why?

Because we have passed the tipping point in a stunning way.

Here is our new reality:

- In four years, children of color will be a majority for their age group—the majority of births have been "minority" children for two years in a row.
- Over 1.2 million public school students were homeless in 2012 (73 percent more than at the start of the Recession)— that's like everyone in Dallas becoming a homeless kid.
- In 2011, more than a million households with children had no cash income and relied on SNAP to survive.
- In all, 16 million children were poor in 2012, nearly half in families that earned less than $929 per month.

DEMOGRAPHICS AS DESTINY

HARD TIMES SINCE 2008 HAVE forced many new Americans to jump into the safety net—and the thusly labeled "Takers" list has jumped year by year in proportion. Time was when moral indignation was reserved for a mere 25 percent of our fellow citizens "on the dole," then a third, and then, during a surreptitiously taped political solicitation dinner, 47 percent and above. It will soon be most of us.

Is it possible for a majority of Americans to be un-American?

I think we owe it to ourselves to make sure that America disproves the cynic's notion that "demographics equals destiny." By the way, our middle class depends on it.

With social misery this widespread and intractable, experienced poverty fighters know we must balance our funding and energies between survival and elevation. No amount of economic stimulus and classroom excellence can trump a kid with a growling empty stomach. It can't be done.

Alexis de Tocqueville long ago lamented that the problem with democracy is that it gives the masses the ability to direct the commonwealth to support dependency.

Arthur Brooks posed the essential question in an aptly timed 2009 *Wall Street Journal* column: "The Culture War Is Over Capitalism." The temptation is to place emphasis on inequality with the War on Poverty. But poverty is just one part of inequality. It requires its own fixes, and its remedies must be applied with that balance of experience and theory.

WHAT CAN BE DONE?

THE FIRST ANSWER IS TO acknowledge Geoff Canada's genius in devising a true holistic process. Here's an example: Most Americans agree that failing schools and declining educational outcomes are a vital ingredient in elevating young people out of the cycle of poverty.

Most Americans also agree on other objectives for poor kids: Getting them to at least graduate from high school if not college, waiting until after their teen years and marriage to have children, avoiding criminality, and getting a job and keeping it.

Such a simple remedy. Poor young people who execute on these targets have a 90 percent likelihood of escaping poverty.

Good news—most people are right about how to avoid poverty's clutches. The bad news is in helping poor kids get there.

So many societal forces prevent this simple view of reality—the road map for getting there is daunting and complex. It's easier to bring back the witch's broom.

For years, poverty-fighting organizations have been working with educational administrators to fix or shutter failing schools. Others have been fighting for choices, like charter schools and education investment tax credits, which help kids in failing schools find other options.

Another focus is on teachers. Outstanding educators transform the classroom experience. The best teachers should be rewarded in every way we can conceive. Compensation is not the only motivator, but it is a good place to start. Another is advancement, like offering teachers greater leeway in course and school selection; sabbaticals; and advanced training in their discipline.

And for the lowest-performing teachers, particularly for those without passion for improvement or adaptation, or an interest in helping kids perform better, perhaps they should spend their time elsewhere than in the classroom.

Sadly, too much argument surrounds these relatively straightforward ways to manage our supremely talented 4-million-strong public school teaching force. School administration and teachers' unions are never more animated than when fighting change.

Great teachers are the most powerful in-classroom determinant of student success. But students spend most of their lives out of the classroom. We need teachers to be at peak performance and fully supported by new technologies when class is in session, but those enhancements cannot survive a dearth of in-home and in-community reinforcement. Many charter schools require a student/parent contract to bridge their longer school-day with the rest of their lives.

Poverty is its own enemy. School dropout rates are ten times higher in poor neighborhoods than in high-income families. Poverty's adverse impacts are most pronounced in early-childhood learning. Without a total intervention at this early stage, these youngsters will never catch up.

Children in poor communities face violence and health risks in greater proportion. Criminal behavior, hunger, homelessness, family stresses, obesity, and asthma, which are prevalent among our poorest kids—all these trump a great teacher once class is dismissed.

Poverty fighting is a war on many fronts, and nowhere is the fight made more challenging than in fixing the misaligned priorities of our K–12 public schools. There is no area of human interaction more resistant to accepting new technology than the classroom.

Every other sort of enterprise has been earlier adopter.

We need to continue to fight to get optimum use of the educational assets we have. New York State regrettably decided against creating an Educational Investment Tax Credit, where any educational donation to any school—public, private, religious, or none of the above—would be deducted from your tax bill. Parents loved the bill, but as so often happens when sensible educational reform comes along, it was rejected. The New York Civil Liberties Union claimed that the proposal violated rules preventing government from subsidizing religion.

Come again? The law said any donation to any school. Thousands of laws allow tax-deductible donations to religious organizations—why pick the one that might lead to greater excellence in religious schools?

It is inconceivable that New York State won't sometime soon come to its senses and adopt the Education Tax Credit. Then others will follow.

The truth is that the monopolists who used to control all public schools are fighting to prevent parents from having choices. No vouchers, no charters, no religious schools.

They will blame businesses, the rich, the middle class, the wayward parents, the churches, the religious leaders—anyone, including the children, who decries the unchallenged authority of the public schools and their unions to dictate how school is taught. Even when charter schools agree to be shut down if they fail to deliver—something no other public school faces as a part of their daily routine—preservationists still insist they have come up with the only right and true way.

The good news is that the tides of change are advancing.

What is needed is more, not less, private-sector involvement in creating good schools. The Bill and Melinda Gates Foundation has made progress in schools by requiring union acquiescence when they make large donations to some school districts.

And while it is barely a trickle, technology that will shift everything is beginning to creep into the classrooms.

In the end, we must bring more Americans along the seams of poverty into the middle if we are to have the healthiest economy and the most just society.

What we need is a class accelerator—an affirmative action program for the poor. These programs must reinforce initiative. But we must balance survival programs affecting hunger, homelessness, and health as we support elevation programs that lift hopes and aspirations like training, after-school, and job-placement initiatives.

We need to acknowledge and respect the new family structure that is so prevalent among the poor. Single mothers with little or no training or child care cannot be castigated for the position they are in. Financial help for single mothers who want to go back to school; job training and mentoring programs; and, yes, free child care are ways that huge changes can be wrought in the poorest communities.

Blaming the poor for being poor is a bad place to start. Claiming, as many have, that the poor are "more comfortable" because of a litany of possessions is equally likely to land you in the wrong spot. Material resources don't suffice and material possessions don't elevate.

Michael Harrington's 1962 book *The Other America* may have played a bigger role than any other text in driving the War on Poverty. Certainly, by the measure of the number of citations by defenders of welfare programs, it stands alone.

But for all of its early warning, it has been the experience of the last fifty years that leads to the essence of poverty. Velocity of poverty has changed everything.

We need to create an opportunity culture to replace a dependence culture. Special tax incentives and outright payments for work and opportunity will incentivize job creation. Public/private partnerships and delegation and outsourcing by federal authorities are the keys to delivering the poor into the satisfaction of a job well done, money well-earned, and yes, as a by-product, entrance into the world of the middle class.

LBJ was right. "Our history has proven that each time we broaden the base of abundance we create new industry, higher production, increased earnings, and better income for all."

CHAPTER THIRTEEN

THE MARCH OF THE
BLACK MIDDLE CLASS

Return of economic segregation

His mother, Ruby, was a domestic *worker her whole life, zealous in her job, and even more enthusiastic about disciplining her son. Maternal concern and exhaustion should have conveyed the depth of her feelings, but it would take years before the restless boy could understand why "I love you" was never uttered in their home.*

By the time he was twelve, his parents' marriage was irretrievably broken. He was shipped to New York from his black Tallahassee neighborhood to live under the watchful eye of his aunt Della. He was a rolling stone, and soon dropped out of vocational high school for a stint in the Air Force, where he completed his equivalency studies and grew to manhood.

Returning to civilian life, he attended secretarial school, studying shorthand and steno. Far from captivated, he landed a part-time spot in the supply room of Saks in New York City, removed from the swells who shopped there but close enough to catch the eye of manager Ernie Riccio. It seemed like he had found his first mentor. The young man worked diligently and was rewarded with full-time employment. Under the older man's tutelage, he modeled his behaviors and started reading the Wall Street Journal. *Riccio recommended his protégé for his first management job.*

Later, the lights of show business shined brighter than the prospects at Saks' supply room and he left his managerial job to start over at the bottom rung, in the mailroom at the eponymous William Morris Agency. It was the first of many reinventions. Charm and enthusiasm helped him work his way into the Music Department—another in a long line of coups. He became the firm's first African American agent.

Earlier than his superiors expected, he signed an emerging duo displaying remarkable promise—Paul Simon and Art Garfunkel. He would become Marvin Gaye's first agent. Promotion followed to running the newly formed rock-and-roll business—a position that brought him into the lives of the Supremes, Helen Reddy, The Temptations, Sam Cooke, and Dionne Warwick.

He had an engaging personality, and his business reflected it. But it wasn't all sunshine. The Holy Grail in the agency game was filmed entertainment, and at the time that was a bridge too far—even for their bright young star.

Then the bluesy notes of South African trumpeter Hugh Masekela wafted into his life. In exile from his native land, Masekela had moved to America, and in 1968 his "Grazin' in the Grass" brought him worldwide acclaim and the need for a great manager.

Sensing golden opportunity, the young agent packed up his second wife and their infant child and transplanted his family to California. While Masekela played Monterey Pop with Janis, The Who, and many greats of the era, his new manager ministered to the trumpeter's moods and business affairs. When the edgy musician dropped him like a bad back-beat, the uprooted now former manager entered "the low point of his life."

Stuck in Hollywood and tiring of the vagaries of the entertainment world, he turned to cooking to calm his nerves. Adapting recipes from his aunt Della, his cookies brought rave reviews and another reinvention.

Borrowing $25,000 from Marvin Gaye and Helen Reddy, her husband and the head of United Artists Records, he leased a storefront on Sunset Boulevard and began promoting. His company, How The Cookie Crumbled, opened its doors in 1975. Within months his gourmet cookies were on sale at Bloomingdale's in New York.

With little money to advertise, he became the company's showman, his flair so infectious that Newsweek called him "the greatest cookie salesman alive."

Within two years, he was producing six tons of cookies every week in a bakery in nearby Van Nuys and another in Nutley, New Jersey.

Growth meant more shares and more outsiders. Endlessly promoting, he marched for years in the Macy's Thanksgiving Parade and into the consciousness of 150 million Americans. Ignoring the advice of investors and staff, he expanded into chocolate sodas and other products. Sales soared, but the world's greatest cookie salesman was, sadly, not the world's greatest manager.

He had developed a bad case of entrepreneurial affliction—founder-itis— not listening to his team, sprinting far ahead of his troops. Red ink ran everywhere. The better business got, the bigger the losses. Backed into a corner, he sold control to the Bass Brothers from Texas for just over a million dollars.

He was stripped of everything but his dignity and a vice chairman title. But neither of those would last. When he was awarded the Entrepreneurial Success Award by Ronald Reagan, he had already lost his company.

In the years that followed, the Famous Amos business was passed around like a problem child, finally coming to rest in the hands of the Shansby Group, who took the cookies from the gourmet niche to the vending machine, warehouse club, and fast-food segment. The product was reformulated and many special ingredients were removed, including founder Wally Amos himself.

After starting another cookie business, he was dragged into court to defend his right to use his own name and likeness to sell what he sold best. But those privileges had been transferred long before. So powerful was the brand surrounding the man that his Panama hat and shirt icons were inducted into the Smithsonian Collection of Advertising History. Embarrassed but undaunted, he repaired to his home in Hawaii.

Bouncing back with a muffin venture under the Noname brand (say, in Hawaiian, "No-Nahhh-May"), he regained some momentum and built a decent business, especially with fat-free sweets.

In 1998, the Famous Amos reformulated cookie company was sold to Keebler, another cookie empire, for $61 million—a huge profit for Shansby *investors. Not a dime of the proceeds went to Amos.*

The following year, Keebler once more altered the formula in two major ways. They brought Wally Amos back to promote the brand. And they gave him back his face and naming rights.

"It took me a while to catch up with my name," Amos enthused afterward—he had been nameless for a decade.

His incognito company was rechristened Uncle Wally's and soon was churning out hundreds of millions of muffins a year, available in thousands of retail outlets across the country.

Today, the still-famous Amos is the author of numerous books, a tireless campaigner for Literacy Volunteers of America and other reading advocacy organizations—because, he explains, both his parents were illiterate. He is never far from a reinvention. His latest venture is an Internet start-up called CookieKahuna.com. At seventy-eight he is a late-stage venture capitalist if there ever was one, and a true Renaissance man.

One of his favorite quotes is "Volunteering is reaching your hand out into the darkness to pull another hand into the light . . . only to discover it's your own."

His is the "face that launched a thousand chips." He must be pleased to have it back.

THE PARABLE OF WALLY AMOS has broad application no matter how unique a character he appears to be.

The march of the black middle class is a story of constant ups, downs, and reinvention. So let's start with an economic panorama. Black Americans benefited from both the civil rights activism and the economic surge of the 1960s. But there was vulnerability in their ascent. Our failure to make fundamental structural changes ensured that the black middle class would remain vulnerable to the inevitable troughs that bedevil any economy and occasionally, as in 2008, threaten to wipe it out altogether.

The Real Problem

THE REAL ROOTS OF THE black middle class stretch a long way back to A. Philip Randolph's March on Washington in the early 1940s. As World War II munitions and supplies production spiked, white employment jumped accordingly. Black workers were all but denied these home front opportunities. Union organizer Randolph imagined a march of 100,000 black workers on Washington to protest their exclusion—for the time, a daring recommendation.

Randolph struck a nerve. Black journalists chronicled the increasing rolls of likely participants, linking "the voteless South and the jobless North."

Suddenly, almost a hundred thousand seemed poised to march.

FDR blanched: "I can't afford to permit you to bring 100,000 Negroes to Washington . . . You can never tell what might happen, nor can I."

On the eve of the proposed march, Roosevelt signed Executive Order 8802, which forbade "discrimination in the employment of workers in defense industries or government." It went on to create the Fair Employment Practices Committee, which despite its lofty ambitions possessed resources far too meager to accomplish much. In fact, the FEPC perished before the armistice, brought down by a Congress bent on starving it to death.

Randolph remains unsung, but he had created something more indelible than a consent order or an impecunious and toothless federal agency. He had placed the employment of black Americans squarely on the political agenda—and once in the arena, the subject proved highly reluctant to leave.

Particularly in the 1960s, fair employment was the glue that held together a strange patchwork of competing organisms: the civil rights, labor, and anti-war efforts, to name just three. Randolph's victory would come twenty years later with the passage of the 1964 Civil Rights Act, whose Title VII at long last outlawed discrimination in both the workplace and American unions.

Haltingly at first, blacks found opportunity at American manufacturers and in trade unions. It was an uphill struggle and federal government intervention was necessary along the way.

A potent example is the action of a group of disaffected African American workers at United Airlines. They filed suit in the early 1970s against both the airline and the unions. The Court found for the employees and imposed a consent decree that fixed hiring goals for qualified blacks and women for supervisory positions at the company and skill positions at the union.

It took court intervention to circumvent the contract seniority argument that unions had been using for so long to exclude blacks from equal opportunities. Other airlines took notice and provided opportunities without the necessity of court order.

But as with any intervention, there are unintended consequences. By the late 1980s, profound economic shifts were occurring and government failed to see the lasting impact on the black middle class it had labored so hard to support.

The elimination of a substantial number of manufacturing jobs hit black workers the hardest. Numerous studies showed significant African American concentration in our most vulnerable industries.

Particularly in lower-skilled jobs, layoffs were swift, certain, and unlikely to return.

What was missing from social planning was risk assessment. If you were an under-educated worker in a low-skilled manufacturing job in a vulnerable industry in the late 1980s, your risk of being laid off or your plant being closed was extremely high. And the odds of finding similar employment were extremely low.

One perpetuating flaw in the way we analyze job creation is that we rarely assess risk factors. These exposures are left out of virtually every conversation about employment numbers. What happened to low-skilled high school educated workers in the 1980s was just a warm-up for 2008. We created an economy replete with low-skill vulnerable jobs and they disappeared.

The white middle class was certainly stressed by recent economic conflagration. But low-skilled black workers falling out of the middle ranks with no obvious avenue of return only widened the disparity for the whole middle class.

SEEING PAST THE NUMBERS

THE PANORAMIC VIEW GIVES A strategic perspective, but it won't solve the problem.

You can't zoom over the economic landscape at 50,000 feet when trying to repair job creation and the erosion of the black middle class. There are too many trends and countertrends, some that deliver advantages to white middle-class families even as they set the black middle class in reverse.

Make no mistake, changing the arc for the diminishing black middle class is a requirement for keeping a robust middle class overall. The problem cannot be ring fenced. As goes the prosperity of our fast-growing minority groups, so goes the wealth of our nation.

It is no longer a matter of fairness; it is an economic imperative.

One of the most powerful engines of rising incomes and middle-class wealth from the post-1970s period to the present is the surge of the two-paycheck family. But low marriage and high divorce rates exclude African American families from this wealth effect.

From 1974 to 2004, the median income fell 12 percent for black men yet increased 75 percent for black women, in part because twice as many black women graduate from college as black men.

A third of African American households are at risk because neither the primary earner nor the spouse has any education beyond high school, according to a Brandeis University Study at the Institute for Assets and Social Policy.

THE GREAT CRASH OF THE BLACK MIDDLE CLASS

THE CRASH OF 2008 WIPED out a substantial percentage of the remaining black middle class. Study after study has come to the conclusion we have discussed already—a generation's advance was obliterated by the Great Recession.

An analysis of Federal Reserve data by the Economic Policy Institute points to a plummeting net worth among black American households. In 2004, the median net worth for whites was $134,000, as compared with

$13,000 for black households. By 2009, white households had dropped 24 percent to $98,000, while the median net worth for black households fell 83 percent to $2,000.

Huge gains made since the Selma days have been reversed. When the overall unemployment rate hovered frustratingly around 8 percent, the black unemployment rate stubbornly stayed at 16 percent.

Even college education, long the potent protector, highlights the dilemma faced by the black middle class. For white college graduates the unemployment rate was under 4 percent. For black college grads it was more than 7 percent.

Changes in high school and college enrollment show encouraging signs. Among twenty-five to twenty-nine-year-olds there has been a thirty-year rise in high school graduations and General Education Degrees (GEDs). There have also been impressive gains for this demographic for college attendance rates. Between 1976 and 2010, African American shares of college enrollment rose from 9.4 percent to 14.5 percent, according to federal data. But African American college graduation numbers, while improving, continue to lag far below white graduation numbers.

The tragically low academic achievement is just a part of the overall gap that is draining the sustainability out of the black middle class.

How Has the Black Middle Class Fared
in the Slow Recovery?

LET'S FACE IT—WHEN BLACKS have two cents for every dollar of white net worth, rebounding is pretty hard.

Social mobility isn't impossible, it's just rare. Concerning those born in the bottom fifth of economic earners, only a bit over half ever make it out, and only about 6 percent move all the way to the top fifth, according to recent Brookings work. (These statistics are lower than those for most European countries.)

A report by the Pew Center in 2007 says that the sons and daughters of the black middle class face a 45 percent likelihood of ending up near poor. Downward mobility translates to this harsh reality:

The majority of middle-class black children will end up with lower incomes than their parents.

While this is happening, two-thirds of white children will out-earn their middle-class parents.

In fact, the same pattern has repeated since we began exporting our manufacturing jobs. In each economic expansion since 1980, the poor grew relatively poorer or at best stayed the same; the middle stagnated or expanded the number of household earners or their home equity borrowing in order to prosper; and the top did relatively better. Most recently, the top did dramatically better.

Carry that over forty years or more and you have more than an undeniable trend. You have a huge and intractable problem brewing: The kind that bedevils solution. The kind that either you fix yourself or events fix it for you; the kind with a chilling inevitability. The kind that inspires historians and poets.

The kind that ends ugly if it doesn't get fixed soon.

We need an American Children's Zone, and we need it now.

TRENDS IN THE BLACK MIDDLE CLASS

THE BLACK MIDDLE CLASS HAS been growing since the 1960s in absolute terms, but numerous studies conclude that the percentage of blacks making it into the middle class stopped increasing in the mid-1980s.

When you break down earners into deciles, things only get worse. African Americans are twice as likely to be in the bottom 10 percent of earners as whites, and that proportion hasn't changed much in over forty-five years. Looking at the bottom fifth, there is some modest good news. Though blacks are still 50 percent more likely to be there than whites, their overall numbers are down.

The result is an oddly bifurcated landscape. In a special PBS broadcast in 1998, "The Two Nations of Black America," Henry Louis Gates, Jr., chair of the Harvard African American Studies Department, lamented, "How have we reached the point where we have both the largest black middle class and the largest black underclass in our history?"

Worst of all, both are heading in the wrong direction.

In her book *Black Picket Fences,* Mary Pattillo McCoy talked about the shift away from the traditional black middle-class couple who were married with 2.5 kids and a pooch. By 2000 these middle-class marrieds lost their status as the majority middle-class black household.

Kris Marsh of the University of Maryland has taken the freshest look at developments in the black middle class. She and William Darity, Jr., coined the term for the emerging group of single and living alone (SALA) households in the black middle class: "The Love Jones Cohort."

The second-largest and fastest-growing segment is the Love Jones Cohort of SALAs. Marsh sees them as the future leadership of the black middle class and the group most responsible for the absolute numbers growth of the black middle class.

Her work also challenges the traditional notion that marriage is the ultimate anti-poverty strategy.

The Love Jones Cohort is a separate trend. The family unit has given way to single black professionals who choose not to marry and/or have children—some not at all and others much later. These SALAs represent the terra firma of the black middle class. Our policies have to take their prominent role into account, but they don't.

We are locked into 1960s models of aid, support, and service. And once again the music has most definitely changed.

It is no longer as simple as finding direct causation between single households and economic mobility. The black middle class is increasingly comprised of people who choose to be single at the same time that the overall profile of African American motherhood is one of a single-parent family structure.

DIVERSITY FATIGUE

MIDDLE-CLASS INTEGRATION FEELS TIRED. Diversity committees at professional firms appear to meet less often and with even lesser fervor. When the great crash hit Lehman Brothers, one of the very first activities to be dismantled was its industry-leading diversity effort.

Race-based admissions and affirmative action are under attack, with the University of Texas traveling all the way to the Supreme Court in 2013 to determine whether it could continue to consider race as one of its many factors in accepting students.

A number of states, like Arizona, Michigan, Nebraska, New Hampshire, and Oklahoma, have banned race-based affirmative action in the past few years, following similar moves before the millennium by California, Florida, and Washington.

Outside the halls of the academy, the story is as much about torpor as anything else. At the nation's biggest companies only about 3.2 percent of senior executive positions are staffed with African Americans, says the Executive Leadership Council. About 12 percent of the nation's working-age population is black.

Just one percent of the Fortune 500 CEOs and about 5 percent of the country's doctors and dentists are black.

What is far more telling is a *New York Times*–commissioned study by Queens College and CUNY showing that the African American proportion among physicians has remained unchanged for nearly twenty-five years.

That study also found that blacks make up about 3 percent of the architects in the United States, and that proportion has been flat for two decades.

For twenty years, the National Association of Law Placement has been tracking the slow but unmistakable growth in minority and women lawyers, but that number fell in 2010.

Diversity has taken a direct hit in the recession. But for all the tiny numbers at the upper echelon, the more telling story is found much further down the line. Competition for superior qualified candidates with diverse backgrounds has never been keener at law firms, consulting firms, and investment banks. But at many of these professional service firms the absolute hiring numbers are down meaningfully since the late great crash.

The Conference Board recently asked senior executives how their priorities had been altered by the financial crisis. One question focused on "achieving diversity and representation in a cross-cultural workforce." Their answer confirmed what can easily be surmised if you talk to business people across the country—or, for that matter, to anyone trying to get an entry-level executive position.

Diversity's gone sideways. Procedures remain, meetings are dutifully convened, tables are taken at charity functions, symposia ad nausea are held, and minutes are dutifully kept. Progress is won by inches, which by any measure of the problem is an anemic response.

Welcome to the slow-walk solution. But in the race to the top, forget about bringing a stopwatch—a Gregorian calendar is a better bet.

A Receding Tide

FOR TOO LONG, WE HAVE refused to tie together the continuing problems of discrimination and foreclosed opportunity for minorities to the steady erosion of the entire middle class. Four decades have passed since the Kerner Commission presciently warned of the emergence of two Americas.

Policy makers and social activists who cling to this separated Americas notion miss the key point. We are one mighty ecosystem. Lack of mobility and discrimination has direct economic impact on the whole body, just like the loss of a limb undermines the capabilities of the whole individual.

Forty years of differential development has taken us well outside the realm of civil rights. Fixing these problems is a matter of national direction. Persistence of these problems influences the ability of the whole nation to govern, adapt, and prosper. And we are timid about identifying and obliterating hidden discriminatory barriers.

The vision of an all-white middle class based on the nuclear family and supported in small measure by minority players on the fringes no longer works. Witness first the rise of the black middle class, joined later by women as distinct members leading their own households, and then Latinos and others—each contributing in their unique way. There is no success for our middle class unless *all* members come along.

Otherwise, we will experience the same cracked façade that gave way once before.

The black middle class has a vital role to play, but it remains fragile. We simply cannot grow our middle class without enhancing mobility for the poorest among us. We have not sufficiently funded, nor have we demanded excellence from, our K–12 education system. Access to higher education has improved, but even the laudable Pell grants are no longer sufficient to cover the spiraling costs of college. Similarly, we have taken a hands-off approach to job training, community college, and local economic development.

Worse, we treat these necessities like expenses rather than investments. We have changed welfare to workfare, but Children's Defense Fund surveys of families who returned to work found they often did so by taking low-paying jobs with no benefits, which forced them and their families to emergency rooms and soup kitchens.

Among the most threatened are the working poor. According to the CDF, nearly a third of people who have left welfare to work have ultimately lost their jobs, and most of those who were working had slipped below the poverty line again.

The biggest problem with vulnerability is that most Americans are unaware or uninterested in risk. And fewer still see race as an issue.

When the Gallup organization polled Americans to identify the number-one challenge facing the country in 1964, at least 60 percent named racial issues. For the same question in 2012, only one percent picked race.

CHAPTER FOURTEEN

AMERICAN MATRIARCHY

A new engine of the middle class

SHE WAS EMBLEMATIC OF THE SURGE *in middle-class families to these suburban frontiers, though from where she sat trying to earn a few extra bucks doing freelance writing, the room was so cold she often wore gloves when she typed.*

Hers had been a long and strange trip to Rockland County, a recently carved suburb of New York City. Born Bettye Goldstein, her childhood in Peoria was hardly ideal. Growing up brainy, assertive, and Jewish kept her Midwestern classmates at a distance. That her look, too, was different—diminutive and thoughtful behind heavily lidded eyes—meant some adolescent girl classmates were even more distant.

High school can be hell.

Her life on the periphery, with few dates and episodes of extreme solitude, furnished Bettye with a sensitivity for mortals on the margins that cannot be taught in books, even to such a brilliant and dedicated student.

She found liberation and her voice in the calm, sequestered halls of Smith College in the wilds of western Massachusetts. She even chose to shed the "e" on her name, considering the appendage a vestigial pretension from life in Peoria.

She became Betty.

Liberation blooms in many forms.

Left to her own devices, Betty found ample intellectual challenge, gradu-ating summa cum laude with a reputation for staunch antiwar positions and a stint as editor in chief of the college newspaper.

A fellowship at UC Berkeley led her westward to the tutelage of the bril-liant developmental psychologist Erik Erikson. More excellence led to an-other promising fellowship. Betty was beginning to create a career consistent with her prodigious talents. As she later recounted, the physicist she was see-ing at the time urged her not to accept the prestigious posting. He may have been intimidated by her arc of flight.

After reflecting about the kind of life women were expected to live at the time, she reluctantly turned the fellowship down.

Though the boyfriend/physicist met his own passing soon after, that fateful decision came back in interviews for the rest of her life. She had come to a fork in the woods . . . and took the road oft taken.

It was a habit she was about to break.

Sitting in the quiet of her rented home, sandwiched between the inces-sant demands of tending to her two grade-school boys, the brilliant scholar who had moved from Berkeley back to Peoria and ultimately to Greenwich Village sought freelance writing assignments for ladies' magazines to fill the time and the house account.

As a street reporter for a labor newspaper she honed her skills at inquiry and expository expression. She had finagled an inordinately long maternity leave after the birth of her first boy, but when she announced her subsequent pregnancy the union chose to dismiss her on the spot.

It was another time . . . back in 1957. And maternity leave meant just that.

An impending fifteenth reunion at Smith College led her to be engaged to conduct a survey of her returning class about the course their lives had taken. Working with two friends, she designed a questionnaire with a series of open-ended questions for her 200 classmates, mostly middle- and upper-class women from across the country.

Her interrogatory ranged from how these women had used their educa-

tion, to how satisfied they were with their life's direction, to how and when they confronted intimate problems with their husband. Her queries covered a great many subject areas, and yet they can naturally be summarized by the single genuine question that lay deep at the root of the entire exercise:

Are you happy?

Like most "independent" surveys, this one had a hoped-for outcome—to disprove the growing cultural myth that self-actualization for women was negatively influenced by pursuit of college and graduate degrees. A well-circulated book titled Modern Women: The Lost Sex by Ferdinand Lundberg and Dr. Marynia Farnham pointed to sexual and gender dysfunction among women of higher education.

Not surprisingly, Smith College was keen to build evidence to the contrary.

At the same time, it would be inaccurate to portray the women of Betty's Smith College class as energetically interested in the outcome of this survey—much less the women of the nation and the world. As those alums dutifully and faithfully answered and submitted their forms, there was no sense of restless anticipation. This study was the furthest thing from a bold new beginning. It was instead just a humble list of questions with ample space provided for reply.

It was just a chance to be heard.

How dangerous could a few simple questions directed to the Smith sisters of '42 be?

What happened next stunned her, which is surprising in retrospect for two reasons—one that she was a brilliant and observant woman, according to all accounts. But the other and more striking reason was that young Betty Friedan was a member in good standing of the very target audience she had set out to survey.

That's how deep the truth was buried.

―――――――――

IN LIFE SO FAR, FRIEDAN acknowledges that when she designed the survey with her friends Mario Ingersoll Howell and Anne Mather

Montero they were creating inquiries for their classmates that they had not truly posed to themselves. The irony, of course, is that the survey did not disprove the notion that education made women dysfunctional—instead, it bore a more powerful message.

These seemingly happily settled, educated women from all across the country were leading lives of desperation, disaffection, loneliness, and pain.

Worst of all were the feelings of resentment from women who were undergoing psychoanalysis and finding that the prescribed remedies (by their mostly male doctors) only added to their sense of isolation.

As she gathered the findings, it slowly dawned on Friedan that there was a major crisis facing middle-class American women. She broadened her inquiry to include women graduates from Radcliffe and other colleges. In time she would survey scores of women with strikingly similar results.

She composed an article and submitted it to the major women's magazines for whom she had been writing—among them *McCall's*, *Redbook*, and *Ladies' Home Journal*. Her essay was rejected at every turn. She tried another version, and then another—each time with similar result.

After her fourth attempt was summarily dismissed, despite ardent massaging and editorial accommodation, Friedan reluctantly reached a couple of conclusions.

First, the subject she had unearthed threatened the very existence of the deeper-into-domesticity magazines for which she had been supplying happy hausfrau stories.

They simply could not handle the truth.

And as she huddled for warmth in her Rockland exurbia she realized that only an independent book format would grant her sufficient latitude and freedom to explore in detail what was unfolding in her research. Her greatest challenge was distilling in a credible and sensitive way the hidden anxiety that coursed through the words of all these women.

Imagine how these Smith alums might have engaged with one another on those spring reunion afternoons in 1957. The smiles and shared laughter belied the searing words they had forwarded in secret, wrapped in the comforting sequestration of Friedan's open-ended questionnaire. None could be truly sure what the other had written. Had they shared the secret? These ladies externally adopted the code of middle-class women everywhere in those days: an omerta shared by a generation's gender: Suffer in silence . . . endure it alone . . . keep a clean home and a smile on your face. Tell no one . . . not even . . . or especially not, your shrink.

Theirs was a deeply suppressed anxiety in spite of its prevalence—which made it the saddest kind of all.

It took nearly five years for Friedan to bring definition and form to this amorphous pain. Armed with a $3,000 advance from publisher W.W. Norton, she lined up three days a week of babysitting help and secreted herself to the Allen Room of the New York Public Library.

It was a painstaking process, involving month after month of listening, reflection, and probing. At last the answer came to her as a great notion. Staring into the opaque angst of so many women, Friedan's first chapter was called "The Problem That Has No Name."

Betty's remarkable work took our nation by storm from its first appearance and for the intervening fifty years. It was titled, simply but prophetically, *The Feminine Mystique*.

Friedan opened her book with an admission: "Gradually without seeing it clearly for quite a while, I came to realize that something is very wrong with the way American women are trying to live their lives today." Later in the preface she faced the mirror: "I sensed it first as a question mark in my own life, as a wife and mother of three small children, half guiltily, and therefore half-heartedly, almost in spite of myself, using my abilities and education in work that took me away from my home."

From the instant of publication in 1963, Betty Friedan's life changed. In time she liberated herself from a restrictive marriage and from the reverie of Rockland County. Once again she settled in New York City, and she became a constant fixture on the lecture and talk-show circuit.

She was forceful and persuasive in the sort of way that led the *New York Times* to eulogize her as "famously abrasive." "She was one of a kind."

For years the only time the book, which debuted on the *New York Times* bestseller list, fell from that permanent perch was when there were simply no copies to be had and the printers hurried to replenish the shelves.

Rarely has one small set of questions uncovered such a trove of emotion or coincided with a gender revolution of such sweeping proportion. Cause or effect is for historians to debate. Did she merely observe the starter's pistol, or did her book itself spark the revolution?

Whatever, her book brought many soaring arrows suddenly into alignment.

No matter her cause or effect; for the women of our nation, change was already on the march.

HI HO, HI HO . . .

WHEN THE UNITED STATES ENTERED World War II, more than 12 million women were already working as a valued quarter of the American workforce. During the period of combat operations another 6 million women took active part in working for the war effort, bringing the total number of women to more than a third of all labor.

Their involvement went way beyond Rosie the Riveter. Much of their specific involvement was determined by their race, class, marital status, or the number of children they had, but their collective impact was profound.

True, women surged into positions in manufacturing, replacing men who had left those workstations to soldier on in the war effort. Half of the women who took on war jobs were minority and lower-middle-class women who were already in the workforce. But the rigors of wartime production meant that many women who were married and with school-aged children were also put to work in the plants. At the time, the very idea of tens of thousands of married mothers working in factories represented a sea change.

Taking nothing from the patriotic fervor that drove these women, a great many of them had traded up from low-paying clerical or basic service jobs to higher-paying manufacturing opportunities. More important, these women proved to themselves and to their superiors that they were more than capable of "manning" the post.

It was not simply a matter of taking up the rivet gun. An army of women flooded the fields of American farms to keep the breadbasket full. And more than 3 million women worked for the Red Cross and another 200,000 served in the country's uniform. (Women's ranks in the defense sector expanded by 460 percent.)

After the war, the cultural division of labor regained some of its earlier composition. But a majority of the women working in traditionally male occupations, both single and married, wanted access to the same job prospects they enjoyed during the war.

Try as they might, there was a significant resetting of the order, and women wishing to continue with their employment were redirected back to lower-paying jobs. Millions more were laid off and told to return to their homes.

Nevertheless.

The effects of World War II on American women could not be reversed. They had proved themselves capable—but a catalyst would be necessary to change a steely mind-set. Many white middle-class families determined that they could raise a family and own a home with a sole breadwinner. During the 1950s, only one woman in every three entered the workforce.

The taboo against middle-class women working may have been broken, but economic momentum sent them back to their kitchens for a while.

In 1960, the FDA approved a drug that brought far-ranging social change. The first oral contraceptive for women found its way to pharmacists of the nation the following year, coincidentally just at the moment when government leadership began to take note of the massive inequalities those women faced at work.

Within months of the Pill's approval, President Kennedy's Commission on the Status of Women began to delve into all manner of workplace issues and to expose in plain sight the wage gap that women had endured more or less in silence. Kennedy's commission also tackled other issues facing women, including education, Social Security benefits, and hiring practices.

It was a target-rich environment, and Kennedy's commission found ample evidence of discrimination.

Within a year, the Equal Rights Act was amended to prohibit gender-based wage discrimination between men and women in the same place of employment. The 1963 Equal Pay Act was passed.

When President Kennedy signed the bill banning wage discrimination, women were earning 58 cents for every dollar earned by a man.

In 1964, President Johnson signed his far-reaching Civil Rights Act, which included language designed to prevent workplace discrimination against women. He went even further, establishing the Equal Employment Opportunity Commission to enforce these rules, and appointed FDR's son to run it.

The courts also tackled the reproductive rights of women. Headline writers called it "feminism's second wave."

But for all of the blossoming regulatory and legal support, women throughout the country continued to face unfair practices as a matter of routine. Something more was needed.

In 1965, despite all the changes pushed through in Washington and across the nation, Betty Friedan and twenty-eight other women on a quest created NOW, the National Organization of Women.

Serving as its first president, Friedan composed the mission for the group: "to take action to bring women into full participation in the mainstream of American society."

But the pace of change was glacial. A frustrated Lyndon Johnson signed Presidential Executive Order 11375 in 1967 banning gender discrimination in federal hiring. And still the wheels of justice turned at a funereal tempo. Later, the Equal Rights Amendment of 1972 was proposed and passed in the House and Senate but fell three states short of the thirty-eight state requirement for ratification by the 1979 deadline.

Even as regulations and laws protecting working women were circumvented, events had taken on their own momentum. History has a funny way of breaking what will not bend.

The rise of the service sector and the parallel shifting in employment roles in manufacturing played to women's strengths in the workforce. So did increased expansion of women's access to higher education.

In the 1960s, 70 percent of families had a stay-at-home parent—most often Mom. That fairy tale lasted until the days of double digits; the three uglies cast a very long shadow.

Runaway inflation, sky-high interest rates, and spiking unemployment in the 1970s made stay-at-home parenting a luxury, a vestige of an earlier economic circumstance. Civil rights gave way to home economics and necessity made women the mothers of invention.

The proportion of women in the workforce increased from 43 percent in 1970 to 59 percent in 2006. Women's relative wages also gained. In 1979, full-time women employees earned about 62 percent of what their male counterparts did. By 2006, before the economic conflagration, women earned just above 80 percent of what comparable men took home.

Looking behind the numbers, it is impossible to ignore the pride-swallowing grind that women have endured. During those intervening twenty-five years, women made extraordinary strides. They made so much progress and built so much momentum that a very basic tide had turned.

And policy makers, business leaders, and even many women are still in denial about how important that passage has been.

For decades we have managed women's issues through the same rearview mirror we've used for most policy—marking progress in increments and exhorting patience. But for anyone daring to peer around the corner, women have advanced their own cause in a striking and immutable manner.

It is time to acquaint yourself with the new Feminomics. The tipping point has already passed.

Women will move from parity to superiority over the short term. And in many measures they already have.

FEMINOMICS AND MIDDLE-CLASS RECOVERY

THE GAME, AS THEY SAY, has changed. That sound you are hearing is the shattering of every glass ceiling . . . now and forever.

In 1970, only about 10 percent of women in the labor force had bachelor's degrees; by 2006, it was over a third.

The Great Recession and subsequent anemic recovery only exacerbated the trends—and few people have taken the time to acknowledge where things stand as a result.

In a phrase, women have built an extraordinary position—now and for the future. And any true rejuvenation of the middle class must involve major acknowledgment of the shift in the balance of gender power that has already occurred.

First, the dramatic reduction of heavy manufacturing and construction jobs disproportionately hit men. From December 2007 until the job market ran aground in February 2010, the economy lost more than 8.5 million jobs. Losses for men were so pronounced in the beginning that it was called a "Mancession," and when the market started to turn it was called a "Shecovery."

The disparity makes sense when you investigate where women started out before things went south. Despite all the progress in the last generation, there are still gender barriers in different parts of the economy. At the beginning of the recession, women held just about half of the non–farm payroll jobs, by any measure an extraordinary accomplishment.

Women did not participate equally in all sectors, holding just 29 percent of the jobs in manufacturing and 13 percent of the jobs in construction.

As these two sectors collapsed, the education and health sectors added 844,000 jobs (almost 200,000 of which were home health and home nursing jobs), which boast women participation rates of more than 75 percent of the jobs. Women also held 57 percent of the public-sector jobs, which initially gained in the early days of the recession.

The stirring result is that by the spring of 2010, for the first time in our history women made up 51 percent of the professional workers in the United States. And 70 percent of American women with children under eighteen are earning a paycheck while raising their children—a position diametrically opposite of where things stood when Friedan went to press.

Women have truly arrived. According to the Bureau of Labor Statistics, women now hold 51.4 percent of managerial and professional jobs (they held 26 percent in 1980).

Over half the accountants in America are women. A third of the physicians are women, as are 45 percent of the associates in law firms; both are tracking to put women in the majority soon. Already women hold half of all banking and insurance jobs.

How are women positioned for the future? Today, women earn almost 60 percent of the university degrees conferred in the EU and the United States. On grades and board scores alone, women could hold even higher percentages in the best-ranked schools than they do. But university leaders prize balance in their coeducation.

Today, there are millions more American women in college than men, and they are headed to supermajority. Why has this happened? As women traded up in the quality of the jobs they could get, the proportional financial return to women for a college education became far greater than for men. Their prior entry-level incomes were dwarfed by what they could earn thanks to higher education and even higher aspirations. As women got better, higher-paying jobs, they also delayed marriage and child rearing.

Women went from looking for jobs to looking for careers.

In graduate schools women are evolving too. In 2005, women earned 60 percent of the master's degrees and about half of the PhDs.

For a while, women focused their undergraduate studies in less immediately "marketable" areas—again the shift has been tectonic. When Betty Friedan first published her book, 40 percent of women got their BAs with a focus on education and 2 percent in business and management. Now it is 12 percent education and 50 percent business and management.

Medical schools now report that women hold 51 percent of the seats, and law schools put women at just under half of their enrollment. For several years running, more than 100,000 women have taken the GMAT tests to get their MBAs. In 1997, about 39 percent of MBA students were women, and by 2007 the number exceeded 44 percent. Harvard, Stanford, and many of the other prestigious MBA programs are admitting record numbers and proportions of women.

For the first time, female economics doctoral candidates at Duke University will outnumber their male colleagues; nearly two-thirds of the entering class of economics PhDs are women, and the national average exceeds 30 percent.

These extraordinary achievements signal increasing responsibilities for middle-class women. They have been focused, intent, and yet flexible. Recalling that 70 percent of families in 1960 had at least one stay-at-home parent, now 70 percent of families have either or both parents working, or are a single-parent household with a sole breadwinner.

In 40 percent of all households in this country women are the sole or lead breadwinners—and that number is increasing.

Yet women still have ground to cover. They comprise only about

20 percent of the math, science, and technology undergraduate majors nationwide, and just 14 percent of Fortune 500 officer positions are held by women (just 3 percent of the CEO slots).

It is always easy to point to the 16 percent of Fortune 500 board seats occupied by women and complain about glass ceilings. But the momentum of Feminomics is simply too powerful to ignore.

The economic empowerment of middle-class women and the millions of younger women who have worked to position themselves for leadership roles in the middle class is one of the great fifty-year accomplishments in our history. In the half-century since *The Feminine Mystique* burst into national consciousness, women have become the vital ingredient in re-energizing the middle class in every area of our society.

The time has come for an economic empowerment zone for women.

This book makes no attempt to designate whether men come from Mars, Venus, or Uranus. It simply acknowledges the fact that women are a key ingredient to middle-class revival here on planet Earth. It ascribes nothing more than motivation, focus, and flexibility to women. Women have simply made the adjustments and the sacrifices to improve their lot—clearly; the increased access to higher education was available to both genders.

Consider the rate of change. At graduations in the 1950 academic year 120,796 women earned college degrees—some 24 percent of the more than half a million college diplomas awarded. By the 2009 graduations, women earned 1,849,200 degrees, making up 60 percent of the sheepskins handed out.

The combined effects of greater absolute numbers and greater share of the total signal a fundamental change in the ability of women to get jobs throughout the U.S. economy. Look at Europe for direction. In the European Union, women have filled 6 million of the 8 million new jobs created since 2000.

For decades, these have been subterranean economic forces. But with the disproportionate dismissal of men the new balance has burst into high relief.

It is far too early to sound the death knell for the male labor force, though the damage was widespread. Since December 2007 men have accounted for seven of every ten jobs lost (half of all job losses came from construction and manufacturing). By February 2010 the share of adult men with a job shrank to 66.6 percent. Until this recession the number had never been below 70 percent since these numbers were first tabulated post–World War II.

Job losses in this recent recession were steeper and more prolonged than in any contraction in the last sixty years. We lost more than 6 percent of payroll at the worst point, compared with 3 percent in the 1981 recession and much smaller dips in other downturns.

A bigger story for men is playing out across the vast public sector and in select industries.

Since February 2010, the manufacturing beast has begun to stir. Abetted by early stages of reshoring and wage-gap compression with China, men have gained back nearly 300,000 jobs in the male-dominated manufacturing sector. Construction, too, has come back from its multiyear hibernation. Men continue to gain in those two sectors, and women's hiring has actually retreated.

Men have gained position, too, in education and health services.

The public sector has been a lagging indicator, adding jobs in the early phases of the recession and only recently beginning to see meaningful cuts. After holding up reasonably well through the recession, the sequestration and other local government budget cuts have disproportionately affected women.

Local governments facing continuing shortfalls in tax revenues and decreasing federal assistance, relief, and stimulus spending means more bad news for women.

The sputtering economy and the lack of any true leadership on job creation have brought the labor force participation rate to a new low for both sexes. Despite recent signs of relative improvement for men overall, worker participation of just 62.8 percent is an enemy of economic progress.

While the women's participation rate is relatively steady at 55 percent, as is always the case digging deeper tells a different story. Department of Labor data in 2008 clearly shows that white women are far more likely to be employed than are black and Hispanic women. Unemployment among young black women has increased to over 20 percent. And today 15 percent of Latina women in the same age cohort are unemployed.

Age matters. Young white women are doing as poorly as young white males—11 percent at least are unemployed.

What all this gender bias has done in the face of male employment meltdown is cause gender rebalancing in selected markets. Federal data shows that men are making increasing inroads in the retail sector, long the province of women. Three years ago, women made up a meaningful majority of payrolls in the retail trade (something that has been true for at least three decades).

Men now account for 51 percent of the retail jobs in the country. Increasingly, men are being forced to be more flexible as the prospects for broad-scale rebounding in construction and manufacturing remain elusive.

Put another way, lower-wage industries like retail, education, restaurants, and hotels have been a disproportionate provider of new jobs. Women typically face more jobs in those sectors, but men are getting tired of waiting.

In spite of the recent rebound in the hiring of men, the trend toward increased employment and purchasing power of women continues. Studies show that female consumers control as much as 85 percent of all purchasing decisions responsible for $7 trillion in spending. This surge in influence reflects a combination of factors. First, in the 1970s women contributed between 2 and 6 percent of the family income. Today, women provide 42.2 percent of the family income, and even more are the primary breadwinners for their family.

An interesting question is whether this shift in earning and purchasing power will be the key determinant of who is in the working class and who can maintain middle-class status. In 2005, the top quintile of families had over 77 percent of their members with two or more wage earners.

Single-earner households were far more prevalent in the lower quintiles, and most often the lead earner was still a man. Women wage earners were responsible for many families remaining in the middle class. And for many others, their wages were the ticket out of working-class status.

Which is why the wage gap has become more than a moral equity issue; it is a vital ingredient of the middle-class revival.

And we are fighting it for many of the wrong reasons.

Our economy is increasingly dependent on building a wider and deeper skill base. Workers who have taken the steps to educate and retrain themselves will be the beneficiaries of this growing war for talent.

The combination of an aging workforce and a renaissance in manufacturing and health care means that the United States will have to make more effective use of its female population. We have heard the statisticians decry the bad economic trade that a college education now represents. They claim that the costs of education are not worth the long-term income benefit.

What these bean counters ignore is that a college education is the best known cure for unemployment. Measuring simply by dollars out today versus earnings in the intermediate term ignores the special flexibility and adaptability college graduates enjoy. Once again risk is left out of the equation—but less and less by women.

Time after time, those who have jobs fare far better in seeking new ones. College graduates are not the first to go in a downsizing. Those recently laid off do far better than those out of work for a protracted period.

Degrees are also an excellent way to position oneself for retraining and career enhancement—in and out of the workforce. There have been studies which show that women are more willing to train for new careers and new jobs once the plant leaves their town or a major employer engages in massive layoffs.

Truth be told, these studies are too recent and too localized to be truly determinative. But what they claim is that men have been more resistant to relinquishing their craft or their profession in search of a new paycheck. That psychology may be accurately portrayed, but the absolute numbers are more telling.

Simply put, when robotics or a shuttered factory obviate the need for an arc welder we need to make the path easier for that skilled laborer to find another job. Because when the manufacturer pulls up stakes in Flint, Michigan, that job is unlikely to ever return.

And so arc-welding jobs in Flint may be gone with the wind as well.

We need to create flexibility when corporations abandon communities—that's how new jobs get formed.

CORE CURRICULUM

SO WE FACE A NEW economic reality—the core of Feminomics.

With millions more women than men attending college, combined with a pattern of greater flexibility for embracing career change and getting the best renewal training during their career, women have become the flex factor in the new labor force.

It makes no economic sense to pay them less.

Increasing women's participation in the labor force and bringing pay to parity will without fail boost our country's GDP.

Corporations will be forced to address the combining of work with child care. The energetic way that women are working and improving their station puts us far past the days of Mommycare. That original path had the mark of female exceptionalism about it. Now the true response is more market driven. Telecommuting, flexible hours, child-related leaves of absence— all will be offered as a matter of course.

Why are the big corporations making such accommodating moves?

Because women are already exerting their newfound economic power. When they encounter roadblocks at their companies they do something that has stunned their corporate "benefactors." They simply quit the inflexible behemoth and start their own companies with greater focus on flexibility.

In the past decade, women have started more privately owned companies than men at a rate of more than two to one. Women-owned enterprises employ more people than the Fortune 500 and have combined revenues in excess of $2 trillion.

Middle-class women are a force of economic nature. And they are just getting warmed up.

But trouble still lurks around every corner for working mothers who are poor. Public and private-sector initiatives have not touched them. These women fail to get the benefits from female-friendly companies. Child care continues to be so expensive that many poor working mothers can barely keep up with expenses. Millions of families must fight to cope with a school-day that bears no relationship to their working lives, and worse, they must engage insufficient and brutally expensive child care facilities.

What is necessary is a cohort of both public and private initiatives to feed the needs of working mothers. It will take years for such steps to be taken. By that time, given the increasing number of single-parent households, women who are sole breadwinners will likely represent the majority of households.

Economic necessity and doing the right thing will converge—not as an example of female exceptionalism but as a matter of economic empowerment.

What are the elements of such a female empowerment initiative?

Expansion of paid family medical leave will be necessary if mothers are to balance their caregiver responsibilities with their breadwinner duties.

Raise the minimum wage to more than $11 per hour and vigorously police gender inequities.

Create incentives for affordable, tax-deductible child care. If we allow a tax-deductible child care program we will empower more women to join the workforce and enlist the aid of many men and women who are marginally employed. Tax-deductible child care is the definition of win/win.

Embrace charter schools and other initiatives where children's schooldays match more closely their mothers' work-days. It simply does not serve our children or their working parents to cling to the vestigial three o'clock dismissal.

Universal pre-K should be a matter of civil right so long as it is tied in to a robust next step in the school system. Study after study cites the benefits of reading to children earlier and to the power of instilling educational curiosity at a younger age.

And for God sakes, if you hire women, pay them. It is past time for equal pay for equal work. The mommy-track discount is an anachronism that ignores the facts. Your average talented worker is someone's mother. Pay her what she deserves.

If you don't, she will quit your firm and start a highly effective competitor.

So play offense or defense—it doesn't matter.

Just do the right thing . . . or she will.

CHAPTER FIFTEEN

The Latino Generation

An American super-minority

I N S O U T H C E N T R A L T E X A S, A M O N U M E N T *stands in the blazing sun about 150 miles from the Mexican border that has developed an unusual capability over the past century or so—it can perplex you. It might even underwhelm you . . . until you know the story.*

After hearing about that edifice for years in folklore and song, memorializing it, lionizing the men who fought and died there, vilifying those who triumphed over the Texans in battle, it is a bit of a surprise to encounter it first-hand. The Alamo has loomed so large, like Plymouth Rock, as a fixture in our nation's consciousness; it's natural to expect a colossus. It's Texan, after all.

Housing myth in mortar and stone is almost an impossibility.

A simple structure, built as a mission to convert and baptize the Native American population, its main wall is 190 feet long by 122 feet wide. It feels more like an old-time parochial school than a fortress.

The siege of the Alamo happened just eight days before the Texas Declaration of Independence was signed in 1836. Texans proudly remember their standoff against insurmountable odds. They reverently recount how a small but mighty group of Texas Freedom Fighters held the line against a Mexican army fifteen times their strength. This hard-won delay bought Sam Houston time to gather an army to make a surprise attack and crush the Mexican Army at the Battle of San Jacinto.

What some remember less frequently are the Tejanos (Texans of Mexican and Criollo Spanish heritage) who fought bravely alongside their Anglo brethren in the doomed campaign. San Antonio, like many cities in the United States today, was founded by Spanish settlers long before the formation of our thirteen colonies. When the Mexican troops gathered outside the walls of the Alamo in late February they were likely unaware of the complex and incendiary keg of history they were about to ignite.

But for some time there had been unmistakable indications of strife.

Almost twenty years before that fateful day, a group of Tejanos, who were Mexicans and some Europeans in the San Antonio region, chafed at what they considered increasingly autocratic Spanish rule. These Tejanos waged a brutal but ultimately unsuccessful rebellion. When their insurrection was crushed, the Tejanos sought support and protection from their American immigrant friends.

Texas, which had been populated by numerous Native American tribes for thousands of years, had always been the darling of imperial powers. From the sixteenth century to the cessation of the Civil War, it had been claimed entirely or in part by no fewer than seven nations.

Another collision was coming. Tough economic times in the United States in the early 1820s and '30s led Stephen Austin, a young Missouri lawyer, to embrace a great notion: Texas land was plentiful and cheap, and Austin's concept was to lure thousands of settlers to homestead in the region. A key figure in Austin's plan came in the unlikely personage of Jose Antonio Navarro, a European by birth but a proud Tejano who served as mayor of San Antonio.

The region had long been a beacon for well-to-do Tejanos. Though many of their brethren were essentially subsistence farmers, other industrious Tejanos eked out a better life by capturing wild mustangs and trading them for supplies in the Louisiana Territories. When the Spanish monarchy claimed these wild horses as property of the crown, many Tejanos lost their livelihood.

A stormy cocktail was brewing. The surge of Anglo settlers in Texas reached 30,000, more than four times the number of Mexicans (Tejanos) living there. Uneasy about the state of their domain, the Mexican government closed its borders to further American immigration (a strange turnabout in American immigration history).

The Mexican government, long considered corrupt, took a turn for the worse with the elevation of Antonio Lopez de Santa Anna in 1834. Santa Anna dissolved the state legislatures and abolished the federal constitution.

The U.S. settlers responded immediately. They feared with some justification the loss of their property and their slaves. That December, Texan and Tejano volunteers led a house-by-house insurrection to drive all Mexican troops out of San Antonio. In a matter of days, every Mexican soldier had been banished from Texas, and on December 9, the leader of the Mexican troops surrendered at the Alamo.

It was not to last.

Santa Anna considered the revolt an affront to his presidency and amassed an army of nearly 4,000 soldiers. Thousands of Tejanos were forced to choose sides—brother against brother; some siding with the Anglos and their independence, others pledging their allegiance to the Santa Anna regime.

El Presidente's army nearly caught the intrepid revolutionaries by surprise. It was a biblical standoff: thousands of Mexican troops facing a combined army of volunteers led by the irascible James Bowie, and the regulars led by a young lawyer named William Travis. The combined Anglo and Tejano forces were less than 200.

Severely outnumbered, the Alamo fighters nevertheless held Santa Anna at bay for thirteen days.

Just after midnight on Sunday, the sixth of March, thousands of Mexican infantrymen surrounded the small fort. Signaling the intensity of his purpose, Santa Anna enveloped his own infantry with cavalrymen to cut them down if they gave way. Scaling ladders were passed overhead, and at dawn were slanted against the walls. Soldiers scampered up by the hundreds.

The Texans persevered and drove back the first wave of Mexican soldiers. Then a second charge was repulsed. Eyewitnesses recount a moment of calm and quiet before a third strike was joined, with every member of the infantry pressing against the embattled freedom fighters. The results were fatal to the Texans; all but one or two were killed.

Outside the walls and along the ramparts, nearly 600 Mexicans lay dead. It was a bloodbath for both sides. Yet so overwhelming was his victory that Santa Anna declared the war all but over.

Just weeks later, Sam Houston, with newly refreshed troops, revitalized by the cry "Remember the Alamo," led a surprise attack on the Mexican

Army in one of the most decisive battles in history. The rout lasted a mere eighteen minutes, though eyewitnesses describe the savagery of the killing that occupied the next several hours. The embittered Texans sought out and killed every Mexican soldier they encountered. The next day, Santa Anna was captured and this time the war was indeed over.

WHILE TEXAS WENT ON TO prosper and become a central source of energy and power for the United States, the Tejano gamble for an independent Texas proved tragic. Following the revolution, Tejanos were overwhelmed by a surge of Anglo immigration. Despite having cohabitated with their Anglo brethren for generations, the new Texas leadership was uneasy with past alliances. Power sharing faded and the new leadership turned its back on the Tejanos, leaving them foreigners in a land they had fought to defend and had long been their own.

Any study of Latino immigration and of the increasing Latinization of American society requires a clear sense of our history at the adjacencies with Mexico and their generations spent among us. Misunderstand that history and you lose all perspective.

Today, San Antonio is like many cities sprung from the head of a small town—it swallows its suburbs as it grows. It has become enormous. You can fit Boston, Miami, and Chicago into its city limits and still have room for Manhattan. Mexican Americans who inhabit the region have a long and complicated relationship with Texas.

Tracing Texas history, it appears that Mexican Americans have legally been considered "white," but inconsistently so. They served in the white units of the segregated Army and Texas National Guard. During the Jim Crow years, they were permitted to marry white (but not black) partners. In the early 1940s, the Texas legislature even passed a "Caucasian Race Resolution" that affirmed their status as white.

Today, the U.S. Census muddies the waters even more: "Hispanic," "Latino," and "Spanish Origin" are each treated as an ethnic category. Race is a separate category on the census, and among the choices is "Some other race." In the Millennium Census of 2000 about half of all Hispanics checked

"White" for race. A significant number of the remaining checked "Some other race."

Petty bureaucracy on the face of it, but deeper meaning lurks here.

In 1984, there were 20 million Hispanics and Latinos in America. Today, they number over 52 million, and many believe that count is too low. Spanish is the official language in at least twenty different countries, and divisions between the wide variety of Spanish- and Portuguese-speaking nations from which American Latinos hail have prevented them from finding a united voice. So far.

We have a very complex spread among our Latino citizens. In San Antonio you have Mexican Americans with a multi-generational link to the United States—some for centuries. They are English speakers and have more than assimilated. But cruise down Interstate 10 South away from the river oaks of Houston and you will find precious little English spoken in the colonies spread in the hot grasslands and scrub that stretch to the border.

As goes Texas, so goes the nation. The Cuban Americans in Florida are still miles from the Mexican Americans in spite of their common language.

It is important to note that Census and other authorities consider Hispanic and Latino as ethnic rather than racial designations. Hispanics as they are counted span many races. To put the 50-plus million Latinos into context, there are 44.5 million African Americans in the United States inclusive of one or more races.

For all their differences, Latinos are increasingly finding common areas of interest driven by a very real political imperative. In some measure, the Telemundos and the Spanish-language media are contributing to the trend toward unity.

First look at two 60 percent slices of the Latino culture.

Mexican Americans comprise about 60 percent of the total pan-Latino community concentrated in key electoral states like Texas and California.

Looking at the pan-Latino group in another way, 60 percent define themselves as Democratic. That would seem to indicate a political block. But it doesn't.

Political science has not rested its case just yet. Certainly, Obama won the majority of the Hispanic vote. The Republicans have demonstrated a great propensity to harm themselves with this audience, exhibit A being the ill-considered law—which for better or worse carries a GOP imprimatur in Arizona—allowing local police more invasive powers in an illegal immigrant crackdown—a kind of Latino "stop and frisk."

But Democrats, be not proud.

One needs to look no further than Florida and the Republican Senate primary in which a young, forceful, and articulate son of Cuba, Marco Rubio, chased popular ex-governor Charlie Crist from the ticket. That Crist would seek the office as an Independent, rather than face a challenge from a "Tea Bagger" of Cuban descent for the Republican nomination, tells you at least one thing: The pan-Latino cake is far from baked.

And the emergence of Senator Ted Cruz as a Republican force in Texas bears watching too. Particularly if you disagree with his politics, pay close attention to what he says and writes. He is extremely bright and appears comfortable with the limelight, even if he polarizes in its glare sometimes. His value added will be far greater than a Dr. Seuss-enlivened filibuster. He possesses a powerful quality—he captures attention for his causes. Don't underestimate him. He wants to be your president.

While Democratic electoral victories in the pan-Latino community are not a foregone conclusion, here is something that is: Whether it is English as a second language at schools; patients' rights; prison and parolee reform; veterans' affairs; or, the most boiling of issues, immigration and naturalization, anyone who has not developed a sophisticated attitude regarding the growing number of Latinos by immigration or naturalized birth will make a bad leader and, worse, pass bad laws—if they can even get elected.

We need policies that embrace both the newly arrived and those who have lived here for generations. Some may immigrate and be your neighbors and co-workers, and some will be your in-laws. Others may be your boss. The time has come for a better plan.

Naming Rights

LABELERS HAVE DIFFICULTY CAPTURING THE complexity of this cohort—"Hispanic" and "Latino" are certainly descriptive with the former using a language and the latter attempting to capture a broader heritage. But neither is particularly useful in distinguishing who is lately arrived and who has been here for generations.

The alternative of two ethnonyms is just a symptom of a broader issue. We have not developed sufficient sophistication for dealing with a complex demography that is growing to majority in numerous areas of the country. While the evolved practice is to use the two designations interchangeably, "Hispanic" refers only to Spanish speakers, which tends to ignore Brazilians. "Latino" technically excludes persons from Spain. To put things in context, Brazil's population approaches 200 million (most of whom are Portuguese speakers) and Spain is just under 50 million. And there are more than three times the number of Brazilian-born Americans as Spanish-born.

It appears Latino has the upper hand for now, but you get the picture—anyone painting with a broad brush will not serve themselves well. This growing group is not well described by using an easy generic, though many policy makers still try and do so.

LATINOS AND THE MIDDLE CLASS

JUST HOW MANY IS 52 MILLION people? Imagine every person in New York State and California speaking Spanish or Portuguese and you get a sense. Soon you may not have to imagine very hard.

For all its imperfections, the 2010 Census Bureau tally carries an important theme with vital influence on today's middle class—Latino Power. Here is the most telling fact about the head count: They were our growth until trouble hit in 2008.

The 50-plus-million Latinos, by birth more than by immigration, accounted for over 56 percent of our nation's growth during the decade.

Latino adults account for one of every six Americans—and, more important for the future, one in four of America's children are Latino.

Whenever a minority group shatters barriers in such raw numbers, it signals an end to stereotype. There exists in large and steady numbers a vibrant, educated, and growing Latino middle class.

Too many of our leaders imagine this group as immigrant, impoverished, and undocumented. When they use such restrictive thinking about our emerging super-minority they serve both themselves and our nation poorly.

Fully 37 percent of Latino families are making between $40,000 and $100,000 a year.

In the two decades before the millennium, the Hispanic middle class grew by more than 70 percent to nearly 10 million people. That middle-class group also gained impressively in terms of educational achievement, household earnings, and home ownership. Before the crash of 2008, at least 64 percent of middle-class Hispanic families either owned or were buying a home, and 20 percent of those households were headed by someone with a bachelor's or advanced degree, according to HispanTelligence.

Close watchers of the complex ecosystem comprised by those 50 million Hispanics have likened the growth in size and scope to the postwar baby boom.

Creating the apocalyptic vision of an unassimilated super-barrio across the Southwest leads to paranoid thinking and polarization. It simply is not so. Now the largest minority group, Latinos are well down the road to comprising a third of Americans in the next generation or two.

The surge in upscale Latinos was certainly harmed by the Great Recession, but their story has been underreported. This group controls 40 percent of Latino spending power. They are young, with an average age under forty-five, and family oriented, many with households of four or more. They congregate; the majority live in the wider Los Angeles region. But they are forming interesting and sizeable consumer markets in cities like Houston, Miami, and New York.

These middle-class and upscale Latinos consume, educate, and buy homes for themselves in a manner consistent with other ethnicities in the rising middle class—with perhaps a bit greater focus on higher education.

But according to a recent Nielsen study in conjunction with the AHAA, the Voice of Hispanic Marketing, middle-class Hispanics are outpacing the rest of the population in job recovery and their employment rates are higher today than when the Great Recession began.

These upscale Hispanics are educating themselves; college graduation rates are up year over year for the last decade. College enrollments are gaining too. Latino and Hispanic young people are trying to educate themselves. But the college numbers are still small. In 2010, more than 23 percent of all elementary and high school students were Hispanic, but the proportion in college drops sharply to just over 6 percent.

There are other important indicia of health for the higher rungs of the Hispanic middle class. According to Nielsen, one in every eight of these half million Hispanic households have at least one member who owns a business.

The Latino Hourglass

THIS MIDDLE-CLASS LATINO STORY HAS been overshadowed by the incidence of extreme poverty and hardship felt by so many, particularly among immigrant families.

It is a complex mix. The U.S. Census tracks twenty different countries of origin, and still more nations through the categories of "Other Central American" and "Other South American."

The top three countries of origin remain Mexico, Puerto Rico, and Cuba, and while these countries' relative positions have not changed, four new countries grew much faster in the last decade. Salvadorians increased by 152 percent, Dominicans grew by 85 percent, Guatemalans increased by 180 percent, and Colombians nearly doubled in population.

Numerous studies relate the dire consequences these Latino families are facing. They are among our poorest and most troubled citizens.

According to Rogelio Saenz, a professor of sociology at Texas A&M University, the disparity between native and foreign-born Hispanics in our nation has shifted into a classic hourglass figure: About 60 percent of those earning below $25,000 are foreign born, and earning above that level, most are native born. Among the well-to-do and the rich, it's an even split between native and foreign born.

For the bottom of that hourglass, poverty is very much the story—fully 23 percent of the Latinos counted by the Census Department live below the poverty line, as compared to a national average of 14 percent.

According to the same census, African Americans and Native Americans had higher poverty rates—27 percent and 26 percent, respectively.

(To be fair, there are many who think the ranks of poor Latinos are much bigger than reported.)

Countries of origin reflect a wide disparity of poverty rates: Cubans have the lowest at 16 percent, while Dominicans have more than 26 percent.

The story of the ebb and flow of immigration is the great American drama. According to Pew researchers, about 45 percent of Hispanic immigrants are here without legal documentation. But the rates of immigration have changed recently. Asians have surpassed Hispanics as the latest and largest wave of immigrants to American shores, pushing our population of Asian descent to more than 18 million. Asians are for the moment the fastest-growing segment of our population.

2008 AND BEYOND

THE PAINFUL PATH TO ILLEGAL entry into the United States rests on the promise of jobs at journey's end. Without that opportunity, even desperate travelers will choose another path.

Hispanic immigration dropped 31 percent from 2007 to 2010. And birthrates fell by nearly as much.

Women all across our country had 6 percent fewer babies after the debacle of 2008, making 2011 the year with America's lowest recorded birthrate since such statistics were first gathered. For all of the general decline, it was immigrant women, and pointedly Mexican immigrant women, who saw the most significant drop—23 percent—between 2007 and 2010.

According to a Pew Research Center report, the declines cannot solely be attributed to foreign-born immigrant women. U.S.-born Latina women had greater birthrate declines during the same period than U.S.-born women of other ethnic and racial groups.

Considered from the high fertility years of the 1990s, the drop for both native and foreign-born Latinas is even greater—nothing short of a steep slide. Distress over economic security can be a powerful prophylactic.

LATINO REBOUND

THIS DICKENSIAN OUTCOME, THE BEST of times and the worst of times—the lower birth and immigration rates; the growth in poverty, hunger, and homelessness in scale and proportion; the slipping of educational accomplishment—means we must consider carefully the role this group will play in the rebound of the middle class.

According to a report from the Institute on Assets and Social Policy at Brandeis University, fewer than one in five Latino families had the appropriate combination of assets—income, education, health insurance, home, and retirement funds—to ensure middle-class financial security. Nearly half of those studied were at real risk of slipping out of the middle class.

Other studies have pointed to the poor recuperative power that exists for anyone who lost or never owned financial assets for the intervening years from that 2008 study until today.

Many middle-class Latinos just slipped over the precipice. Hispanics had the largest decline in household wealth—more than two-thirds—during the Great Recession.

It would be a mistake to underestimate the role that this group will play in returning our middle class to prosperity. They retain a commitment to educating their children, and even with meaningful (and probably unsustainable) decreases in birthrate, the Centers for Disease Control in Atlanta counted 346,000 births to Latina women in 2011.

Immigrants and their families will continue to be dominant factors in the growth of our nation, because there are many Latinos who have weathered the storm particularly and relatively well.

Yet all that is told is a tale of one city.

Watch for emerging young leaders of the pan-Hispanic Americans. They are successful, educated, and beginning to develop the powerful idea that they need to lift their fellow Latinos if they as a group are to take their rightful place in running things.

A polarized approach to anything involving the huge and growing populace of Hispanics in our nation, whether it is health care or immigration, is misguided. The Democrats enjoy an advantage, certainly, but faced with a group that is only just discovering its voice, it is far too early for the left to gloat or for the right to give up. Jeb Bush and other mainstream Republicans have the capacity to embrace great numbers of this electorate.

In time, particularly with the intense concentration of Hispanics in select states, they will constitute a major voice in our national dialogue.

It is as certain as the tides.

As economic vitality returns, so will the birth and immigration rates for this vibrant and dynamic part of our national heritage. Together we march to the day when a third of Americans will claim Latino descent and, more powerfully, when major cities in California, Texas, Florida, and New York become magnets for concentrations of middle-class Latinos.

These metropolitan centers will soon tip the balance in their states. Other emerging Latino markets, like Honolulu, Salt Lake, D.C., Oklahoma City, and Raleigh, will follow suit.

These next twenty-five years will be the Latino Generation.

CHAPTER SIXTEEN

G, Myself, and I

America's place in global manufacture

Eight high-speed motorcycles formed a *spear as if to pierce the wind.*

But the townspeople of Savar knew that parting the sea of Bengali workers was their primary motive. Nestled in the sweet spot behind the advancing phalanx, a local muscleman known as a "mastan" rode his scrambler like he was astride a Saracen steed.

Pressing both on middle age and the tight leathers stretched across his belly, he had an imperial bearing born not of respect or high office, but resentment and fear. He led by taking.

Local media referred to him as a thug, and political enemies pointed to drugs and arms dealings. He had clawed his way up from nothing.

It was a family affair. His father had sold off a meager scrap of farmland to buy an even simpler slice of in-town Savar real estate. As the small city absorbed industrial growth, that land soared in value. The older man sold off a slice and started a mustard oil business.

The muscleman was connected, not least by his close affiliation with the Awami League, the ruling party in the region since the 1970s.

Savar draws its name from a Muslim phrase, "the lord of all things." About a million souls toil there beside the Bangshi River, which wends its way across the soft alluvial landscape to the Bay of Bengal. Workers' wages are just over a dollar a day, so being lord of all things doesn't require much.

Like many nations, Bangladesh was born in a bath of blood. Independence in 1971 cost a million lives.

In the age-old manner of imperial mapmakers, East and West Pakistan were carved out of the Indian subcontinent by men in conference rooms far removed from realities of the street.

Two Pakistans were united by a common religion in Islam, but divided in far more powerful ways—by culture, physical features, and nearly a thousand miles of Indian territory. As history often narrates, the minority in the West had disproportionate power and wealth, and the East was the denser, poorer population. Gravity ultimately took hold. After elections put East Pakistanis in increasing control, the inevitable civil war was finally joined.

Bangladesh resulted, now the eighth-most-populous country in the world.

Land became precious in the new state. Imagine the United States as a huge blanket, and by lifting the ends more than half of the population slides into a single state the size of Iowa. That's how densely populated Bangladesh is today.

Land for uses beyond farming was rarer still, because huge rivers like the Ganges and the Jamuna and endless tributaries threaded through the soft soil in search of the Bay of Bengal. Southern Bangladesh is a warren of deltas and tributaries, making the development of large cities nearly impossible throughout the coastal Sundarbans.

Seeking enrichment, the mastan had more than party affiliation to help him. After a mentor, Murad Jong, won a seat in Parliament's 2008 elections, the muscleman was appointed a convener for a youth unit of the Awami League. He saw his new role in an expansive light, though the job came with little portfolio other than the requirement to mobilize flash strikes, called "hartals," to suit the party's agenda. Such demonstrations were his specialty.

Another was seizing land.

Both skills were needed because Bangladesh had entered a new race—to the bottom. It offered the globe's garment industry millions of workers willing to bear any privation to make underclothes for the West in return for the lowest wages in the world.

Low wages meant pugnacious pricing for goods—T-shirts in 2015 could be had for half the cost of those in China.

Double-digit increases in Chinese wages led the global garment trade to seek towns like Savar. In due course, Bangladesh's 5,000 factories churned out an astonishing $19 billion of garments a year for export, making it the second-largest apparel maker after China.

Garments shot to 80 percent of the country's exports in 2012, reshaping the entire economy. Four million workers, 85 percent of them women, struggled to find these $40-a-month opportunities. For many, it meant escape from the stockade of farm life and from rural subservience in arranged marriages. Meager though the money was, it provided poor Bengalis their first suspicions of social mobility.

And with a population of 165 million, anyone who complained about conditions could be replaced instantly. So very few did.

This is the soft underbelly of the global supply chain. Don't be fooled by the clipboard or the PowerPoint presentation—it is hard to know all there is to know about how goods are manufactured. It is a murky world of subcontractors and sourcers, where despite best efforts, working conditions are sometimes the kind anyone would consider inhumane. Imagine trying to regulate an industry while $20 billion a year sifts through the nation's fingers. Cash flow like that papers over many sins in a place like Bangladesh.

Yet there were hurdles. Since so little of Savar was conceived as an industrial mecca, engineering entrepreneurship flourished.

Public servants relied on thugs to mount demonstrations when necessary to achieve their goals. Patronage meant turning a blind eye to land seizure and false permitting. In building after building, heavy machinery vibrated in structures designed for another use entirely. Inspections, when they came, were circumspect—focused on child workers and other issues easily dodged by manufacturers.

The gangster imagined new vistas for himself on a couple of parcels of land beside a small pond in Savar.

Still, his unique skills were required to close the deal.

In one case, he was accused of seizing the land outright and sending thugs to the owner's home to seal the arrangement. In another, land with a pond was acquired by simply counterfeiting a deed and taking possession.

It was a time-tested strategy, and for a while it worked brilliantly. The local municipality granted him a permit to build a five-story structure, *though it had no authority to do so. The state-run regulator would later claim that Savar is not an industrial zone and for that reason no factory could be housed in the newly constructed plaza.*

The official was shocked—shocked—that there were reports of manufacturing in this establishment.

The mastan filled the pond and wetlands with sand and rubbish and built a five-story retail and office building, which filled quickly with small factories manufacturing directly or via subcontract for Benetton, Primark, and other well-known retail brands. Much of the output was subcontracted, making it nearly impossible for Western retail brands to trace—and even easier to deny.

Business was booming, so three additional stories were added and a ninth floor was in mid-fabrication. Engineering experts reported that "extremely poor-quality iron rods and cement" were used and the upper floors cantilevered over the street to create an even bigger footprint than the lower floors.

Mohammed Sohel Rana, the strongman whose name was embossed in red letters above the entrance, kept his offices on the ground floor. Tenants manufactured on the upper floors—and five factories employed about 3,500 workers there at wages of about twenty-five cents per hour.

On Tuesday, April 23, 2013, third-floor workers were startled by a loud splitting noise—like a falling tree. Terrified by the appearance of major cracks in the wall, workers fled; an engineer was summoned. Local press was drawn to the commotion.

The engineer who declared the building unsafe was a reasonable judge; he had helped design the structure.

The mastan declared to reporters that namesake Rana Plaza would stand for "a century."

The next morning, men at the premises threatened uneasy workers with dismissal and loss of April wages if they did not get inside. All this delay put managers far behind their aggressive quotas.

At 9:00 a.m., as is common in Bangladesh, electricity stopped flowing.

In the momentary darkness, Bengali workers heard noises familiar to them from many years of brownouts. Heavy generators throughout the building started rumbling. But the familiar suddenly gave way to the terrifying: walls collapsed, floors gave way, and upper stories piled full force onto swaying concrete slabs below, which then gave way . . . and so on . . .

In moments, the building collapsed into itself. During the next days more than 2,000 dusty, terrified workers were pulled from the wreckage. But no amount of energy could save the 1,127 victims sandwiched between floors.

Everywhere in Bangladesh angry workers demanded to know why their women endured such danger to make clothes for the West. Irate protesters took to the streets.

Their wail went viral.

That night, Rana's mother died of a heart attack. Days later, the mastan was caught in Jessore fleeing to the Indian border. Murad and other government inspectors were arrested and detained.

The engineer who declared the building unsafe was also arrested for his role in the building's construction. The government's response had all the feel of a turning page.

Aftershocks from the worst disaster in garment-making history were felt in capitals throughout the world.

But in the end the tragedy was theirs, not ours. We never really owned it—we outsourced it.

———————

BITTERNESS IN BANGLADESH WAS PALPABLE. Five months earlier, during a fire at the Tazreen Fashions factory, laborers were ordered to keep working even after alarms sounded. More than a hundred souls were consumed in a sea of flames. In April 2005, another factory in Savar had collapsed, killing sixty-four and injuring more.

Western retail brands were caught off guard, but should they have been?

Benetton denied a relationship with any factories in the building but changed course when their labels and documents showing their orders were found in the rubble. Kolpana Akter, of the Bangladesh Center for Workers' Solidarity, who helped create a safety accord signed by thirty-one Western retailers, was ironically touring the West describing workplace horrors. She developed a powerful antidote to big-brand denial: crawling into damaged and burned-out factories to photograph designer labels on charred garments. Facts are as stubborn as she is.

Loblaw, the Canadian chain, and Primark, the British low-price retailer, each acknowledged using a factory in the building and formed a compensation fund for victims and their families.

Other brands dodged the bullet.

Disney, unallied with Rana factories, had recently decided to end production of branded merchandise in Bangladesh. The country accounted for less than one percent of the $40 billion of branded merchandise Disney sells each year, but even a single percent was not worth the reputational risk.

Ladies and gentlemen, meet the mouse ears conundrum.

Major retailers and brands face an uncomfortable dilemma. Customers expect huge cost savings on quality goods and, within reason, cleanliness of the working conditions at manufacturing plants.

Balancing these extremes is vexing, because many third-party evaluators and authorizers fail to sufficiently check items like a factory's engineering integrity. Marry to that the penchant for subcontracting parts of the manufacturing process and it gets difficult for even the most earnest brands to police their suppliers.

As countries like Bangladesh, Cambodia, Vietnam, South Korea, and many others seek more business, they can expect even stronger reactions from the world's biggest brands. Reputational hits after events like the Rana Plaza disaster change the economic calculus.

Up to a point.

In spring 2013, nearly two dozen retailers and platinum brands met in Germany to determine how to negotiate greater safety at the factories in Bangladesh.

When brands such as Walmart, Gap, Carrefour, and Li & Fung are in the crosshairs, they react. Across the world, labor organizers are pouncing on Bangladesh. But don't be swayed by public relations.

For Western stockholders this was simply not our tragedy.

Loblaw's stock moved up sharply right after the disaster; both Walmart's and Primark's parent companies hit five-year highs in the weeks after the floors collapsed. (Benetton had gone private the year before.) Shareholders had other things on their minds. And the death of 1,800 Bangladeshis since 2005 making items for Western consumers was overwhelmed by more compelling reasons to buy the stocks.

Consumers owned the clothes, not the tragedy. These garments are made, as the old saying goes, by "hands we never see, by folks we rarely consider." In the end, shoppers care most about saving.

Other voices were heard.

The prime minister of Bangladesh called for an increase in the minimum wage; Pope Francis called it "slave labor," and lesser lights than Mickey Mouse reconsidered Bangladesh.

The outcry raises a basic question: Just how much additional margin on a pair of Western underwear might be needed to fund decent wages and reasonable conditions?

Peanuts in the scheme of things: some analysts say as little as 2 or 3 percent.

Can you imagine the resilience of a 3 percent price increase making it all the way back from a suburban Cleveland retailer to a poor Bengali woman toiling in a steamy factory in the city of Savar?

And what percent of the ultimate retailer profit is that stingy 3 percent addition?

All of it—because textile manufacturing has been in a decades-long race to the bottom. It's a business of profitless prosperity.

And what might happen if Bangladesh's goods started costing more?

The stealthy search for another "lord of all things"—the dark promise of lowest-cost production, Charon the ferryman, your guide on the river Styx, undertaking a quest for the glory of the cheapest undies man ever wrought.

We have watched textiles traverse the path from cottages to mills to modern factories to abandonment. Along those pathways, ethnicity handed their loom on to the next ethnicity in an immigrant's rite of passage. The expedition wandered from New England towns of Lowell and Nashua to the Carolinas and the deeper South, and then to destinations ever farther from our shores.

In its odyssey, the garment trade is always searching for the next flag of convenience. And when the chartered accountants prepare their T list of blame when disaster strikes, who will shoulder the responsibility? Accommodating governments, factory managers, property owners, subcontractors, the endless array of jobbers, sourcers and intermediaries, inspectors and third-party evaluators, trade and decency associations, global brands, platinum and lesser metal retailers . . .

Or should the ultimate blame lie with the American middle class and aspiring Western consumers at every level of our society?

This quest is for the soul of everyday low prices.

You are looking at a massive shape-shifting global enterprise. Major sourcer Li & Fung has as its chief asset a sprawling network spanning more than 60 nations and at least 15,000 suppliers. This massive organism is teeming and dynamic—a direct descendant of consumer choice. Modern supply-chain management means that production shifts quickly from one supplier or locale to another.

And when it does, it takes a prized commodity—jobs. For Americans even more is lost, because manufacturing is a job multiplier in a way that, say, government employment is not.

Apparel manufacture is different from the mass production of other goods . . . and the same.

The ever-shifting pressures of style, color, seasonal turn, and capricious teenage tastes make the creation of today's hottest "look" a challenge to Western brands. Deciding the instant that you read these words what must be in the stores in eight months to a year from now transforms your supply chain into a supply-chain gang. Factories in the emerging world appear and disappear like paranormal spirits and often involve little more than electrical power, worktables, and sewing machines.

And, of course, an able and hungry work force.

Once upon a time, American factories needed eight months and longer to manufacture and deliver a million units of a fleeting fashion item like a bubble dress or a clingy tube-top number.

With global sourcing, the goods can make it from designer sketch to the Mall of America in a mere six weeks—at a slice of the old price.

As the textile belt unbuckled, southern states bled garment jobs to East Asian dynamos like China and India. Other American industries whistled through the graveyard, presuming and perhaps hoping that engineering or process complexity, even local regulation, would serve as sword and shield against the specter of globalization.

Their hopes were misplaced—as out of date as a bubble dress and every bit as dangerous to wear in public.

Other industries chased cheap labor too. And lower tax rates. And more accommodating regulatory requirements in labor, energy, and pollution. And perhaps a little less scrutiny.

Soon everything from autos to pharma to sophisticated semiconductor, computer, and robotics equipment sought offshore manufacture. For some American factories their chief purpose shifted from end-to-end manufacture to the less heady work of final assembly and test. Pulling parts from all over the world and assembling and quality-controlling the resulting automobile meant the traditional label of "an American car" was suddenly a less apt description.

Then we started measuring manufacturing in a one-sided way—and made decisions accordingly. Cockeyed.

THEY WENT THATAWAY

AN OBVIOUS SIGN OF AMERICAN manufacturing decline has been the loss of jobs—but there are other, equally important measures of our might: manufacturing output and competitiveness. They are as important to our economic position as jobs, and these haven't declined.

In the early 1950s, U.S. manufacturing employed about 14 million Americans. By 1979, that number exceeded 19 million. Since that peak, U.S. manufacturing employment has steadily shrunk to below the 1950s levels. Then, thanks to the Great Recession, the bottom fell out.

Not surprisingly, jobs got all the attention—and because of that we missed a few things. Hence we created fewer jobs.

During that same half century American demand for manufactured items exploded and the nation's population more than doubled. Some might call that promising.

What about manufacturing output? Since 1975, U.S. manufacturing output has more than doubled, while jobs are down by nearly a third.

Job losses are painful but do not mean that America has lost its competitiveness. We are a manufacturing behemoth. The average manufacturer is more than three times more productive over the period.

Steelmaking is an example. In 2011, fewer than 100,000 workers produced almost 10 percent more steel than 400,000 workers did in 1980.

Naysayers who trumpet that America doesn't make things anymore should acquaint themselves with the facts. We make different things today with different processes, and sadly for the American worker, it takes a lot fewer jobs. But we are still a world leader in manufacturing. And as developing economies lose their wage advantage we are seeing the first exciting signs of manufacturing rebirth, a re-sourcing of American manufacturing.

But we are not immune to economic trials.

During the agonies of 2008, American manufacturing ground to a near halt. But the rebound is highly illustrative—since the depths of 2009 to late 2012, manufacturing output rose more than 20 percent, but only 4 percent more manufacturing jobs were added during the same period.

Here lies the jobless recovery.

What accounted for the loss of all those jobs?

We have been inadvertently killing them for decades. And, even more painfully, neither business leaders nor politicians have been willing to address these unintended consequences. They'd rather point fingers than fix things.

Understanding why these jobs died will help us re-create new ones.

The police lineup has many suspects: Wall Street, manufacturing CEOs, lobbyists for foreign manufacturers and governments, outsourcers, robots and computers, Walmart, trade deficits, corporate tax rates, currency manipulators, bureaucrats and regulators, emerging markets, working poor, the unions, the community colleges, American workers . . . and, of course, Wall Street again.

And don't forget the federal government, Democrats, Republicans, the Tea Party . . . the middle class, and Wall Street.

A complete picture helps us make choices. This is a movie we have seen before—in farming—but with meaningful differences—especially for the middle class.

In the spring of 1935, almost 7 million farms were planted in the

United States. Today, about 2 million. Though most are family owned, consolidation and concentration have changed the face of farming. In 2007, just 188,000 farms accounted for 63 percent of ag sales.

True, agriculture has slipped to about one percent of GDP and less than one percent of all jobs, but America is still a world agriculture power, ranking third behind China and India. American farms and other agricultural operations still feed the world. But farmers are aging—60 percent of the farmers in this country are fifty-five and older. And labor rolls continue to dwindle.

There is little hope for a true renaissance in agriculture, but manufacturing is an entirely different matter—even if the patterns look the same.

Rather than stop at the jobs-versus-output standoff, let's consider two more angles: what manufacturing means to our overall economy, and American demand for manufactured goods.

How Much Is That T-Shirt in the Window?

IN 1965, MANUFACTURING ACCOUNTED FOR half of the U.S. economy. By 1988 it was down to 39 percent, and in 2012 it was under 12 percent. Think of it—number two in the world and just 12 percent of our GDP. Our economy is a monster.

The service economy and the information, digital, and mobile ages dominate our economic complexion. But manufacturing still has a major role to play.

While America passed its baton to these new services American consumers and businesses kept purchasing manufactured goods. For the last ten years demand for manufactured goods as a share of total U.S. demand has increased. Through good economies and bad, Americans love manufactured items.

Pay no attention to reports from the CBO or economists who point to the shrinking relationship between real manufacturing output and GDP. The declines in output have been more than met by the surge in net imports in the manufacturing sector.

We still want stuff . . . and somebody has to make it.

So we order in, and export jobs in the process. Currency battles have helped the cause.

Now China is losing its wage competitiveness and lower-end manufacturing is drifting away from them. But they are also seeing drift on the higher end. Who picks up those great new jobs?

Unless something is done with the mismatch of our output versus our demand, jobs will suffer—especially in periods of weak economic growth.

And when manufacturing jobs disappear, social mobility suffers, the middle class shrinks, and white-collar jobs follow suit. In the first five years after the millennium and before the '08 meltdown, GM had already furloughed more than 40 percent of its white-collar workers.

Two forces explain what has been happening here: globalization and outsourcing.

These two run together, but they are different. Globalization is really about mobility. Imagine you are a CEO of a large business and you can move capital and technology anywhere in the world. Add the flexibility to move goods, services, management, and even labor wherever you wish. Such flexibility enables companies to craft manufacturing, sales, and support networks which have as their chief goal a higher return on investment (ROI) for the shareholders.

ROI—the ultimate yardstick of corporate prowess. It is the board's final responsibility—the fiduciary obligation to maximize shareholder wealth and often their own. Globalization is like input chess: Move the pieces around the globe to beat ROI targets.

Make it cheap and sell it dear.

Outsourcing is a distant cousin, in many ways a narrower and stingier program with the same objective—improving economic return. Offshoring, as it is also called, means that another country now performs a function or service that was once handled domestically. It's a world of contract manufacture where price per unit is the chief talisman.

The key to globalization is a network of trade agreements that serve to eliminate barriers, tariff or otherwise, to free-flowing goods. Americans faced many hurdles in achieving favored-nation status, but they knew how to bargain with a long-term perspective, something of a lost art.

These arrangements began simply enough. American manufacturers opened up foreign markets by promising to invest, build, or acquire manufacturing capacity abroad. As trade began to flourish, Americans, often with their local manufacturing partner, began to serve not only the foreign country's home market but ours as well. That's when the trouble started.

GATT, the General Agreement on Tariffs and Trade, was forged in 1947 by the United Nations and was to have been absorbed into the ITO (International Trade Organization), which never took flight. Instead, in 1994, GATT was superseded by the World Trade Organization.

In the beginning, freezing and eliminating tariffs kept GATT engaged. American economic growth was unimaginably robust as overseas markets opened up for our goods. When communism fell, billions of people who had been walled off from our country's feasible marketing universe suddenly became potential customers. In the early years, these communist nations faced massive under-employment and lacked meaningful purchasing power. But the largest of these countries possessed untold capacity to build American economic might.

All we asked was to let us build things there for sale in our market—and ultimately in theirs. Here's why: American businesses realized that a full 95 percent of the world's customers are not here, but there—as was the highest-percentage economic growth.

Here's the rub. We had to partner with these foreign countries and patiently grow their consumer markets—because having 95 percent of the customers doesn't mean much if they can't spend money. China realized quickly how this process of maturing a consumer market could work to their advantage. Others nations followed.

Our approach was to commence with local manufacture and on-the-job training of their people in exchange for producing cheap goods for export. Everybody wins . . . but China won just a little bit more.

After GATT and later NAFTA (North American Free Trade Agreement, in 1994), the equation changed. Armed with freedom to shift capital, technology, manufacturing, and intellectual property anywhere in the world, business leaders searched for the manufacture of *quality* goods at the lowest price.

But what was really going on was a competition for a share of the

American middle-class opportunity.

Jump ball for the American dream.

Countries had many ways to compete for the ability to make goods: regulation, taxation, work rules, child labor, non-tariff barrier removal, and investment flexibility were just a few. But none could match the benefit that cheap labor brought to the equation at the time.

For low-end items labor rates are still the trump card.

A few world thinkers grew anxious about the sea change created by globalization and outsourcing. Their worries fell on deaf ears.

British financier Sir James Goldsmith authored *The Trap* in 1993. He and others testified before Congress that the ability to freely manufacture "there" in order to sell "here" would have profound and lasting impact on our home-country employment.

In a Delphic prediction, Goldsmith argued that the long-term result would be increasing concentration of wealth, massive disruption in manufacturing employment, particular hemorrhaging on a local level and a dislocation of the will of the major companies from the needs of society— and, most potently, the steady dissolution of the middle.

Prosperity would be tilted toward the few, they predicted. And while the markets would naturally soar, the middle class and the working poor would miss out.

Massive expansion of corporate profits occurred when jobs once performed by Americans were aptly managed by workers earning a wage forty times lower when capital, technology, and all other inputs were held equal.

The freedom of movement that is the essence of global free trade raised natural questions, and they are little different today.

How can a chief executive and a board of directors choose to manufacture any place but where quality goods can be made cheapest and that offers the highest return on investment—even if it means job loss in America?

Is it right to judge the health of an economy simply by the size of the profits of its major corporations?

Re-importation created a different case.

When companies use cheap overseas labor to manufacture goods for re-importation, what they are saying to their home-country workers is that they are too expensive and that the company is dis-employing them to manufacture there and sell here. With re-importation, higher corporate profitability is created without a matching expansion of jobs in the home country.

Or, more properly, without a matching program to create more jobs along the food chain. What has happened instead is that the value added provided by American workers is cleaved off their paycheck and is shared instead with the much cheaper foreign laborers and with the stockholders.

Guess who gets most of the pie?

Ronald Reagan's chief of the Council of Economic Advisors, Murray Weidenbaum, explained that companies outsource to gain entrance to overseas markets certainly, to reduce the cost of producing products, and to enhance their competitive edge in the global marketplace. The last point is the most important to American corporates—it is a global donnybrook, and being a high-cost manufacturer seals a corporation's fate.

In the end, outsourcing allows companies to save money in production while providing cheaper goods for American citizens.

Again the last point is the most important. Americans lust for cheap, quality goods, and whole retail ecosystems have been created to cater to this need.

Economists and proponents of outsourcing point to the intersection of these two important points—the global arms race for lowest-cost manufacture and the ability to provide everyday low prices for the American consumer. They say that higher corporate profits result from free trade and that those increased profits mean more new and higher-value-added jobs are created domestically.

And lower-cost items mean that Americans are better off. Excess funds mean more consumption, and therefore more investment and hiring by domestic companies.

In fact, a batch of studies initially confirmed the economic theory that exporting jobs abroad creates even more and better job opportunity here because by buying cheaper our savings could be redeployed into higher-return activities.

For a while these economists were right . . . until they weren't.

Job Divorce, American Style, 2008

IN 2008, TRICKLE DOWN BECAME melt-down. At best, we had hit the reset button, with a long, torturous cycle necessary for workers to crawl out of the wreckage.

What happened was a divorce of corporate mission from the interests of American society as a whole. American companies prospered mightily for decades, but American workers at all levels shared increasingly less of that prosperity. We have seen a surge in stock prices and in corporate cash and profitability since the crash of 2008, with modest growth in jobs.

Corporate cash has really exploded. Holdings of the thousand biggest nonfinancial companies at the end of 2012 surged to $1.5 trillion, nearly doubling from the $820 billion held in pre-crash 2007. Fifty companies held 62 percent of the total, and five companies—Apple, Microsoft, Google, Cisco Systems, and Pfizer—amassed more than a quarter of the cash. Apple alone had nearly 10 percent of the total—almost $150 billion. By early 2015 and their $18 billion blowout quarter, the largest profit ever earned by any company in history, that Apple stash only got larger.

Through 2015 the corporate cash has kept building—perhaps portending massive mergers, and causing activists like Carl Icahn to demand that some of the money be returned to shareholders.

This jobless recovery (fewer new ones than can accommodate population growth) points to a sluggish economic experience for labor and middle management while the multinational itself prospers. Creative destruction of manufacturing jobs brings neither white-collar expansion nor the opportunity to retrain displaced American workers.

At best, the agonizing pace of trickle down and redistribution means that over a very long cycle, maybe as long as a generation, creative destruction may lead to economic rebirth somewhere else.

Not necessarily here.

Manufacturing is a bad-to-worse scenario where significant job losses occur in economic downturns and only modest gains are created, if any at all, in recovery.

An intervention is required.

Economists gamely point to some white-collar and new-technology job expansion. But those meager improvements have been dwarfed by the stock market's surging enthusiasm for the renewed profitability of American corporates. (The stock market [S&P] has more than doubled to an all-time high from its nadir in March 2009.)

But real wages are down.

We were wrong on the community level too. We all know towns bound up in reliance on a major local employer. When those communities face downsizing or abandonment, there are rarely replacement jobs or training initiatives to complete the virtuous circle described by the arc of free international trade.

Since 2001, nearly 5 million manufacturing jobs are gone—an astonishing 29 percent loss in a decade. Some 42,000 factories have been shuttered. Whole industries have left the United States. (In 1980, 1.3 million Americans worked in the apparel industry and fewer than 150,000 do so today.) And other industries are suffering in a way that signals trouble down the road. The culprit?

Well, one may surprise you. Undercapacity.

Factories at low capacity simply cannot compete on cost per unit, since overheads must be absorbed by fewer units. There are only two solutions: generate more through put or consolidate your factories. Thousands of factories across the country are hovering in this purgatory, operating at less than optimum capacity and hoping for a surge in demand.

Undercapacity is bad for job watchers, since boosts in manufacturing do not bring increased capital expenditure and a flood of new jobs—instead, current capacity absorbs the increase with marginal job growth.

There were a number of studies in mid-decade concluding that more jobs came to the United States from other countries than we sent abroad. That's tough to gauge.

Truth be told, we really never measured the number of lost jobs in any granular way—few are the multinationals who would volunteer how many jobs they have exported to low-cost countries. These move in the dead of night.

And it is far from easy to assign increases in hiring somewhere else to the labor losses in the manufacturing sector.

It's what economists and priests call a leap of faith. And what little we have of it does not seem justified.

The loss of manufacturing carries with it another major sting with particular vituperation for the middle class. Manufacturing typically accounts for 70 percent of our spending on R&D. It also carries with it the glorious economic creation called the multiplier. Studies vary widely in describing just how many additional jobs come and go with the addition or subtraction of a manufacturing job. (A range of .40 to two additional jobs, but some studies go even higher.)

Whatever the number, every manufacturing job requires more blue and white collars to manage, sell, source, extract raw material from, distribute, and store the product.

Economists are in a tizzy because many secretly suspect the government may have mis-measured the true impact of surging imports and outsourcing. If that is the case, then we have understated our import dependency and overstated our output and competitiveness.

Never confuse a recovery of economic indices with a real recovery.

And what has been the result? Hourly wages have declined in real terms, and economic value added in manufacturing has increasingly gone to shareholders and management.

Today, many of these workers are never destined for the middle class, where once upon a time they might have been. We have traded social mobility for a cheap pair of underwear and a tube top.

For Whom the Bell Tolls

FEWER WELL-PAID BLUE-COLLAR WORKERS AND fewer two-paycheck households means that the middle class shrinks. Once upon a time, upper-middle-class aspirations and white-collar careers were comfortably outside the rim of concern that affected manufacturing workers.

No longer. Increasingly, manufacturing workers have been the leading indicator—a wheezing canary in the mines.

Before 2008, white-collar employment held up and selectively (by industry) increased as manufacturing steadily slipped. At the upper end, real wages were increasing even as middle-class and laborers' real wages declined.

But the steady shift in the way we manufacture and, equally important, purchase manufactured products from overseas sources ultimately infringed on the higher reaches of the middle class.

Corporates slashed their white-collar workforces. It was one thing when "undereducated . . . stuck in the past" blue-collar workers watched their jobs ship off to destinations east. But it was quite another when X-ray technicians, pharmaceutical engineers, and CPAs watched their livelihoods ship out.

Forrester Research takes the fifteen years commencing in 2000 and forecasts 3.3 million job losses overseas, many of them high paying and white collar.

By the way, offshoring white-collar jobs is sometimes a lot easier than moving manufacturing. Gone are worries about shuttering factories, a village collapse, shipping-lane pirates, or labor problems at home. There aren't many picketers in the executive suite. White-collar workers carry no tariffs and their footprint is merely a desk with connectivity—all easily moved in times of duress.

And quietly done.

Here's the rub for CEOs: If corporates are continually rewarded with higher stock prices for creating a jobless recovery with lower real wages, then what inducement do they really have to massively increase American employment or to bump compensation?

Our tax policy is an industrial policy. Same with our free-trade initiatives. We induce CEOs to move productive activity elsewhere. And it can hurt a lot more than simply a lost job. America lost more than a quarter of its tech jobs in the last decade. And the National Science Board recently reported that a growing percentage of research and development operations have been moved overseas too.

That's a negative multiplier.

Is it right to ascribe job losses in a cause-and-effect way to the growing and massive U.S. trade deficit? In this parlance we have literally exported jobs in exchange for cheap goods. There are numerous analysts who see matters in that straightforward manner.

Perhaps too simply.

Some see shrinking manufacturing jobs as a natural evolution of a service superpower. A growing service sector usually means the country has growing per capita income. The trick, of course, is that it is not useful to look at manufacturing as a single industry. Many sub-industries lend themselves more naturally to robotics and other technology; others stubbornly resist the ability to squeeze out labor content.

Not all of the manufacturing jobs lost were simply exported to low-cost locales. Productivity increases brought on by computer and robotics technology meant that fewer laborers were needed to run the factory.

And, in a plus for the middle class, increasing IT and other tech-support jobs had the look and feel of higher-value-added vocations coming as a direct result of the productivity enhancements in manufacturing.

That has helped the economy even as jobs marched out the door. Nearly three quarters of U.S. real GDP growth in the 2000–07 period came from increases in productivity and the rest from employment gains.

That's something worth aspiring to—a manufacturing renaissance built on American industrial productivity. But that also means less good news for jobs.

America's purchase of cheap manufactured goods is often identified as the chief reason that job losses have been so severe. It is such a temptation to blame this jobless recovery on trade deficits.

Our counterparties have a habit of keeping their currency weak to help their exports. Other tricks, known as offsets, require that you build a local factory in order to get access to some of their goods. That's why so many tech companies locate factories in China.

THE TARIFF TRAP

PLEASE DON'T BE PERSUADED BY those isolationists who say the answer to our jobs problem is as simple as swapping one for another, or placing massive tariffs on cheap goods.

If you are unconvinced, look at trade deficits for manufacturing in-dustries by group from 1989 to just before the Great Recession. The trade deficit grew by about $700 billion during this eighteen-year period.

The largest deficit growth ($237 billion) was oil and gas, obviously having little to do with poorly paid overseas workers or unfair labor prac-tices. The second largest was computer technology ($109 billion), which may have a labor advantage but certainly requires higher-value-added manufacturing.

These don't have the feel of the Bangladeshi problem writ large; the battle for manufacturing jobs has many more weapons.

G, MYSELF, AND I

AFTER WATCHING THE RISE OF the Chinese export monster, countries around the world are printing more money to weaken their cur-rency and boost their export competitiveness. U.S. and European policy makers are naturally distressed that such a round of currency devalua-tions might destabilize the fragile global recovery.

Trouble is, any question of currency devaluation is a bit ticklish for industrialized nations that have already embarked on a path to boost their home economies with accommodating monetary policies which carry as a side effect the weakening of their currencies.

Quantitative easing by the Fed—QE ONE/TWO/ETC has already caused angst and envy among financial policy makers, because buying back our bonds has kept interest rates low and the greenback weak even if the primary target was to inch us toward recovery. Europe has re-sponded by deciding to deliver a no-growth economy in 2015, which is keeping the dollar strong.

Mario Draghi, president of the European Central Bank, has commit-ted to his own version of QE—committing to a trillion Euro asset pur-chase program to combat deflation. The markets cheered. Suppose every-one chose quantitative easing by buying back their own securities?

Japan has also amplified its government securities purchase program in Prime Minister Shinzo Abe's massive attempt to boost his country's economy. As a by-product it weakened the yen. Judging by his campaign rhetoric, the yen reaction was the opposite of an unintended consequence.

As the old saying goes (approximately), emulation is the sincerest form of strategy.

The G-7 nations (United States, Japan, Germany, France, United Kingdom, Italy, and Canada) have all agreed that unilateral currency intervention isn't kosher and that free-market economics and the purity of exchange trades require noninvolvement—except of course when the life of the child is at stake.

But deep inside they each believe that their currency is too important to leave entirely to the whim of the markets. However, what these countries, including the United States, have been doing is very different from China's intervention.

Chinese Take Out

NOT TO BE OUTDONE, CHINESE local governments have piled up $3 trillion in debt, in sync with the nation's intense investment-stimulus program. Borrowings now dwarf its GDP (debt to GDP was 125 percent in 2008 and is well over 200 percent today).

China watchers resort to increasingly dramatic language to cast doubt on China's investment-driven growth model. I like "debt bomb" best. No one is making a bigger bet on themselves than the Chinese—which leads one to ponder their command of two simple words: Bad debt.

But when the government controls the banks, the brokerages, the companies, and the regulators, there is always room for negotiation.

Summertime and the credit is easy, fish are jumping, and the lending is high. At the end of 2009, Chinese credit was $9 trillion; today, it is over $24 trillion. To put that growth into context, imagine every loan by every financial institution in the U.S. banking system—that figure is smaller than the $15 trillion increase that China borrowed in the last five years.

Keep your currency weak and invest passionately in your home infrastructure.

This is the world of G-Me. Forget the G-7 and the G-20. Economic physicians say heal thyself.

Are these self-centered G-Me strategies the key to climbing out of the 2008 dustbin?

The answer is not about economic theory but instead about economic destiny. With only so many bets to make, some nations have decided to bet on themselves.

Free-spirited monetary policy plus stimulus of the home market is the new black.

Overreliance on monetary maneuvers has worked thus far for the United States without the attendant inflation that inhabitants of the textbook world tend to obsess over.

But for highly indebted nations, good things like inflation come to those who wait.

Renaissance Fair

A MORE LASTING WAY TO win than a clandestine currency battle fought in plain sight is to actually create your own renaissance.

The biggest problem with the proponents of the manufacturing renaissance is that America never really experienced the dark ages, just cycles of pain.

If you ignore a few recession-plagued years after World War II, U.S. manufacturing has achieved new heights for years in all the measures we have talked about—output, value added, productivity, return on investment, and profits (OK, episodically).

Just not jobs.

Proportionately manufacturing did decline, but it is important to distinguish a slowing in growth from a slowdown. Service businesses exploded while manufacturing simply grew. (Obviously, when the bough broke in 2008 it was a cradle-and-all situation.)

Some people simply refuse to look at the bigger picture—and rely exclusively on the loss of jobs as the only indication of our manufacturing prowess. But employment cannot be the sole barometer of well-being in manufacturing—not when value added has been in upward trajectory for so long. It was only in 2011 that China pushed past the U.S. as the leading manufacturer.

The Boston Consulting Group (BCG) and others foresee a wave of manufacturing jobs returning—a super-Renaissance if you will. It's one of those part right/part wrong scenarios but worth examining.

The essence of their thinking is this:

Years of double-digit wage hikes in China have eroded the labor gap between us. Blended with the energy dividend of cheap domestic natural gas and the availability of vast reservoirs of shale oil in the Bakken, American manufacturers are wise to reshore jobs and processes from China et al.

Some breathlessly forecast more than 5 million reshored jobs by 2025.

The problem with their analysis is that it is exactly correct.

We do have a shrinking disparity between pay stubs and a widening one for natural gas costs. BCG sees a convergence of average wages between the United States and China in 2015.

What has been happening in real terms is that the cost of average employment in China has been rising while the cost of labor in real terms in the United States has been flat.

But anyone operating in the real world of China trade and manufacturing knows that these are two important—but just two of many—inputs necessary to determine where best to manufacture.

Take the example of technology companies—high-value-added enterprises with skills we possess. One of the biggest challenges for a reshoring is getting these tech companies to break their supply chain.

Suppose you are in the small computer or TV screen or mobile device business. For a generation the semiconductors, memory, and other components necessary to build your products have been manufactured in Asia. Chinese policy makers have made little secret of the linkage of building factories in their midst and access to scarce resources and products. These offsets matter when constructing your supply chain.

Beware the analysis that creates a couple of magic benchmarks that, like levees in a dam, will suddenly flood back when the proper heights are reached. It is never that simple, particularly when we have not been manufacturing many of these items for more than twenty-five years.

Finally, consider the most basic economic question: Where are the most new customers? Judging by the massive and growing spending appetites of the Chinese, there is a true inducement to keep your capacity local for the day when the slumbering giant awakens.

President Xi has spent enormous political capital in the hopes of introducing true market forces into the rigged game of planned Chinese capitalism. If his wish is to create a vibrant Chinese middle class that purchases goods at a rate that begins to approach that of the American consumer, why would American manufacturers pull up stakes and trudge back home now?

After a generation of patience, it would be putting away our cymbals at the moment of crescendo.

What has happened is that many of the indicia of a Renaissance are episodic and we are hoping for a trend. Every time an economist sees two dots they draw a line through it.

Certainly, there are glimmers of good news in the car business. BMW, Volkswagen, Daimler, and other world auto brands have ramped up production in the United States. Caterpillar has expanded in Texas, and NCR is moving back some production of ATMs to Georgia.

Even the Frisbee has been zipped back across the Mexican border for a major part of its production.

But for every BCG study predicting a Renaissance in American manufacturing are realists who say that the rebound is temporary, a result of economic malaise everywhere on the planet.

OUR TIME TO SHINE

THE NUMBERS ARE ENCOURAGING, BUT pragmatics suggests they won't last without help from all of us.

The truth is, we should want BCG consultants to be right. We need them to be right. And the thing to do is move heaven and earth to make them right.

Once and for all, we must decide to support a rebound in skill manufacturing. Not the old-style widgets for pennies with low skill and poor returns on capital. That won't be a tide that lifts many boats.

We need a grand aspiration that captures the next wave of manufacturing—3-D printing, robotics, and the cutting edge of technologies in production, resources, parts, basic materials, nano-technology, bioengineering, aeronautics, and, yes, even in considering Amazonian drone delivery—if not to individuals at home, at least between businesses.

There is a new manufacturing model, and it is ours to devise and create. Pharmaceutical and biotechnology, super-materials, intelligent automotive, mobile applications—the wave is way offshore, and it is approaching.

We need to acknowledge that our leaders on both sides of the aisle have been dancing a pantomime of job creation.

New manufacturing will not be the job panacea that old manufacturing was. We have fallen prey to the age-old problem of mislabeling and generality. Worse, we miss the obvious: the down-waging of the American middle class.

Recession has taken the core out of the middle earners. According to the San Francisco Federal Reserve, mid-wage occupations earning between $13.80 and $21.13 per hour made up 60 percent of the job losses during the recession, and they made up just over 25 percent of those added in recovery.

Manufacturing renaissance is the key to fixing a piece of our dwindling middle class.

But nothing is more important than jobs . . .

CHAPTER SEVENTEEN

LA GRIPPE

The United States of underemployment

DEEP IN THE CITY, LONG AFTER *urban sprawl had absorbed the ambling cow paths, a three-acre oasis stands as the sole reminder of what had been there before. Wrapped in wrought-iron fencing, the lushly planted plaza is adorned by a centerpiece fountain that is bisected by diagonal walkways like an amulet between crossed swords. The ornately arched Newberry Library presides over bordering Walton Street, and also the flowering of the park's feisty oral tradition.*

Chicago has a rich history of debate and oratory—the sort of fiery speechmaking that turned colorful characters into anarchists.

Long ago the park swarmed with speakers of every persuasion, especially on warm summer nights. Buttressed by left-leaning mainstays like Lucy Parsons, whose husband was hanged in the Haymarket affair, and feminist/ Marxist (or was it Marxist/feminist?) Martha Biegler; unionists like Big Bill Haywood and many other soap-boxers from the International Workers of the World; the grounds played host to throngs who came to enjoy speechmaking as a contact sport.

After the 1920s and '30s the radicals were joined by thousands of other speakers well-known and unheard-of—Clarence Darrow, Carl Sandburg, and Slim Brundage, beat poet laureate of the park and sometime manager of the oh-so-exclusive speakeasy Dill Pickle Club.

The grounds had been christened Washington Square, but the cacophony when thousands gathered to listen and heckle led locals to fittingly dub the park Bughouse Square—bughouse being period-speak for a mental institution.

Into this ward wandered a young boy who got swept up by the chorale. "I came up the year the Titanic went down," he would often recount. He was Bronx born, the third son of a tailor and seamstress Polish immigrants who bolted to Chicago in search of greater opportunity. Settling into their rooming house at the corner of Ashland and Flourny on the Near West, the elfin son filled his ears with the tales and conversations that whirled between the lobby and the square nearby. Later, his parents purchased the Wells-Grand Hotel on the Near North. There among the guests began his real education.

Voices like these, arriving and disembarking from every stop and station, served as the chorus of his life; but it would take the lad some wandering before he found his own voice. And ours.

Bored of bond counting for the U.S. Treasury, the young law school graduate found refuge from legal ministrations in FDR's Works Progress Administration's Federal Writers Project. He was a journeyman of his craft, writing scripts, working in soap operas like "Ma Perkins" and "Road of Life," and appearing in repertory theater.

At Chicago Rep, his given name was the same as the star's, so he temporarily borrowed another from Chicago literary character Studs Lonigan. Seven decades later, he still hadn't returned it. He found work as a disc jockey, spinning eclectic tunes from jazz to country on a show he called "The Wax Museum."

The always-short-of-cash bachelor encountered Ida Goldberg, a Wisconsin social worker. "She made a lot more money than I did," he recalled. "It was like dating a CEO. I borrowed twenty bucks from her on our first date. I never paid her back."

She would become his most important audience, and his wife of sixty years.

He found his voice and a larger audience at a burgeoning fine-arts radio station where his brand of conversational interview with folks large and small struck a nerve. His daily hour-long show ran from 1952 to 1998—an unprecedented forty-five-year uninterrupted run.

His questioning style was tough-guy tender, marinated by all things Chicago. For guests, he uniquely shied away from actors and politicians, though he made exceptions. Once, after an hour-long interview with a young Marlon Brando, the actor was so bemused by the questioner that the typically reticent performer insisted on spending another hour.

The diversity of his guests is hard to fathom: Martin Luther King, John Kenneth Galbraith, Gloria Steinem, Louis Armstrong, Aaron Copland, Bob Dylan, Tennessee Williams, Leonard Bernstein, Carl Sagan, Federico Fellini, Buster Keaton, Dizzy Gillespie, Janis Joplin, Frank Zappa, Gore Vidal, Brian Wilson, Martha Graham, Marc Chagall, James Baldwin, Buckminster Fuller, Maya Angelou, and Zero Mostel—thousands from every walk.

Studs Terkel's preoccupation was not what they did for a living but what they did for a life.

Over 9,000 hours of interviews were saved by the Chicago History Museum. Listen to any of them. They are like long-meter hymns. He was a master listener, panning for gold dust in the lives of his guests. His questions had the uncanny ability to gently unlock and reveal, and the gravelly growl grown soft with the passing decades cooed and cajoled in such a respectful way.

His was a unique instrument. So special, in fact, that Andre Schiffrin, the publisher and editor of Pantheon Books, approached him in the 1960s. Would he be willing to turn that sensitive ear and that gently penetrating query into a series of conversations about life in Chicago?

What followed was a book called Division Street, *which was a series of seventy conversations with Chicagoans from every walk of life transcribed into a bound volume of oral history. The compendium was a runaway success.*

What followed was an epoch spent transcribing the American soul. No life was off-limits for the mosaic Terkel was piecing together: prostitutes, Klansmen, executives, poets, teachers, cops, firefighters, soldiers, prizefighters, and jazz singers—anyone who lent color to the warp and woof of the American fabric.

Division Street *was code for the schisms in our society, and Terkel feasted on stories he first encountered in Bughouse Square. In 1970, he compiled* Hard Times, *a Depression-era memoir, followed by his seminal book*

Working: People Talk About What They Do All Day and How They Feel About What They Do *in 1974. It would become his best-known work—and was even adapted to a Broadway musical.*

Terkel spent three years interviewing more than 130 people about their jobs—not just about their daily bread but their daily meaning. Each interview took a day or two. These were real talk, nothing subconscious or careful. Except for a small handful of famous people like actor Rip Torn, everyone was given a pseudonym.

His questions were edited out of the final book, but if you listen to the raw tapes you can hear the gently probing master: "What's your typical day like?" "What's the first thing you do?" "Why do you say being a housewife is the bottom of the totem pole?"

To that last question, when the woman answered "Anyone can do it," he gently replied, "Not everyone can be a great mother."

His affection is genuine and relaxing—never gotcha journalism. Just a conversation.

The Working *tapes have ample reserves of gripe and grouse about employers and bosses. But the patient inquisitor keeps delving, and time after time when the smoke of animus clears, profound meaning surfaces. A twenty-five-year night-shift waitress says, "I feel like a ballerina"; an interstate trucker with 2,500 trips hauling steel says, "Every load is a challenge, and when you off-load it . . . you have the feeling of being vital in the whole cycle of the manufacturing process."*

A priest talks about saving souls and helping solve social problems: "I was a fisherman pulling people out of troubled waters. Trying to bring them back to life with artificial respiration and Band-Aids. Then I'd put them back on the other side of the river into the same society that pushed them in."

Terkel's genius was unlocking the eloquence in everyone. His life's work was finding the best in ours.

Actor Rip Torn: "I've done jobs I wasn't particularly proud of . . . You try and make it a little better for your own self-respect. That's what's changed in the nature of work in this country—the lack of pride in the work itself. A man's life is his work . . . Even in Mexico there was something unique about the road work. The curbing is not laid out by machine, it's handmade. So there's little irregularities. That's why the eye is rested . . . because it's crafts-

manship. You see humanity in a chair. And you know 7,000 didn't come out in one day. It was made by some man's hands. There's artistry in that, and that's what makes mankind happier. You work out of necessity, but in your work, you gotta have a little artistry too."

———————————

BY 2014 . . . SIX YEARS AFTERWARD, malaise still gripped New York City like a flu that would not let go. The nation was seeing green shoots of rebirth in September 2014, but for so many Americans the song remained the same. A new underclass had been created. Lungs everywhere rattled as yet another winter of discontent bore down on them.

Like an art house film with *Forgotten* somewhere in the title, wide swaths of American citizenry were stuck in the nightmare of joblessness and misery. Everything was reduced to its most basic. The average age of a homeless person in New York City slipped to nine.

Think of it—do you remember being nine years old?

For all the rebounding markets, the detritus of the mortgage explosion could be found like a trail along the everyday streets anywhere you traveled.

America's jobless numbers contained this powerful central irony:

The evaporation of wealth in the stock market and the housing industry in 2008 was, over half a decade later, still haunting people who had never owned a stock or a bond or a house in their lives.

A BREAK IN THE INACTION

MIDDLE-CLASS JOBS HAD FLOWN AND an unemployed class faced more dire prospects that were seemingly immune to market correction: long-term joblessness, what the news networks now call "food insecurity"—the artist formerly known as hunger—and a new one for the folks at home, "underemployment."

"Underemployed" is one of those terms of art, not science, to the extent that someone somewhere considers economics a science. (It's actually more like dueling expert witnesses in a crime-of-passion trial.) It reminds me of an old Studs Terkel line: "I quote Einstein whenever I can because nobody ever wants to argue with *him*." Just hire an economist to support your point of view, and carry on.

New York City's underemployment rate for the first half of 2013 surged a full percentage point past the state's rate to a whisker under 15 percent. Pick any period and the problem remains: Joblessness was proving intractable despite what the overall movement in unemployment numbers indicated, and like a virus it was mutating.

Many leaders still clung to the take-two-aspirins-and-call-me-in-the-morning solution: More demand equals more jobs, by which prescription you simply fix demand and we're all set; but others began to wonder if something more structural might be at fault.

So who are these "term of art" underemployed? Clinical as if dipped in ice, the figure counts that new underclass of workers officially unemployed; those working part time who wished they had more hours (call it 100 percent of part timers); and those lost souls who are no longer counted as unemployed but who are willing to work. This last group they now call, with infinite understatement, "discouraged workers."

What is emotionally missing from this odd catch-all is the fundamental shift these underemployed are facing. After bruising losses of decent middle-class jobs paying $50,000 to $80,000-plus and a probably permanent shrinkage of Wall Street jobs, came a trickle and then a flood of new jobs that paid lower wages, often without benefits.

Boosters claimed that from the spring of 2008 until the start of 2014, New York State saw a net gain of more than 100,000 jobs.

A rebound, right? But many of the job gains were concentrated in New York City in low-wage industries like restaurants, retail, and home health services.

And the story can't end there. Population growth means that even though the state was ahead a hundred grand on these less-good jobs, it was still short more than 150,000, according to the Fiscal Policy Institute's study of the state's Department of Labor data.

In a nutshell, we have replaced great jobs with fewer jobs in low-paying sectors. And many who saw their hours reduced lost both benefits and wages but were still not eligible for unemployment funds. All of which makes it hard for New Yorkers on the margin of employment to build anything resembling a stable future.

The missing word is *risk*. Everything about the job prospects for the underemployed involves more risk.

And just how hard can you work if you are one of the nearly 50 million Americans who are "food insecure"?

THE BROKEN CIRCLE

IN THE OPENING PAGES, I described how Henry Ford reacted when faced with the dilemma of a sluggish economy just as he was introducing the Model T. Blasting through all convention, he simultaneously raised wages and shrunk the workday. He was widely derided as a socialist who would destroy his company.

But Ford was a canny entrepreneur and also a believer in social justice. Or maybe he was long-term greedy versus short-term greedy.

He knew that low wages dog a market with uncertainty and risk—purchasing suffers and growth is stymied. Steady income and decent pay have the exact opposite effect, because all customers are workers and if they are confident they will want, for example, goods like a Model T of their own. And damned if they didn't.

We have lived in this virtuous circle of confident, well-paid workers buying more merchandise, which in turn feeds business expansion, capital expenditure, and more hiring. It wasn't until the 1960s that economic math was put to the phenomenon. Arthur Okun devised a law which seems today un-prosecutable but had worked for the United States for generations.

Okun theorized that a drop in the unemployment rate of one percent required a 2 percent increase in GDP above its natural rate to earn it back—and, of course, vice versa. He quantified the natural relationship between inputs of labor and total output.

But the Yale professor's rule of thumb has failed us.

From 1948 to the oil embargo of 1973, the productivity of non-farm-workers nearly doubled, as did average hourly wages. But a sea change occurred in the late 1970s. Despite a productivity increase of over 80 percent from the embargo to 2011, average wages rose by just over 4 percent. If you include the benefits that were awarded, total compensation rose only 10 percent over the period (this according to the Economic Policy Institute).

Imagine two curves:

On one is the growth of corporate profits, which trended upward in the 1990s and the millennium, hitting a 2006 peak as a share of total income not seen since before World War II. It's just a beautiful line pointing, as we love to see, to the northeast.

On the same chart is another line tracing the proportion going to wages and salaries. This goes southeast, the opposite direction, down to the lowest level since the rather ominous date of 1929.

And then came the Great Recession. Gone were Henry Ford's steady jobs and rising pay. Gone, too, is the virtuous circle.

Rising pay won't lift the economy by itself. In Germany, average hourly pay has grown five times faster since the mid-1980s than America's has—and the Merkel economy is still struggling.

What's missing is the Ford ingredient. Time after time, we have seen the economy lift when the middle class enjoys a reasonable slice of the gains. Today they are starved for the kind of jobs and the kind of opportunities and the kind of training that has made our nation soar.

Today's dilemma isn't just replacing the 8 million jobs lost during the dark days. We need to accommodate the population growth since 2008 too. And we are in denial about how that can best be done. Obviously, demand must grow, but we also have structural issues that must be urgently addressed.

Every politician pays lip service to caring about job creation, but our national political establishment is basically a spent force. No one in Washington looks farther down the road than the next primary or ballot box. Politicians have squandered too much political capital on turf battles and prosecuting the longest wars in our history to confront the enemies within. Here, every chess game ends in stalemate, and the president and congressional leadership have proved themselves incapable of true engagement and compromise. Nothing gets done.

Worse yet, we can't even agree on the nature of the problem.

BOTH RIGHT/BOTH WRONG

WE NEED TO UNDERSTAND WHY the jobs outlook is so frustratingly resistant to recuperation. We are using old-time tools to fix a newfangled problem.

The debate is whether the high unemployment we are facing is cyclical, brought on by weak demand and lingering effects of the recession, or structural, which means that there is something fundamental that has changed that, if left unchecked, will establish a new normal rate of joblessness.

People argue their corner—structural versus cyclical—to extremes, when in fact both are right. And wrong.

After studying the matter extensively, I find it is nearly impossible in real time to discern how much weight is attributable to each. Hence the dilemma, because different solutions work more effectively depending on what is the true cause.

Cyclical unemployment is influenced by the return of demand to the economy. It's as if the line is slack and by pulling on both sides and tightening the cord, the economy grows and jobs happen. Much of the expansionary policy of the government has been directed toward getting the slack out of the economy. And if you force yourself to be undemanding as to time and tangible results, the plan is limping along.

Fortunately, under Ben Bernanke and, more recently, Janet Yellen, we have had an expansionist Federal Reserve. Under their leadership, the Fed seems as concerned about jobs and standards of living as they have historically been about combating inflation. (In 1978, Congress passed the Humphrey Hawkins Law, which gave the Federal Reserve the dual mandate of protecting the value of the dollar while trying to bring about full employment.)

The Honorable Ms. Yellen famously declared on Capitol Hill, "I'm committed to achieving both parts of our mandate."

If anything, she and her predecessor have been dovish on taming inflation. But the Fed has had to step up, because both Congress and the president have been entirely too passive in the face of catastrophic unemployment and its financial repercussions.

Talk about a squandered opportunity. Any leader in the Congress or the White House who had truly made jobs and middle-class well-being the centerpiece of both their words and deeds since 2008 would have achieved heroic status.

After all, the warnings had been there for everyone to see for a long time.

No matter how you slice it, America's jobs crisis began fifteen years ago, long before the subprime blowup knocked the entire economy akimbo. Our job-creation machinery had already begun to sputter and, in some sectors, break down.

In "The Phantom 15 Million" in the *National Journal* in 2011, Jim Tankersley outlined the issue. Step back and take a look at the pattern between the recession in 2001 and the meltdown in 2008. The American economy enjoyed solid if slower GDP growth; soaring corporate profits; buoyant equities markets; lending super-liquidity that financed a company buying spree by both corporations and private equity firms; and a real-estate expansion as never seen in our history.

It was a classic example of the great four-word Wall Street lie: "It's different this time."

Based on past experience, such explosive growth should have meant surging employment. Not this time.

With all this growth, unemployment was naturally low, but productivity enhancements, technology, and globalization meant lagging job growth. Demand was anything but slack at the time. Nevertheless, jobs had already become a bit of a problem—but we were in denial.

And then the axe just fell. The Great Recession effectively wiped out every job created in the twenty-first century.

Suddenly, everyone was focused on staunching bleeding everywhere at the same time. The body economic was facing ten types of trauma.

Bail out Wall Street. Nationalize parts of the derivatives market like the credit default swaps (insurance against downward movement in bonds, which threatened to topple insurer AIG). Take over Fannie and Freddie to try to nationalize the mortgage-repackaging business necessary to keep mortgage originators originating. Bail out and transfer ownership of major American auto companies. Reassure our counterparties around the globe. Oh yes, and prosecute two of the longest wars we have ever fought.

History will judge whether that precise moment was best to spend so much political capital overhauling our entire health care industry. In retrospect, the music had completely changed but the president and Congress wanted to dance the dance they promised during the hard-fought election race—health care came first, and then jobs.

But we campaign in poetry and we govern in prose.

Was there room for both a health care and a jobs initiative on the docket? We'd all like to believe that the American people and their leaders are broad-gauged enough to manage both.

But we didn't. By dint of specific performance—jobs created, programs adopted, infrastructure built—we did not measure up. Not Democrats. Not Republicans. We have all left our middle class to suffer largely in silence. Goodies were being passed in many directions, but for the middle it was a frugal repast.

Swing and a Miss

IT IS TIME TO BEAR down on the problem of jobs; in fact, we are years too late.

As the 2000s opened, the U.S. Bureau of Labor Statistics projected that 22 million net jobs would be created in the next decade (a lower number, by the way, than what had been created in the 1990s). But anyone really watching could see at the moment of their prediction that things were already changing. When the job market in the United States peaked in 2008 just moments before the financial crisis, manufacturing had already shed 5 million jobs since the decade before.

Job growth in the 2000s was already the lowest since the 1970s, even before catastrophe struck.

Cyclical and structural unemployment rained down. In the first quarter of 2009, nominal GDP plunged, falling at the fastest rate of any year since 1938. We are talking about a far more threatening and powerful shock than the previous two recessions. This was a demand shock unlike anything we had experienced in decades.

For cyclical unemployment advocates this was proof positive. Folks, they were 100 percent right. Demand collapses on a frightening scale, combined with loss of credit liquidity, plunging home prices, and massive excess vacant and foreclosed housing inventory meant cyclical unemployment was a given.

But here is when we let the symptoms of one totally mask the equally powerful structural issues that had been building for years. In the parlance of the emergency room, we treated for Trauma One and largely ignored Trauma Two.

The most charitable assessment could be that structural unemployment must be addressed slowly and cautiously and our leadership chose a stealth approach. But a B-1 bomber would be easier to detect.

Finding the Right Bottom

Whenever people speak about "the bottom," ask which one they mean. It helps with the cyclical/structural argument we're having here.

During major economic downturns there are always at least four bottoms, which come in sequence and rarely turn upward at the same time. (By the way, the questioners won't usually be able to tell you which they mean—except maybe to say "you know . . . the bottom bottom.")

It doesn't work that way.

Bottoms typically come like this: The stock market dives first. It is anticipatory. Similarly, the market is usually the first to turn upward, foreseeing better times ahead. If you believe the economy is going to turn positive in six to eight months, invest at that very moment. If you wait until the economy turns, as most people do before investing, you have missed a huge proportion of the return.

Corporate earnings vary—they plunge second or sometimes third—it just depends how nimble companies can be. CEOs have gotten very used to moving promptly. These days, corporate profits are so tied to serious cost cuts (read layoffs) and belt cinching that you can see major profit improvements even as the economy continues to flag. So corporate profits will typically turn down second and then back upward before the economy lifts.

The economy usually comes third, after the stock market and

corporate earnings. Watch for downturns after a market plunge. Similarly, the economy rebounds after the market and corporate profits have turned north. Always a lagging indicator.

The all-important jobs bottom typically comes last. That doesn't mean jobs aren't weak beforehand; the unemployment rate often worsens after the depths of a recession. And a jobs rebound is always stubborn about declaring itself.

The Bureau of Economic Research's "Business Cycle Dating Committee," which has the task of calling the end of recessions, has pegged the demise of the Great One at the middle of 2009. In the following few quarters, the economy grew at an uninspiring but creditable rate of more than 2.7 percent on average. The fourth quarter posted a 5 percent-plus uptick, but trending is a more sensible way to measure our progress.

At the time of the economic turn the unemployment rate was 9.5 percent. In a matter of months, despite this economic growth, unemployment spiked to over 10 percent, and a year later it was gallingly still only improved to 9.5 percent.

Jobs bottomed last, right on schedule—but they were grindingly slow about returning.

Fifteen million people, and their families, and the stores, mortgagors, landlords, health care providers, and food markets that serve them were all caught in a vise that would not release.

Cyclical theorists recalled the same behavior after the end of the 2001 and 1991 recessions. In both cases, unemployment was higher twelve months later. In the 2001 recession, unemployment did not peak until fifteen months after the economy had bottomed.

Could it be that something structural was diminishing our recuperative power to create jobs?

BALANCE SHEET BLUES

FORGET THE END OF THE recession in 2009. The Dating Committee was right on the recession's time of death, but they should have looked at people's accounts.

By almost any measure, there is still a balance sheet recession that has been washing over the nation.

Not in generations has the structure of everybody's balance sheet had to adjust so profoundly.

That powerful change has brought a new action to economic center stage: deleveraging (cutting debt on the balance sheet).

What occurred on the surface in 2008 was the bursting of an asset bubble where both prices and availability had been fueled by easy debt. Fair enough. People who shouldn't have or could not afford to were provided the opportunity to purchase houses beyond their means.

But consider the broader action of deleveraging. Even with zero interest rates, banks, Wall Street firms, corporations, even private equity, leveraged-buyout shops, and hedge funds are all shrinking their balance sheets. So are philanthropies, local governments, pensions—everybody's doing it. Banks are still levered at a high rate if you look at a hundred-year sweep of history.

They are doing so because shrunken asset prices now mean their debts are a higher portion of their net worth. And everybody deleveraging, no matter how slow and subtle, means that risk is seeping out of the system.

Because *risk* has become a four-letter word.

But even with asset price surges like the stock market (and the Fed's accommodating near-zero-percent rates), corporates and individuals are still deleveraging. This is a fundamental structural change. It is hard to see how Wall Street will ever be the same again.

Can you imagine the response of bulled-up investors in 2006 if they could have borrowed at under 2 percent? Asset investment would have screamed. Leverage would have ballooned.

Today, not so. Apart from local clouds on the middle-class horizon, like surging student-loan debt and a renewed vigor in credit-card borrowing, we are witnessing a slow letting of the air out of the debt balloon.

The panic-prone worry about a deflationary spiral, but given the rebound in housing and the Fed-supported surge in the stock market it does not appear to be a valid concern. Frankly, broad-scale deleveraging by all sectors of the economy would be massively deflating. Credit colleagues Bernanke and Yellen for taking a wise and brave approach.

But soon, very soon, tapering will have to seriously kick in. An economy based on near-zero rates is an expensive luxury for a government to maintain. P.S.: Other governments are catching on and emulating the Bernanke/Yellen approach.

SLACK BEHIND THE NUMBERS

IT'S HARD NOT TO SHOUT Hail and Hosanna when the unemployment rate dips below 6 percent. In 2010, it was over 10 percent. But there is still so much slack in the system, which this incomplete measure fails to highlight.

The ranks of the long-term unemployed have not thinned much. More than 5 percent of the labor force—a huge number—is comprised of people working part time because they have to and want to work more.

The slack in the system has led Janet Yellen to maintain that only a "small portion" of the remaining unemployment can be attributed to structural issues like the mismatch between workers' skills and the millions of jobs currently available in the country.

Again ignoring Trauma Two.

The answer, sadly, cannot be found in the Hail and Hosanna number at the opening of this section. Unemployment is falling for many reasons, but we are barely keeping pace with population growth even as we are producing more jobs—forgetting what kind of jobs they are.

Why aren't jobs improving faster?

The answer comes in two places where we have not typically looked: the labor participation rate and the hourly wage rate.

LABOR PAIN

SOMETIME IN THE CLINTON ADMINISTRATION a conclusion was reached that people who had gone too long without a job were no longer called unemployed. I guess it all depends on what the definition of is, is.

Those who were more than a year removed from their last job would be pulled out of the unemployment ranks so as not to spoil it for the rest of them. What resulted, to be fair, is a somewhat better indication of how the more-employable workers were faring in the job market.

But it also conjured up this notion of the great unwashed who were neither unemployed nor employed. It also brought into higher relief a useful measure called the labor participation rate, the active portion of our economy's labor force—those working plus those actively looking for work.

Unemployment rates and the labor participation rate have been moving down in tandem. (In comparison to our current hugely improved 6 percent unemployment rate, the *peak unemployment* of the early-2000s recession was 6.3 percent, and when the 1991 recession ended unemployment stood at a peak of 6.8 percent.) Today's vast improvement has only gotten us to their peak level of pain; things are still very rough out there.

So as unemployment continues to edge down, the fraction of the people out of work for over a year flirts with an all-time high. In the 1990s, we saw actual labor participation rates of over 67 percent.

By mid-2014, that rate had slipped to a thirty-six-year low of 62.7 percent.

What that translates to is more than 92 million Americans not in the labor force—up from 80 million in 2008. But a closer look shows that over 4 million people—about a third of the unemployed—have been jobless for at least a year.

Stubborn unemployment issues hide behind the vastly improving headline numbers.

What is the government's answer to this discrepancy? For her part, Chairman Yellen says the large number of long-term unemployed is primarily a cyclical matter. That long-term unemployed and the high number of part-timers who crave more hours constitute more slack in the system.

She's not all wrong.

Others say many aging boomers have been out of work so long that they will never reenter the workforce. Still more point out that the sectorial and geographic reallocation of jobs is consistent with recovering from such a massive economic shock. Certainly, deleveraging and a slowing of construction indicate that there will be far fewer jobs in finance and construction than there were before 2008.

Calling the long-term unemployed ready for work doesn't match what we are seeing either. Many of them are simply not prepared for the new reality. If they were in fact ready for action, the continuing improvement in the economy would draw more of them into the workforce. Boomers don't get lazy that fast.

These poor participation rates defy the growth in corporate profitability and the renewed capital expenditure we are seeing companies undertake. Vast arsenals of cash could be a leading indicator. Employees in skilled jobs are not just-in-time inventory that you hire in a flash. Highly skilled jobs are apprenticeships, crafts where hiring is done in anticipation of training and employee development. With all of the revenue growth and enhanced profitability at American corporations, job mobility and placement should be improving, and the great unwashed who have been benched for a year should come into the game.

But that is not what is happening. The opposite is.

THE NEW ABNORMAL

LET'S FACE IT; WE ARE years into an economic turnaround, with quarter after quarter of positive performance. Demand may still be weak, but we are facing a structural shift as well. There is a new normal for the natural unemployment rate, and it is showing up in the shrinking labor participation rate.

Even as the slack gets taken out of the system, wages will remain weak. Monetary policy will diminish in its effectiveness. You cannot buy your way into a jobs turnaround. We have over-relied on the Fed to face the array of traumas in the job market.

Fiscal decisions and structural imperatives need to be faced by the executive branch and Congress, not swept under the carpet. We need the fierce urgency of now in the form of a jobs czar. We've needed it for years.

WASHINGTON'S WAGE WAR

WHY AREN'T WE MOVING HEAVEN and earth to get the American middle class back to work?

The government clearly plays any number of roles in the economy, but we need to urgently reimagine the federal government's broader part in the labor market. The quantitative easing and other creative measures by the Federal Reserve belie an unimaginative response by the other elements of our federal leadership. The continuing fierce debate, or should I say avoidance of debate, on extending unemployment insurance and raising the minimum wage largely misdirects our attention away from the central question posed above.

Sure, the policies under consideration will affect the incomes of some Americans, but they won't do much to expand opportunities and bring more people back into the labor force.

If we took all the heat generated by politicians claiming they would march into hell for the middle class, you could warm a major metropolis on a cold winter's night. But their actions combined wouldn't generate enough light to brighten a broom closet.

Surely, someone in Washington is capable of a more ambitious agenda.

Let's start with low-wage earners and work our way upward.

For years I have been following a program called Single Stop, which helps low-income families harness the power of benefits, including the Earned Income Tax Credit (which supplements the income of low-wage earners and encourages them to earn more), and other benefits to which they are entitled. The group's execution has been extraordinary, even if the basic notion is a simple one. Fact is, they conceived of a way to bring an array of services to low-wage earners, raised nonprofit grant money, and brought meaningful improvement to thousands of families.

Is there any reason that the government can't fund dozens of Single Stop locations in every major American city? And if you co-locate Single Stop in a soup kitchen, you convert survival initiative into an elevation initiative at the same time.

Why doesn't the government take the EITC, which has brought so much well-being to so many working families, to single workers too? Unlike welfare, these are work incentives. If you have developed something that works in one pocket, why aren't we trying in another?

It is not a failure of imagination entirely. It's a failure of will.

Let's go one better and spend some money helping people further up the chain.

Why not extend the range of people covered into the hovering poor? Taking more people who are working and encouraging them to do more by reinforcing better earnings, or reducing taxes, or both, may be just the thing to keep them out of poverty's clutches.

We need to build more bridges into the middle class. And we need to be super vigilant about monitoring all disincentives to work. There is no reason a single mother should have to choose between working and child care payments. Through tax incentives and programs, working women must be supported.

Let's tackle unemployment insurance. Forget the original intent, which was to bridge a difficult period in a family's life when the major breadwinner lost work. Almost everyone can be persuaded that allowing unemployment insurance to broaden its span during the darkest days and years since the collapse of 2008 was a wise and humane thing to do.

But the program took on a life of its own, expanding into something so vast, for a period so far beyond the initial intent. It was inevitable that mythology would gurgle up about it.

The first fable is that $300 a week would become a disservice because a recipient could become lazy and disincentivized to work.

An exhaustive study spanning thirty-five years by the Federal Reserve Bank found that unemployment rates are not significantly affected by the existence of unemployment benefits.

First enacted in June 2008, the Emergency Unemployment Compensation (EUC) program added 20 weeks to the existing 26 weeks of insurance benefits. Over time, the benefit was expanded to accommodate four tiers, enabling a maximum of 99 weeks. Despite the transitory intent back in 2008, Congress extended the EUC several times until a Senate-passed initiative was tabled by the House in December of 2013.

To give you a sense of scale, more than 1.3 million unemployed workers lost benefits.

But are there other kinds of disservice such a long-tailed benefit causes, recognizing what a help $1,200 a month can be to a family in need? Anyone out of the workforce for a year has meaningfully hampered their job search. It's patently unfair, but many companies only interview candidates who are currently working; others require applicants to have worked in the prior six months.

But rather than debate the Catch-22 requirement to have a job to get a job, there are empirical studies that deserve a second look. The New York Federal Reserve Bank did a study to test the theory that increasing unemployment insurance puts upward pressure on wages since luring people back to work has gotten so expensive.

Conclusion: You are deprived because you are deprived.

The economic consequences are equally predictable: Higher compensation means lower corporate profits, which stifles job creation; hence an increase in the unemployment rate and a decrease in the job participation rate. The hotly debated Diamond-Mortensen-Pissarides model predicts just that. And as a corollary, an end to the EUC benefit should lead to an increase in job openings.

How did this theory hold up in the real world?

The response of the jobs market after the cessation of benefits late in 2013 certainly co-indicated the economic theory. The number of job openings across the country surged 20 percent by June of 2014. What is more important is the rate of change in job openings, which has meaningfully expanded over the rate of prior years.

One of the study's authors, Fatih Karahan, put it succinctly: "The expiration of the extended benefits increased the willingness of firms to hire, leading to the large increase in job openings in the first half of 2014."

What the author does not say is that the government could be doing more to build that bridge to the middle class for all of these long-term unemployed who want to continue earning a living.

DISABLED DISABILITY

BURIED INSIDE THE SOCIAL SECURITY system is a well-intentioned black hole of regulation and benefits that act as disincentives, are sadly misguided, and are most certainly abused.

The whole world of disability insurance needs reevaluation. The notion should be a simple one, and we are way off course. If you are seriously disabled, you should be helped. Some people are incapacitated; yet there are others whose impairment is not so severe that they cannot work.

We should help people who have claimed disability find a way to train and prepare for a return to the workforce in a manner consistent with their ability to contribute. Disability insurance was not meant to be a work-avoidance payment.

After the Reagan years, the disability rules were changed, altering both the intent and the behavior of workers on disability leave. The incentives were so markedly changed that the number of people reporting disabilities who continued to work has fallen by 50 percent.

The entire program was designed to help, and now there is simply too much incentive to remain off the job—even when people want to go back to work. Too many of the incentives have been misaligned.

BARE MINIMUM

THE RAGING DEBATE OVER WHETHER to raise the minimum wage is a pox on both our houses.

So much hot air and energy has been expended that one might conclude that this centerpiece strategy would do a huge amount of good for a large number of people.

You be the judge.

About 144 million Americans were working as 2014 began, a little more than half of them on a per-hour basis. Of the total, 2 percent (3.3 million laborers) were paid at or below the minimum wage set by the federal government. (There are exemptions that allow employers to pay below the minimum wage—full-time students, tip earners, and certain categories of disability. About half the states, the District of Columbia, and municipalities like Seattle have enacted higher minimums, and these workers are not included in the total either.)

Does the federal government increase the minimum often enough? Since Ronald Reagan's presidency the minimum wage has been raised seven times.

President Obama noted in his 2014 State of the Union address: "Today the federal minimum wage is worth about 20 percent less than it was when Ronald Reagan stood here."

Hang on a second. Wasn't the hourly minimum wage $3.35 throughout Reagan's two terms of office? And today, after seven bumps, the federal minimum sits at $7.25—more than doubling pay. How does that equate to a 20 percent drop?

Obviously, it is because the dollar's buying power has been weakened by inflation and currency fluctuations. Think back to Nixon Agonistes and our shift to fiat currency. We have hiked the nominal rate we call the minimum wage over and over, and the level simply hasn't kept pace with the shrinking dollar.

Whatever nominal rate we choose, isn't it smart to consider the real issue? A fluctuating dollar and inflation means that we are in an ongoing bet to see how the overall economy will treat our entry-level workers.

If we have been increasing the federal minimum wage every four or five years and are still losing ground, then optics rather than real income is playing a role. No sooner is the ink wet on an increase than it is out of date.

THE PRODUCERS

ABOUT FORTY YEARS AGO THERE was a disconnect between workers' wages all along the income curve related to the increase in productivity.

Much of the surge in wealth for investors, including retirement systems and plans that benefit the middle class and lower-income earners, came because workers kept less of the rewards of the surge in productivity and the profits that generated.

Minimum-wage advocates, including the increasingly formidable

Senator Elizabeth Warren, have trumpeted a study that points out that the minimum wage, if tied to worker productivity, would exceed $21 an hour. This figure is increasingly cited as proof that workers have not shared in the productivity gains they helped to create.

What is irritating is that a reasonable point overall is bent like a blues guitar note to fit the minimum-wage debate.

The study tracks productivity increases generated by all workers rather than the increases of the minimum-wage earners. Having all employees share in more of the income they created—reasonable point. Having the tiny minority of minimum-wage earners share in that productivity increase seems less valid. Why not measure productivity increases in minimum-wage earners just to test the thesis?

The Bureau of Labor Statistics tracks food service-sector productivity, which as a proxy seems in the range of reasonable. How did they do? Between 1987 and 2012, the food service sector grew at 0.6 percent annually, according to the BLS. The nominal rate of increase in their pay from Reagan to now has been about 3 percent per year ($3.25 to $7.25).

So, forgetting the dollar weakening as a fiat currency, the productivity notion raises a question: How much should other workers' enhancements, including those in engineering, high tech, and construction with few minimum-wage earners, subsidize entry-level employees?

One final point before taking a more micro approach to the problem. The minimum wage has taken a nominal journey from $.25 in 1938 to $7.25 today. Since those early days, we have lived through a dozen recessions and many more market swoons.

Many people talk about the strong relationship between boosting the minimum wage and overall employment, especially in tough times. If such a correlation were true, then the unemployment rate would have risen during the 1960s and declined in the 1970s and 1980s.

In fact, the exact opposite happened. Be very uncomfortable when dogma is cited about the performance one to another. Theory and reality rarely collude. More often they collide.

So Who Are These Workers?

It's not as easy to figure out who these workers are as it might appear.

First, there are at least five times more minimum-wage workers today than in 2007. That screams velocity.

In 1980, minimum-wage workers in the United States peaked at 4.7 million, earning $3.10 an hour. They represented 15 percent of all hourly workers.

Remember those heady days of 2007? The number of minimum-wage earners had dropped to just 267,000. (It is important to note that the 1.5 million below the minimum wage of $5.85 did not see the same massive drop in numbers.)

The total represented about 2.3 percent of all hourly paid workers.

Since the Great Recession, the number of minimum-wage earners has surged fivefold to more than 1.5 million, and the number of below-minimum-wage earners has grown from 1.5 to 1.8 million.

That combined group represents 4.3 percent of the nation's hourly paid workers, a near doubling.

The rate-of-change debates are also kind of irritating. Yes, the proportional number of minimum-wage earners has shrunken meaningfully since 1980. But can you at least acknowledge that the trend since the recession hit has been pretty profound and counter to the thirty-year cycle?

This debate goes back to the ebullience over the diminishing unemployment number. In truth, too many of the jobs that have been created are not the type to promote economic stability. At $7.25 an hour, 40 hours a week, workers barely clear $15,000 a year, and most work less than 40 hours.

Yet we crow and take victory laps when we cross the 6 percent unemployment threshold.

Threading the needle of all this hype requires delving a little deeper into the details on minimum-wage earners. They may surprise you.

Teenagers comprise about 31 percent of minimum-wage workers. They are not a group we should blithely toss off. If there is a minimum-wage hike, they may well be the most harmed by any slowdown in hiring that might occur.

Remember the law of unintended consequences? (If there isn't one, there should be.)

That law would caution against doing something that might harm the folks you least want to hurt. Teen unemployment was over 25 percent in 2013 and is hovering around 20 percent today. Black teen unemployment, especially in the inner cities, is at catastrophic rates. Most cannot find work. Go to an inner-city neighborhood and you will see what a harvest we are going to reap. Street corners do not provide the kind of after-school benefits we are after.

Whatever we do with the minimum wage will at best be neutral with respect to helping poor teenagers. And it could be a great deal worse. Some may enjoy a bit more money to bring home. But that good news barely dents the far more pressing problems of poverty and high drop-out rates.

The next 24 percent of minimum-wage earners after the teen cohort are between the ages of nineteen and twenty-five—meaning most of the minimum-wage earners are not the main breadwinners for their families.

At least two-thirds of minimum-wage workers are white, and nearly half are women.

Almost two-thirds are part time; a majority work less than thirty hours a week. As has been widely reported, food service, hospitality, and retail comprise almost 70 percent of the jobs. BLS says 36 percent lack a high school diploma, though most are still enrolled in school.

Christina Romer, UC Berkeley professor of economics (President Obama's former Council of Economics chair), uncovers interesting additional information. About half of the group is part of a family making $40,000 a year or less.

TO HIKE OR NOT TO HIKE

SO WHAT HAPPENS IF WE increase the rate?

First, spending by those who earn it will increase. Study after study predicts little of any increase will go toward savings.

Second, it is clear that a hike will bring relief to some of the hovering poor. But demographics challenge the notion that poor working families will be massively helped by a minimum-wage hike. A small number are African American, and the average family incomes are above the poverty rate. But less than a quarter of those earning minimum wages are currently at or below the poverty line.

Members of private-sector unions (average member wage is $22 an hour) may also benefit, since their baseline wages are often tied to prevailing minimum-wage rates.

There will be knock-on additions up the line as the many millions of earners just above the minimum get their pay adapted over time to reflect the new compensation reality.

It is pretty doubtful that all this spending will create a lot more jobs, but some have strenuously argued that it is theoretically possible.

Lower employee turnover has been cited as a benefit—hard to argue with that—increased pay may increase loyalty. But consider that this group has surged fivefold in six years. The recession of 2008 created a counter cycle in the steady trend of diminishing part-time minimum-wage rolls. It is safe to assume that many of this cohort will seek higher paying full-time employment once the economy turns—so any increase today has a high likelihood of diminishing returns.

Quo Vadis?

THOSE WHO SAY RAISING THE minimum wage is just a liberal attempt to redistribute wealth from business owners to their employees are right. But they are missing the bigger picture. Everywhere we have all been paying and donating vast sums of money to help the poor and the hovering poor survive.

Go to any soup kitchen. Visit any food-donation pantry. Go to a Navy base.

At any of those places, you will find members of a growing club: junior Navy personnel living on food stamps; working mothers trying to pick through the shelves at the pantry to feed their families; elderly having a breakfast or a lunch at their local center.

These are working Americans who, in addition to the white teenage suburban kids trying to save for college or for repairs to their rusting car, are trying to live the kind of decent life they hope for.

Yes, a minimum-wage hike will be intrusive on profit-and-loss statements. Yes, it may speed the day when someone invents a robotic burger flipper and makes some minimum-wage labor obsolete. And even though it will help at least the hovering poor slightly, the Earned Income Tax Credit is a better approach. By raising its levels, those with low incomes would receive a government payout. The tax credit would go to poor and hovering poor, and not to relatively better off college students, spouses, and retirees. It has been called cumbersome, but Single Stop is more than capable of helping folks through the accounting.

Here is the dirty little secret of the minimum wage:

Companies that pay low wages count on others of us to subsidize them—other businesses, other individuals through charity, other taxpayers. When full-time workers and part-time workers seek the public safety net or the kindness of strangers so that they can cease being "food insecure," then all of us are actually subsidizing the profits of their employers.

It is no different from a company that pollutes and leaves us to pay for the abatement, or sells sugar-filled products and leaves us to cope with the aftermath of obesity.

We have gotten too accustomed to letting narrow, selfish economics define the way we treat some companies and their profit motives. Society has to become a better tax collector. There are public costs which we are all happy to share—military, roads, schools, and more. But should we support the income stream of a master franchisee of a fast-food behemoth because they can get away with paying substandard wages?

It is not clear that raising the minimum wage will make a profound difference. I called the debate a pox on all our houses precisely because its influence will be on so few people; because it may be negative for some of the people we would most like to help; and mostly because it won't really do much to ameliorate the afflictions of the poor.

It is so frustrating that this subject has become the centerpiece of the debate. It will not mean a major increase in whatever mojo we need to get the molecule spinning. As usual, we are selecting what wallpaper pattern we want to use, when we should be looking at the foundations of the house.

It is a glancing blow disguised as a terrible swift sword. A largely palliative salve to a festering wound. And, given the last seven times we have tried this solution, the effects will be short lived.

Congress is hopelessly deadlocked on this issue, but don't fret about their paralysis. Expect many of the remaining twenty-plus states and a host of marquee municipalities to finish the job anyway. Then we can move on to more consequential and lasting solutions that don't necessarily involve the government.

CHAPTER EIGHTEEN

BACK TO WORK

The new abnormal of job creation

SUNDAY MORNING JUST BEFORE CHRISTMAS AND *it seemed the year 2008 had turned against just about everyone.*

Talk about your annus horribilis. Markets were swooning. Banks were bursting like piñatas, slammed again and again by the sharp stick of plunging stock and asset prices. And a mountain of bad mortgages had piled so high that the summit was out of sight.

It was a dark time for everyone.

So a little high anxiety inhabiting a southern California entrepreneur's Sunday reverie went completely unnoticed. Moguls on the rocks are hardly sympathetic characters in the best of times, and in 2008, nobody cared.

Everything personal and professional was muddied into the same soup as he stirred in bed. His companies were failing and choking for money; his bankers were unable to advance funds; divorce was bearing down on him.

In the early Los Angeles light, he cast his mind back to the simple things that had propelled him to that point.

After college graduation, like many of his Wharton classmates, he had moved to Silicon Valley, sharing an apartment in Mountain View with three roommates. He stated to friends then that the three areas that most captured his imagination were the Internet, space exploration, and sustainable energy.

But while he dreamed of uncharted realms he found opportunity instead in sectors long overlooked.

He quit a Stanford PhD program, deciding to build a company in newspapers instead. With his brother he devised software that helped bring old-style media companies on-line by providing accessible business directories and maps. When the business, Zip2, was purchased by Compaq Computer, he was launched.

The ink had barely dried when he founded his next company, in financial services—another old-line business ripe for rethinking. Called X.com, it specialized in the world's second-oldest profession—transferring money; again, on-line.

He became particularly intrigued by another small player, Confinity, which had recently developed a money-transfer business called PayPal. Though it was only months old, the entrepreneur saw enormous promise in PayPal's ability to transform an ancient industry, and after a quarrel with his partners, he pursued the business, acquired it, and took it all the way to the bank.

eBay was trying to develop Billpoint, its own solution, but the canny operator had stolen the march. PayPal grew and hired at a rapid clip. Two years later, eBay concluded it was better to join than fight and paid $1.5 billion for the privilege.

A dozen years later, eBay announced a spin-off of PayPal as an independent company.

In 2002, he decided that if humankind were to truly be a multi-planet species, the government's tired approach through NASA would never lead to a commercially viable alternative. Manned space flight was attracting visionaries like Richard Branson and Jeff Bezos of Amazon. But he determined to build more than an ecotourism business and pursued instead a credible commercial alternative.

Just a year later, he surmised that the automotive landscape was near barren despite lip service by the major players to hybrid and electric cars. So he launched an electric-car company.

He was widely derided for both ventures. Fool hardy. Wasteful. Filled with hubris. Un-American. Brash.

None of this stopped him from starting a third company, SolarCity, in the energy arena in 2004.

That fateful Sunday morning in 2008, his motorcar company sat on the brink of death. Far from creating products and jobs and a more sustainable planet, the only thing Tesla had sustained was a river of red ink.

And the first three launches of his rocket ship venture, Space Exploration Technologies (Space X), had all failed. (Astronauts Neil Armstrong and Gene Cernan each voiced harshly public criticisms of the Dragon program.)

Just when it seemed nothing more could go wrong, the investment bank behind SolarCity could not honor its financial agreement.

Some Sunday. But fortune favors the brave.

The very next day, NASA called Elon Musk with a billion-dollar contract offer for Space X.

In time, Space X launched a rocket that brought the first commercial vehicle to the International Space Station. Since then, the billion-dollar contract with NASA to supply the space station has been boosted by a third.

SolarCity is now a publicly traded solar-panel designer and installer run by his cousin.

After investing $70 million of his own money to get his car company rolling again, Tesla took off like a Fast and Furious movie.

His start-up became a magnet for money. He convinced the Department of Energy to grant nearly a half a billion dollars to Tesla and then took the company public, raising an additional $226 million. He quickly secured another $50 million deal with Toyota Motor Corp., and an additional $60 million deal to create an electric RAV 4 EV.

Turning to the Tesla battery, the heart of the vehicle, he secured a $30 million partnership with Panasonic. In September of 2014, Tesla picked Nevada as the site for its 10-million-square-foot, $5 billion giga-factory, which will employ 6,500 workers and generate more than 22,000 jobs.

By 2015, Tesla Motors had surged to more than 6,000 employees apart from the battery operation and enjoyed a market value of $28 billion (to GM's $48 billion). By that time, SolarCity had climbed to more than 6,000 workers too. SpaceX had over 3,000 employees as 2015 commenced, and exciting expansion was planned.

Musk's latest ideas? High-speed rail transport and space travel. Behind every dream another job.

"If humanity doesn't land on Mars in my lifetime I would be very disappointed," he has said. And to an audience at SXSW he confided, "I would like to die on Mars . . . just not on impact."

―――――――――――――

A CATEGORY FIVE JOBS HURRICANE hit the middle class and a half dozen or more years later all we have done so far is hand out water and blankets.

The time has come for a curative jolt that addresses both slack demand in the economy and structural changes we have disregarded as things plunk along. We need to create jobs that catapult, not kick the can down the road.

Let's start with the need to create true allegiance among business, government, and philanthropy to build a potent new middle class. That same spirit animated everything we did as a nation in postwar 1940s and '50s.

States should be encouraged to form workforce investment boards; industrial-sector consortia should meet with universities and government leaders in their regions; and so on. We need jobs czars at every level of government.

Let's make jobs a true national priority.

We first need to identify industries where we have a commanding lead and competitive advantage, and once identified, do whatever we can to fortify them. Included are certainly aeronautics, defense, and space; software and service; computer and communications; digital and mobile media; Internet search and online services; entertainment; materials sciences; and medical devices and health care services, biotech, and pharmaceuticals. These should be industries where we care less about protection and more about doing whatever we can to advance their leadership.

R&D expenditures in these industries are matters of national interest. Any advancement of their collective industries serves a greater good. What incentives can we create to deliver those societal benefits?

There are other businesses that are emerging or need to be reconsidered on both a national and a regional basis. We are on the precipice of an American energy renaissance. Washington has not embraced the enormity of the shale dividend from a geopolitical or a monetary basis. The shifting of the American energy landscape from a massive net importer to a world-class exporter and super-producer can tilt the axis of our entire economy. The drop in the commodity prices to $44 a barrel and perhaps lower should not prevent us from seeing the bigger picture. But we are awfully quick to plug at the well-head because of short-term price action. Taking nothing from the valid environmental concerns, petroleum development comes in decade-long cycles. We can't let a year or two drive all of our analysis.

Similarly, we have starved stem cell and regenerative medicine as other nations have rushed to fill the gap. The practice of medicine as we know it may extend for another generation, but the promise of self-regeneration and self-curing is a mission too big for America to miss.

We are abandoning nuclear power in the least thoughtful way imaginable. We are down to about 100 nuclear power plants. No nation generates more nuclear power than the United States. But the average age of our plants is more than forty years. It takes nearly a decade to get one built, though we have not brought a new one on stream since the Three Mile Island incident in 1979. This strategy of avoidance and delay would make sense if nuclear power weren't such a massive contributor to our current grid—some states get most of their power from nuclear generation.

And when the summer sun bakes the earth, and the air conditioners hum, will these maturing forty-something plants be given a chance to act their age, or will they be forced to produce at full output? We are pursuing a nonlinear strategy with a potential outcome that is all too linear.

The forces behind alternative energy seem to have lost their verve; the pure cost economics are a strain. But no balance sheet other than the federal government's is big enough to carry the development load for solar, wind, tidal, and nuclear energy.

There are more micro-opportunities that have been shifted from the government balance sheet into the commercial sphere. These seem to make sense. More and more, space is becoming businesses rather than government's final frontier. Biotechnology and basic science is finding other ways to promote itself as National Institutes of Health (NIH) grants are slowing. And personal aviation, a huge and growing market dominated by the United States, has increasingly become a commercial development activity.

Batteries to run automobiles and other former carbon-emitting devices are also in the private sector's wheelhouse now.

What has to happen is better collaboration and incentives on the public–private partnerships necessary to maintain our national lead.

City-States

WE LIVE IN AN AGE of cities.

Mayors are an increasingly potent force, because cities must confront demons like joblessness in real time. Government shutdowns and the tabling of bills, or remanding urgent matters to endless committee work, are luxuries cities cannot abide. States spend endless hours fighting for and splitting federal subsidy, while mayors get out there and execute.

They have to—a mayor's spin cycle is overnight. They may campaign on rhetoric, but they govern on execution.

The 388 metro areas in the United States make up 85 percent of our population and over 90 percent of GDP. The top 100 cities create three quarters of our GDP.

If anything, developments in the United States understate what is happening in the world at large. Forty cities and their surrounding areas generate two-thirds of the world's economic output. And, in a challenge to our current thinking, a McKinsey study predicts that 440 emerging world cities will generate nearly half of the economic growth by 2025.

Economic development has gone through a sea change. International trade can no longer tolerate endless diplomatic encounters between ambassadors and their bosses country to country. Trade has turned into a city-to-city exercise.

There is nothing inevitable about globalization; we and other national governments have put up barriers before—and it could happen again. Congress recently postured that it would not honor the agreed-upon increases in the International Monetary Fund (IMF) financial commitment. Protectionism can be contagious, often with disastrous consequences.

We will still tally results on a sovereign basis. And trade agreements like the Transatlantic Trade and Investment Partnership (TTIP) and the Trans-Pacific Partnership (TTP) will still volley back and forth among the White House, Capitol Hill, and the sovereigns in the respective theaters—with each capable of tearing up the deal at any time.

But mega-cities competing and collaborating in the global marketplace is where trade is headed.

Economic development, the true creation of jobs in your town, in your metroplex, in your MSA (Metropolitan Statistical Area) or other regional organism, is the new path forward. Anyone truly in the business of creating jobs and industries has watched in appalled awe as sovereign governments have forfeited their leadership position on job creation. Nations don't build nations anymore.

In the late 1990s, over a quarter of foreign direct investment went to the United States. That figure has plummeted by a third since then.

We should not fear these offshore organizations. We want foreign companies to locate subsidiaries here. Today, they represent less than one percent of all U.S. firms, but they employ about 5 percent of private-sector workers, spend 11 percent of capital investment, and pay $71,000 on average—a third more than the economy-wide wage.

Wining and dining throngs of corporate titans will not create jobs for your city. Economic development teams bolstered by local and regional business organizations must find the site selectors wherever they may be around the globe. Feeding these powerful site selectors with insights about your locality has swelled into a huge activity—still pursued quietly, for the most part. It's a huge market; between $60 and $80 billion in tax abatements and community benefits are doled out to corporate settlers every year—often with the doors closed.

Cities compete in a global context and deliver by making their local resources sing. Like a great middle class, great cities do not just happen. They are created on purpose, with great deliberation and collaboration among the public, private, and philanthropic realms.

On-line marketplaces like StateBook and commercial real estate websites like CoStar are just beginning to open up these closed conversations. Their data, tools, and analysis are the new weapons of choice. But ESRI and Nielsen's Claritas provide raw data and some clever mapping for site selectors and companies seeking to expand or relocate. And a seemingly endless number of local economic development organizations (EDOs) provide their own websites.

Online marketplaces do more than bring a technocrat some transparency. In a very real way they level the playing field so communities can compete on a more equal footing.

So stop waiting for your U.S. senator to deliver you jobs. Most of them have never created one. Preventing base closures they can manage, but attracting the new BMW plant or the new Tesla battery facility will require a masterful execution by other parties first.

If the new normal is the rise of the mega-city, an outstanding example is the Greater Houston Partnership. Forget everything you think you know about Houston. Something profound is happening in Texas way beyond the oil patch.

A generation ago, the Greater Houston Partnership was created among the big three local business organizations: the Chamber of Commerce, the Economic Development Council, and the World Trade Organization. In the unruly world of Texas politics they have used their convening power to face big-city problems and opportunities in a way that should be emulated. They tend to their problems and opportunities broadly and globally, even as they are keenly focused locally.

Job creation is a global competition, won locally.

Houstonians have watched their role broaden to include workforce development. It has become a talent management game. Their principal focus is on winning the development trifecta—creating high-end jobs, mid-wage jobs, and attracting a huge cohort of college graduates. In building this cadre of great jobs and a surge in trained young people, the city's focus has to be as much on 2025 as 2015. It's a marathon and the course runs around the world today.

Houston now has the third-biggest consular corps of any American city.

Who would have imagined such a thing a dozen years ago? Over a thousand representatives from ninety-four nations are living in Houston, and they are not there because of proximity to the State Department.

Paul Hobby, the organization's engaging chairman, says earnestly, "We find ourselves in a special time and a special place . . . a time where we no longer think about international trade in a country-to-country perspective, but as a metro-to-metro affair. Our job is simply to make Houston the best city in the world to start or build a business."

If your region has no such planning and economic development effort, then you will have a tough time creating more jobs. Even if you have a Silicon Valley in your locale, you won't prosper long if you tolerate a pedestrian economic development authority.

Finger pointing is a poor way to win, though a lot of municipalities try. There is no American exceptionalism when creating jobs, no beneficent government authority. There is only you and your neighbors. And anyone who has ever created a job can tell you it is the ultimate "us" exercise.

Long ago Texas governor Jim Hogg beamed these words: "Beautiful cities create beautiful citizens." Today, he might well agree that the reverse is also true.

THINK SMALL

HOW TO SUCCEED IN BUSINESS? Just find the start-ups that will become Google and back them.

How tough can that be? Well, of the 7 million small firms in this country, most have no real interest in being Google. Less than one percent (about 60,000) account for 40 percent of the new jobs in the economy.

Finding them in the haystack is a trick. But they are out there. And the best way to discover them is to let them declare themselves. First, they hire people. These high-growth firms add on average about eighty-eight employees a year; slower players add just two or three.

Start-ups, for example, account for 3 percent of total jobs but provide nearly 20 percent of the new jobs. This single statistic demonstrates how powerful a start-up culture can be for job creation.

Elected officials love to lump small businesses together; they can reach more voters that way. But it makes more sense to attempt to understand how things work.

Companies that employ nineteen workers or fewer—about 90 percent of all U.S. businesses—create jobs at almost twice the rate of larger companies. But looking closer, the strongest growth comes from organizations less than four years old.

Do you feel these start-up enterprises are getting their due these days?

These high-growth companies are in every major market, not just Silicon Valley and Seattle and New York's Flat Iron District. And they are not all high technology. Health care services, transportation, energy, construction, shipping, retail, financial—all industries have their high-growth new entrants.

Many of these start-ups will falter and fail. But over and over, the few that do break out more than make up for the business failures. The trick is for government to provide oversight and liquidity and processes to get help to entrepreneurs. But government should stay out of the business of picking winners.

Historically, bureaucrats have a pretty poor record of picking winners and losers, even when they can influence the outcome—much better for government to create the environment for small businesses to flourish and then let rockets fly.

Every state and municipality should have a designated group whose responsibility is to streamline permitting and regulatory review processes. Many municipalities require licensing before someone can do manicures and pedicures—surely your metro region has similar restrictions in job creation. Clear the way for small business. There is no more powerful way that states can be of service.

Government at all levels can be more realistic about regulation. Why isn't there a more effective small-business jobs champion driving the federal and local authorities to cut the enormous burden of filing and regulatory requirement? Once upon a time, when someone brought an exciting new business idea to a region or municipality, they'd roll out the red carpet.

Today, they roll out the red tape.

Here's another example of a needed change. A brilliant youngster from India or China comes to MIT, or CalTech, or some other franchise institution. With luck they stay on for a master's or a doctoral degree at Harvard, Texas, the University of Virginia, or the University of Chicago. They are brilliant; they are trained—often with NIH or another U.S.-based granting organization. They may have worked at Johns Hopkins, where former New York City mayor Mike Bloomberg has made nine-figure donations and grants.

After all that investment, what's the first thing we tell them when we hand over the sheepskin?

"Go home."

Bloomberg's view? "It's the dumbest thing I have ever heard."

We have trained them, housed them, helped finance them. Many times they have performed research or served as interns, lab assistants, or post-doctoral researchers; and just when they are primed and ready after a fancy graduation ceremony, we just as unceremoniously bid them adieu.

So they build their careers elsewhere, either back home or somewhere else.

Think of this outcome on a return-on-investment basis: we have educated many of these hardworking geniuses at State-supported institutions—on our dime. And who is enjoying the fruits of our investment? We have got to become more imaginative in managing the talent that flows through our fingers.

Whenever immigration pokes its head up, the armies of the night blow back with all their might, but not all applicants to stay here are equal. Why not make a selective judgment rather than a broad brush slur? Some possess the ability and the drive to lead others, to start businesses, to create jobs. Sadly, for so many of these talented folks, we will never know.

THE SAME BOAT

ANOTHER APPROACH IS CLUSTERING—DRAWING together disparate talents into an effective whole.

Karen Mills of the Small Business Administration recounts how she was contacted by Maine's governor John Baldacci when the Brunswick, Maine, naval air station was cited for closure. Her brainstorm at the time didn't float many boats: She formed a cluster.

"Who is less likely to cluster than Maine boat builders?" she said with a laugh later. But after pulling together researchers in composites from the University of Maine, strange magic started to happen. The crafting of lightweight and new-material hulls that were faster, lighter, and more durable resulted.

In the last few years, the SBA has incubated forty such clusters, in cities like Akron and Cleveland around flexible electronics, in other regions around food. The result has been networks of companies and communities focused on advanced manufacturing, new technology, and, oh yes . . . jobs. Done right, these can be hives of regional activity creating competitive and technology-driven small businesses.

Armies of Angels

Providing capital is another way that individuals can help. Too much emphasis by government and the Fed has been on the price of credit.

Pricing is rarely the issue—sometimes companies are uneasy no matter how cheap the rate. Credit for start-ups and early-stage companies comes and goes. For early-stage enterprises, it mostly goes. For companies at the edge of credit quality, terms can be pretty hairy in the best of times. Often, an outside loan guarantee is the only thing that can ensure access. The government has been talking about a $30 billion loan program. But too many entrepreneurs consider it cumbersome and inflexible.

Government should be a pump primer—not a venture capitalist.

Providing tax incentives for individuals to lend money to or invest capital in early-stage companies is a way to spread the opportunity broadly. Investors in early-stage companies who hold for three years or more ought to get a big tax break.

Folks freak out about granting tax benefits, because it sounds like you're feeding the rich. But it's more accurate to say we are manipulating them for the greater good. Frankly, the give-up is slight when you consider the number of capital losses generated most of the time in start-up land.

Let the wealthy take the risk of backing nine losers for every one winner. When they hit, everybody benefits.

Facebook's IPO brought enormous capital gains to the state of California's coffers. And there will be more Facebook capital gains taxes to collect for generations. In that sense, we are all Facebook friends.

We have to find ways of manipulating the wealthy and their investment schemes to benefit the greatest number of our citizens. Loans and equity purchases in start-up companies can create a lot of jobs, build community between the company and the state or state-sponsored organization, and lift more people into the middle class.

But total returns on the winners will still be exceptional. Limiting benefits to the first $20 million of capital keeps mammoth institutions from cannibalizing and turning the investment into a tax dodge versus a business-creation exercise. It supports instead the angel investors who are traditionally more involved during those crucial, risky start-up years.

GOVERNMENT SHOVELS

EVERY AMERICAN WHO TRAVELS OUTSIDE this country reports the same findings. We are in a competitive infrastructure race and we have lost our pace. We are so tied up in what is shovel ready that we are using the implement all wrong.

One of the few places the federal government can wield influence is by clearing out obstacles rather than building speed bumps. Everywhere you look (or drive or fly), we are the picture of decay. Every four years, the American Society of Civil Engineers grades America's infrastructure like a school report card. In 2013, the country got an overall D+, which is a boost from a D in 2009. To reach an acceptable level, we'd have to spend $3.6 trillion by 2020, a shortfall of $1.6 trillion relative to what is projected.

The United States is one of the few leading nations that operates without a national policy to define major infrastructure projects with private funding.

What is most disarming about our lack of drive is that these projects pay dividends now in the form of good jobs (most in the 25th to 75th percentile), and also later in their contribution to overall productivity and competitiveness.

Without straining, most Americans could come up with worthwhile projects ranging from the simplest to the complex.

At a minimum, couldn't we institute a true speed-to-shovel-ready program for the hundreds of projects that are languishing in the vast purgatory of process?

Could we enlist major players who might benefit directly in the funding of these projects? As an example, could we seek financing from union pensions where the projects are likely to benefit their own rank and file? Other nations have set up national infrastructure banks and bond-issuing authorities. Marrying that financial might with private enterprises can get major projects paid for.

Why not enlist the American people in the solution as we did with War Bonds long ago?

So many areas need upgrading. Studies range from a trillion to trillions of dollars, but who needs another study? Let's pick a few major spots and carry on. "We inherited such superb infrastructure from our parents' generation—what is our legacy?" asks a well-known TV analyst.

The three pipelines of the future seem an obvious place to start—broadband and fiber-optic backbones; pipeline and natural-gas-transmission capability; and electric transmission lines.

The majority of today's transmission infrastructure was built before 1990 and is woefully out of step with the advance of alternative power generation. Throughout the country the grid is plagued by congestion and reliability issues.

Track the growth of renewable energy, another national priority, and you'll see that a collision is coming. We will ultimately generate more clean power than can be transmitted down the lines.

Another clamoring need is the transportation infrastructure. When Joe Biden called New York's La Guardia a third-world airport, he said it all.

DEATH BY STRANGULATION

FOR SMALL BUSINESS THE SARBANES-OXLEY law is a departure from common sense. For companies with market values well below a billion dollars, having public shareholders is barely worth the aggravation. It's very short sighted of the regulators to be so overly protective of investors that job-creating engines are choked off from public capital.

Sensible exemption of certain parts of the act will help newer companies come to market. These public companies are researched and followed intensely by investors and traders. Hiccups happen, but for the vast majority of enterprises management adheres strictly to the rules of the SEC and the NASD and FINRA and the alphabet soup of enterprises trying to root out evil.

The bridge of capital from ideas to a broadly held mature public company is where the government should focus—not on picking a winning stock or high-tech enterprise. The markets often dictate whether capital will flow to one industry or another.

Seed capital adjusts according to risk.

In 2014, venture capital was being raised at a $26 billion annual rate, approaching 2008 levels but a far cry from the $106 billion raised in 2000 when the Internet bubble was inflating. Nevertheless, many seasoned venture capital players are concerned about the major burn rates—how much cash is being spent by start-ups to build their businesses quickly. But these young companies have to make the big private capital bets because the public market alternative simply won't work if you are too small. Regulations are so expensive for a young company to follow.

Today, early-stage biotech and some information services companies are suffering dry spells. So have the angels fallen from some early-stage funding.

These death valleys could be helped by additional government support—tax breaks for individuals and investment organizations that invest in IPOs and hold them for a year or more.

Cutting red tape and helping ease the burden of seeking patent protection are possible and useful avenues for government and business to take. But let's face it: None of these will happen without intrusive steps.

Abandonment Issues: Adult Retraining

WHEN EMPLOYERS ABANDON MUNICIPALITIES OR shutter factories or meaningfully downsize, they do so with near impunity.

A lingering obligation to retrain and help those in the community that has for so long been a provider of home, hearth, and citizenry should become a part of the corporate social compact. Today, the circus can simply pull stakes and leave town. Shouldn't the abandonment for outsourcing or other reasons include a more constructive exercise? We have seen how globalization separates a company from its community, if not from its nation of origin. Fair enough. But there have to be costs associated with beating a hasty retreat.

What happens with the hundreds of thousands of furloughed manufacturing workers sitting on the sidelines? Do we consign them to the heap like obsolete equipment? Why not instigate a GI-style bill to retrain and prepare them for new opportunities? We could make that a condition before a shuttered manufacturer departs.

If a departing manufacturer left behind environmental hazards, we would require a cleanup. What could be more toxic to jobs than an abandoned community? It is time for a massive rethink for experienced workers and veterans who need training to take the next step.

Corporations have to play a greater role in cleaning up after they leave town. We have made the process friction free—and in many cases long before, during the original solicitation phase of site selection, tax advantages and other goodies were used to entice the corporation to develop in that community. Shouldn't there be a toll on the way out?

Training may take six months to a year for some disciplines. Others may take longer. But the notion that we would consider a forty-something worker with maturity and experience to be a depleted asset to be abandoned like an old factory is beneath us as a nation.

AMERICAN IDLE

IMAGINE EVERY WORKING AMERICAN PLUS everyone else who is either searching for a job or training to hone their skills standing before you. Then add all the kids in college whose next stop is supposed to be the working world. Behind them stand legions of high schoolers and little ones down the line. Like a vast plain extending to the horizon, you have hundreds of millions of people bursting with energy and potential.

No nation on earth can convene such a brimming pool of talent and enthusiasm, with a collective future so bright your eyes would be burning. We are blessed as a nation with every gift but the gift of collective will.

We have no shared vision for that vast array of souls—no searing passion to get them trained and schooled and fed and housed and hired. Visible tangible problems tend to get all the attention. Garbage is collected, roads are plowed, and children get picked up by school buses.

But the invisible systemic problems that once were our strong suit have long been overlooked. Why? Because nobody really owns the problem, when in fact everybody does.

Now picture in your mind the great wide sea of American business, a colossus of economic might, a shape-shifting organism with astonishing momentum.

Today's business shares many things with the industry that brought the postwar American middle class to life. Yet the force that brings so much heart to American enterprise is its power of reinvention. Today business's brand is broken. Where have their leaders been to point the way forward since 2008? How many have found a way to rebuild a relationship with Washington? How has the divorce been reconciled?

It's time for business to reconcile with the American people—to re-energize their penchant for reinvention.

Innovation, technology, and passion have led that journey before, and they can again.

Technology has done so much more than just make companies efficient. Technology's journey from back-office support function encased in a sealed-off room, to the dedicated office building, to the desktop, to the laptop, to the palmtop, to the ultimate—technology and solutions have become fully woven into the fabric of the product.

Today, all companies are Internet companies, all products are software products, all customers are communications links, and all the data and customer behavior and experience are locked up in the essential brand that the company and its products and its employees represent. Brands are social networks.

Inside industries like pharmaceutical and bioengineering and transportation and energy is core chemistry and biology that drives better performance. We have honed our businesses with flowcharts and inventory and parts management. We have created supply-chain efficiencies and distribution wheel-and-spoke networks. We store data in the cloud and manage person-to-person interaction through voice data and video literally at the speed of light.

We have created a marvel of efficiency and just-in-time everything. Money has been reduced from a dime to a digit, and we can express it in any currency or form anywhere on the planet in a millisecond.

Whole new trading and investment schemes and data transfer and tools analysis are conducted so fast that they occupy the space between the wallpaper and the wall.

Efficiency has been wrung out of every interaction and every chain of activity. We are surging ahead, corporate profits are screaming again, and corporations are seated on mountains of cash.

We have thought of everything.

Except the one thing that cannot be managed to "just-in-time"—talent.

Our technology progress has gotten too fast for the labor pool and the talent-creation organisms throughout our culture to keep up. We have created the two hardest invisible problems to solve: We have a talent mismatch and too few workers to meet our dramatically expanding needs.

Forget the notion of slack demand and the intrusive Fed, there is no monetary policy or economic assumption that can fix these twin problems. These are structural flaws with our economy.

The answer requires the gift of will. And a little imagination.

The American Paradox

WE HAVE A HUGE MASS of unemployed, underemployed, and discouraged workers at the very moment that increasing numbers of companies have job openings they cannot fill.

For every economist who debates whether we have a structural problem in our employment future, I cite this example and will extend it to a social outcome.

No company on the planet spends more on research and development than Microsoft. Over 83 percent of their budget is spent in the United States. They have thousands of high-paying job openings in research and thousands more in other parts of the programming function, and they simply cannot fill them.

And the number of unfilled jobs is growing.

Pay is better than good, benefits are competitive. But the jobs remain unfilled. And there are studies proving that these tech jobs have a multiplier effect—as many as four people get hired somewhere once Microsoft fills the opening.

The gap at Bill Gates's company is widening, and so it is all across the country.

Study computer-related occupations. Their unemployment rate has fallen to 3.4 percent—that's *below* the definition of full employment. So how are we doing on the talent-creation side in computer science?

In the decade ending in 2020, it is projected our economy will produce over 1.2 million new computing jobs. Can you imagine a more robust opportunity? A review of the nation's computer science majors tells us that the annual college graduation rate among this group is running at about 40,000. They might call that an "epic fail."

That massive shortfall leads to a new economic reality that constitutes an enormous threat to the middle class.

Today, unfilled jobs can easily migrate. Microsoft cannot wait forever —R&D is the soul of their business. If we cannot fulfill their needs . . . There is no safe harbor in a higher skill base. Jobs all along the value chain can be shifted to another locale.

That means something bad today and worse tomorrow. An unfilled job today robs us of the employable moment—that happy occasion where someone says, "You're hired." But longer term, this seemingly tolerable miss is far more pernicious. If that job migrates and multiplies, are we seeding a new global competitor in an industry we created and were the world leaders? Can the very same competitive threat extend to other dominant American industries where we might be ceding superiority to another nation hungrier for a middle class?

A talent exodus is an excellence exodus. We cannot allow that to happen.

Bioscience, engineering, aeronautics and space, stem cell research, alternative energy, battery, and other electronics industries where American superiority has been sustained are now threatened by the structural mismatch that so many dismiss.

Estimates vary, but there are 3.7 million unfilled jobs today, according to the U.S. government. Our current system cannot generate the skilled workers or graduates to meet the demands of the digital age. Many of these jobs are unfilled because of geographic mismatches, and still others because of disparity in income growth.

What is becoming clear is that this disequilibrium is not being solved by the tightening slack. Measures that successfully bridged the gap in decades gone by are not delivering answers today.

One study suggests that we need to array the changes in jobs across the spectrum—from robotics and smart machines, which once simply automated but now manage production functions. We need to plot where smart machines are headed and train for that destination. Another study calls for the redesign of transaction processing and information-management jobs. These skills too are evolving quickly.

And the latest wave, which is the fastest growing and most impactful in creating a middle-class renaissance is the *complex-interaction jobs.*

Since the 1990s, these knowledge economy jobs which involve interactions with technology, customers, and clients, and that require judgment and situation-specific customizations, have been the fastest-growing category of employment. Salespeople, managers, all manner of professionals like accountants, lawyers, architects, doctors, teachers, and those in advertising, media, and marketing—all are included. Interaction jobs span high- and low-skill ranges, and more than 5 million such jobs were created in the first decade of the millennium.

Raising the productivity in these high-interaction jobs is an intense focus across the business landscape, here and abroad. A key feature of these jobs is their ability to be migratory. Ubiquitous broadband and wireless technology has turned the interaction worker into more of a virtual asset.

Virtual suits—a white-collar worker's worst nightmare.

In reality, this kind of labor has become a highly transferrable variable cost, rather than the immovable fixed expense we have come to expect. The threat to the middle class of our nation can be summed up in a sentence.

The interaction jobs that define white collar are far more moveable than we ever realized—ironically, far more nimbly moved than factory-worker jobs because so few fixed assets need to be moved to accommodate them.

The middle class has become virtual in a way we never could have imagined.

Across the entire OECD, part-time and temporary employment has grown 1.5 to 2 times faster than total employment since 1990. Jobs in the future will be strikingly different from what we have come to accept as the norm. Worker skills will need to evolve at a faster pace than they currently do—and unskilled labor will continue to shuffle off to the poorest nations.

All across the globe the fates of high-skilled and low-skilled workers will continue to diverge. These fates will separate particularly as more demands are made of skill-based employees to keep up with technology and workplace advances and redesign.

The disparity in unemployment rates between those who do not graduate from high school and at each successive educational level of attainment will continue to expand.

There are reports by McKinsey and others that call for dramatic shortfalls in our talent pool by 2020—1.5 million fewer college and graduate degrees than employers will need, and more than 6 million too few high school graduates than can be employed.

We will have massive shortfalls in all STEM-related fields (that is science, technology, engineering, and math).

What will be the impact of all these trends?

The greatest threat to the American economy—our middle class will be left behind.

We have a barbell of unemployment, with babes and boomers on either end. If we cannot quickly change our talent-management process, too many of both will be permanently impaired.

At minimum we will have unfulfilled opportunity for GDP expansion. Industries that the United States has long dominated will look to other regions for support and jobs. Some may initially be at lower real wages than the American corporations, so there may not be a hit to corporate earnings equivalent to that in the overall economy.

But failure to address these key invisible initiatives will create far more visible problems.

What the long-term implications of the erosion of national competitiveness may be are worth pondering. But this next generation is facing a steady ceding of American financial and production superiority to other nations.

Corporations are the ultimate adaptable beings. If they are people, they are without doubt the most selfish people you will ever encounter. These major corporations are truly multinational, and they will shape-shift to find the talent they need wherever it may grow. Their prospects will not dim.

But the policy considerations we make today and the actions we take in the very near term will have profound impact on how much we cede to other nations. The center of this circle will be the middle class. The jobs that we have come to regard as the bedrock of the middle class will certainly migrate to the countries that most actively pursue them.

TEENAGE WASTELAND

WHAT IS THE RISK WHEN youth unemployment is high and growing, particularly when it is approaching majorities in some demographics? Surely a generation of opportunity is lost and an annuity of pain has been created. But the risk fully written is more than lost GDP or unfulfilled expectations. These are the seeds of Arab Springs. Massive youth unemployment is the greatest risk to the status quo imaginable, and it is time we got really serious about it.

The costs will be far more than a percent or two in lost domestic product.

In the United States, a staggering 6.1 million people between the ages of sixteen and twenty-four are neither in school nor in the workforce—that's like every living soul in Los Angeles and Philadelphia. Managing this cohort will cost the taxpayers nearly $100 billion a year. If there is any single group that we cannot ignore it is this potent but lost generation of talent. Turning their fortunes around will be vital to economic stability.

Let's examine the disconnect between educators and business, two spheres that circle each other tolerantly as long as one is never allowed to become too influential in the life or direction of the other.

According to a McKinsey study called "Education to Employment, Designing a System That Works," fewer than half of employers believe new graduates are adequately prepared for entry-level positions in the working world. When asked the same question, just under 90 percent of educators think these graduates are adequately prepared.

What may explain the divergent perception is poor communication in both directions.

One-third of educators report that they are unable to estimate the job-placement rates of their graduates. And one-third of employers say they never connect with educators.

Part of the problem is that students have sufficient education, but not in the fields that employers covet—two often-cited areas are STEM degrees and vocational education in secondary and community colleges.

The most obvious divergence between these two institutions occurs when graduates are looking for jobs beyond their schooling or expertise. But new fields of study and on-the-job training can be pursued to match company requirements. Far more vexing is the mismatch of theory and practice that employers are increasingly reporting.

Companies report that their students have too much academic knowledge and too little practical or real-world training. Companies prize entrepreneurial and problem-solving skills and the ability of students to comfortably interact with all types of colleagues and to advocate their point of view in a collaborative way. These interactive and reasoning attributes are more valued today than any specific knowledge of an industry or deep command of a subject matter.

Government has proved it cannot solve the skills gap alone. Business can bridge the gap by working to help shape educational and vocational programs. How? By developing accelerated training programs to retrain unemployed workers with years of experience in advanced manufacturing.

Employers are working with community colleges on hiring. It is time to go to the next step to shape their curriculums to meet the current and future needs of employers.

STEM Winders

WE HAVE A MAJOR PROBLEM in STEM education and training. There are a number of actions that can alleviate the problem. We have to strengthen the entire K–12 experience. Right now we are experiencing a million dropouts a year, and more than 60 percent of K–12 testing is at or below base level.

We are managing to the wrong test.

The real measure should be how effectively we are engaging students to embrace the next generation of science well before they enter the job market. Computer literacy is as important as basic English-language skills. Many resist the Common Core because it smacks of national interference in local education. But the counterargument must be made persuasively.

Our kids face enormous global competition for the very jobs their parents hold today, and even more for the millions of great technology-based opportunities that are highly prized worldwide.

The test we should be teaching is for our children to be able to compete effectively on the world stage. For that to happen, we must endorse the STEM disciplines by bonuses and differential support. Graduate students who teach STEM should get subsidies in the form of tuition reimbursement or additional fellowships and research grants.

Faculty in STEM should enjoy benefits for taking on that role—

perhaps bonuses, sabbaticals, and technology support to broaden their impact to more students and more schools.

We have a crisis in college completion. Over 70 percent of high school graduates enter some form of advanced education or training within twenty-four months of getting their diploma. But somewhere along the line their enthusiasm wanes or the expense proves too great and they stop their progress.

Far too few part-time students complete their degree inside of eight years. Three-quarters cannot complete the degree. For two-year associate's degrees, which should be more attainable, the numbers are even worse—92 percent of part-time students cannot complete the two-year program within a four-year period.

Obama administration plans for a $60 billion program to grant everyone two years of free community college tuition will spur a rush to register. But the concept ignores a stunning reality.

Just 4.1 percent of City University of New York (CUNY) first time enrollees at their six community colleges earn a diploma two years later. Hostos Community College in the South Bronx has a two-year graduation rate of 1.4 percent, the lowest in New York City. Some point to the $4,500 full-time CUNY tuition as a part of the problem. But there's more.

Nearly 80 percent of New York City high school graduates applying to CUNY fail the admissions tests and need some type of remedial classes.

The quickest way to ameliorate what is a dual unemployment rate (8.8 percent for high school grads and 4.1 percent for college) is to move mountains to get more high school and college completions. Leaving hundreds of thousands a year to lead lives of double-digit unemployment through their twenties is an unacceptable solution.

Steps necessary to complete more college include subsidies for STEM studies. Universities need to ensure that freshman preparedness programs are offered to all engineering and science students. Studies by Spencer Stuart have shown that such prep courses double retention rates.

Another way to encourage completion is to grant employers rebates and deductions for promoting school attendance while on their payroll. Many working students simply cannot balance both. Those students often complain that the total costs of education dwarf their ability to pay.

Why not have a ten-year period promoting STEM degrees?—a super focus decade for moving the STEM needle in our nation. Let's provide 50 percent of tuition reimbursement for any student who satisfactorily completes the STEM course requirements on a timely basis.

A report by the Association of Higher Education says that undergraduate research projects can significantly increase the likelihood of a student's completion of the program. The federal government is constantly providing funds for research—tying undergraduate involvement, and in certain cases direct funding, could bind more students to the notion of completing their degree.

In the same vein, corporations must find ways to partner with schools and universities to create more internships and student engagement in the STEM disciplines. It is not simply a matter of getting these students to attain a degree; it is also a matter of retaining them in the programs.

Only 8 percent of college freshmen end up graduating with a STEM degree. The number in Europe is double that, and in Asia higher still. In China the number exceeds 30 percent.

The Wrong Pipeline

FORGET THE KEYSTONE. WE HAVE spent so much worrying about that stretch of pipe when the most desperate needs are for another pipeline entirely. The talent pipeline.

There are two essential thrusts. One is to finally get serious about excellence in inner-city schools and about tying those institutions to the next length of pipe. For some it will be college and university, for others trade school or junior college, for still others it will involve taking veterans and others who have left academia and devising programs that trains them to re-engage as a valued employee.

This first challenge can only happen when business, government, and education get together. Who can possibly convene such a group? Today it must fall to the universities to be the conveners. Or it can be economic-development organizations like the Greater Houston Partnership. Too much mistrust between business and government obfuscates the ability to get all sides talking—but we have to start in earnest.

The second employment initiative is the STEM pipeline, a subset of the overall talent pipe with many of its own idiosyncrasies that we need to address—and not only at school and college levels.

There needs to be a combination of approaches if we hope to bridge the major STEM shortfall we are experiencing today. The talent strategy has two components: import and self-made.

A bold new plan embraced by Microsoft and other technology-industry leaders bridges the gap and provides a funding source for major support of STEM initiatives. Establish a new program of H-1B STEM visas to meet the technology employer's crucial unmet hiring needs to enable them to remain competitive and continue to innovate. There are currently caps on H-1B visas and those were established in 1990, an eternity ago in the context of the workplace needs today.

Establishing an additional 20,000 visas per year for advanced STEM-degree holders would be huge enablers to the tech community. And the tech world should pay for it. Another part is to provide for recapture of 30,000 unused green cards that for one reason or another get voided after a span of time.

Remember, these visas are to fulfill the needs of companies large and small who say they cannot find what they need in the U.S. market.

This plan keeps great jobs here and fills our coffers. Hint: Make companies pay for it.

Charging $10,000 each for those and the additional H-1B visas would generate over $500 million every year, or $5 billion for the ten-year program. That's more money than the federal government is spending on the Race to the Top program.

Directing these moneys to improve the American STEM pipeline will pull corporations directly into the solution of their own problem.

AMERICA'S GOT TALENT

EVERY SINGLE SUGGESTION OUTLINED ABOVE means that school authority, corporate governance, and political span of control will have to compromise. But workforce development and talent management are by far the key ingredients for maintaining American leadership—particularly in the new economy.

It would be easier to stand still. But leaders like the Greater Houston Partnership and the Michigan Economic Development Corp. and other local initiatives have not flinched from the responsibility to create a robust job market in their regions.

Admitting our shortcomings and managing all of the tender territorial disputes will be a magnet for criticism. But competing ideals will have to co-exist if we are to turn around what has been a decades-long divergence from the thoroughfare we hope to travel.

We cannot make the old system well fast enough. We need a new one. The education-to-employment system is not working optimally because we have been reluctant to manage at the adjacencies. But at those very margins lies a fertile field filled with opportunity to compromise and drive away job killers that have become habit.

Imagine for a moment the world that you inhabit—your own little ecosystem. What small yet wise things are within your grasp to change or influence? What subtle additive impact can you bring? It may be no more than teaching an evening or two in a business school, or it may involve hiring a trainee when you really don't need one, or sending someone talented to business school or college.

The competitive arena is so vast and the problem so intractable that indeed no one does own it, even if we all should. It is in this pressured and polarized state where change faces the Hamlet choice. Often it is not the bold plans of a Microsoft or a federal government initiative that make the difference. True change in creating a new economic reality comes from individual warriors who bring no more to the conflict than the ability to make a single cut. Do I or don't I?

Each of us can make a single cut in our own way, according to our own resources. Collectively we are a huge army.

And as we all know, nothing slays a dragon better than death by a thousand cuts.

CHAPTER NINETEEN

_____ Middle Earth _____

The world's exploding middle class

Clenching a pipe in his mouth, *the stork-like scientist stepped out of the bunker into the predawn air. Silhouetted against a hive of activity inside, he scanned the sky and grumbled, "Mid-July high desert and another damn week of rain." His team scurried making final preparations. Moments later, he was joined by the general whose sole ambition was to soothe some frazzled nerves. Everyone was tightening; it was almost time.*

Strange, the general reflected, that years of intense research, trial, and error after error could lead to this: a rain delay. His mind wandered to the early days of the project.

Back then a group of transplanted scientists ventured into the desert mountains to explore a ghastly new proposition—one so exasperating and bursting with risk that they couldn't leave until their design was built and fully tested.

They worked for a new branch of the Army Corps of Engineers under Major General Leslie R. Graves, established as the Manhattan Engineering District only days before the attack on Pearl Harbor. A great many tributaries flowed together to create the project. An Italian émigré physicist, Enrico Fermi, met with Navy officials at Columbia University in 1939 to share his vision of matter. Not long after, the world's most famous scientist wrote to President Roosevelt describing his own relativity on the subject. The fed-

eral government responded by committing $6,000 for research. Hardly a ringing endorsement.

Intellectuals took until 1942 to persuade the U.S. government that the Axis enemy was working on its own solution. Fear finally sparked someone senior in the War Department to clear cobwebs and to seriously fund the study. Six thousand dollars quickly turned to billions.

At the University of Chicago the following year, Fermi set off the first chain reaction, which soon created another chain reaction altogether. Lanky Dr. J. Robert Oppenheimer, in trademark pipe and flat-brimmed hat, launched a research project at the Los Alamos Laboratories, constructed in the northern New Mexico desert far from all prying eyes.

That stark, mountainous frontier provided Oppenheimer and his team key ingredients for their work—secrecy, temperate weather, and the right amount of solitude. What wire was tripped to cause their budget to explode? Intelligence sources feared Germany was about to create a weapon so destructive that their domination would be assured.

What was required was the invention of a whole new explosive involving enriched uranium and plutonium. The Nazis were reliably reported to be working on the purification of uranium-235. The job of the Manhattan Project was to beat them to it.

Natural uranium was not much help in the process. This heavy element is always on a journey, its bulky atoms slowly wasting away until after a few billion years all that remains is a chunk of lead. Nature provides uranium with three isotopes: the majority U-238 and the far less prevalent U-235 and U-234. Oppenheimer's interest was in the less than one percent of uranium that is U-235, which is fissile, meaning one neutron blasted into it can kick off a chain reaction that is not linear but geometric. The progression can be so powerful that mortal reaction occurs in a millionth of a second.

Oppenheimer was joined by a score of the finest minds on earth—more intellect and ego can scarcely be imagined. Niels Bohr, David Bohm, Enrico Fermi, Edward Teller, Klaus Fuchs—a Mount Rushmore of scientific prodigy. Years of planning, trial, and development followed.

Temperatures soared in the desert, and in the laboratory too. Under dire threat of German breakthrough, these scientists debated fission (atomic bomb) techniques versus fusion (hydrogen superbomb) techniques without the traditional comforts of tenure or notoriety. It was pure science in a hellish race to the apocalypse.

Time was not on the scientists' side. The hydrogen bomb would have to wait while two atomic bombs were designed.

Even before the first was tested, a second was dispatched under cloak of secrecy to the Pacific. The hope was to create a bomb so biblical that its destructive force would shred any ambition to return fire. Time was running out.

Against this backdrop, Allied forces conceived Operation Downfall, the large-scale invasion of Japan. Allied casualties from an invasion were estimated to reach one million—plus another 10 million Japanese casualties, including civilians. Allied planners anguished for another way to end the war.

The scientists needed a remote place to test their device, affectionately known as the Gadget. They found it in the ominously named desert plain Jornada Del Muerto—the Journey of the Dead Man, more than 200 miles from the Los Alamos Lab and a very long way from the general populace.

A 100-foot steel tower resembling an oil derrick was erected. It was late June 1945, and as if on cue a rainy pattern commenced. Rain could wash nuclear fallout from the sky, obliterating the true measure of the blast aftermath. Nothing approaching the scope of this test had been done before. In late May, 108 tons of dynamite was detonated near the test site Trinity. Clearly, something more profound was needed.

By July 12, component parts that would become the Gadget were brought to a farmhouse at MacDonald Ranch. The plutonium core was carried in a shock-mounted case by a team sergeant as if he were carrying a six-pack of beer. How little was understood about what was about to happen.

At long last, a huge hooded cauldron held by massive tongs was hoisted gently off the back of an open truck. Apart from the ginger treatment, they could have been unloading a cement mixer. Final assembly of the Gadget was done in the roasting heat of July 14 inside a canvas tent at the base of the tower. Men scurried in their underwear. Gently, the plutonium core was inserted into the explosive shell of the Gadget.

There was no real fear of detonation; the plutonium sphere would later be encased by symmetrically placed explosives. The Gadget without its detonators was hoisted to the top of the test tower. As night fell, scientists finished the assembly in the inky darkness reserved for remote deserts. Delicately, detonators were installed. Dr. Norris Bradbury, assembly supervisor, wrote in his log: "Look for rabbit's feet and four leaf clovers. Should we have a chaplain down here?"

The team's apprehensions went further than a momentary blast; this was, unusually, a full-scale test—no time for baby steps. Was there some sort of catastrophic chain reaction the scientists had failed to consider? Radioactive fallout was expected, but its range and duration were unknown.

Oppenheimer and crew waited for a nearly windless, dry moment. High, puffy clouds brooded in the darkness. Rain continued intermittently. By three a.m., the observation shelter was buzzing. Tempers lurked just under the surface. Other groups were scattered for miles to observe the blast and track the impact on the distant populace. Santa Fe lay somewhere out there in the darkness, 120 miles away.

A dozen scientists fussed with details. Another handful of military and intelligence specialists observed from the back bench. With each successive radio call counting down to the moment of the blast, there were brief pauses and a resumption of kinetic energy. Intervals came more quickly, minute-long gaps turning to seconds . . .

A blink before 5:30 a.m., the test bomb was detonated. Instantly the blast-site temperature was 10 million degrees. Light pierced the darkness like a rising sun. Everything within half a mile was vaporized, the light so intense an observer ten miles away was temporarily blinded. A hundred miles away, a blind girl reported seeing the flash. Observers at the back of the shelter were knocked over by the compression waves. Calling the test Trinity, Oppenheimer had unleashed dark deities. Quoting from the Bhagavad Gita Krishna, he muttered prophetically, "I am become Death, the destroyer of worlds."

Seeing the unparalleled force and destruction, a number of participants petitioned against proceeding with the atomic plan. But just three weeks later, on August 6 at 8:15 a.m., the B29 bomber Enola Gay, piloted by Col. Paul Tibbetts, dropped a device named Little Boy on the Aioi Bridge in Hiroshima.

Less than a minute later, over 66,000 people were dead and 69,000 injured, many mortally. In that split second, more died than the total num-

ber of American fatalities in World War I. A mile diameter marked total destruction. Within two and a half miles, every flammable thing burned. And a cloud of quiet radioactive ash settled on an unsuspecting populace throughout the city.

Bomber copilot Robert Lewis exclaimed, "My God, what have we done?"

Seventy hours later, a plutonium bomb called Fat Man was dropped on Nagasaki. Though the bomb missed its target by more than a mile, nearly half of the city was leveled. Forty thousand died in an instant.

The next morning, Japan surrendered.

WE HAVE ALWAYS BEEN AN extraordinary country—never more so than at the time of the launch of the postwar middle class. Consider our humanity after World War II.

America was in sole possession of ultimate weaponry. Never mind the lab work and the slide-rule claims of other nations. We owned the martial high ground.

Imperfectly, we used nuclear weapons twice to devastating, permanent effect. Imagine what Hitler would have done with such an arsenal. We could have turned the world into a slave camp if we had chosen to. For that brief shining moment we had the superiority of unchallenged might.

Not even the Roman Empire held such sway.

So did we drive for domination: a *Pax Americanus*? Quite the opposite. Our cultural DNA, then as now, was formed by the double helix of grace and power, might and fairness.

Instead of concertina wire and patrol dogs, we chose the Marshall Plan. Our greatest warriors, like MacArthur, spent their gloaming years rebuilding Japan and many parts of Europe. No nation in history has ever held such advantage and instead chosen to be so humane.

The world that helped us create the defining middle class was so much simpler. We drifted from a global split between Allied and Axis powers into another duality, the Cold War Spy vs. Spy.

Americans born after Levittown see the world the same way as the two-faced Roman god Janus, who looked at the year behind him and the year to come. But while we peer deeply into the past, we look faintly at the road ahead, too guided by what has gone before, too unwilling to adapt.

Today, the world is not beating a path to our door; they are trying to beat us to the punch. There is a plurality in everything and we have not fully adjusted to the new competitive reality.

We stand at a defining moment, like 1945. There are major differences between 1945 and today, but the similarities matter now. We still possess the greatest military fighting machine on the planet, but in an age of terror and nuclear capacity, superiority is relative. After 2008's crash, our economy remains the largest and most resilient. Again, superiority is relative.

Just as we resisted playing the domination card in postwar affairs, let's take the lead around the world now, with economic and social development that bolsters our middle class. These days we do the opposite of "speak softly but carry a big stick." Shock and awe rarely does either for very long. Let's change our approach. Forecasters see a new world middle class growing to more than 4 billion people—shouldn't we lead that surge rather than watch it pass us by?

Exploding Middle

Study the number of major countries in the developing world with a keen eye on creating their own middle class. Then ask, does Adam Smith's invisible hand limit the number of genuine middle-class jobs the planet can accommodate? Can we possibly create enough jobs that reward endeavor with material comfort and the prospect of upward mobility through the generations?

The implications for the United States are profound if the world middle class is a limited proposition.

Item one is jobs. The issue is, every workweek another million souls join the planet. It took from Adam and Eve's first encounter until 1930 for the global population to reach 2 billion people. Then things got moving. By 2014, the population had more than tripled to 7.25 billion, with a target of 8 billion by 2025 and 10 billion by 2050—a five times multiple in 120 years.

Since 1930, this is one area where the world exceeded all targets. (Not sure what this says about our spare time.) Paul and Anne Ehrlich forecast the stuffed phone booth in their 1968 treatment *The Population Bomb*, which foresaw 9 billion people by 2050 (too low) and hundreds of millions of deaths beginning in the seventies (too high). All sorts of dire predictions came and went, and we kept finding room. But what about jobs?

Spin the dial forward to 2025, when we will boast a global population of more than 8 billion. Let's try right here to find as many people work as we possibly can: Take the top 500 companies in the United States; add 700 more in Europe, 1,000 in the Asian nations, 1,000 in the rest of the world, plus 800 for new technology—making 4,000. Let's imagine they employ 100,000 people on average apiece, a generous number given trends in productivity, consolidation, robotics, and so on. All these giant companies would employ fewer than 400 million people in total. Okay, 7.6 billion to go.

Include every army in the world—that only adds another 100 million. Government employees everywhere equal 300 million more. Small businesses add 130 million in America, plus 250 million for Europe, and 600 million for the rest of the world. Throw in another 500 million farmers and you just clear 2 billion total jobs. Double every number and we still barely get above 4 billion.

Here's the rub for anyone thinking about the middle class: In a world of over 8 billion people with just 4 billion jobs, what are the other 4 billion going to do? Conceding 2 billion for the elderly and the very young, that still leaves another 2 billion without work.

Today, it is more useful to look at where the growth is originating, because the trend is all about emerging nations.

Developing countries account for just under 6 billion people; by 2050 it will be more than 8 billion. In a Dickensian paradox, growth is expected to be most dramatic in some of the least-developed countries. By century's end, the UN expects the economies of thirty-five of the least-developed nations to triple and some to grow fivefold.

The International Labor Organization reports that 3 billion are employed in the world today. Nearly half are "vulnerable employment"—self-employment or work contributed by family members.

A couple of disturbing trends directly impact our middle class. First, every year 40 million more people look for a job. With more than 200 million unemployed workers globally today, that means we will need to create at least 600 million jobs in the next decade just to return to pre-Crash proportions. That's like finding a new job for every single living soul in Europe over ten years.

A second tricky proposition is the fact that 900 million of the jobs in the world pay less than $2 a day, by anyone's measure a poverty line for working poor.

Can America re-create its middle class with all this global growth and competition? Earlier I posed a question: Is the middle class an endless sea of opportunity or an infinity pool with water constantly pouring off and recirculating to another part of the pool?

My answer is, I don't believe in limitless opportunity. Too many outside forces intrude. Thoughtful forecasts have middle-class numbers approaching 5 billion people, and they point to an eradication of poverty on a massive scale and an explosion of promise across the globe.

Appealing as these studies may be, I just don't see it. The huge proportion of informal workers in the world—non–paycheck earners who toil in family shops or in the shadows of small businesses in their village—will benefit from middle-class expansion. But they lack staying power.

Middle-class stability that feels something like our own will come to billions around the globe. But for the remaining billions I believe the future will be lived somewhere above the $2-a-day poverty mark. That is progress, sure, but nowhere near enough to have strong recuperative power if trouble strikes. The world is a dangerous place, and assets that propel nations—like minerals, energy, manufacturing prowess, or an industrious populace—are a magnet for bullies, whether they wear fatigues, robes, or pinstripes.

If low-cost manufacturing is their high card, many of these nations' competitive advantages will be short lived. For the mineralogically endowed, supply chain, distribution, or military repression may deplete them. Deep in every get-rich-quick national story are dark moments when power and greed trump what's good for the people.

Economists marvel at the latency of the world's workers. But we need to create 50 million jobs a year just to stay even. That number will grow.

However delicious the daydream; the world does not distribute fairly. Middle-class surges often bring greater expectations of health care and clean government, but those rarely fall into place. In the infinity pool, America must compete for its middle-class well-being.

CONSOLIDATION NATION

THE NOTION THAT EVERY COUNTRY that wants a middle class gets one feels cheery—but not particularly real.

Look at the Darwinian capture of market share. Natural selection means that some nation is always willing to pay less, build cheaper, pollute more, inspect less, and otherwise shave quality and safety to deliver a lower price. And just as some nations are happy to race to the bottom, others are racing to the top, leaving room for others to take their place in the food chain.

The chessboard of the developing world is teeming with fluctuations in stature and human drama. The World Bank and the CIA's use of Purchasing Power Parity concepts can equalize and level set the wages of the world, but they cannot equalize the wages of sin, of war, and the unending march of productivity. Through all of the spinning in the developing world, growth is interrupted by periods of retrenchment and consolidation. Few economies march straight into the sky.

As fortress Europe was born, American investment banks swept into the city in London and other capitals because they smelled consolidation. Centuries of independent national business planning meant Europe's same-sized economy as America's had twice as many car companies, three times as many major drug companies, and so on down the line. Consolidation followed.

This matters to the middle class because consolidation creates redundancy and redundancy begets unemployment.

Some European countries were benevolent about discharges, so workers got soft landings. Others weren't so cordial. Real wages stopped growing. Shops shuttered, factory whistles fell silent, duplicative assets were sold or abandoned, and the middle class stalled.

Emerging tigers are not immune. Asian state-owned enterprises are webs of patronage begging for rationalization. India and China together boast more than 85 million private companies, most starved for some form of capital, many hidden outside the clear view of consolidating markets. As these countries grow their middle class, consolidation and reduction of redundancy will happen there too.

Marry these consolidations with offshoring and technology replacements for work functions once performed by hand and you get job compression—especially on middle-class job growth. The point is, America still has a commanding position because we are farther down this road. But unlike those scientists in the desert, we are dawdling.

Poor Little Rich Nation

TODAY'S NEW ECONOMIC JUGGERNAUTS ARE different kinds of host cultures for a growing middle class. For generations, Western countries held their heads high as the economic powers. Their demographics were a few rich people, a majority middle class, and a large but still minority poor. Overall GDP and GDP-per-capita were high. Both the country and the people were well off. Developing nations considered these Western nations rich. But definitions have changed.

China represents a new model of economic prosperity. It will be the richest nation without having anything like the highest GDP per capita. (It is the 84th-poorest country per capita. India is 53rd and Pakistan 49th.) China's capita creates its huge GDP: a vast number of people blessed by small but growing earnings.

China is the second-richest economy, with the highest number (or close) of poor, the most sick, the most disabled, the most elderly, the most retired. China is a poor little rich nation. Think back to the great empires—Roman, British, and precursors. Their vast spread incorporated colonies teeming with the poor and just a few captors in control. No one lived in the middle—that middle class is why China is a new model indeed.

Other developing nations are emulating China's growth story. They will elevate many people from a dollar a day to something that on a purchasing comparison feels like lower middle class.

We must surf this wave, not fight it. Abroad, a vast and growing middle class with expanding waistlines and expectations awaits. No nation on earth has keener insight into these expectations than the United States. If there are limits, as I believe, to the number of good middle-class jobs on the planet, we need to compete by feeding the wants and needs of the global middle class, not only our own.

Our trump card seventy years ago was our military and manufacturing might. Now we lead too often with our arsenal. How much energy have we expended flexing arms rather than investing first? We have more major brands than our competing nations added together. We lead in technology, distribution, branding, and strategic planning. But beyond all that we have an instinct, a command of the subject matter.

We were weaned on middle-class mores. Together, we wrote the book.

Each nation is different by law, religious custom, and populace. Who knows better than the United States how a small middle class grows and matures, and what nurtures and sustains it? Who has crafted more global content messages that travel across borders even when that content is illegal or provocative?

Yet our first instinct is to turn defensive, even hostile. We have academics, politicians, and unions fighting trade deals, levying tariffs, and generally acting like the little Dutch boy, finger in the dike, protecting us from the world outside. They accomplish exactly the opposite.

Preventing American workers from buying offshore goods, and picking trade fights that reduce the appeal of our goods to foreign regulators, is the opposite of the right thing to do. The middle-class miracle may not be limitless, but it is absolutely gigantic and it is happening out there right now. There is a second mountain of worldwide wealth creation besides well documented surge in the one percent—the global middle class.

I say we get our baton, take our place at the front of the parade, and lead it down the boulevard.

The Third Wave

THE CHALLENGE FOR US IS to feed the global business story of our time—the third wave of middle-class economic growth.

We should sell them goods, feed them, clothe them, manufacture their goods here, or manufacture our goods there—even their goods there. Capturing as much of the new worldwide middle-class market as we possibly can will be great for our economy and a boon to our middle class. Their products might replace our own, and some jobs may drift overseas. But the secret the dozing sentries have missed is that many of our jobs are going there anyway because that is where the vast majority of the economic growth is going to be for the next century.

On balance, we worry too much about the sanctity of our technology and our intellectual property—bluntly, the world of the uncopied app, the impenetrable formula, and the knockoff-free product is over. Product cycles boasting unique selling propositions have shrunk. Today, secrets get downloaded. The crushing of proprietary content is the new economic reality. A phish, a worm, or some fauna from the bizarre menagerie of the World Wide Web is rummaging through your data as you read these words.

I suggest using an entirely different kind of web, one that attracts customers to our products. Speak to offshore manufacturers and they know how to make it just like we do, but for reasons of economics, engineering, supplier, materials, or just profit margins they choose to go a cheaper way.

We must change our behavior now while we bravely consider the world-view of the new middle class.

The Great Convergence

WHAT IS HAPPENING HERE IS a great new convergence, with direct impact on the middle class. A new convergence implies that there once was a great divergence—and there was, back when China was the Middle Kingdom. According to historian Niall Ferguson, the average Chinese was richer than the average Westerner in the year

1500. By 1970 came a great divergence, and the average American was twenty times richer than the average Chinese. Ferguson conducted similar studies contrasting the United Kingdom and India, with nearly identical results.

Things are changing. Today, the average American is five times richer than the average Chinese—and that number is expected to halve before long. Eastern nations, what Ferguson calls the "resterners," are tightening the gaps—driven by belief.

One point says it all. Today, the average Korean works a thousand hours a year more than the average German. Think of it—at least three hours more every day. That only happens when you are driven by belief.

How to make sense of the dizzying array of converging inputs? Between 2012 and 2020, over a billion potential new workers will look for jobs—and most will find one in the developing world. Some economies are stalling while others soar. Populations are shrinking while others boom. And a rarely considered new "youth bulge" hit developing countries just before the world markets collapsed.

The youth bulge?

Every year, the world gets the joy of experiencing another 120 million sixteen-year-olds—89 percent of whom are in developing regions. They are the next middle class.

What Does the World's Middle Class Look Like?

NOTHING DELIGHTS THINK TANKS AND economists more than pinning down a new cohort such as the global middle class like a butterfly on wax. Labeling debates rage. But some proposed middle-class earnings ranges don't even overlap.

Esther Duflo and Abhijit Banerjee of MIT picked earnings from $2 to $10 a day. And widely quoted expert Homi Kharas of Brookings sets his low point at $10 per day, the MIT study's upper level. Doctors do differ don't they?

Some use the advanced-country median income of $31,000, or roughly $85 a day. Only a tiny minority in developing countries qualify by this measure. Besides, people earning seven times less have figured out how to buy a car.

With Purchasing Power Parity, $2 a day does not buy much, even in the poorest country in the world (Zimbabwe). And accounting for all the PPP imaginable, ten bucks a day is a long way from Levittown.

The Organization for Economic Co-operation and Development (OECD) defines this middle class as making $10 to $100 per day, a group they project to rise to nearly 5 billion people by 2030. They forecast that spending by this group will rise from $21 trillion now to $51 trillion by 2030. (That $51 trillion is greater than the combined GDPs today of the United States, Europe, China, and Japan.) The global middle class is serious business.

Income, as we have discussed, is a pretty poor measurement because comparable pricing is so difficult. And a huge proportion of the world's workers do not get a pay stub—so they cannot tell you what they earn. Consumption won't work very well either, nor do taxation levels, because both vary from country to country. Imagine comparing a poor Chinese with a very high savings rate to an American middle-class member who never conceives of saving a dime.

One simple, practical rule of thumb for identifying this new middle class is automobiles. In the developing world there is no easier measure of relative affluence. Car values adjust to home-country economics, creating an unscientific but useful purchasing-power comparison. As an example, the average car in India is twenty years old, versus about half that for the United States. Once cars in circulation are measured (annual registrations help), then estimates of per-household family size are gauged—different again between China and Nigeria. By this measurement, about 600 million people in the bigger developing nations are middle class, and this figure is growing. These measures can be influenced by massive new-car purchases made in the biggest developing nations—creating a car barbell of very new and very old models.

What does this tell us? The growth in the rate of automobile ownership in the BRIC nations (Brazil, Russia, India, and China) was more than 14 million cars in 2010. Using the household multiplier, that means 46 million people were added to the middle class that year—that is the equivalent of the population of Spain.

There are other markers for the world's middle class. The Walmart effect on manufactured items means that TVs, computers, and other household items have gained greater ubiquity. Cell phones lead that charge, obviating wire line service in much of the developing world. Today, there about 6 billion active cell phones, 4 billion in developing countries—and a significant minority of those owners do not have access to a regular power supply.

Emerging middle class members have expectations beyond material goods: Better education and more available health care (a sizeable shortcoming in even the most advanced of the developing nations). They have something else in abundance that should be familiar: hope.

Pew Research conducted a massive 40,000-person survey in thirty-nine countries in mid-2013, asking the touchstone question for middle-class aspirations: "Will children in your country be better off than their parents?"

The developed world answered with a resounding "No." Just 33 percent of Americans thought their children would be better off, a high-water mark for the West. The United Kingdom's answer was 17 percent, Japan's 15 percent, and France's une petite 9 percent.

The developing world brought staggeringly different responses: China's was 82 percent (frustrating because they wanted an A) and Brazil's 79 percent—with a large majority of "Yes"es in Nigeria, Indonesia, and many more nations.

The United Nations is more expansive, likening the third wave to the Industrial Revolution. The new middle class has propelled the developing economies of the BRICs (Brazil, Russia, India, and China) to approach the size of the G7 economies. Reports throughout the financial sphere say that by 2050 a clutch of these new tiger economies will account for almost half of world output, vastly outstripping the G7.

Other studies say that by ten years hence, North America and Europe will drop from half of total output to a third.

At a recent World Bank meeting, country team after country team presented business plans with a shared core thesis, driving economic growth by building a strong middle class. Not since the Wild West medicine shows has there been a more universal elixir. A strong middle class is the new black.

New Middle-Class Benefits

LIFE EXPECTANCIES ARE RISING IN even the poorest developing nations. Middle-class growth has lifted more than a billion people from poverty by any definition. Having America help these countries build a middle class may seem counterintuitive. But the best way to grow us is to grow them.

Tapping this potential is the key. For example, the number of cars per thousand people in India is 10 and in China is 27, compared to over 500 for Germany and 450 in America. The great convergence means India, China, and other nations will strive to catch up. Who better than the U.S. middle class to drive them there?

Unlike the United States, in many of these developing countries the gap between the rich and poor is shrinking. Before, they had no middle class and childhood was threatened. In our lifetime, the mortality rate of infants who died before their first birthday has fallen by more than 60 percent. Two million fewer children die every year than as recently as 1990. Vaccines, cures, infant formula, and medical awareness are just creeping into many of these countries.

Hunger is at all-time highs, but many countries are finding better ways to feed their people. The average calorie intake has risen for many of these developing countries from below the recommended minimum of 2,000 calories to nearly 2,700.

Literacy has completely changed for the latest generation of developing nations. Forty years ago, most adults in the developing world could not read—an enemy of every kind of progress. Today, two-thirds of developing-world adults read and write.

The only true measure of job well-being is the employment-to-population ratio. In 2007, it stood at 61.2 percent, and it is approximately 60 percent today. OECD reports conclude that young people are three times more likely to be unemployed globally—bad news when you consider the global youth bulge. Europeans call them NEETs: Not in Employment, Education, or Training.

Nations that invest in youth with both education and value-added skills will create the next middle class. NEETs in the youth bulge are the enemy of progress. (Remember America has over 6 million of them.) All other inputs—money, technology, manufacturing know-how, intellectual property, brands—are highly transferrable. Large cohorts of trained and ready young people are not. If you have them, you win. Everything else can be shipped in via FedEx or wire transfer.

Nations like India plan to spend three times more money in the next five years on higher education than they did the last five years. China plans to spend more too. We are in an entirely different kind of arms race, one that we cannot afford to lose. The team with the best-educated, most motivated middle-class workforce wins.

The new middle class are also urbanites. In a decade or so, 60 percent of the world's population will live in metropolitan regions. Still, for all the momentum the costs of many basic needs—like food, water, and energy—will skyrocket. Consumption patterns of the middle class invariably lead to increased use of these basic life ingredients. Add to these the desire for better, more consistent and available health care and there are clear opportunities for the American middle class to prosper. We excel at delivering all of these services.

The global middle is not only huge but hugely diverse. The new global middle-class nations, like the BRICs and the TIMBIs (Turkey, India, Mexico, Brazil, and Indonesia), each have their own unique social profile. Sweeping reference generalizations, like Asia and Africa, must be reconsidered in a more targeted manner. Each is so different. Japan: rich, shrinking, aging, immigration-disavowing; China: aging, urbanizing, industrializing in a get-rich-slow mode; India and Indonesia: huge, administratively bumbling, choked by massive ineffective bureaucracy, too much brawn and not enough economic development brain; South Korea: hungry, driven, focused, has created some business superpowers; Nigeria and South Africa: combined nearly a trillion in GDP, still poor, still a nineteenth-century worldview of mineral development, still stung by their own legacies; Brazil: an energy superpower that just blew by the

UK in economic might, blessed by huge growth and restrained by staggering poverty.

Each presents unique opportunities for our middle class. Each, too, represents a competitor if we continue our "repel boarders" trade mentality, or worse, we stay obsessed with our home markets.

But there are a few things that these and other nations have in common. They are struggling to recover from global recession, their numbers are expanding, they have youth who want to work, and they are becoming increasingly urbanized. Their demand for stability in goods, services, and infrastructure is our true middle-class opportunity. They are dying for things we know how to give them.

There is another common denominator beneath the surface of all these different national stories—something we can use to our advantage, thrumming like a background hum—never articulated, rarely mentioned. Listen; watch their behavior and you will sense it.

Insecurity

CONSIDER IT A DUAL AWAKENING. Just as developed countries realized that their middle class is shrinking and their wages are fading, the youthful middle class of the developing world is stretching their wings. It is a tableau of contrasts: One group's expectations are dwindling but resilient; another's is expanding and yet vulnerable and insecure.

Purchasing Power Parity compares poverty levels between the United States at $13 and the rest of the developed world at $2 a day. But PPP doesn't buy security. It doesn't account for risk.

Continental South America and Africa, with nations at different stages of economic development, deem most of the jobs held as informal. That means there's no paycheck but instead work in the family or in some small business. Workers cannot answer basic questions like "What did you earn last year?" and "What will you make next year?" They move, clean, store, and arrange things. Their job evaporates and they move to another informal opportunity.

Whatever social protection systems exist, they simply do not save these workers. At least a billion are this vulnerably employed.

In Africa, the signs we take of a secure and stable income like the purchase of durable goods simply do not happen—even in countries with growing-middle-class consumers. In South Africa, for example, 83 percent of households do not own a car.

Another slowly changing factor is the rare example of university degrees. We are spoiled. Eighty-eight percent of Americans have completed high school and 42 percent have achieved an associate's and/or a bachelor's degree. According to the *Huffington Post,* only 6 percent of the world's adults have gotten a college degree. Brazil leads the developing world at 11 percent; others are single digits.

Here's a big difference in the new middle class from the American version. Precarious employment means unstable income and timid consumption in the developing world. Furtive steps *follow* the achievement of material well-being. Chief among them is that emerging middle classes have no recuperative power—particularly in times of economic strife. Americans borrow and spend through economic vicissitudes. All those years, through good times and especially bad, the consumer represented 70-plus percent of the U.S. economy.

The developing world's middle class has no such appetite yet.

Please don't confuse middle-class growth with social progress. Emerging middle classes do tend to demand more freedoms and better services from their government. But their political preferences can veer toward the protectorate and the populist, which may slow the pace of social reform. Rebellion and unrest can quickly turn the fortunes of a developing-world middle-class family upside down. So they keep their heads bowed.

Divisions creep in between those wanting greater freedom and those who just want support and service from their government. Most often if the money is good, folks make compromises—Americans tend to forget that.

Anxiety is the essential difference between the middle class of the developed and the developing world. We forget that too.

Not Like Us

NOT ALL MIDDLE CLASSES WILL look like us. Resist the temptation to look at the rise of a middle class and democracy as cause and effect. Economic and political freedoms are not inextricably conjoined.

In 1989, Francis Fukuyama published a thoughtful piece called *The End of History*, which predicted that the fall of communism would lead to the inevitable victory of liberal democracy. There are grains of truth in the essay. But we Americans tend to see the world through our eyes, through our beliefs and our experience. Those will be imperfect guides as countries pursue their own brand of capitalism, their own unique style of liberalism, and their own ways of determining how their governments should be run.

Watch profound changes create dreams for liberalization of laws and conduct. Those are natural occurrences. But looking deeper, restrictive regimes take menacing steps to encourage economic growth while keeping a lid on freedoms.

The mantle of liberty has been frayed in places like Thailand and Ukraine. Other, newer democracies like Iraq and Afghanistan took toddling steps only to backslide into their old ways, or even back beyond the starting line into some new nightmare.

Many hoped that the Arab Spring signaled progress toward adoption of Western ideals we hold dear and that seem consistent with an informed middle class. But counter signs indicate a willingness of new middle-class families to compromise as long as their prospects improve.

How else to explain the Brazilian middle class's response to the state taking greater control over the oil industry after foreign firms pushed too hard? Putin's "Back to the Future" doctrine has elevated him to the highest approval ratings he has ever enjoyed. Indonesians have embraced stricter interpretation of Islamic laws in anti-pornography regulations and the formation of halal cities, where food must be served under stricter guidelines.

There is a new nationalism in the air. The great convergence has led many to presume that political and social philosophies will merge. In bursts people who are armed with intelligence, money, education, and future prospects and who are more traveled than their countrymen have a natural tendency to push against restrictive regimes.

But taken as a whole, sanctimony has clouded our judgment, our military spending, our nation-building ideas, and our ability to create a stronger middle class. We see middle-class replication and immediately our eyes turn to the dewy recollections of Levittown.

In these early innings, consider the contrary. Convergence of income has not equated to shared values in democracy.

Globalization has shown more middle-class members to be proud of their nation, not our nation. Pew Research found more study in contrasts: Middle-class members of these foreign countries were generally in favor of open elections and the free speech that accompanies them. But people were willing to trade prosperity and protection for those vaunted Western ideals.

Considering how far so many have come, and how fast, perhaps that is not so surprising.

CHAPTER TWENTY

The Cyclone

High winds in the developing world

IN THE DYING DAYS OF APRIL *2008, the first spring storm gathered in the Bay of Bengal. As warmer waters intensified the brew, the near-stationary depression made an unexpected turn east, developed a concentric eye, and blossomed with an unthreatening name—Cyclone Nargis (the daffodil). By May Day things escalated, the eye widened a dozen miles, and sustained winds hit 135 and higher. By midnight, the daffodil made landfall—and a twelve-foot surge blasted the Burmese shoreline.*

Burma, now known as Myanmar, is one of Asia's poorest countries. Once the pearl of Southeast Asia and the world's leading exporter of rice, Myanmar's rule by repressive military junta left the country isolated and mismanaged, a stagnant pool surrounded by economies rushing forward at rates of 8 percent and higher. Economic growth had reduced poverty across the developing world, but time passed Burma by. Poverty was baked in.

Nargis slammed the densely populated Irrawaddy Delta with catastrophic force, precipitating at least 138,000 fatalities. Labutta Township alone suffered 80,000 deaths, and many believe the junta stopped counting as the toll mounted. At least 55,000 are still unaccounted for.

The tiny economy sustained at least $10 billion in property damage. Burma had no safety net. Worse, at least 2.5 million were suddenly homeless. Burst sewage mains flooded the rice fields, ruining the country's cash *crop. Four days later, the military junta refused to allow foreign aid workers or military units to operate in the country. A French UN ambassador said the action could lead to a "true crime against humanity."*

UN Secretary General Ban Ki-moon met with junta leader General Than Shwe for hours, and an agonizing three weeks after landfall, aid workers were finally allowed to enter, but not their ships. On June 5, after weeks of waiting, a USS Essex–*led American carrier group reluctantly withdrew from the Burmese coast after repeated denials of entry, its massive aid cargo undelivered. Weeks had passed and only a minority of the millions suffering had received any form of aid.*

These marked the last days of the junta.

A hundred pounds of fierce determination and ladylike poise was waiting in Rangoon. Trouble had been brewing for a long time. Back in 1990, free elections brought the National League for Democracy Party 80 percent of the seats. As chairwoman placed under house arrest, Aung San Suu Kyi had to again endure junta refusals to cede power. There were no victory celebrations.

Her father was the founder of the Burmese Army who later negotiated independence from the British Empire, only to be assassinated by rivals months later; and her mother was ambassador to India and Nepal. Young Suu Kyi, ever a daughter of Burma, spent her years at Oxford and the University of London planning a return.

The wait was longer than she ever imagined.

Over a two-decade period she would spend fifteen years under house arrest and incarceration. Shunning the option to visit her dying husband or receive the Nobel Peace Prize and other accolades, Suu Kyi suffered in detention, fearing that any departure would foreclose a return to her beloved homeland. Her sons, Kim and Alexander, separated by oceans and the years from their mother, served as her emissaries abroad.

After the storm, pressures on the military regime led them to swap their uniforms for political garb. Suu Kyi was at last released in 2010, and was elected to Parliament two years later. The military wrote regulations prohibiting her—as a widow, with children living abroad—from running for president in 2015. But she intended to seek higher office.

No citizen in the reborn Myanmar's history enjoyed more international support.

Changes like the dissolving junta, the elections that followed, and Suu Kyi's release led to an easing of economic sanctions. But opening the doors a crack only showed how disastrous the fifty-year rule of the military had been. As of 2013, according to the Human Development Index, Myanmar had one of the lowest-ranked levels of human talent development in the world.

Myanmar's emergence from economic isolation and despair provides a unique window into the massive transformative power of the middle-class miracle. It is a perfect petri dish.

Between 2012 and decade's end, the country expects to double its middle class to more than 15 percent of the populace. Consumers in Myanmar are among the most optimistic in the world. Ninety-three percent believe their children will have a better life than they do, compared to single digits for some Western developed nations like France.

Liberalization of company ownership and local investment is being encouraged in infrastructure, banking, insurance, and textiles. The government acknowledges a drastic shortage of hotels and is pushing to expand health care and food services.

In March 2012, a draft foreign investment law emerged, the first in decades. Foreigners will no longer require a local partner to start a business in the country, and will be able to legally lease but not own private property. The draft law also stipulates that Myanmar citizens must constitute at least 25 percent of the firm's skilled workforce, and with subsequent training, up to 50 to 75 percent.

In very short order, a significant migration from the agrarian base to the industrial has commenced. For years, the only factories were government-run enterprises with abysmal quality and no consistency of product. The wealthy and emerging middle class demand better brands. Since national distribution networks are antiquated and unreliable, almost all supply-chain adjustments offer quantum-leap improvement.

As a result of these inefficiencies, the wheel of modern retailing—

complete with world-known brands—has not begun to turn. Mom-and-pop shops still dominate the landscape. But that, too, is changing fast. Though still early stage, diet and other consumer trends are changing, too, as is the demand for new kinds of food. Food imports are increasing at 40 percent per annum.

Durable goods and appliances that consume significant electricity must wait until a modern power grid can be created. It may take decades for the large rural populations to consider renovating their kitchens.

But almost any facilitating technology in point-of-sale retailing, distribution, storage and manufacturing, transportation, and construction makes outsized impact in Myanmar today.

The population of 64 million makes Myanmar the twenty-fourth-largest country in the world. Placed at the strategic crossroads between India, China, and the rest of Southeast Asia, Myanmar remains an untapped major market. But not for long.

Economic growth is predicted to sail along at high single digits. Parts of the Myanmar economy are virginal. With nearly the lowest per-capita earnings in the world (under $3 a day), small increases are having enormous impact on the overall economy.

In 2012, the Asian Development Bank formally began re-engaging with Myanmar to finance infrastructure and development projects in the country. Investment is moving in force.

Cash costs in Yangon (formerly Rangoon) for cars are at least $20,000. And seven-figure apartment sales are not unusual. Wealthy Burmese are ready to pay cash to join the modern world. The emerging middle class will not be far behind.

The Myanmar Spring is upon us. Once a closeted and inefficient society revered by Rudyard Kipling for its nonchalance about keeping pace with the world, and then held by a power-mad junta in suspended animation, Burma is busting out as modern Myanmar.

It faces internal battles as majority Buddhists persecute and expel Muslim Rohingya minorities in what looks startlingly like ethnic cleansing. But human rights and economic growth are not always bedfellows in the emerg-

ing world. And poppy crops that fed the world's heroin trade have flourished once again. Economic rebirth often leads to painful adolescence.

Myanmar provides the perfect case in point for Americans to cease their complacency about forging a more powerful middle class. Once Myanmar's walls came tumbling down, the journey to middle-class prominence, which took Americans a generation, leapt from the starting gate. If we don't mobilize, the countries of the emerging world will bound into the breach.

We are too quick to dismiss Southeast Asia as a whole. But consider it the double/double.

With a population double that of the United States, and an economic growth rate double as well, Southeast Asia will be the ASEAN Economic Community in 2015 with a free-trade pact that will put a booster rocket on their individual countries' progress. Consider the combined impact of Vietnam and Myanmar. Their total population of 150 million exceeds that of any nation in the EU and enjoys a 6 percent GDP growth rate. These two nations represent the new middle-class frontier. Vietnam's middle class is expected to rise from 12 million to more than 33 million from now to 2020. That means Myanmar and Vietnam will soon have more middle-class members than the entire population of Spain.

Unilever and Coca-Cola have opened manufacturing facilities in Myanmar, and Ford will be open for business there soon. Vietnam is surging ahead, with Samsung opening a billion-dollar facility and Nestlé building a $240 million coffee-processing factory with designs on serving the entire region.

Is it possible that virginal Myanmar and war-rebounded Vietnam can serve as a wake-up call for the American middle class?

Look at the miraculous turn in Myanmar and the middle-class spring that is bursting forth all over the developing world. Not every player will make it to major middle-class status. But if principalities like Myanmar are determined against all odds to try, then it's time we did too.

Older economies, like those of Europe and the United States, are too far down the road to pay much attention to these puny upstarts. It's easy to feel superior and entitled. But people all over the world are advancing—with us or without. On beaches everywhere the combers are marching, searching for ways to create their own version of the middle-class glory days we once enjoyed. And where have the developed world leaders stuck their heads?

They are missing the greatest convergence in the history of man.

———————————

PART OF THE MYOPIA IS they are using the wrong yardsticks. If you expect that the United States holds lunar sway on how each individual nation nurtures its own version of a middle class, you are in for a surprise.

BRICs, CLICKS, AND TIMBIs

WHAT DO BRICs BRING TO the party? Four distinct trillion-dollar economies with over 3 billion people. These countries frame the discussion of whither the middle class.

Not long ago, we saw the world as America versus Asia. The West versus all the rest. Such distinctions don't work today. People looking at Asia as a single effort fail to appreciate the huge differences between East Asia and South Asia. It is very hard to see how China and India could forge a consensus view. They are so entirely different.

At the same time, expect Indian prime minister Narendra Modi to emulate many of China's growth initiatives. Japan's prime minister Abe is doing likewise, with low interest rates, lower value of the yen, a drive to boost export prowess and performance—rebooting a slack manufacturing economy and using that momentum to drive excellence and service economics.

Watch for careful dialogue between China and India, each warily considering the other.

There is a new acronym in town. The decade-old BRIC incumbent versus the upstart TIMBIs (Turkey, India, Mexico, Brazil, and Indonesia). Russia misses the cut because its workforce and population are shrinking; China got pink-slipped because it is graying.

My counsel is to pause before jettisoning the Russians and the Chinese.

People are always ready to dismiss Russia, with 2 percent of the world's GDP, a shrinking population, and a shrunken nation. Never underestimate them; history has many times, with eventual regret. Vladimir Putin is the re-joiner of lost Soviets. Hard-liners have persuaded him that the dissolution of the USSR was Russia's darkest hour. Economic resurgence on dramatically higher oil prices through early 2014 mask this deep wound festering inside him. Plunging oil prices means Russian bonds and equities have collapsed too, as the country appears predicated on $70 oil and higher. But Russia is rarely simple, so look at them differently. The cost to "lift" the oil is germane. The total costs of oil include many billions of spent investments in infrastructure that will cover many years of production. Putin learned long ago that covering variable costs also covers many other sins.

Watch Putin's control of the message, how tightly wound he is, and how dismissive he is of the West and its leaders. Putin's approach is entirely different from China's. It is political, military—trending toward annexation. Middle-class concerns come second. Pride in the heart before bread on the table.

Mother Russia wants him to be the father of the new USSR. And whatever mama wants . . . With energy and mineral might, and military right, Putin will elevate his nation even if it suffers an economic sideways movement in the process.

GRAYSIA

WAGS CALL CHINA "GRAYSIA"—LIKE Japan, only more so. Shortly there will be more old Chinese than there are Americans. How a country with no safety net will manage a growing unproductive aging population is in part answered by the Chinese savings rate. That is the rainy day for which all those Renminbi were stashed in mattresses.

Do not be distracted by the argument that China will become old before it becomes rich. That seasoned saw is used by countries forced to care for their aging unproductives. China is a new world. Age limits are expanding, as is effective productive life. Asia's middle-class elderly will not go gently into that good night. Retirement is not on their minds. Saving is. Work is.

The heft of China's growing middle class will be the truer indication of its capability than the age curve of the labor force. The middle class will provide economic stability, even if savings impairs Western-style consumption.

Focus carefully on China's military strategy. It seeks hegemony over a new perimeter. Any nation that built a 5,500-mile-long wall around its territory obsesses over boundaries. The Chinese know exactly what they are doing in this regard. Whether it is an oil rig off Vietnam, a dispute over uninhabited islands with Japan, protein squabbles with the Philippines over fishing on the Scarborough Shoals, the paternity of Taiwan, creating defensive air and no-fly zones over disputed airspace, or cyber-spying on U.S. companies with whom they are doing trade deals—China has a plan.

It has a swift sword at its side, but it has not been principally militaristic. China's goal is local hegemony, not world domination; bullying squabbles, not outright warfare. Think of this perimeter as the new Great Wall surrounding the East and South China Sea. From that base China plans to create the largest middle class in the world. It will be difficult, since consumption rates hover at 30 percent and investment spending has been outsized. No nation on earth is spending more on its infrastructure. And if you want to see where China's foreign policy is headed, follow their checkbook.

Unlike our Soviet recollections, China has no plan to bring its governing philosophy to the world, no need to annex country after country. No expansionist jackboot. Think instead: regional warlord, and serving as workbench to the world, and obsessive capital infuser, and partnerer to pursue their competitive commercial agenda. Capital and co-investment are their weapons of choice.

Given cozy state-run banking relationships, two words will bedevil the Chinese middle-class miracle: bad debt. But controlled economies have a weapon that free markets don't when facing bad loans—extend and pretend. (It is much easier when you sit on both sides of the negotiating table.)

Every year, 15 million people move from farms to China's hastily constructed cities. Their goal is a middle-class style of life. Impediments like an aging population, corruption, and lack of true market dynamics between the government and the SOEs (state-owned enterprises) will cause the middle class in China to expand more episodically. But fully expect their middle class to dwarf the total population of the United States before long. Fifteen million people a year are betting their lives on it.

Looking Beyond the Obvious

RESIST THE URGE TO FOCUS only on China, since everybody else does. If only half of their plan goes right they will be an economic juggernaut for middle-class expansion. Truly understanding the global middle-class opportunity and what it offers the American people means forcing yourself to watch a fast-forward movie called the developing economies.

Take a much trickier case—a thornier nation or two—as potent examples.

Consider Nigeria, by so many measures an imperfect regime. Huge disparity in well-being between the North and South fuels kidnappings and terrorism—the folks who brought you Boko Haram. Over 62 percent of Nigerians live in extreme poverty, but at 173 million today, the country already has nearly as many people as the United Kingdom, France, and Italy combined. Nigeria's economy has surged to more than half a trillion dollars, even as violence and unrest has stalled its petroleum growth. And what can you say about a nation whose president's name is Goodluck Jonathan? (Sadly in April 2015 his namesake's good luck ran out, and he was thwarted in a re-election bid.)

His flawed young nation has become the biggest population and economy in Africa, as well as the seventh-most-populous country in the world. While the state gets more than 70 percent of its revenues from petroleum, the economy is not just about energy. In their recent rebasing in which the IMF, World Bank, and the African Development Bank were brought in as verifiers, just 14 percent of the country's GDP is derived from oil.

The country has been posting 7 percent growth and has many ingredients to drive it higher: low debt, low budget deficits, and nearly 40 billion barrels of proved oil reserves.

Nigeria's stark contrasts—a surging state with abject poverty and mineral riches—are a tale as old as time. Criminality and corruption are bumper crops. But globalization has collapsed the time frame from colonial rule to self-determination. Nigerians have seen the movie of life on the frontier of the oil patch. They will be ethically flexible, they are willing to import more pollution than most any EU nation, they will face marauders like Boko Haram, and they will live for as long as they can with the huge income and well-being differentials between their regions.

Nigeria may not be center stage the way that China and India are today. But that is precisely the point. They will become a force to be reckoned with, and our robust trade relationship and significant foreign direct investments face competition.

China recently inked a $13 billion railroad deal and a $3 billion infrastructure loan there. China's Africa push revved up over a decade ago. They invested more than $5.5 billion in 2008, though slowing growth on both sides reduced the annual rate to $2.5 billion in 2012. The Chinese currently preside over a $30 billion credit line to African countries.

It should come as no shock that Africa supplies about 20 percent of China's oil needs.

Make no mistake; we are competing with China for energy and more from countries like Nigeria. China leads with its checkbook, whether it is building roads in the Sudan or cricket stadiums in the Caribbean. Feeding our middle class means making sure that we have full relationships and trade agreements with emerging nations. China is signing these at a rate of three times our own pace.

Future shocks are hard to predict. But this is no time for American austerity. China and other leading countries are making massive commercial bets on the emerging nations' middle class. It is nearly impossible to pick the winners in this new market version of the World Cup. That's why a portfolio of investment and trade partners is so sensible.

Let's stretch this notion of a thousand flowers blooming and examine another place that has been living under history's bell jar—an economy as far from the notion of middle class as we can imagine: Ethiopia, a name synonymous with famine and despair.

"Rider on the Black Horse"

That's how Ethiopians describe the nightmare of advancing starvation. They have faced wave after wave throughout their history.

Searing images, dry heavens, skeletal mothers and distended children, the gauntest cast of eye—these are the faces of famine. In 1974 they were inconvenient truths, and so they were ignored.

Emperor Hailie Selassie's troops escorted the dying and the starving from the city limits of his capital, Addis Ababa. He denied the galloping black-horse rider by sweeping it from view. Even his own countrymen were shocked by *The Hidden Hunger*, a Jonathan Dimbleby documentary that brought Ethiopian starvation into the world's living room.

Hunger was just one of the reasons for the Selassie overthrow. The military junta, the Derg, broadcast documentaries showing the royal family feeding expensive meat to their pets. The Derg allegedly killed the former emperor by smothering him with a wet pillow, and then turned their attention to dispatching fifty-eight of his most influential generals and ministers.

Mengistu Haile Mariam quickly established a Marxist military regime that horrified the West and usurped foreign funds and food aid for his army and for weapons.

The black-horse rider kept cantering on.

When drought returned in 1981, the West remained indifferent to the warning signs. Things worsened, and by 1984, disease devastated Sidamo—the Ethiopian breadbasket. When the rains chose not to visit in that spring, there was no escape for the hungry nation. The black horse rider took them by the hundreds of thousands.

Famine topples regimes, so the conspiracy of silence from a prior decade was reprised with callous nonchalance. When asked about his starving people, Prime Minister Haile Mariam replied dismissively, "What famine?"

Lack of rain was just part of the problem. A lead economist for the World Bank said later, "This crisis is man-made." Droughts had been dogging the country for years— the politics of famine were the main culprit. Ethiopia had been conducting a civil war against Eritrea for decades. And the West had been warily watching the incursion of communism, making it complicated to parse through its own diplomatic response.

In global political theater starvation rarely plays the lead, even when it harms a cast of thousands.

Kenyan photojournalist Mohammed Amin captured the stark horrors confronting the Ethiopians and also the indifference of the government to the famine that killed nearly a million in 1984 and '85.

The regime had finally sent out warnings in March 1984. By summer hunger held Ethiopia in its claws. Worldwide relief agencies responded but were stymied at every attempt. Foreign governments turned their back on the unfolding disaster despite claims that 6 million Ethiopians, mostly women and children, were at risk.

By October, hundreds of thousands had died. Still, foreign governments were troubled by Russian involvement in Ethiopian matters. Margaret Thatcher took a hard line on aid and American policy makers discredited the African communists. The regime had expelled American military missions seven years earlier after all.

Finally, in the late fall of 1984, the Western powers relented, but hunger is an impatient mistress—nearly a million souls had already died from starvation.

The Ethiopians had so little to lose that they forged alliances among former competing fronts and together they ran Prime Minister Mengistu into the waiting arms of Robert Mugabe in nearby Zimbabwe.

In 1991, Meles Zenawi took vigorous charge and would hold control until his death in 2012. (He was followed by Hailemariam Desalegn, with equally tight hold on the reins.)

Under both regimes foreign aid was welcomed, but Western nations soon tired of the passing plate.

A gallows-humor joke is told in Addis Ababa that the prime minister is asked if he is worried about the lack of rain in Ethiopia. In the story the prime minister responds: "We're not worried about the rains in Ethiopia. We are worried about the rains in the United States and Canada."

THE ETHIOPIAN WAY

HUMAN RIGHTS WATCH CALLS ETHIOPIA one of the most repressive and hostile media environments in the world. Its spy and surveillance apparatus rivals the most sophisticated and intrusive in modern history. (Someone must be showing them how.)

Shrewdly, Ethiopia has offered to play local police officer for the region, hosting a U.S. military base and on occasion sending troops to fight the Islamist al-Shabaab in neighboring Somalia. Odd for a China-style planned society.

Oxfam ranks Ethiopia near the bottom of its world rankings of worst-fed countries, narrowly eclipsing Chad and Angola. At the same time, U.S. Food for Peace grants have been on a steep decline from nearly half a billion dollars in 2009 to under $100 million in 2014.

More than 70 million of the country's 90-plus million citizens have no electricity. Three-quarters of the roads are dirt. And the automobile ratio is one for every 330 people.

And yet under the repressive Meles Zenawi regime Ethiopia has been transformed. For at least the last ten years the country has enjoyed double-digit economic growth. Inflation has been sloppy, hitting 60 percent in 2008 and 40 percent in 2011. But it has since settled down to high single digits.

This is certainly not a regime that counts open dialogue among its chief goals. Of the 547 members of parliament, just one belongs to something that feels like an opposition party.

Anyone studying the approach will sense an Asian-style control to the economy. The late Prime Minister Zenawi was unambiguous: "There is no connection between democracy and development."

The prime minister had a clear vision and an articulated national goal to turn Ethiopia into a middle-class nation by 2025—defined by the World Bank as $1,430 income per capita. It was laughable at first, as was his opening press conference decades ago, where he defined success as three meals a day for his people.

While he missed both targets during his lifetime, for all the degradation of freedoms and human rights shortcomings, progress happened. There is a middle-class message here.

Just before his death, the country's per-capita income reached $410, up from the very depths a generation before.

Many obstacles remain. Unemployment runs about 27 percent for young people. But despite these hurdles Ethiopia remains a development darling, and it is creating millionaires faster than any country in Africa.

According to McKinsey Global International, emerging markets see major retail expansion once income per capita reaches $750. Ethiopia is inching toward prosperity.

A unique feature of the Ethiopian way is that they offer short contracts to foreign business operators. Call it a semi-privatization. France Telecom secured a twenty-four-month deal to run Ethio Telecom, one of the few government-owned communications monopolies in Africa. When the two-year term ended, a refreshed and refurbished business was returned to Ethiopian hands.

For that reason Walmart and other compelling corporate partners are circling and watching—waiting for the opportune time to try to strike their own deal.

The new leadership has admitted that it must modernize its supply-chain and distribution networks and encourage better price competition—if for no other reason than to tamp down inflation, which constantly growls on the periphery.

Beverage giant Diageo purchased one of Ethiopia's state-owned breweries and will produce a million bottles a day of Meta beer. With the emerging middle class and its attendant thirst, the company hopes to double production inside of three years.

African Truth and the Ethiopian Middle Class

IN AN EFFUSIVE RECENT REPORT the Africa Development Bank cheered that the number of middle-class Africans has tripled in the last thirty years to more than 313 million of its billion people. They cite the shift to a salaried business culture from agriculture as the principal reason for the seismic shift.

The report cautions that the new middle class contains a large "floating class," which has at best an insecure foothold.

Their middle-class numbers have doubled since 1990. But the definitions give pause to their enthusiasm. "The middle class is usually defined as individuals with annual incomes of greater than $3,900" in PPP terms.

This group is subdivided into a floating class of $2 to $4 spent a day, lower middle of $4 to $10 a day, and upper middle in the range of $10 to $20 per day. (The floating class is much larger than the other two combined.)

By this optimistic yardstick, 21 percent of Ethiopians are middle class. Over half are in the floating category. But by their measurement 4.8 million are lower middle and 2.7 million are upper middle class. Eight million out of 90 million is astonishing progress; not long ago, there were barely a few thousand.

From the gates of hell a generation ago, an unmistakable, small, and growing middle class has emerged in Ethiopia. Like many emerging nations in the region, Ethiopia combines the modern and the medieval. But the rate of growth is as demonstrable as the gut determination behind it.

Standard Bank and others have taken a decidedly more skeptical approach to the ADB findings—placing the total number closer to 50 to 60 million of middle-class Africans spread over a wide array of economies. Not surprisingly, they are highly concerned about the stability of the floating class.

There is risk in the middle class emergence throughout Africa—it cannot be denied.

But even Standard Bank named Ethiopia and ten other nations as home to millions of middle-class households and reported with confidence that their trends will continue for at least the next fifteen years.

Long Shots

PROSPERITY FOR OUR MIDDLE CLASS will come only if we make a portfolio of bets—even some with long odds. Emerging countries will not sit back and let America simply inherit what we believe is rightfully ours. They do not believe in entitlement. Nor will these nations embrace a democratic way of life just because they can purchase Wonder

Bread and Velveeta.

The forces of middle-class advance are being nurtured in nations all across the globe in ecosystems entirely distinct from our own. None of these countries take middle-class ascendancy for granted. In this respect, the American cheese stands alone.

In 1945, America faced unique historical circumstances. And we devised a plan. Circumstances in 2015 are also unique, but this time we can't agree on a strategy. China, as we know, has a plan. But even if China fails, there are India, and Nigeria, and Brazil, and Bangladesh—and maybe even sorry old Europe—that can steal a march on competitors. And coming up on the rail are rank outsiders—countries like Myanmar and even Ethiopia, which most Americans couldn't find on a map.

If these countries can comfortably forecast a doubling of their middle class in six years or less, what does that say about the American drive to do the same?

It's time we realized the dualities we are facing: Consuming nations are potential competitors; meaningful allies will not always be business friends, yet their need to advance may provide us a way out of our middle-class doldrums.

Diplomacy will be tested like never before, in part because some pretty unexpected players are making astonishing progress. The world economy is nothing if not a competition, and right now, as beautifully positioned as Americans are, we are looking for solutions in homebound remedies that are palliative and self-medicating—and nowhere near a cure.

America's Choice

Stay the course or restore our middle class by
immersion in the emerging world

As the ninetieth day approached, the *boy began to steel himself—time to disconnect again. His father was a dedicated journeyman back when public servants did just that—lived to serve. His job as mapmaker for the U.S. Coast Guard and Geodetic Survey meant gathering information and making precise surveys for a couple of months before moving on to the edge of the next map.*

His crew of assistants and data gatherers moved with him, as did his loving family. "It was like a circus caravan without the elephants," the boy recalled. Every three months, he got a new home. By the time he reached seventh grade, the boy was moving to his twenty-fourth state.

He credits his peripatetic childhood with helping him adapt. "I learned how to go into new situations, survey the landscape [like his dad] and deal with people." The experience would serve him well.

His empathetic and outgoing nature led him to journalism studies in Missouri and eventually to advertising, where his enthusiasm caught the attention of clients. After he supervised major relationships at PepsiCo and Frito-Lay, it wasn't long before the client beckoned.

In time he was running their restaurant business, an important but smaller subsidiary of the soda and snacks behemoth. Toward the end of the last century, Pepsi spun the business off to its shareholders, preferring to focus on their core opportunities.

Almost immediately, the young manager faced the challenge of uniting three iconic brands that were each struggling and highly mistrustful of one another. Bringing the operators of Kentucky Fried Chicken (KFC), Pizza Hut, and Taco Bell into alignment tested him like every new town had for all those years as his father's caravan traversed the country.

But his travels were only beginning.

Under this new CEO, and independent ownership, the company blossomed and relations with the hardworking middle-class franchisees thawed considerably.

But the cheerleading pitchman could not ignore the prospects for the three brands he was charged with advancing. Everyone suspected that U.S. gains were going to moderate and that significant growth required bolder vision and new strategic direction.

David Novak, the Yum! Brands CEO, had lectured and spoken endlessly about dreaming big—surveying the scene and making a bold bet. Now it was time to practice what he had taught.

He gathered his team together to hear reactions to his plan. Novak saw a huge new worldwide middle class evolving, and he wanted them as customers. His idea was to take his three primary brands and transform Yum! into the largest quick-serve restaurant in the world, ahead of the Golden Arches guys.

Few believed it was possible, or advisable.

"China is the biggest retail opportunity in the twenty-first century," he argued. Focusing his team on China, India, Russia, South Africa, and selected European markets, he paid particular attention to the insights of his franchisees—a cardinal rule for brand extension into bold new places.

"They think like entrepreneurs," he wrote. Their proverbial nest eggs are on the line every day.

By the end of 1997, Novak had opened a hundred restaurants in China, where eating at an American-style fast-food chain was seen as a status symbol. Quickly, he learned it was vital that local management and owners be free to tailor their offerings to suit local markets.

In China, consumers demanded greater variety, spicier taste, and 24/7 availability. In India, sauces and flavors are important, and Taco Bell doesn't serve beef there. In Dubai, food is prepared so it is halal—ritually compliant with Islamic law.

Yum! introduced pizza delivery into China in 2001 and now serves twenty-eight cities. That was just an hors d'oeuvre.

Early successes led to many more openings in a wide array of countries and to market leadership positions in Malaysia, Indonesia, Vietnam, and Africa.

There were plenty of mistakes along the way: bad products, mispricing, and cultural insensitivities. But nothing was more damaging than run-ins with the State Food and Drug Administration in China over suppliers using expired meat. First in 2012 and then in 2014, Yum! was hammered by bad press for the behavior of one of its primary chicken and beef suppliers. Another report of drug use in chicken raising by suppliers in 2013 caused KFC China's sales to plunge 37 percent in the following month.

Novak was outraged but undaunted.

He has clear eyes on the global middle-class prize. Today, Yum's biggest market is no longer the United States. Novak oversaw the opening of over 4,700 KFC restaurants and 1,200 Pizza Huts serving over a thousand cities in China, by far their biggest market.

They are the largest and fastest-growing restaurant company in India too. Yum! predicts that India will become the largest-consuming middle class in the world by 2030. Their India growth has tripled in the last five years to nearly 400 KFC stores. Across all brands, Yum! projects having more than 2,000 restaurants in India in five years.

As Novak stepped into the executive chairman role in 2014, having brought the Louisville-based company to the world's largest middle-class eating establishment, with 40,000 restaurants in more than 125 countries— many where it is the leading chain—he naturally turned reflective.

What can you say about the temerity of a marketer who opens Taco Bells in Mexico City?

Three quarters of Yum's profits come from overseas—that's statement enough.

When asked in a USA Today interview if Yum! could still be called a U.S. company, Novak paused for a moment and said, "We want to be the defining global company that feeds the world."

Opportunity will not come to us—we must seize it. That's the message of Yum's success.

A defensive island strategy won't work, because our home market is nowhere near large enough to sustain us. Our most successful enterprises reach across borders for most of their economic opportunity. Changes in Europe, and the emergence of BRICs and TIMBIs and other new economies, mean that America must adapt its behavior, its laws, its business strategy, and its global mission.

For dozens of nations the middle-class opportunity is now. America cannot dither. For now Brazil and Nigeria are principally commodity and agricultural exporters, both anchored by too much poverty. At least one of them, if not both, will evolve into a broader-based economy. We cannot rest on our market position. Companies that win loyalty among this emerging global middle class will return massive benefits to their home markets, their investors, their financial and supplier counterparties, and to their middle-class employees.

Everything about these relationships will be more complex. Control of massive multinationals only gets tougher. For the manufacturers who choose not to make it at home, they will have to invest to make it elsewhere. Our middle class will stay strong by feeding the needs of the world's evolving middle class, not by staying homebound.

How to Win the Middle-Class Opportunity Abroad

Here are ten ways to capture the world's growing middle-class opportunity:

Lead the world's industrial flow. Japan and South Korea have learned to trade up the technology and value-added curves. Robotics installations have doubled in China in the last three years. Japan and South Korea and Taiwan have created true world-class conglomerates, boasting thirteen of Asia's top fifteen exporters.

India, Indonesia, and many developing countries have the raw material but not the industrial presence of the Asian giants. If they are clever, they might gain economic ground that China is ceding. India's Tata Group runs underperforming businesses at home and impressive global winners, like Jaguar Land Rover (JLR) and TSC, an expansive IT enterprise. Both India and Indonesia have the workforce and motivation to partner and be guided to the next level.

What are we doing about it? GE has been India-focused since the Jack Welch days, as have other Western multinationals. Where are American policy makers? India's new prime minister, Marendra Modi, is being heavily courted by China and other major players around the world. The first time he tried to visit the United States in 2005 before becoming prime minister, we denied him a visa. His late 2014 visit went a bit better.

Opportunities abound to partner and build the infrastructure necessary to create middle-class economies in these countries. Invigorating their distribution, railway, telecom, and road infrastructure will draw manufacturing jobs. It will drive usage and consumption. It will lead their consumer inexorably to our products and services.

So where is the United States?

To optimize our middle class, we must fully embrace the development of theirs. Parochial thinkers will say we are giving away our secret sauce. They fail to realize that we are creating a market for our products, our services, and our technology. Sitting back and watching China trade up the technology curve, leaving room for these other nations to slip into their "spot" without playing some role in that evolution is the old model for American trade relations. Unless we earnestly engage with India, Indonesia, and these emerging tigers, we will cease to participate in the growth of the world's middle class.

We already compete nose-to-nose with the likes of Toyota, Samsung, and other mature Asian companies. They rival any of our best enterprises in size, profitability, and product capability. China is hard on their heels, but only a handful of their companies possess anything like the scope of our biggest players. Either we compete with these nations or we partner with them. But if we ignore them, we will suffer; our middle class will be spectators—atrophied and glum on the sidelines.

We need a coordinated strategy for each of these economic counterparties.

Cater to growing middle-class demands in the developing world. Remember, many of these nations are facing changes we have digested at a measured pace over decades at their own warp speed. Our expertise is the opportunity. We can help these nations achieve their goals and our quality goods will be ready when they need them. As a middle class develops it demands quality for its money, including products that pollute less, deliver more, and break infrequently. Who makes more of these quality products than we do?

Innovation versus Emulation. Developing nations are so far removed from the technology edge that small steps toward the frontier turn into quantum leaps. In many ways, advanced countries bear a bigger burden of higher expectations and less allowed flexibility whenever they innovate.

It requires the strain of major innovation to move our giant economy forward in a meaningful way. Emerging nations can see massive improvements merely by emulating steps that we have already taken and implementing them locally. Bringing our new discoveries to the emerging markets is the best hope for our middle class, and theirs.

Emulation is the sincerest form of flattery. These developing nations have flipped the classroom. For centuries wealthy nations surged ahead, grew stronger, and differentiated by the sheer size of their lead. The gap has collapsed like a thoroughbred's lead in the stretch. The new timetable has crushed manufacturing advantages and minimized educational distinctions; time and space have merged into a tighter and tighter cycle. We are being watched just as we are watching them. One noted Internet venture capitalist in Shanghai opined that "I'm sitting in China; somebody is going to copy me in the U.S. I'm sitting in the U.S.; somebody is going to copy me in China."

Innovation advances are the key to the developed world's advantage. Apple iPhones dominated in China, having sold 23 million units in 2013, and then a Chinese upstart Xiaomi (pronounced "Show me") founded in

2010 sold over 18 million without running a single advertisement. Xiaomi has since surged to be the biggest smartphone seller in China and third in the world.

Innovation requires endless creativity, calculation, and parsing through cognitive dissonance for the breakthrough idea. Critical thinking trumps rote memorization and rigid thinking. Steven Jobs had it with "Think Different." It is time-consuming, with many failures for each breakout success.

Emulation, like most release 2.0s and movie sequels, should not be underestimated. Its impact can be enormous. For the urgently growing, need-to-be-fed developing nations emulation can collapse product and service life cycles from years to months.

Big-country advantages become less gigantic. The global middle wins because they have few legacy systems that hold them back from embracing change. Think of it as *innovation acceleration.* For example, when wireless technology leapfrogs older, more plodding and expensive installations, like twisted-pair copper wire telephony systems, innovation accelerates an emerging country's growth. Some emerging nations can skip a generation of technological advance altogether, save billions in installation expense, and level the playing field in the process. Innovation comes faster in the developing world. If we take twenty years to get ahead, they now take five.

Use American brand power. No one is better suited for this challenge than American companies and their employees. Take brands—not everyday local products, but the platinum brands and killer and misdemeanor apps found in many categories. With them we can both build and drive the worldwide consumer boom.

Interbrand, one of the world's largest brand consultancies, has for years developed an annual list of the 100 most valuable brands.

Once considered little more than a logo, a recollected jingle, or a snappy ad campaign, the great brands have become engines for whole families of global products and businesses. The greatest brands inspire worldwide trust and consumer awareness. They are the strategic arsenal in any attempt to penetrate a new market—especially one with a somewhat vulnerable and mistrustful new consumer.

In the post-digital world there is no such thing as a domestic company. All products are global, even if they never leave a single zip code. All brands reach far beyond their consumer.

In the top ten global brands, according to Interbrand, South Korea and Japan each have one—unsurprisingly, Samsung and Toyota. In the full 100 list, all of Asia has just 10 percent. Leave out South Korea and Japan and there are none. Pause for a moment. The biggest, fastest-growing consumer markets on the planet (excluding South Korea and Japan) do not have a single entry in the top 100 brands.

The United States dominates the list.

For the American middle class and those who would like to protect it, that screams opportunity. We have begun adapting our major brands to capture the consumer there. And others have imitated us while we waited.

BOOF burgers was started in Iran in 1995 and spread to Malaysia and other markets. It features a McDonald's-style menu, which now includes other Western-style fast foods like fried chicken and pizza and French fries. If we don't innovate, others emulate.

Variations on our own brands are breaking into developing markets: KFC Vegfare in China, Dinner Tang mealtime drink in Latin America, and my favorites, Green Tea Oreos in China and Blueberry Oreos in Indonesia.

Leading with our strengths leverages our middle-class position and consumer power. Remember, the emerging middle class wants to trust its products, and many of the local offerings suffer from inconsistent quality and even toxicity. Just what was that powder in the formula that the Chinese were feeding to their infants? Their new middle class will not tolerate toxic products for their children.

Leading with our trusted brands has other benefits too. Without consumer trust there can be no premium pricing, no line extension or new-product introduction—no lasting customer relationship. Decades of investment elsewhere in the world will boost our nation's market positions in these developing nations. It is a middle-class momentum play. We buy it and they will too. Just with some local adjustment.

BOOF has made great headway in Islamic regions with a post-Ramadan breaking-fast meal with your selection of favorites.

Will pursuing these markets elevate our entire economy? Certainly, if we succeed it will benefit more than just the middle class. But rather than defend with barriers and tariffs, why not surge forward on our strengths?

Service the world. If products are an entry point, then services follow. We possess more insight into servicing a consumer market than any nation on earth. Marry our technology skills with the sales and service mentality that drives our business at home and you can smell opportunity. Services don't require massive industrial infrastructure. Remote management and technology hubs mean we can be nimble as we adjust to growing demand for services.

The transfer of funds and industrial secrets, intellectual property, killer apps, design changes, product refinements—all are a mouse click or a keystroke away. So are services.

In the developing world, middle-class families who have never used services suddenly can't imagine living without them. It is natural that Alibaba and other Internet players in the developing world are testing financial services. The rate of change will be dizzying, but the appetite for a broad spectrum of services provides a magnificent opportunity.

Heal the sick. Emerging middle classes demand access to affordable, consistently offered, quality health care. They rarely get it. A study in India predicted that 100 million people in the country could have diabetes by 2030. Currently, up to 8 percent of the population does, yet most go untreated. American success in the health care sphere is far more apparent from abroad than at home. By any measure, the United States is the gold standard for drug development, preventative health care, and standards of care. How mature is the developing world's health market?

The market value of health care for all of the stock markets combined in Asia except Japan is barely one percent.

It is a wide-open opportunity.

With Japan included, health care is still only 4 percent. As a proportion of Asian GDP it is minuscule. Africa's numbers are even lower. Explosion of health care in the developing world's middle class is the closest thing to a sure thing that exists in the world today. Let's turn our health care system into an engine of growth rather than the thorn we all grouse about.

In virtually every area of health care and delivery—in implant technology and joint replacement, in surgical approaches and acute-care treatment, services, data analysis, elder care, imaging, distribution—the United States is without peer.

Look at the developing and other nations of the world and see who is aging fastest. Ride your bike by the Bundt in Old Shanghai, travel the French Concession, and check the parks around Beijing. Imagine every living American is seventy years old—that is China in short order. China is a health care entrepreneur's holiday. Add other aging nations, like Thailand, South Korea, and Taiwan, and you get a sense of the opportunity.

In fifteen years, there will be hundreds of small villages in northern Japan without a single woman of childbearing age. Their aging populace is our opportunity.

A diminishing working age population always has difficulty when supporting a growing population of elderly. Age pyramids all over the world are inverting. Efficient and affordable health care armed with the highest technology will become a requirement of the world's middle class. By 2021, health care will exceed 20 percent of America's GDP— let's export our genius. Look at India, Brazil, and some of the erstwhile tigers held back from their expectations because they have too many poor and sick among their population. Solving these urgent national priorities will boost their middle class and ours.

Export our management, technology, and execution expertise. Developing countries are flying down a road that we used to travel at the speed limit. Mobile-phone platforms skip over wire line installations. Sky TV preempts cable plant. Mobile has become the first screen, not the PC. Tablets replace laptops and over a billion of the 6 billion cell phones are already smart phones in the developing world. Let's enable more countries to skip a grade.

Things move so quickly that our nimble networks and our software dynamism can be a major help. Justifiable concerns surround intellectual property and, by some countries' consumers, an unwillingness to pay. Piracy is frustrating, but the issue remains.

We still have much we can share about supply-chain management and logistics with the developing world. We have created vast retail networks and our top ten Internet retail players are bricks-and-mortar players like Walmart.

In 2014, China passed the United States as the world's largest Internet retail market. Unlike in the United States, market China's top ten Internet retailers have no bricks-and-mortar retail establishments. They live in a virtual retail world. In Japan, only one of the top Internet retailers has a meaningful retail presence. Perhaps they have something they can teach us.

Take advantage of structural weakness and inefficiencies. Both India and Indonesia need a recapitalization of an aging and poorly built industrial plant. And these countries were born shovel ready. Partnering, acquiring, investing, joint venturing—all are ways that our capital and expertise can build demand for our resources.

Throughout greater Asia, structural inefficiencies surround state-owned enterprises (SOEs) and family-controlled businesses.

In the 1980s and '90s, Europe went through a massive privatization campaign. Turning the German phone company Deutsche Telekom, or British Gas, or Total of France, into competitive private players had the virtue of passing capital gains to the people and of creating competitive enterprises out of protected monopolies. These painful steps were first condemned, then welcomed by the middle class. Deregulation brought competition, better pricing, better service, and, in time, more jobs.

Competition on the world stage necessitated these government spin-offs. Developing countries like Mexico, with Tel-Mex, and Brazil (still majority owner) with Petrobras followed suit—again to gain access to international capital, to create international financial brands, and to turn the management and ownership of the enterprise over to public institutional and individual shareholders.

This semi-privatization model has been followed by China with its SOEs. Linkage to the Communist Party, the government, and in some cases the military, is very tight in these companies. Regional governments often hire an SOE to build projects directed by the Party. Crony lending by state-controlled banks is the coin of the realm. SOEs enjoy robust credit availability, but smaller companies lack access to capital. These giant enterprises directed by a tightly controlled party apparatus can't be nimble and flexible. Senior executives are often Party members and are reluctant to ruffle feathers. This cozy situation is an opportunity for Western capital, and it is far from limited to China.

There are 85 million private and small businesses in China and India, almost all of them starved for capital. Most are stuck, by code and regulation, serving local markets. When the market uncovers these buried gems, a consolidation like none the world has ever seen will certainly follow—just not anytime soon.

Bring them here. Developing countries have not fully entered the world of export marketing. Fewer still manufacture here. Western multinational company exports account for a majority of sales. Not so the Asian multinationals, which hover around 30 percent of revenues.

But that tells only part of the story. In many of these developing countries, a few individual companies account for huge proportions. In India, Reliance alone accounts for more than 14 percent of the country's exports. South Korean giant Samsung comprises 17 percent of the nation's exports. If we can't feed every bit of their consumer boom, then let's build up their companies with our assets and our finances and bring their greatest products to our shores.

Winnovation. The developing world is a city of two tales. Not everything is as it is recorded or even as it appears. The popular press often cites a few statistics to cement Asia's position in the hierarchy of technology giants. They count 29 percent of global research and development as being spent in Asia. They also point to Asia filing for 41 percent of the world's patents. Sobering numbers indeed.

Yet who are their high-tech behemoths? Huawei is clearly on the march, but it is viewed by many nations as a pawn of Chinese military policy and is therefore foreclosed from entry into the American network architecture. Samsung has grown enormously, with profitability rivaling Apple's. But there are many tired entries, like Sony and Panasonic, that once held greater sway.

Hon Hai Precision of Taiwan (which trades as Foxconn) is the world's largest contract manufacturer. But for all of the high-tech manufacturing done in China and other countries in the region, where are Apple's value-added revenues actually booked? In the United States, even if the tax rolls show Apple on the Emerald Isle.

For all of the excitement around online behemoth Alibaba, or YY, the $3 billion social network in China, there really isn't a start-up culture fully developed in China. Japan has Rakuten as its leading Internet commerce company, and Softbank, which owns large positions in Alibaba and Yahoo. South Korea's Naver is their leading search engine.

Some of these names are expanding globally. Rakuten bought a global messaging platform called Viber, and Softbank led by Masayoshi Son, purchased control of Sprint and Clearwire, which went on to acquire control of T-Mobile from Deutsche Telekom, merging the number-three and -four wireless companies in America.

But missing from the spinning top of Asian innovation is sufficient flow of capital to these enterprises, particularly if you exclude Japan. Only 28 percent of Asian-listed companies are controlled by institutional investors. The balance are state-owned enterprises and family conglomerates, or other forms of company groups controlled by a combination of both.

American comprehension of innovations in many areas can serve our economy well in the Asian sphere. We understand venture funding and entrepreneurial capitalism. Getting markets opened to us is understandably tricky. But there are innovations in industries more mundane yet still important besides the robust opportunities in the entire health care space, mobility, technology, and communications.

Watch television or movies anywhere in the developing world and there are legion opportunities to bring our unique Western culture to that market. Bollywood makes more movies than Hollywood, but where are their global brands?

We have much we can teach the Indian drug industry about quality standards. But their ability to employ highly educated, experienced drug industry experts at a fraction of the costs we pay bodes well for their industry. Companies there have moved on from stuffing capsules and packaging to creating molecules. There have been setbacks with Ranbaxy and other drug manufacturers in India, but their speed-to-market with drugs and in building and permitting is singularly impressive. A huge opportunity there is bringing our supply chain and retail health care expertise to address their virtually nonexistent pharmaceutical retail distribution system.

Study these countries. Innovations for them are run-of-the-mill for us today, including hotels, consumer services, fast foods, and automobiles.

Seizing these opportunities will help their economies grow as it will help our own. The lifting of our boat will serve the middle class most of all, because we are talking about bringing value-added competitive product to an increasingly canny consumer of the developing middle class.

Finally, try something really different. Let's collaborate with competing countries on a goodwill mission where profit, military advantage, and a diplomatic upper hand are not on the agenda (even if they really are).

Everything we do with China, Russia, and Brazil is a kind of competition. Let's try, instead, a grand cooperation. Let's work together with one of these nations to eradicate malaria, build a water-filtration system, renew untillable land for agriculture, and provide drinking water to villages across another poor nation. Let's create a food bank together, or a training program for low-end manufacturing, or any other community good some poor nation requires.

Our penchant is for territorial imperative and better earnings per share or superior weaponry. Should we exercise a different muscle just occasionally with these emerging dynamos? If nothing else, when products are dumped, nations are annexed, military maneuvers upset the balance, or political rivals offend, we will have some shared objective that is just for the betterment of another nation.

The point is that our middle class will be inextricably tied up with these other nations. We will service, supply, and, yes, compete. They will steal our intellectual property and we will penetrate their markets. We will lend to each other, supply each other parts, and soon there will be no such thing as an American Apple Computer laptop or German BMW or a Korean Samsung television. Each product will become a shared creation, even if the companies making the good or service owe allegiance to one principality over all others.

Every product is a world product, and the Internet will make every middle-class consumer part of a huge global cohort who are competing and collaborating, buying and selling to each other at the same time.

What we need is a well-worn path of community good that links these disparate nations and prevents what might appear like a Western bloc of the United States and Europe, or an Eastern bloc of Russia and China, or a Southeast Asian, or an Indian, and so on.

We have developed a prescribed set of relationships with other countries—military, diplomatic, regulatory, commercial, trade, economic, but almost never spiritual. Thinking of any great nation, no one save perhaps the chief executive maintains the overall relationship. We need another dimension.

The role of our national outreach in making our middle class a lasting imperative means we need a way to break the logjam when all trails between us and our competing nations have grown cold. Working together to feed starving families in the Sudan, or launching a communications satellite to promote better dialogue—these more spiritual linkages may be just the thing to prevent a breakdown when the relationship gets too complex and constrained in every other way. The key word is engagement. It is through engagement with new and existing partners abroad that the way forward is to be found.

CHAPTER TWENTY-TWO

Mojo Found

How you change everything

SOMEWHERE IN THE HEAVENS A LONG *time ago the gods gathered in high council to discuss a critical issue: where to hide the greatest of all their gifts, courage, to keep it from being discovered by inquisitive mortals who walked the earth.*

Debate at the tribunal was animated and intense. Answers volleyed back and forth across the table without resolution.

One deity suggested hiding courage at the top of the highest mountain, another opined it should be hidden behind an impenetrable jungle thicket, another deep in the darkest cave, still another at the bottom of the sea.

In every suggestion, the other gods were convinced that mankind would somehow find their secret. No matter how challenging the obstacles they imagined, the gods feared that mankind would overcome them. The tribunal was frustrated and deadlocked.

Finally, an elder stood and the bickering crowd fell silent. "You are thinking about this all wrong. Don't hide it where it is hardest to find. The answer," the old deity offered, "is to hide courage in a place where mankind will rarely think to look."

He paused to let the baffled gods ponder in silence.

"Let's hide courage deep in the human heart. They won't look there until every other option is exhausted."

AFTER A LONG JOURNEY TOGETHER, we come to the precipice of the infinity pool. There is a vast middle class in the world today, and a vaster one still tomorrow.

Many rejoice in ever-upward curves of middle-class growth to 5 billion souls, and in their idyll, poverty as we know it comes to an end.

How can we possibly provide that many middle-class people with something to do for a living? Try as I might, I can't find 4 billion good jobs on the planet.

Seeing suffering firsthand as we quintuple the earth's population in just 120 years, I can only dream of such an outcome. Quantum leaps in productivity and well-being are so appealing, but the portrait I see is shaded by enormous vulnerability.

Scan the horizon—an extraordinary vision is coming to life.

Wander through old Europe, the beautiful land of so much American patrimony. It is the ghost of Christmases to come. Study events there and reflect on what it portends for us.

Their middle class is fading, and dividing between a cascade of nations that have and many that have not. Marginalized by parochial attitudes and economies of smaller size, there is a stark necessity to maintain unity even as there are calls from the periphery to disunite.

The greatest threat to the EU middle class is not that they fail to hold together the union, but instead that the greater European middle class fails to make it through at all unless as some ward of the state.

Divided they will fall.

At their absolute best the Europeans may find moments of solidarity under a sole monetary authority, but having eighteen different fiscal authorities and national interests makes rebounding so strenuous. By comparison, America has élan.

And if Utah or Colorado were to stumble and fail to meet their obligations, can you imagine Americans rushing to the IMF looking for a multibillion-dollar bailout?

We have so many gifts that we have not opened yet.

Sometimes gifts come from a wholly unexpected source, proving once again that we must always be ready for the unpredictable.

There is a saying in the oil patch (or there should be)—when oil is worth $100 a barrel, there is oil everywhere.

Huge surges in oil prices attract innovation, technology, and exploration. By 2014 and 2015, thanks to oil sands technology, America had gone from the world's biggest consumer of oil to being at the same time one of the world's biggest suppliers. That shift created an outsized supply response. The fifteen-year super-cycle of ever upward oil prices driven by China's and the emerging markets' unquenchable thirst came to a shuddering halt and oil prices plunged for a dozen straight months.

As often happens, big producers hedged, protecting themselves but causing others to misprice. In a downward spiral with many big players hedged to protect against the worst, prices have a habit of overshooting their trend in one direction or the other.

In 2015, OPEC chose not to serve as swing producer and cut production to adjust supply. This time they kept on cranking no doubt a reaction to their declining share of world production—about 40 percent—down double digits percent from their heyday.

For all of the barrel-half-empty economists, this price drop represented the biggest redistribution of wealth from oil producers to oil importing nations and especially into the pockets of the U.S. middle class that we have seen in decades.

Petroleum and chemical companies suffered and some exploration budgets were curtailed. But the middle class as a whole got a Christmas bonus all year long.

Other benefits we have to plan for. The developing world is an entrepreneur's dream—reaching out to copy us, compete with us, and trade with us. They will play every role from confidante to archrival. The challenge we face is to take what makes us great and use it to help them along the path they have chosen.

Ironic, isn't it? By helping them we help us.

We live in times where the ironic, not the obvious, is often the best way forward. But the obvious has such mass appeal that good choices are hard to make and harder to execute.

A central irony about economic conflagrations that result from over-borrowing, overspending, and overconfidence is that the only proven way out of the mess is to borrow more, spend more, and build more confidence. Austerity is the obvious and ineffective course that satisfies no hunger and quenches no thirst. Just look at the nations that have tried it.

Certainly, the types of spending must differ meaningfully, but you cannot fad-diet your way to better economic growth and fiscal health.

You have to spend on the right things.

In the same way, there is a central irony in the developing world. It is counterintuitive for us to feed their local business markets and find their nationals jobs in order to make our middle class more successful, but that is precisely the way forward.

You risk being marginalized if you ignore these upstart nations; and preempted if you are lackluster in building trading relationships there; and obviated for a very long time if someone else partners with them first.

For too long we have led with guns, and it is time for the United States to come first with butter.

If we help fulfill their belief in a better middle-class life there will be American jobs created to maintain, sustain, and track the behavior of these emerging national markets.

One look at the minuscule health care spending among developing nations and a whole world of opportunity there will feed our middle class here.

Within reason.

Just as new manufacturing won't deliver the sheer number of jobs that an old-style steel mill might have, these global companies will prosper differently as they support middle-class growth overseas.

But robust headquarters teams, R&D and branding activity, new product development and technology infrastructure can result from American enterprises propelling the middle classes of the emerging world. We become the bridge of ideas and capital to the developing world.

Sure it is a different course for us, but that is the way the river of commerce is flowing.

Economic isolationism is a bridge to nowhere.

If we don't enjoy absolute superiority, as we did in 1945, we certainly have first-mover advantage. That won't last long.

Happily, everywhere in the world you go, there is an abiding confidence that we possess something special that drives us to higher ambition and accomplishment.

The challenge is to run toward the problem, not away from it. That is the best path for our middle class. Painful though it is to acknowledge, not everyone in America is going to make it. I don't just mean the long-term unemployed, who have been consigned to the margins both statistically and practically, but potentially millions of others who aspire to a middle-class life. Compared to the 1950s, there is just too much international competition today, and foreign governments willing to do whatever it takes to pull a populace out of poverty.

There are the baby boomers who haven't saved enough who won't be able to get back in the workforce. There are the high school graduates who don't want to settle for a job worse than their parents' and end up farther back than that. There are people whose single piece of bad luck is crippling. The prospects for a young person entering the job market today can be frightening, and it's unlikely that the graying population will vote for politicians who want to make it easier for the kids.

It's even possible that untouchable entitlements will eat up more of our budget and we end up with a massive upended pyramid of older and old, protected by a safety net that leaves anyone under sixty-five exposed to the elements. "Hang on tight, son," says the old boomer to the infant. "Help is on the way."

Like it or not, generational fairness will have to be part of the suite of solutions to rebuild our middle class.

Let's not become the historical object lesson. A vibrant middle class is the key to economic stability. We also know that our home market is nowhere near capable of sustaining what we have, not to mention what we want to have.

The answer lies over there, and there and there. We need to be willing to risk what we have or we may well lose it all. "Help me help you" is the only course for us to take. We must let go of the trapeze bar that carried us here, and float suspended in midair with the confidence that another bar is arcing our way.

Today we stand in a position no different from when the Levitt brothers scanned the vast fields of the Long Island prairie. There may be oceans that separate us from the proximal dream of middle-class resurgence.

But put yourself through the process of comparing gifts. We are blessed with the greatest universities, the most educated workforce, the most developed capital markets, the most robust network of early-stage capital players, the most protective defense apparatus, the most open society, the most well-funded research and development laboratories, the most powerful economy, the best health care system, the most prodigious government funding mechanism for basic science and research, the leading space program, the most computer literacy, the greatest sense of entrepreneurship, the highest overall standard of living for the most people, the most gifted young people when it comes to critical and imaginative thinking, and a long parade of other firsts and bests in every measure in every class.

We also have something that may be a bit tired, a bit of an aging character, but it is still strong inside us: the spirit that drives all of that excellence listed above. It is handed down like a mantle from generation to generation. We still venerate it, even if we don't see it tangibly as often as we used to.

It may even be that we take it for granted.

After visiting and studying nations of the world who model our success and interpret it to fit their own idiosyncrasies and their own inertial guidance systems, a burning question is all that separates us from the greatest middle-class expansion we have ever experienced.

Has our American mojo truly been found?

The answer, as with the opening of every chapter of this book, lies with the power of the individual. Imagine what small and tangible thing you can do to build a stronger middle class. Combining those powerful individual histories is our best laid plan.

So many middle-class Americans have searched deep in their souls these last fifty years. Support systems they counted on have one-by-one faded into the mist. But America's middle class is resilient and determined. Even as new players come into the arena, there is a continuing sense of self, of duty, of legacy, of belonging.

It is born not of entitlement but determination, not desperation but hope. It is a fire that won't extinguish. And the most powerful force on earth is a soul on fire.

That spirit is a commitment, one to another, a vow . . .

and an obligation.

America has every gift but the gift of will.

All we need is a vast display of individual courage.

And despite what the gods intended, each of us knows exactly where to find it.

Notations

Sources and further reading

In the course of writing this book I studied innumerable books, articles, web entries, documents, and interviews and pored over video, radio, audio tapes, and other broadcast media. This section is not intended to be an exhaustive bibliography, but rather I have detailed some of the most useful sources I found in my research. You will note that I frequently searched for and found diametrically opposing views from respected sources. These opposition pieces helped test my assumptions and I used them to knit together the story of the American middle class and its place in the dynamic world of global growth. I hope that anyone who wants to study this fascinating subject in greater detail will find this list helpful.

Chapter One: *Paradise Lost*

Among the biographies of Carlos the Jackal are *Carlos: Portrait of a Terrorist,* by Colin Smith (New York: Holt, Rinehart and Winston, 1977), *Jackal: The Complete Story of the Legendary Terrorist, Carlos the Jackal,* by Jack Follain (New York: Arcade, 1998) and *Tracking the Jackal: The Search for Carlos, the World's Most Wanted Man,* by David Yallop (New York: Random House, 1993). For newer perspectives and revelations, start with "Rescued from the shredder, Carlos the Jackal's missing years," by Tony Paterson, *The Independent*, October 30, 2010.

Newspapers like the *New York Times* and major European papers covered the events extensively (check individual websites for searches). Interesting to note that TV reporting was pre-CNN, and video logs are useful but nowhere near as global in scope as those we experience today. For this and other subjects check the AP—the video archive is at aparchive.com.

Chapter Two: *The Invasion*

Joseph F. Spears, "The Golden Nematode Handbook. Survey, Laboratory, Control and Quarantine Procedures," U.S. Department of Agriculture, September 1968. Great for the biology and habits of the pest (at usda.gov).

There are many useful books, papers, and articles—the subject of the rise of the middle class after the war has been widely covered. "Levittown: Documents of an Ideal American Suburb," is a great resource from the late historian Peter Bacon Hales of the University of Illinois, Chicago, available at http://tigger.uic.edu/~pbhales/Levittown.

See also Francisco Buera and Joseph P. Kabowski, "The Rise Of the Service Economy," National Bureau of Economic Research, 2009. Doris Kearns Goodwin, "The Way We Won: America's Economic Breakthrough During World War II," *The American Prospect*, Volume 3, Issue 11, September 1992. Marx, J.D. (2011). American social policy in the 1960's and 1970's. Retrieved 2014 from http://www.socialwelfarehistory .com/eras/american-social-policy-in-the-60s-and-70s/. Herbert J. Gans, *The Levittowners: Life and Politics in a New Suburban Community* (New York: Columbia University Press, 1982). Richard Lacayo, "Suburban Legend William Levitt," *Time* magazine, December 7, 1998. Clare Richfield, "The Suburban Ranch House in Post-World War II America," (thesis) Barnard College at history.barnard.edu/sites/default/files/inline/clare-richfield-thesis.pdf. Michael A. Fletcher, "Middle Class-Dream Eludes African American Families," *Washington Post*, November 13, 2007.

Seismic wartime production shifts and FDR's unyielding leadership together won World War II. Plentiful resources illustrate manufacturing changeover, other's, iron presidential will. Manufacturing details of Liberators at Ford's Ypsilanti plant and the facts about creating fleets of Liberty ships are drawn from the primary sources listed, and I acknowledge the sheer force of the details. Sharing FDR's and Churchill's passions and mating rituals relied on different, though related, materials. Both sets of sources helped me weave the fabric of manufacturing with presidential passion. Here and in other chapters we learn this blend forms the bedrock for creating the middle class then and now.

The U.S. Merchant Marine site (usmm.org) provides details on Liberty ships and the race to build one fast, the SS *Robert Peary.* "A Bomber an Hour, Production at Willow Run," *Strategos* (Newsletter of Lean Manufacturing Strategy) at strategosinc.com. *Tanks Are Mighty Fine Things* by Wesley W. Stout, Periscope Film LLC, 2013.

For more on Churchill's approach to FDR, a great read is *Dinner with Churchill: Policy Making at the Dinner Table,* by Cita Stelzer (New York: Pegasus Books, 2012). See also "Churchill at the White House," by Eleanor Roosevelt, *The Atlantic,* March 1, 1965. "Christmas Message 1941" from the Speeches of Winston Churchill at WinstonChurchill.org. A wonderful treatment is *In the Dark Streets Shineth: A 1941 Christmas Eve Story,* by David McCullough (Salt Lake City: Shadow Mountain, 2008).

Jill Lepore, "The Force: How much military is enough?" *The New Yorker,* January 28, 2013. Report of the Special Committee on Investigation of the Munitions Industry (The Nye Report), U.S. Congress, Senate, 74th Congress, 2nd sess., February 24, 1936. Joseph Persico, *Roosevelt's Centurions: FDR and the Commanders He Led to Victory in World War II* (New York: Random House, 2013) is a complete and fascinating look at FDR's advisors and war counselors. Robert Higgs, "Government and the Economy since World War II,"(Independent Institute, 2005). Cecil Bohanon (Ball State University), "Economic Recovery: Lessons from the Post-World War II Period" at Mercatus.org. Paul Krugman, "1938 in 2010," *New York Times,* September 5, 2010. An investment professional's unflinching and studied take is *The War State,* by Michael Swanson (North Charleston: CreateSpace Independent Publishing Platform, 2013).

Chapter Three: *Chocolate Milk*

Many local and national news organizations gave the Daisy Myers story lots of print. It has been covered from every perspective, and individual viewers tell their own story too. We were still learning as a nation and "not in my backyard" was very much in effect when the unrest broke out. It is fascinating to track the change of perspective. The most poignant telling, of course, is Mrs. Myers' own account: Daisy D. Myers, *Sticks 'n Stones: The Myers Family in Levittown* (York, PA: The York County Heritage Trust, 2005). If you are interested in an accurate, reflective view of the time, also consider *Levittown: Two Families, One Tycoon and the Fight for Civil Rights in America's Legendary Suburb*, by David Kushner (New York: Walker Books, 2009). The author does an exceptional job of marshalling these many voluminous resources.

Also read the articles of Mike Argento of the York, PA *Daily Record* who has written about the family and Mrs. Myers with an especially deft and sensitive touch. Considered through the prism of today's racial anxieties, they paint a fascinating look at how far we have come, but how much further we have to travel.

My great regret is that Mrs. Myers went to her rest in December 2011 during the writing of this book, and I was never to have the privilege of meeting her.

On the black middle class, the first ports of call are *Black Bourgeoisie*, by E. Franklin Frazier (New York: The Free Press, 1957), which excites a storm of controversy still, and *The New Black Middle Class*, by Bart Landry, (Oakland: University of California Press, 1988).

Chapter Four: *Dream Stealer*

Few Americans have been subjected to the forms of media coverage, debate, and dialogue the way Martin Luther King has been. At the same time, there is an incuriosity about the way he died that simply would not stand up in today's hypermedia world. What is left is for us to draw our own conclusions. This book's treatment of Dr. King and his role in building up America's middle class was derived by looking at many media, including speeches, radio and television interviews, public domain websites, documentaries, print interviews, books, periodicals, and oral history recollections.

For a self-serving start try *Who Killed Martin Luther King? The True Story by the Alleged Assassin,* by James Earl Ray (New York: Marlowe & Company, 1992).

Evan Thomas of *Newsweek* covered the story and the doubts about Ray with insight and a resistance to conspiracy theories that lacked supporting evidence. Check YouTube for numerous interviews with Ray, including Dan Rather for CBS News and Bill Boggs. Frank Gerold, *An American Death* (New York: Doubleday, 1972). Hampton Sides, *Hellhound On His Trail* (New York: Doubleday, 2010) provides a crime story description and contributes real drama to the assassination and the FBI manhunt. Larry Copeland of the *Philadelphia Inquirer* provides ample play-by-play analysis in many articles: "Unusual Alliance Seeks a New Trial for Ray," February 20, 1997; "Ray's Push for a Trial Advances," February 21, 1997; and "King Family Urges New Probe of Killing," April 3, 1998. Tim O'Neil, "James Earl Ray, King's Assassin, Was Small Time Robber Here," *St-Louis Post Dispatch,* April 15, 2012. "James Earl Ray, Convicted King Assassin Dies," CNN, April 23, 1998. William Bunch, "Conspiracy Theory Won't Be Laid To Rest," Daily News, April 24, 1998. Richard Pearson, "Ray's Fight to Prove His Innocence Is Over," *Washington Post,* April 24, 1998. For additional research the transcript of the assassination and conspiracy trial is available at the King Center at thekingcenter.org/KingCenter /transcript_trial_info.aspx.

There are many books, articles, and Dr. King's own speeches which trace his linkage of civil rights for African Americans, poverty, and war. Civil rights was the first stop in his vision of transforming society. A lot of scholarly attention has been focused on his civil rights imperative, but fascinating studies have tied his actions and visions to economics and well-being for all poor Americans. In Memphis the intersection is covered thoughtfully in the book *Going Down Jericho Road: The Memphis Strike, Martin Luther King's Last Campaign* by Prof. Michael K. Honey, (New York: Norton, 2007).

Also recommended is MLKONLINE.net, a public domain resource for Dr. King's speeches, videos, quotes, and biographical entries. MLK was named *Time* magazine's Man of the Year on January 3, 1964. "The Last Days Of Martin Luther King, Jr.," *Time* magazine, January 9, 2006. *"Roads To Memphis,"* American Experience (PBS). See resources pbs.org/wgbh/americanexperience/features/further-reading/memphis-further-reading.

Also recommended are the papers and articles on Governor Otto Kerner's eleven member commission set up to create a broader government and public understanding of racial disorder in the country and its causes. Rarely are such blue ribbon panels as insightful and prescient. It is a shame more Americans did not pay closer attention to their findings.

Note that in keeping with historical accuracy the word "Negro" is reproduced only when in quoting from the period as used by Dr. King and others in the movement. I recognize the word is deemed inappropriate, and it has been excluded in all cases after that period.

CHAPTER FIVE: *LOVE/HAIGHT*

YOU OWE IT TO YOURSELF to watch Janis Joplin as a young woman singing at her early performances. These can be found at numerous sites including YouTube. Save the Monterey 1966 Pop Festival for last. In one of the films Mama Cass is shown in the audience being bowled over by Janis' prodigious instrument.

Also read the reminiscences of Linda McCartney and Grace Slick to get a picture of the vulnerability and strength of Janis: "Janis Joplin Biography," at the official Janis web site (www.officialjanis.com).

Ed Ward, Geoffrey Stokes & Ken Tucker, *Rock of Ages: The Rolling Stone History of Rock and Roll* (New York: Summit Books, 1986). Elton N. Gish, "History of the Texas Company And Port Arthur Works Refinery," www.texacohistory.com. For more on the Counter Culture Movement read the various works of Ken Kesey, and MortalJourney.com; Popculture.com and archive "The Student Protest Movement of the 1960s," at Colorado.edu/AmStudies/Lewis/2010. These are great general overviews.

Also Nick Kotz, "When Affirmative Action Was White: Uncivil

Rights," *New York Times,* August 28, 2005. Sheila Weller, "Suddenly That Summer," *Vanity Fair,* July 2012. I also commend Dick Cavett's interviews with Janis Joplin and John Lennon.

See *Time* magazine's January 5, 1970, "Man and Woman of the Year: The Middle Americans."

For the sixties: Rebecca Jackson, *The 1960's: An Annotated Bibliography of Social and Political Movements* (Westport, CT: Greenwood, 1992) contains dozens of outstanding books and references if you care to pursue more. Also Mark Kurlanksy's book: *1968, The Year That Rocked the World* (New York: Ballantine, 2003). The treatise spans the globe from Prague to the Mexico Olympics to Cuba. It is an epic world journey reflecting a single year . . . and little of it and yet much of it reflects the American middle class, but he captures Memphis events, King's struggles, and the emerging beat nation in the most unique way. It is where I found the Eldridge Cleaver send-off to MLK.

Time magazine's "Man of the Year" for 1967 was "Twenty-five and under" and the article "The Generation Gap" filled in the gaps on SDS and student unrest and provided detail on membership beyond what was used in the book. The Port Huron Statement for the Students for a Democratic Society is from the SDS national convention June 11-15, 1962. In *Boom! Voices of the Sixties* (New York: Random House, 2007), Tom Brokaw provides a companion to another book which helped form the spirit in my Introduction and early chapters, *The Greatest Generation,* (New York: Random House, 1997).

CHAPTER SIX: *THE THREE UGLIES*

GOLD ATTRACTS BUGS. THERE ARE hundreds of newsletters and blog enthusiasts as well at some true thought leaders like John Ing, the Canadian gold expert whose opinion is widely solicited by many worldwide market participants. As gold is a volatile commodity, many online participants like mining.com and owninggold.com have the most interesting perspectives on it. There have also been thought-provoking more conventionally published sources for the work in this chapter.

Eric Rauchway, "How Franklin Roosevelt Secretly Ended the Gold Standard," Bloomberg News, March 21, 2013. Michael Kitson, "The End of an Epoch: Britain's Withdrawal from the Gold Standard," at wordpress .com, 2012. Nathan Lewis, "Is A Gold Standard Good Or Bad For the Middle Class?" *Forbes* magazine, October 10, 2013.

For a great book that traces the history of the U.S.'s money supply, gold and currency management and prescribes some tough medicine going forward, read *America's Fiscal Constitution: Its Triumph and Collapse* by Bill White (New York: PublicAffairs, 2014). For an extraordinary financial history, which gets a bit broad in its sweep since it is a companion to a TV special, read Niall Ferguson's *The Ascent of Money: A Financial History of the World* (New York: Penguin Press, 2008).

For oil: Andrew Scott Cooper, *The Oil Kings: How the U.S., Iran and Saudi Arabia Changed the Balance of Power in the Middle East* (New York: Simon and Schuster, 2011).

Released sensitive White House documents classified by Henry Kissinger about meetings attended by the Shah of Iran, Kissinger, the Iranian ambassador Zahedi and Richard Helms, U.S. Ambassador to Iran offer a treasure trove of insights into the Shah.

OPEC.org offers a wide array of background materials and data.

"OPEC/1973 and the Arab Oil Embargo of 1973-74," by Brian Trumbore, Editor, Stocks and News.com, for Seven Sister's revenue sharing. "Time to Lay the 1973 Oil Embargo to Rest," by Jerry Taylor and Peter Van Doren, CATO Institute, October 17, 2003 at cato.org. Action Forex's "1973 Oil Crisis" at actionforex.com. Maggie Koerth-Baker, "Why Your Car Isn't Electric," *New York Times,* October 7, 2012.

Sixdaywar.co.uk offers a concise timeline of the fast-moving events.

Michael Barone, "GM Strike Marks the End of an Era." *US News and World Report,* September 29, 2007. Susannah Cahalan, "Saudis Gone Wild," *New York Post,* October 7, 2012. An American Chauffer traces the mores of Saudi Royal Family members abroad. "1973 Oil Embargo and Gas Crisis," MILEPOSTS Garage at automotivemileposts.com gives American car company and consumer reaction to the embargo. "Energy: Nixon's Decisive New Energy Czar," *Time* magazine, December 10, 1973. William E. Simon, *A Time for Reflection: An Autobiography,* (Washington, D.C.: Regnery,

2003). The Energy Information Administration: "25ᵗʰ Anniversary of the 1973 Oil Embargo," 1998. YnetNews, "The Yom Kippur War (1973)," November 11, 2008.

CHAPTER SEVEN: *FLYING THE HUMP*

NUMEROUS BOOKS, ARTICLES, AND INTERVIEWS have been written and conducted, and a few film documentaries deal at least in part with what Theodore White, the noted historian, called "the skyway to hell." Some books are *Flying High, Remembering Barry Goldwater* (New York: Basic Books, 2008) by the incomparable William F. Buckley, Jr. Steven C. King, a hump pilot himself, penned *Flying the Hump to China* (AuthorHouse, 2004); others are *Last Known Position,* a novel by W.L. Heath, written in 1949; William Diebold, *Hell is so Green: Search and Rescue Over the Hump in World War II* (New York: Lyons Press, 2011). The Hump might be the greatest story rarely told.

For Goldwater, read his *The Conscience of a Conservative* published in 1961 and now available in a number of editions. Mary C. Brennan, *Turning Right in the Sixties: The Conservative Capture of the GOP* (Chapel Hill: University of North Carolina Press, 1995). To unlock the true emergence of the conservative movement, in addition to voluminous magazine and newspaper articles, research and review was conducted in the writings and weekly articles of George Will; the numerous and erudite essays of William F. Buckley; the research and newsletters produced by CATO and the Heritage Foundation, some thoughtful places like roguecolumnist. com and William Kristol's writings. Rick Perlstein, *Before The Storm, Barry Goldwater and the Unmaking of the American Consensus* (New York: Hill and Wang, 2001). Never have there been more varied obituaries, before and after Goldwater's actual death.

Among the many articles, books, and insights on Nixon, one powerful one was David Stokes' January 12, 2009, entries at the NixonFoundation .org titled "Nixon Was the Architect of the GOP's 1966 Recovery," where he recounts the future president's battle back from two ignominious defeats by campaigning tirelessly for his fellow party members, culminating in the famous spaghetti supper I mention at the El Morocco nightclub in New York City. The way he writes, it's as if you were there.

Also listen to WNYC's broadcast of Nixon's 1966 appearance at the Overseas Press Club to lay out his position on Vietnam.

The 1968 election was a hurricane with more moving pieces and so many fabulous articles and perspectives—to get a sense of the whirlwind:

The Nixon Presidential Library has numerous citations outlining the 1968 campaign, as does Rick Perlstein in his book *Nixonland: The Rise of a President and the Fracturing of America* (New York: Scribner, 2008). (Perlstein continues his epic series on the rise of American conservatism with *The Invisible Bridge: The Fall of Nixon and the Rise of Reagan* (New York: Simon & Schuster, 2014). Also see *The Deadly Bet: LBJ, Vietnam and the 1968 Election* (Lanham, MD: Rowman & Littlefield, 2005) well told by Walter LaFeber.

The LBJ to Nixon transition played against the most dynamic backdrop imaginable. Fortunately some of our finest historians are drawn to both characters. Particularly rich is the lode of great books on Johnson. There is Doris Kearns Goodwin's *Lyndon Johnson and The American Dream* (New York: St. Martin's Press, 1976); Robert A. Caro's towering and ongoing four-some of *The Years of Lyndon Johnson* books from *1982's Path to Power* (New York: Alfred A. Knopf, 1982) to *The Passage of Power* (New York: Alfred A. Knopf, 2012). If anything, his insights improve with time. Also Robert Dallek's *Flawed Giant* (New York: Oxford University Press, 1998).

CHAPTER EIGHT: *TALL PAUL AND THE TAMERS*

PAUL VOLCKER'S FLY FISHING PASSION was netted long ago by many great writers like Monte Burke of *Forbes,* Nick Lyons (his multiple books and infinite number of articles on fishing), Louis Uchitelle in the *New York Times*, and Michael Corkery of the *Wall Street Journal.* At least three out of four would prefer actually fishing to writing about it so well. But Volcker's reputation was cemented when he auctioned off a chance to share an excursion on the Beaverkill with his six-foot-seven-inch cast for the RFK Center for Justice and Human Rights. It was a big seller. Like all fishing whoppers a bunch get told about Volcker and fishing. A favorite is this one: The Federal Reserve Bank of Kansas City hosted its 1978 to 1982 annual conferences at many different sites at many different times of the year, each time with an economy of attendance. They were casting about—how could they make their mark?

Then came the ingenious idea that trolling an August session in Jackson Hole in front of sitting Fed chair Paul Volcker might lure him and others to the session and to the delights of the Snake River. Hence goes the fish tale, and the world famous Jackson Hole Economic Symposium was hatched.

Volcker has been profiled by every major publication in the world. An especially compelling interview is an unadorned and modestly edited sitting under the "Commanding Heights" banner of PBS. The lengthy conversation spans some of the trickiest issues the man faced in beating inflation and it illuminates the soul of the Fed chairman. I have quoted from it numerous times because unlike many Fed leaders, Volcker is so plain spoken and direct. I recommend the entire piece without fear of overdone econo-speak. It is as Volcker is—unadorned and skillful.

Other sources—Reagan's tax plans and their impact are hotly debated enough to make even taxation interesting. Deep reading about the period will lead you to one conclusion—Reagan raised taxes. But many supporters have been resourceful in refuting what seems so clear. Here are some of the feeder articles and pieces—but you may have to make up your own mind.

Jeanne Sahadi, "Taxes: What People Forget About Reagan" CNN Money, September 12, 2010. Floyd Norris, "Tax Reform Might Start with a Look Back to 1986," *New York Times,* November 22, 2012. "The Real Reagan Economic Record: Responsible and Successful Fiscal Policy." Heritage Foundation, March 1, 2001. "The Second American Revolution: Reaganomics," The Ronald Reagan Presidential Foundation and Library. "Retrospective on the 1981 Reagan Tax Cut," edited by Andrew Chamberlain, June 10, 2014. Steve Benen "The Biggest Tax Hike in Modern History," *Washington Monthly,* September 29, 2011. Will Bunch, "Five Myths About Ronald Reagan's Legacy," *Washington Post,* February 4, 2011. Lee Edwards, PhD., "The Origins of the Modern American Conservative

Movement," Fred Hutchison, Heritage Foundation Research, November 21, 2003. "The Founding of the 20ᵗʰ Century Conservative Movement: The restoration of traditionalism." Renew America, March 17, 2008.

For contrary positions: Marc MacDonald, "How Ronald Reagan Unwittingly Laid the Groundwork for the Death of Capitalism," beggarscanbechoosers.com, February 9, 2012. Leo W. Gerard, "Mourning in America: Death of the Middle Class," *Huffington Post,* November 16, 2010. Paul Krugman, "Debunking the Reagan Myth," *New York Times,* January 21, 2008. Glenn Kessler, "The Historical Myth That Reagan Raised $1 in Taxes For Every $3 in Spending Cuts," *Washington Post,* December 14, 2012. Bruce Bartlett, "Tax Increases and Bull Markets," *New York Times,* August 8, 2013. "Reagan Raised Taxes," Bruce Bartlett provides color in the *Daily Howler* in 2003 (at dailyhowler.com). Michael Moore, "30 Years Ago: The Day the Middle Class Died," *Herald News,* August 12, 2011. Annalyn Censky, "How The Middle Class Became The Underclass," *CNN,* February 16, 2011. Bob Herbert, "Reagan and Reality," *New York Times,* February 14, 2011.

Books for further insight: Ronald Reagan, *An American Life* (New York: Simon & Schuster, 1990); Lou Cannon, *President Reagan, The Role of a Lifetime* (New York: Simon & Schuster, 1991). And for balance: Will Bunch, *Tear Down This Myth: How the Reagan Legacy has Distorted our Politics and Haunts our Future* (New York: The Free Press, 2009). Bruce Bartlett, *The New American Economy: The Failure of Reaganomics and a New Way Forward* (New York: Palgrave, 2009).

Post Reagan. Michael Marriott, "Pennsylvania Senate Race Kicks Off, Presaging '92 Presidential Campaign," *New York Times,* August 30, 1991. John H. Cushman, Jr., "Senator Heinz and 6 Others Killed in Midair Crash near Philadelphia," *New York Times,* April 5, 1991. Douglas A. Blackmon, Jennifer Levitz, Alexandra Berzona, and Lauren Etter, "The Birth of a Movement, Tea Party Arose From Conservatives Steeped in Crisis," *Wall Street Journal,* October 28, 2010. Andrew Barrett, "The Conservative Movement Has Been a Failure," Ricochet .com, April 10, 2014. FactFile—The Size of the Federal Workforce, January 23, 2012; FedScope, Office of Personnel Management; Bureau of Labor Statistics. Mike Patton, "The Growth of Government: 1980 to 2012," *Forbes* magazine, January 24, 2013. Camille Tuutti, "Counting Federal Employees is no Simple Task," FCW.com, September 13, 2012. Thomas B, Edsall, "A Republican Left Turn?" *Opinionator* Blog, March 27, 2013. Saul Friedman, "Don't Call Today's Republicans 'Conservative,' Goldwater, Dirksen et al Would Be Insulted," *Huffington Post,* September 12, 2013.

CHAPTER NINE: *THE ONE PERCENT PROBLEM*

FOR J.R. "JACK" SIMPLOT: HIS obituary appeared in the *Washington Post,* by Adam Bernstein, May 27, 2008. Also obituaries in the *New York Times:* "J.R. Simplot, Farmer Who Developed First Frozen French Fries, Dies at 99," by Douglas Martin, May 28, 2008 and in the *Los Angeles Times:* "Billionaire made fortune in frozen potatoes," by Claudia Luther, May 26, 2008. Mike Walden, "Ridin' high with J.R. Simplot," *The Oregonian* at OregonLive.com, first published June 30, 1966. Kristen Moulton, "Idaho Potato King Jack Simplot Mulls Slowing Down At 90," *The Seattle Times,* April 13, 1999. See also numerous articles about Simplot, his hat, his former house, and his impact on his home state by Tim Woodward a canny political journalist with the *Idaho Statesman.*

Niall Ferguson's *The Ascent of Money* was helpful again. Essential reading is Thomas Piketty, *Capital in the Twenty-First Century* (Cambridge: Belknap Press, 2014). *The Financial Times* looked at Piketty's data and took issue. See Chris Giles and Ferninando Giugliano, "Thomas Piketty's Exhaustive Inequality Data Turn Out to be Flawed," *Financial Times,* May 23, 2014. "Picking Holes in Piketty," *Economist,* May 31, 2014. "Working For the Few," Oxfam Research Study on Wealth Disparity, 2013.

Hope Yen, "Student debt hits record 1 in 5 U.S. households," *USA Today,* September 27, 2012. Halah Touryalai, "$1 Trillion Student Loan Problem Keeps Getting Worse," *Forbes* magazine, February 21, 2014. "The True Size of The Student Debt Crisis," Demos.org. Joseph E. Stiglitz, "Inequality Is Not Inevitable and Inequality Is A Choice," from the

New York Times series *The Great Divide* June 27, 2014, and October 13, 2013 respectively. Jeffrey M. Jones, "Americans Set 'Rich' Threshold at $150,000 in Annual Income," *Huffington Post,* December 9, 2011. Laura Saunders, "Baby You're A Rich Man," *Wall Street Journal,* December 28, 2012. Tami Luhby, "The wealthy are 288 times richer than you," *Wall Street Journal,* September 11, 2012. Derek Thompson, "How the Richest 400 People in America Got So Rich," *The Atlantic,* July 12, 2012. Dean Kalahar, "What is Rich and Poor in America?" Real Clear Markets, December 13, 2011. Kevin D. Williamson, "The Working Rich," *The National Review,* January 20, 2014.

Read back many years of Forbes 400 and you get a sense of exploding wealth. Jeanne Sahidi, "Wealth of 1.8 million Americans tops $2M," CNN Money, March 2, 2012. G. William Donhoff's *Wealth, Income and Power,* Seventh edition (New York: McGraw Hill, 2013) is a detailed resource for numbers and trends, global reach. Steve Hargreaves, "America's Rich Get Richer—How Income Inequality Hurts America," CNN, September 25, 2013. Emmanuel Saez and Thomas Piketty, "Income Inequality in the United States 1913-1998," *Quarterly Journal of Economics,* February 2003. Edward Nathan Wolff, "The Retirement Wealth of the Baby Boom Generation," *Journal of Monetary Economics,* January 2007. (Wolff is a prolific NYU professor and a great resource for anyone exploring the topics of wealth disparity and middle class prosperity. He also subscribes to the notion that rumors of the death of American competitiveness are overdone.) "29 Valuable Facts About Millionaires and Billionaires," retrieved from randomhistory.com—a good starting point to lead to other sources for deeper analysis. Robert Frank, "Millionaire Population Grows by 200,000," *Wall Street Journal,* March 21, 2012. Tyler Cowen, "Does Wealth Equal Power?" *Political Science,* December 2011. Dr. John S. Atlee with Tom Atlee, "Democracy: A Social Power Analysis," The Co-Intelligence Institute. "1 in 5 Americans rich (for a while)"—Associated Press coverage of Mark Rank's *Chasing the American Dream,* 2013.

Paul Krugman is an economic force of nature with a potent perspective that should be studied regardless of where you stand on the political spectrum. It is especially worth considering if you do not agree with him. See, for example, "For Richer," *New York Times,* October 20, 2002. Doug

Donovan, "Obama to Renew Call To Limit Charitable Deduction," Philanthropy.com, October 2014. Stephen D. King, "When Wealth Disappears," *New York Times,* October 6, 2013. (King is also the author of *When the Money Runs Out: The End of Western Affluence* (New Haven: Yale University Press, 2013), where he presents a different view of western expectations than my book). "NY AG eyes charity calls," *Bloomberg,* February 2014. "Should We End the Tax Deduction for Charitable Donations?" *Wall Street Journal, The Journal Report,* December 17, 2012. Ross Douthat, "Divided By God," April 8, 2012. For a fascinating take on veterans and service to others: "How Service Can Save Us," by Joe Klein, *Time* magazine, June 2013.

CHAPTER TEN: *THE ONE PERCENT SOLUTION*

W.L. GORE, "AN INNOVATION DEMOCRACY," in Gary Hamel, *The Future of Management* (Cambridge: Harvard Business School Press, 2007). Ann Harrington, "Who's Afraid of a New Product? Not W.L. Gore," *Fortune,* November 10, 2003. Nick Hanauer, "Memo: From Nick Hanauer, To: My Fellow Zillionaires," *Politico,* June 2014. Matt Taibbi, *The Divide: American Injustice in the Age of the Wealth Gap* (New York: Spiegel and Grau, 2014). Lesley Stahl, "The Cost of Cancer Drugs," *60 Minutes,* October 2014. Eduardo Porter, "Business Losing Clout In A G.O.P. Moving Right," *New York Times,* September 4, 2013. Anat R. Admati, "We're All Still Hostages to the Big Banks," *New York Times,* August 26, 2013. William B. Harrison, Jr., "In Defense of Big Banks," *New York Times,* August 23, 2012. Neil Shah, "Stagnant Wages Crimping Economic Growth," *Wall Street Journal,* August 26, 2013.

CHAPTER ELEVEN: *THE RENAISSANCE*

LANGSTON HUGHES, "HARLEM," INTRODUCTORY POEM to *Montage of a Dream Deferred* (New York: Henry Holt & Co., 1951). Histories of various poets from the Academy of American Poets, at poets.org for Countee Cullen, Arna Bontemps, Paul Laurence Dunbar, Claude McKay; also suggest Anthony Watson, "Double-Bind: Three Women of the Harlem Renaissance," at poets.org. Langston Hughes, "The Weary Blues" (1926), *The Collected Poems of Langston Hughes* (New York: Vintage, 1995). NAACP in-house magazines, *Opportunity* and *The Crisis*. Welcome to Harlem.com, West Harlem History.

Miriam B. Medina, "Cruisin' The 50s in a Volatile East Harlem," ezinearticles.com.

Gordon Parks has been a photo essayist for *Life* magazine and his work has been exhibited many times, including at The Fralin Museum of Art, The University of Virginia, in the fall of 2014. His Harlem Gang Leader photo essay and "A Harlem Family Life" powerfully convey what words cannot. "Poverty In The United States: A Snapshot," The National Center for Law and Economic Justice at nclej.org. NYCDwellers.com, Spanish Harlem. John Noble Gregory, *The Southern Diaspora: How the Great Migrations of Black and White Southerners Transformed America* (Chapel Hill: University of North Carolina Press, 2005). "Crack Is Still Wack," Ephemeral New York, May 18, 2009, at ephemeralnewyork .wordpress.com. "A Brief History of the Drug War," Drug Policy Alliance at drugpolicy.org. Other reading: Rensselaer Lee, *The White Labyrinth: Cocaine and Political Power* (Transition Publishers, 1991).

The crack epidemic in Harlem was widely covered by New York and national publications. Peter Kerr wrote with great insight for the *New York Times* on the subject in the mid-1980s before taking on the scourge by leaving journalism to join and promote the work of Phoenix House and later the Markle Foundation. Kerr articles to read are: "Growth in Heroin Use Ending As City Users Turn To Crack," September 13, 1986; "Crack Addiction Spreads Among the Middle Class," June 8, 1986; "Submachine Guns and Unpredictability Are Hallmarks of Crack's Violence," March 8, 1988; "Crack and Resurgence of Syphilis Spreading AIDS Among the Poor," August 20, 1989. For another view read Craig Reinarman and Harry G. Levine, "Crack Attack," from *Crack in America: Demon Drugs and Social Justice* (Oakland: University of California Press, 1997).

CHAPTER TWELVE: *THE ZONE*

GEOFF CANADA HAS BEEN THE subject of significant media coverage, TED Talks, and a writer of his own books such that he has become a leading national figure in the movement to bring opportunity to America's poorest kids. In 2009 his "Baby College" brought the Harlem Children's Zone to the attention of ABC News and soon after their broadcasts a national audience. He was featured in *Time* magazine's 2011 "Time 100" edition and his social reform work in Harlem was center stage. He was prominently featured in the acclaimed documentary *Waiting For Superman* (2010). His books are very worth reading: *Fist, Stick, Knife, Gun* (Boston: the Beacon Press, 2010) and *Reaching Up For Manhood: Transforming the Lives of Boys in America* (Beacon Press, 2000). His story has been well told by Paul Tough in *Whatever It Takes: Geoffrey Canada's Quest to Change Harlem and America* (Boston: Houghton Mifflin, 2009). For further research study the Geoff Canada/Stan Druckenmiller talks given at numerous colleges and universities around the country. For data and analysis see the Children's Defense Fund's Overview of the State of America's Children 2014. School Enrollment in the United States, U.S. Department of Commerce, United States Census Bureau. NoKidHungry .org, Share our Strength for the impact of hunger on American children.

The fifty-year anniversary of the War on Poverty brought an avalanche of coverage, opinion, dialogue, debate . . . with little listening. There is a treasure trove in the media, academy, and blogosphere. A handful of useful treatments on all sides of the equation follows: Eduardo Porter, "In the War On Poverty A Dogged Adversary," *New York Times*, December 18, 2103. Bob Beckel and Cal Thomas, "Focus on rescuing the poor children," *USA Today*, January 20, 2014. Robert Samuelson, "How We Won—and Lost—the War on Poverty," *Washington Post*, January 12, 2014. "The War That Failed," *New York Post* op-ed, January 12, 2014. Robert Rector, "How the War on Poverty Was Lost," The Heritage Foundation, January 7, 2014. Sean Michael Winters, "The War on Poverty," National Catholic Reporter, January 9, 2014. Paul Krugman, "On Fighting the Last War (On Poverty)," *New York Times*, January 8, 2014. Annie Lowrey, "Changed Life Of the Poor: Better Off, but Far Behind," *New York Times*, May 1, 2014. Richard

Wolff, "Racial equality still falling short—50 years after the Civil Rights Act many gaps remain," *USA Today,* January 20, 2014. Nicolaus Mills, "America declared an 'unconditional war on poverty' 50 years ago, but you'd never know it," *The Guardian,* January 7, 2014. Paul Krugman, "The War Over Poverty," *New York Times,* January 9, 2014. Gene Perry and Tina Korbe Dzurisin, "Face-Off Over the 'War on Poverty,'" in OklahomaWatch.org, January 11, 2014. "Trillions Have Been Wasted On Poverty Programs That Don't Work," Investor's Business Daily at Investors.com, August 26, 2012. Mike Konczal, "The War on Poverty Turns 50: Three Lessons for Liberals Today," *New Republic,* January 7, 2014. Annie Lowrey, "50 Years Later, War on Poverty Is a Mixed Bag," *New York Times,* January 5, 2014. Scott Winship, "Actually We Won the War on Poverty," Politico, January 24, 2014 . . . And on and on for all sides of this complicated argument.

"Take Care," East Harlem, Community Health Profiles, New York City Department of Health and Hygiene, 2006. Carl Bialik, "Hurdles for the New Line on Poverty," *Wall Street Journal,* September 21, 2013. Poverty Tracker, Income, Hardship and Health in NYC from Columbia Population Research Center and The Robin Hood Foundation, Spring 2014. Mark Rank, "Poverty in America is Mainstream," *New York Times,* November 3, 2013. Valerie Straus, "Public education's biggest problem gets worse," *Washington Post,* October 17, 2013. Lawrence J. Vale, *Purging the Poorest: Public Housing and the Design Politics of Twice-Cleared Communities* (Chicago: University of Chicago Press, 2013). "Won't Work for Food," *Wall Street Journal* editorial, September 21, 2013. Kim Severson and Winnie Hu, "Cut in Food Stamps Forces Hard Choices on Poor," *New York Times,* November 8, 2013. Jennifer A. Marshall, "Incentives Matter in Fighting Poverty," Heritage Foundation, January 8, 2014. Naomi Schaefer Riley, "Gift from God. We need to save the Catholic Schools that rescued so many New York kids," *New York Post,* May 18, 2014. "The New Diversity," *New York Post* editorial page, May 10, 2014. John Podhoretz, "Scalia's Plain Truth On Affirmative Action," *New York Post* editorial page, April 23, 2014. Lee C. Bollinger, "A Long Slow Drift From Radical Justice," *Wall Street Journal,* June 25, 2013. John Hayward, "Paul Ryan Calls For A New Approach to The War On Poverty," Human Events, March 4, 2014.

Chapter Thirteen: *The March of the Black Middle Class*

The Story: The Cookie Kahuna at cookiekahuna.com. Wally Amos and Leroy Robinson. Wally Amos, *The Famous Amos Story: The Face That Launched a Thousand Chips* (New York: Doubleday, 1983). Eden-Lee Murray and Neale Donald Walsch, *The Cookie Never Crumbles* (New York: St. Martin's Press, 2001). Brenna Fisher, "The Recipe for Achievement," *Success* magazine, May 1, 2010. Amanda Gold, "Gary Shansby: Building his own brand," sfgate.com, April 15, 2012. "No Longer Famous, Wally Amos Still Baking," Associated Press July 13, 2007. "Chocolate Chips Equal Love," Reference for Business, Encyclopedia of Business. Wally Amos, The Motivational Speaker Hall of Fame at getmotivation.com. John Kell, "The Cookie Comeback of 'Famous' Wally Amos," *Fortune,* June 26, 2014. Wally Amos, Blue Feather Management, Speakers series biography. Also Key Speakers and the American Speakers Series biographies Ken Schachter, "Wally Amos Face of LI Muffins Tries New Cookie Venture," *Newsday* Business, June 18, 2014. Wally Amos, "Famous Amos on raising capital," *Inc.* Magazine, April 1, 2009. Dana Canedy, "A Famous Cookie And a Face to Match; How Wally Amos Got His Hand And His Name Back in the Game," *New York Times,* July 3, 1999.

The Economics of the Black Middle Class, A Briefing Before The United States Commission on Civil Rights Held in Washington, D.C., July 15, 2005. Joseph E. Stiglitz, "Equal Opportunity, Our National Myth," *New York Times,* February 18, 2013. Sam Fulwood, "The Rage Of The Black Middle Class," *Los Angeles Times,* November 3, 1991. Mary Pattillo-McCoy, *Black Picket Fences, Privilege and Peril Among the Black Middle Class,* Second Edition (Chicago: University of Chicago Press, 2013). Kris Marsh, "Where is the Black Middle Class? You don't have to look far" (About the Love Jones cohort and SALAs), January 9, 2102, and "Don't Be Fooled, Housing Segregation is Still a Reality," February 9, 2012. InAmerica, CNN. Cynthia Tucker, "As black middle class rises, black underclass falls still further, *Baltimore Sun,* December 10, 2007. For a counter-perspective read William Julius Wilson, *The Declining Significance of Race,* Third edition, (Chicago: University of Chicago Press,

2012). Kay Hymowitz, "Fractured black families. An absence of fathers virtually assures that poverty and failure will continue," *Washington Post,* December 10, 2008. Charles Lane, "An endangered racial compromise," *Washington Post,* October 11, 2012.

Kris Marsh, William A. Darity, Philip N. Cohen, Lynne M. Casper, Danielle Salters, "The Emerging Black Middle Class: Single and Living Alone," *Social Forces,* December 2007. Sam Fulwood III, "What The Black Middle Class Still Owes The Civil Rights Movement," The Root.com, April 3, 2008. Craig Chamberlain, "Class Rights," University of Illinois, College of Arts and Sciences at las.illinois.edu, February 2010. Outlines the work of Professor Clarence Lang who holds that the civil rights movement was never as unified as it has often been portrayed. Clarence Lang, *Grassroots at the Gateway, Class Politics and Black Freedom Struggle in St. Louis, 1936–75* (Ann Arbor: University of Michigan Press, 2009). Malik Miah, "Race and Class: Downturn Undermines Black 'Middle Class,'" Solidarity, March 10, 2009. Shelby Steele and John E. Jacob, "The State of Black America," Annals of America series, Encyclopedia Britannica, 1988. Barbara Ehrenreich and Dedrick Muhammed, "The Destruction of the Black Middle Class," *Huffington Post,* September 3, 2009. Wallace Turbeville, "Financialization and the End of our Great American Middle Class," demos.org, February 10, 2015. The African American Middle Class, BlackDemographics.com. The History of Civil Rights from Integration to Nationalism. Essortment.com.

PBS Frontline: The Two Nations of Black America—Are we better off? A discussion led by Henry Louis Gates, Jr. Amazing lineup of African American Leaders discussing race, economic segregation, and the black middle class. Eric Arnesen, "Civil rights and the Labor Movement: A Historical Overview," Teamster.org, February 7, 2012. John Podhoretz, "Why Court Can't Right Race Wrongs," *New York Post,* June 25, 2013. Nelson D. Schwartz and Michael Cooper, "With Affirmative Action Ruling Near, Blacks' Progress Remains Slow," *New York Times,* May 28, 2013. James Baldwin, *The Fire Next Time* (New York: Dial Press, 1963).

Chapter Fourteen: *American Matriarchy*

Betty Friedan, *The Feminine Mystique* (New York: W.W. Norton & Co., 1963). Margaret Fox, "Betty Friedan, Who Ignited Cause in 'Feminine Mystique,' Dies at 85," *New York Times,* February 5, 2006. Betty Friedan, *Beyond Gender: The New Politics of Work and Family* (Washington, D.C.: Woodrow Wilson Center Press, 1997). "Betty Friedan Interview," The First Measured Century at PBS.org. Janet Maslin, "Looking Back at a Domestic Cri de Coeur," February 18, 2013. Rosie The Riveter: Women Working During World War II, National Park Service, nps.gov. Rosie The Riveter, History.com. Woman at Work After World War II, Tupperware!, WGBH American Experience at pbs.org. "Child Care During World War II," ForgeofInnovation.org. "Women's Liberation Movement," created by Nancy Sink, Novaonline.nvcc.edu, December 2008. Women in America, Indicators of Social and Economic Well-being, Prepared by the U.S. Department of Commerce and the Office of Management and Budget for the White House Council on Women and Girls, March 2011. "The Women's Movement," United States History, Countrystudies.us/united-states/history.

Mitra Toossi, "A century of change: The U.S. labor force, 1950-2050," *Monthly Labor Review,* May 2002. Susan G. Hauser, "The Women's Movement in the '70s, Today: 'You've Come a Long way,' But . . . ," workforce.com, May 15, 2012. Lisa Quast, "Causes and Consequences Of The Increasing Numbers Of Women In The Workforce," forbes.com, February 14, 2011. Yenisse Alonso and Vickie Brint, "Women in the Workplace," thehumanequation.com, 2007. "New Data on Women in the Workforce," *Occupational Outlook Quarterly,* excelle.monster.com, May 16, 2008. "United States Department of Labor, Women's Bureau, Women in the Labor Force in 2010. Fortune 500 Board Seats Held by Women," Knowledge Center, catalyst.org. "Six Facts about Women in the Workforce," at divinecaroline.com, October 2010. "Single Mother Statistics," Single Mother Guide, 2013. "Children in Single-Parent Families By Race," Datacenter, kidscount.org, February 2014. "Census Shows Whites are in Minority Among New Births in U.S." Associated Press, June 23, 2011.

Jennifer Keil, "Women, the Recession, and the Impending Economic Recovery," Graziado Business Review, 2009. Eduardo Porter, "Stretched to Limit, Women Stall March to Work," *New York Times,* March 2, 2006. David Leonhardt, "Men, Women and the Great Recession," *New York Times,* August 11, 2011. Paul Wiseman and Christopher S. Rugaber, "Women outrun men in regaining jobs since recession," September 12, 2013. Don Lee, "Newly created jobs go mostly to men," *Los Angeles Times,* July 15, 2012. Susan McCullah, "Working Women and the Recession," ezinearticles .com, October, 4, 2011. Terry Keenan, "Disappearing male workers are not a joke," *New York Post,* January 12, 2014. Rashida Maples, "Women Have Recovered After The Recession Better Than Men," hellobeautiful .com, December 24, 2013. Hanna Rosin, "Who Wears The Pants In This Economy?" *New York Times,* September 2, 2012. Eileen Appelbaum, "Women's Employment in Recession and Recovery," Center for Economic and Policy Research, May 10, 2011. "Women in the workforce: Female Power," *Economist,* December 30, 2009. Annalee Newitz, "Three ways that women are about to change the world," i09.com, June 30, 2010. Maya Wiley, "Feminomics: Race, Gender and Poverty in Economic Recovery," Next New Deal, December 24, 2009.

CHAPTER FIFTEEN: *THE LATINO GENERATION*

THE DRAMATIC BATTLE TO THE death at the Alamo presents historians a challenge because virtually all participants and potential primary sources on one side perished. Many books and fine articles have been written and they have found accounts by witnesses, Mexican soldiers' accounts, and bystanders like Susanna Dickinson who is reported to have hidden in the church during the battle. The heroism of the defenders creates gripping narratives and, of course, controversy and debate such as whether Davy Crockett died in battle, was captured, or was executed afterward.

Books that powerfully describe the events at the Alamo include: James Donovan, *Blood of Heroes* (New York: Little, Brown & Company, 2012). William Groneman III has written eight books on the Alamo. See also Todd Hansen, *The Alamo Reader* (Mechanicsburg, Pa.: Stackpole

Books, 2003); William C. Davis, *Three Roads to the Alamo* (New York: HarperCollins, 1998); Stephen L. Hardin, *Texian Iliad* (Austin: University of Texas Press, 1994).

"Pew Finds Many Children Fall Out of the Middle Class as Adults." This report drawn from the National Longitudinal Survey (NLSY) taking the 1979 cohort who were 14–17 and lived in their parents' homes in 1979 and 1980. Their economic status was assessed in 2004 and 2006 when they were between the ages of 39 and 44. From the Pew Charitable Trusts at txnp.org. The associated report: "Downward Mobility from the Middle Class: Waking up from the American Dream," from the Pew Charitable Trusts.

Hispanic or Latino Populations, Centers for Disease Control and Prevention at cdc.gov. U.S. Census Bureau 2012 Facts for Features special editions (Hispanic Heritage Month) and also 2010 Census Briefs: The Hispanic Population 2010 issued May 2011. (These stats are updated regularly—see census.gov.) U.S. Office of Management and Budget: OMB Bulletin Guidance on Aggregation and Allocation of Data on Race for Use on Civil Rights Montoring and Enforcement, March 9, 2000 at whitehouse.gov/omb/bulletins_b00-02. CDC Report: Mortality Rates by Race/Ethnicity, 2011. See cdc.gov for plentiful data. "Many Latinos Live Below Poverty Line, Census Data Shows," Fox News Latino, February 22, 2013. Hispanic-Latino naming dispute, Cyclopedia.net. Sandra Lilley, "Report: U.S. birth rates hit record lows, largest drop among immigrant Latinas," nbclatino.com, November 29, 2012. D'Vera Cohn and Gretchen Livingston, "U.S. Birth Rate Falls to a Record Low; Decline is Greatest Among Immigrants," Pew Research Center, November 29, 2012. Kirk Semple, "In a Shift, Biggest Wave of Migrants Is Now Asian," *New York Times*, June 18, 2012. Mark Hugo Lopez and Daniel Dockterman, "U.S. Hispanic Country of Origin Counts for Nation, Top 30 Metropolitan Areas," Pew Research Center, May 26, 2011. Tony Castro, "Latino Population: Hispanic Birth Rate Hits New Low," by Tony Castro, Voxxi at voxxi.com, updated December 3, 2012.

Robert R. Brischetto, "The Hispanic Middle Class Comes of Age," *Hispanic Business Magazine,* December 2001. John Benson, "Why You Can't Pigeonhole Latinos Into One Social Class, Voxxi at voxxi.com, January 25, 2014. Kim Piston "'Upscale Hispanics' Could Help Heal the Economy and Rebuild the Middle Class," Voxxi at voxxi.com, updated July 29, 2013. "Building One America: Strategies and Policies for Defending and Expanding the Middle Class in Metropolitan America," 2012 at buildingoneamerica.org. (Member institutions of Building One America are Brookings Institute, Kirwan Institute for the Study of Race and Ethnicity, and the Poverty and Race Research Action Council among many others.) Rosa Ramirez, "Blacks, Latinos, Asians Losing Middle Class Ground," *National Journal*, August 31, 2012. Esther Cepeda, "A Latino Middle-Class Challenge," GazetteXtra, March 31, 2011. Halimah Abdullah, "Hispanics Remaking the Deep South," McClatchy Newspapers, April 22, 2011. Hispanic Trending—Documenting Latinos' Imprint in America (hispanictrending.net) has hundreds of useful articles with many localized and regional reports outlining changes in Texas, Florida, and other states and municipalities.

John Benson, "Education is key for the middle class, and Latinos are going to college more than ever," Voxxi, January 21, 2014.

Chapter Sixteen: *G, Myself, and I*

"Bangladesh factory collapse blamed on swampy ground and heavy machinery," AP, theguardian.com, May 23, 2013. Sabir Mustafa & Shyadul Islam, "Profile: Rana Plaza owner Mohammad Sohel Rana," *BBC News* Bengali Service, May 3, 2013. Shahriar Asif, "Factory owners to blame, claims Rana," *Priyo News*, April 29, 2013. Matthew McClearn, "Global Report: The Uncomfortable Truth About Bangladesh," *Canadian Business*, June 6, 2013. Syed Tashfin Chowdhury, "Babies among rising Bangladesh death toll," *Asia Times online*, April 26, 2013. Matthew Green and Serajul Quadir, "Insight: Anger at Bangladesh factory disaster turns spotlight on MP," Reuters, May 9, 2013. Steven Greenhouse, "Some Retailers Rethink Roles in Bangladesh," *New York Times*, May 1, 2013. Sarah Stillman, "Death Traps: The Bangladesh Garment-Factory Disaster," *New Yorker*, May 1, 2013. Sohel Uddin, "Bangladesh factory collapse: Why women endure danger to make clothes for the West," *NBC News*, May 26, 2013. "Bangladeshi Minister: Factory Collapse Not 'Serious,'"

Voice of America, May 3, 2013. Jim Yardley, "The Most Hated Bangladeshi, Toppled From a Shady Empire," *New York Times,* April 30, 2013. Steven Greenhouse, "Retailers Split on Contrition After Collapse of Factories," *New York Times,* May 1, 2013. "Meet Sohel Rana, The Most Hated Man in Bangladesh," Vice, May 2, 2013. Jonathan Fahey and Anne D'Innocenzio, "Retailers Face Tough Decisions After Bangladesh Factory Collapse," AP, May 12, 2013. M.T. Anderson, "Clothed in Misery," *New York Times,* April 30, 2013. Steven Greenhouse, "3 Retailers Give to Aid Bangladesh Workers," *New York Times,* March 29, 2014. Steve Greenhouse and Elizabeth Harris, "Battling for a Safer Bangladesh," *New York Times,* April 22, 2014. Ian Urbinia and Keith Brandisher, "Linking Factories to the Malls, Middleman Pushes Low Costs," *New York Times,* August 8, 2013.

McKinsey and Company Study, "Growth and competitiveness in the United States: The role of its multinational companies," June 2010. Veronique de Rugy, "U.S. Manufacturing: Output vs. Jobs Since 1975," Mercatus Center, January 24, 2011. National Association of Manufacturers, "Facts About Manufacturing in the United States," at nam.org. Emily Chasan, "Apple now holds 10% of all corporate cash: Moody's," *Wall Street Journal,* October 1, 2013. Linda Levine, "Offshoring (or Offshore Outsourcing) and Job Loss Among U.S. Workers," *Congressional Research Service,* January 21, 2011. Sherle Schwenninger and Samuel Sherraden, "Manufacturing and the U.S. Economy," *New America Foundation,* July 13, 2009. Robert D. Atkinson, Luke A. Stewart, Scott M. Andes, and Stephen J. Ezell, "Worse Than the Great Depression: What Experts Are Missing About American Manufacturing Decline," *Information Technology and Innovation Foundation,* March 2012 at itif.org. "Geography of Poverty," at ers.usda.gov. Face the Facts USA, "Factories Bounce Back, Hiring Hangs Back," August 16, 2012.

Outsourcing is a lightning rod, and to do the subject justice research papers from all sides of the argument have to be considered. Effective position papers have been presented by the Economic Policy Institute, which counts among its supporters many organized labor donors. There have been some valuable studies done and articles published by the conservative-voiced think tanks and study organizations. Piecing together a sensible perspective happens best by casting a wide net. These citations and notes reflect that process.

Harbhajan S. Kehal and Varinder P. Singh, editors, *Outsourcing and Offshoring in the 21ˢᵗ Century* (Hershey, PA: Idea Group, 2006). Atul Vashista, *Offshore Nation* (New York: McGraw-Hill, 2006). "How Outsourcing Affects The U.S. Economy," *Directory Journal,* April 16, 2013. Dr. David M. Anderson, "Outsourcing; The Reality for Cost Reduction," half-costproducts.com, August 2011. Steve Hargreaves, "The Case For Outsourcing Jobs," CNN, September 14, 2012. Richard A. McCormack, "Output Growth is 50 Percent Lower Than Reported," *Manufacturing News,* September 12, 2013. Eliot Morss, "The Loss of American Manufacturing Jobs: What Are The Facts?," *Seeking Alpha,* February 21,2011. Harold Myerson, "Free Trade and the Loss of U.S. Jobs," *Washington Post,* January 14, 2014. Adam Nager, "Why Is America's Manufacturing Job Loss Greater Than Other Industrialized Countries?" *Industry Week,* August 21, 2014. Michael Moran, "Team America Needs A New Game Plan," *Global Post,* April 4, 2014. Alec Friedhoff and Howard Wial, "Bearing the Brunt: Manufacturing Job Loss in the Great Lakes Region, 1995-2005," Brookings Institute, July, 2006.

See also numerous articles from the Economic Policy Institute, including Josh Bivens, "Shifting blame for manufacturing job loss," April 8, 2004. Also by Bivens: "Trade Deficits and manufacturing job loss: Correlation and causality," March 13, 2006. Robert Scott, "Displaced Minority Workers Suffered a 29.6 Percent Drop in Wages from the Growing Trade Deficit with China," October 10, 2013. Also by Scott: "Kerry Drinks the trade Kool-Aid, but trade agreements do NOT create jobs," March 29, 2013. Danielle Kurtzleben, "Middle Class Losing Ground," Pew Research Center, August 22, 2012. Roert Morley, "The Death of American Manufacturing," *The Trumpet,* February 2006. Patrick J. Buchanan, "Who Killed the Middle Class?," *The Imaginative Conservative,* April 18, 2013. Howard Wial, "How to Save U.S. Manufacturing Jobs," CNN, February 23, 2012.

Ron Hira and Anil Hira, *Outsourcing America* (New York: AMACOM, 2005). James Goldsmith, *The Trap* (New York: Carroll & Graf, 1994). Milton Friedman, "The Goldsmith Standard, Review of *The Trap* by Sir James Goldsmith," *National Review,* November 27, 1995. Winterman "Lessons From a Billionaire—Goldsmith's *The Trap,*" *Asset Manager,* February 20, 2009. See Goldsmith's Interviews with Charlie

Rose in 1994 (at YouTube) and testimony before Strom Thurmond's U.S. Senate Commerce Committee Hearings on GATT in the same year. Kathy Chu, "Not Made In China," *Wall Street Journal,* May 1, 2013. "A Growth Agenda: Four Goals For a Manufacturing Resurgence in America," *National Association of Manufacturers,* 2013. "Made in America, Again," Boston Consulting Group, 2011. James R. Hagerty, "Why U.S. Manufacturing Is Poised for a Comeback (Maybe)," *Wall Street Journal,* June 1, 2014. Rebecca O. Bagley, "What's Next For U.S. Manufacturing?" *Forbes,* August 1, 2013. Gabrielle Karol, "Apple's New Arizona Factory: More Signs of a U.S. Manufacturing Renaissance?," *Fox Business,* November 5, 2013. Don Brunnell, "A Renaissance in Manufacturing," *Association of Washington Business,* October 31, 2013. Keynote address by Nicholas Pinchuk, CEO of Snap-on Tools, Manufacturing Summit, October 25, 2013. Eammon Fingleton, "Reports of America's Manufacturing Renaissance Are Just a Cruel Political Hoax," *Forbes* magazine, November 13, 2013. John Maywell, "Beyond the BRICS: How to succeed in the emerging markets (by really trying)," *PwC View,* Issue 15. Daniel Ikenson, "The Myth of a Manufacturing Renaissance," *Cato Institute,* May 1, 2013. Rana Foroohar, "Made in the USA: Manufacturing Is Back, But Where Are The Jobs?" *Time* magazine, April 11, 2013.

Many media outlets reacted to a major Morgan Stanley report titled "U.S. Manufacturing Renaissance: Is It A Masterpiece Or A (Head) Fake?" published in 2013, including *Business Insider's* Rob Wile. Brian Snyder, "The American Manufacturing Renaissance is a Flop," *Reuters,* April 8, 2013. Philip Odette, "Manufacturing's Renaissance Depends On Skilled Workers," *manufacturing.net,* October 28, 2013. John W. Thompson, "The Manufacturing Renaissance and the Middle Class," *ComputerWorld,* September 30, 2013. Brad Plumer, "Is U.S. Manufacturing making a comeback—or is it just hype?" *Washington Post,* May 1, 2013. Also by Plumer: "Goldman Sachs: Sorry, U.S. Manufacturing isn't coming back," March 25, 2013. Scott Paul, "A Manufacturing Renaissance? Not Yet," *CNBC,* April 19, 2011. Steven Greenhouse, "At a Nissan Plant in Mississippi, a Battle to Shape the U.A.W's Future," *New York Times,* October 7, 2013. Nathaniel Popper, "Old Economies Rise as Emerging Markets' Growth

Falters," *New York Times,* August 15, 2013. "10 States Losing White Collar and Blue Collar Jobs," *The Atlantic,* July 14, 2011. Jeff Black and Simon Kennedy, "Draghi Committs ECB to Trillion-Euro Asset-Purchase Plan to Fight Deflation," *Bloomberg,* January 22, 2015. "Comeback Kid. America's Economy is once again reinventing itself," *Economist,* July 14, 2012. Sophie Quinton, "In Manufacturing, blue-collar jobs need white collar training," *National Journal,* February 26, 2012. Brad Plumer, "How the Recession Turned Middle-Class Jobs into Low-wage Jobs," *Washington Post,* February 28, 2013. Veronique de Rugy, "Destroying Jobs in Order to Save Them," *Reason.com,* July 14, 2009. Howard Gold, "White Collar Recession, Blue Collar Depression," *Market Watch,* October 23, 2103. Ilya Leybovich "American and Chinese Consumers Prefer 'Made in the U.S.A.,'" thomas.net, December 6, 2012. Matt Jarzemsky, "3-D Printers Come in View," *Wall Street Journal,* December 12, 2013.

CHAPTER SEVENTEEN: *LA GRIPPE*

STUDS TERKEL, *WORKING* (NEW YORK: The New Press, 1974). Also: *Hard Times* (New York: The New Press, 1970), and *Division Street, America* (New York: Random House, 1967). Rick Kogan, "Studs Terkel Dies," *Chicago Tribune,* October 31, 2008. William Grimes "Studs Terkel Dies at 96," *NewYork Times,* October 31, 2008. Stuart N. Bronfman, "Why Studs Terkel's Working World No Longer Exists," *Forbes,* June 12, 2012. Scott Eyeman, "To remember—and be remembered," *Palm Beach Post,* January 11, 2008. "The Bughouse Square Debates," speakerscorner.org. Studs Terkel: "Conversations with America," Chicago History Museum. There are books and articles that begin to capture the man, but nothing can compare to listening to recordings of Terkel's enormous body of work at the Chicago History Museum. There are thousands of hours available—take a random walk through his legacy. No interviewer in history has more recorded interviews with a wider array of people and nothing tells the story like the patient questioner himself.

"Left out in the cold," *Daily News* editorial, February 9, 2014. John Aidan Byrne, "City's Not Working," *New York Post,* September 8, 2013.

"Worse Than Jimmy Carter," *New York Post* editorial, September 6, 2013. Hedrick Smith, "When Capitalists Cared," *New York Times,* September 2, 2012. John Cassidy, "Ten Takeaways from Janet Yellin's Big Day," *New Yorker,* February 11, 2014. Ryan Cooper, "The Fed Needs New Tools to Fight Unemployment," *Washington Post,* February 11, 2014.

Ezra Klein, "We Have Unemployment, Not Structural Unemployment," *Washington Post,* August 31, 2010. "Structural Unemployment, Jobs for the Long Run," *Economist,* May 21, 2012. Matthew Boesler, "Janet Yellin Has Taken An Odd View Of The Labor Market, And It Has Big Implications For Fed Policy," *Business Insider,* February 11, 2014. Gary Burtless, "High Unemployment: Cyclical or Structural?" Brookings Institution, May 22, 2012. "Is America facing an increase in structural unemployment?," *Economist,* July 23, 2010. Tyler Durden, "Janet Yellen Discovers Okuns Law is Broken, Confused," zerohedge.com, February 11, 2013. "Do Unemployment Benefits Expirations Help Explain the Surge in Job Openings?" Federal Reserve Bank of New York at libertystreeteconomics.newyorkfed.org, September 30, 2014. Rick Moran, "Surprise! Ending unemployment benefits increased employment: Fed," *American Thinker,* October 2, 2014. "The Causes of Unemployment go beyond the state of the economy."

Read the last four years of the Hays Global Skills Index to follow the structural skills mismatch and talent gaps we are seeing widen. These numbers are sobering. (At hays-index.com). "The State of Working America, 12th Edition," Economic Policy Institute, Cornell University Press, September 2012. Neil Shah, "Good Sign For Jobs: More People Quit," *Wall Street Journal,* February 10, 2014. Ben Casselman, "Job Gap Widens In Uneven Recovery," *Wall Street Journal,* November 12, 2013. Robert Stack, "Hike the Minimum Wage? Show Me How," *Wall Street Journal,* April 12, 2014. Mark Weisbrot, *Newport Daily News*, September 21, 2013. "Pay Hasn't Kept Up With Economic Realities." James Sherk, "Most Minimum-Wage Jobs Lead to Better-Paying Opportunities," Heritage Foundation, January 21, 2014. Sarah E. Needleman and Daniel Lippman, "Business Stung by $15 Hourly Pay," *Wall Street Journal,* December 12, 2013. Annie Lowrey, "Hold the Cheese," *New York Times,* December 22, 2013. The following are all from the *New York Post* "The Wages of Cheeseburgers," July 29, 2013; "The Wages of Chagrin," August 6, 2013; "The Wages of

Humor," February 18, 2013; "The Wages of Spin," June 6, 2014; "The Wages of Walmart," February 22, 2015.

CHAPTER EIGHTEEN: *BACK TO WORK*

MICHA KAUFMAN, "DRIVING DISRUPTION: TESLA is Building Cars Out of Software," *Forbes* magazine, October 16, 2014. "Elon Musk named Fortune's 'Businessperson of the Year,'" *Fortune,* January 22, 2013. Video Interview with Elon Musk. Charlie Rose, *Bloomberg,* November 9, 2011. Marlow Stern, "Interview: Elon Musk," *Newsweek,* updated October 20, 2011. Zachary Shahan, "Interview with Elon Musk and Brother Kimbal Musk," *CleanTechnica,* January 14, 2014. Also Video Interview with CNBC on the "Disruptor 50," July 9, 2014. Video interview with *Wired* magazine's Jason Paur, April 26, 2012. Marlow Stern, "Elon Musk and the Revenge of the Electric Car," *The Daily Beast,* April 25, 2011. Zach Ho, "Tesla's CEO and Billionaire Elon Musk Talks About His Five Secrets to Success," *Vulcan Post,* June 7, 2014. Ross Andersen, "Exodus: Elon Musk Argues That We Must Put A Million People On Mars If We Are To Ensure That Humanity Has A Future," *Aeon* magazine, September 30, 2014. Mark Harris, "PayPal Tycoon Bounces Back," *Sunday Times,* October 31, 2010. Jennifer Reingold, "Hondas in Space," *Fast Company*, February 2005. Hannah Elliott, "Elon Musk On The Biggest Week Of His Life," *Forbes,* May 25, 2012. Amanda Wills, "SpaceX Pulled Off the Nearly Impossible," *Mashable,* April 30, 2014. Katie Sola, "SpaceX Rocket Malfunctions, Then Explodes Over Texas," *Mashable,* August 22, 2014.

Tod Newcombe, "The Rise Of Cities And The Mayors Who Run Them," governing.com, September 12, 2013. (I hold a minority stake in one of the private companies listed, StateBook.) "Urban World: Cities and the Rise of the Consuming Class," McKinsey Global Institute, June 2012. "Taking Action, Building Confidence," President's Council On Jobs and Competitiveness Interim Report, 2012. Will Yakowicz, "Young Businesses Not Small Businesses, Create Jobs," *Inc.* magazine, February 25, 2014. President Obama Address to Winning the

Future Forum on Small Business, Cleveland State University, February 22, 2011. Sarah Pringle, "Cities Walk With Gangplank to Spur Small Business Growth," *Cronkite News Service,* September 17, 2012. Sangeeta Bharadwaj Badal, "How Large Corporations Can Spur Small-Business Growth," *The Gulf,* December 2012. Karen Mills Profile, *Maine* magazine, December 2009. Beth Solomon, "Spur Job Growth Through Small Business Lending Surge," *The Hill,* January 24, 2014. Laurie Kulikowski, "Facebook Works to Spur Small-Business Growth," nuwireinvestor.com, October 24, 2011. James Cassel, "A Wish List to Spur Growth of Small Businesses," *Miami Herald,* December 28, 2011. Newt Gingrich, "Job Killers Vs. Job Creators," Human Events, July 21, 2010. "Who Creates Jobs? Small vs. Large vs. Young," National Bureau of Economic Research, August 2010. "Restarting The U.S. Small-Business Economic Growth Engine," McKinsey Global Institute, November 2012. "Moving People to Work," Manpower Group, 2012.

Niels Bottger-Rasmussen and Krsitian Rode Nielsen, "Lack of Jobs and Lack of Talent . . . Welcome to the Great Mismatch!" *Scenario* magazine, January 2014, "Help Wanted: The Future of Work in Advanced Economies," McKinsey, March 2012. Randall Eberts, "Human Capital and Productivity: Toward Quality Job Creation," W.E. Upjohn Institute for Employment Research, June 2014. Joseph Coombs, "Will Skills Gap Chill A Warming Job Market?" *Society For Human Resource Management Newsletter,* April 6, 2012. Schumpeter, "The Great Mismatch," *Economist,* December 8, 2012. Asohka, "What Government, Business and Individuals Can Do to Tackle European Unemployment," *Forbes,* October 2014. Thomas L. Friedman, "It's a 401(k) World," *New York Times,* May 1, 2013. Catherine Rampell, "A Sharp Rise In Americans With Degrees," *New York Times,* June 13, 2013. Glenn Hubbard, "Where Have All The Workers Gone?" *Wall Street Journal,* April 5, 2014. "A National Talent Strategy," Microsoft at microsoft.com, 2014. The Company has become an amazing resource for great ideas and collective actions.

Chapter Nineteen: *Middle Earth*

THE NEXT THREE CHAPTERS DRAW their energy and focus from the emerging global middle class and the endless debates about what is driving this worldwide phenomenon. Optimists see five billion souls elevated from poverty, a diminishment of terrorism as a result and the creation of a second mountain to compete in many ways with the rise of the one percent—a powerful and massive middle class in the emerging world. Debate rages over every element of the optimists' position, and many opposing sources are listed here; but about one thing there can be no argument. A vast new cohort of middle class members is sprouting from the most unexpected places, transforming the economic balance of the earth's axis. As with all vigorous debates each side should be examined because there is another certainty whenever a change this massive is beginning to occur: No one knows for sure where things are headed.

Devin Powell, "A Visit to Trinity, Where the First A-Bomb Was Tested in 1945, Turns Up Radiation Still," *Washington Post,* June 3, 2013. "Trinity," Nuclear Weapon Archive, updated March 12, 1999. There are several film clips of the Trinity test and preparations in the archives. See also a summary of the "Symposium On The 50th Anniversary Of The Trinity Test" sponsored by the National Academy of Sciences and The Department of Energy, July 1995. Many historical web sites and articles cover Trinity and later tests, but for sheer power of the art try the *New York Times* archives for the reporting of William L. Laurence who found epic poetry in his pursuance of the story: "Huge New Atomic Gun To Tear The World Veil," October 24, 1939. "Atomic Scale Nears Intangible Reign," April 27, 1940. "Drama Of Atomic Bomb Found Climax in July 16 Test," September 26, 1945. And for haunting and haughty images, see *Life* magazine photographer Loomis Dean's stark renderings of mannequins in the desert—they are vintage certainly but the black and white images are iconic.

Numerous reports from the United Nations Population Fund and also the Food and Agricultural Organization. The Commission On Population and Development held a Session in

April 2013 on New Trends in Immigration. Lisa Evans, "Global Employment: What Is The World's Employment Rate," *Guardian*, January 25, 2011. James Hopkins, "Human Population Crisis," cosmosmith.com, 2012. Doug Struck, "The Avoided Topic: How Do We Stop More Babies?" *Boston Globe*, May 2, 2014. Howard Steven Friedman, "10 Countries With The Largest Projected Population Growth," *Huffington Post*, updated April 1, 2012. "Global Employment Trends For Youth, 2013: A Generation At Risk," International Labour Organization at ilo .org, May 8, 2013. "The Rise and Spread of the Consumer Class," Worldwatch Institute, 2013. "State of the World Population, 2014: The Power of 1.8 Billion," The United Nations Population Fund, 2014. "Preventing A Deeper Jobs Crisis," International Labour Organization, February 10, 2012. "The Future Of Global Muslim Population," Pew Forum on Religion and Public Life, November 20, 2014. Eric Rosenbaum, "Megatrends," *CNBC* Special Report, August 8, 2013. Linda Yueh, "Rise Of The Global Middle Class," *BBC News*, June 18, 2013. Lily Kuo, "The World's Middle Class Will Number 5 Billion by 2030," Quartz, January 14, 2013. Shimelse Ali, Uri Dadush, "The Global Middle Class is Bigger Than We Thought," *Foreign Policy*, May 16, 2012. By the same authors, "A New Measure Of The Global Middle Class," *Vox*, June 2, 2012.

"Beijing to Cut New Car Registration by Two Thirds," *China Post*, December 24, 2010. Steve Clemons, "The New Power of the Global Middle Class," *The Atlantic*, February 21, 2012. Rana Foroohar, "An Unstable and Less Liberal Global Middle Class," *Newsweek*, March 5, 2010. "Competing for the Global Middle Class," *strategy&*, January 8, 2012. "Global Trends 2030: Alternative Worlds," U.S. National Intelligence Council, December 2012. Daniel T Griswold, "More Like Us: The Growth of the Global Middle Class," *The Globalist*, February 22, 2010. Peter Finn, "Report Sees Middle Class Growing, Islamist terrorism subsiding by 2030," *Washington Post*, December 10, 2012. Alan Murray, "Surge," *Wall Street Journal*, July 18, 2013. Stephen Fidler, "Two-Track Future Imperils Global Growth," *Wall Street Journal*, January 22, 2014. "A World To Conquer" *Economist*, May 31,2014. Amartya Sen, "Why India Trails China," *New*

York Times, June 20, 2013. Geoffrey Gertz and Homi Karas, "The New Global Middle Class: A Cross-Over from West to East," *Brookings*, March 2010. "The Future Of Everything," *Wall Street Journal*, July 8, 2014. Isabel Ortiz and Matthew Cummins, "When The Global Crisis and the Youth Bulge Collide," Unicef report, February 2012. George Will, "Rancid 'Recovery' Is Failing the Young," *New York Post*, May 31, 2014.

CHAPTER TWENTY: *THE CYCLONE*

JANE PERLEZ, "U.S. AND CHINA Press for Influence in Myanmar," *New York Times*, March 31, 2012. "The Lady and The Peacock: The Life of Aung San Suu Kyi," podcast by the Woodrow Wilson Center hosted by Peter Popham, May 27, 2012 (and a book of the same title, published by The Experiment, New York.) "In Myanmar, Daw Aung San Suu Kyi Granted a Passport," *New York Times*, May 9, 2012. "Aung San Suu Kyi Voices Concern Over Burma Violence," *Guardian*, October 4, 2011. Randy James, "Aung San Suu Kyi," *Time*, May 15, 2009. Steve Erlanger, "In Isolation, The Burmese Vote and then Wait . . . " *New York Times*, June 30, 1990. "Burma Junta Releases Democracy Leader Suu Kyi," *Fox News*, November 13, 2010. "Burma Democracy Icon Calls Her Detention Illegal," *Toronto Star*, November 18, 2010. "Aung San Suu Kyi—A Life For Myanmar," *Deutsche Welle*, April 8, 2014. Other stories from *Deutsche Welle*: "The Uprising of 1988," August 8, 2013, and "Gauck Pays tribute to Burma's Aung San Suu Kyi," February 11, 2014. "Cyclone Devastates Myanmar, 10,000 Feared Dead," *ABC News*, May 5, 2008. "Myanmar: Cyclone Nargis 2008 Facts and Figures," International Federation of Red Cross and Red Crescent Societies, May 3, 2011.

Shein Thu Aung, "Middle Class in Myanmar to Double by 2020," *Myanmar Business Today*, December 30, 2013. "The Middle Class in Vietnam, Myanmar Double," *The Nation*, December 23, 2013. Stephen P. Groff, "Middle Class Myanmar?" *Huffington Post*, September 5, 2012. "Vietnam and Myanmar: Southeast Asia's New Growth Frontiers," Boston Consulting Group, December 17, 2013. Also by BCG, "Off The Beaten Path: Looking Beyond the Growth Thesis in Southeast Asia," December

6, 2012. Alan Taylor, "Myanmar's War on Opium," *The Atlantic,* February 2012. Motokazu Matsui, "Myanmar's Middle Class," *Nikkei Asian Review,* December 11, 2014. Thomas Fuller, "In Myanmar, The Euphoria of Reform Loses Its Glow," *New York Times,* July 4, 2014. Jane Perlez, "For Myanmar Muslim Minority, No Escape From Brutality," *New York Times,* March 14, 2014. "Myanmar Retail: An Unseen Opportunity?" Invest in Myanmar, December 7, 2012. David I. Steinberg, "Reexamining Growth and Poverty in Myanmar," In Asia (The Asia Foundation), June 25, 2014. Andrew Goodman, "The Opening Up of Burma: Burma's Foreign Investment Law," *Thailand Law Forum,* January 10, 2013. Tim Hume, "Aung San Suu Kyi's 'Silence' on the Rohingya: Has 'The Lady' Lost Her Voice?" CNN, May 31, 2014.

Elisa Griswold, "On the African Front," *New York Times,* June 15, 2014. John Defterious, "Nigeria: How Violence Threatens Revival," CNN, May 7, 2014. Geoff Dyer, "Beijing Invites U.S. to Link Up Over Africa," *Financial Times,* August 6, 2014. Wayne Arnold, Drew Hinshaw, "China Takes Wary Steps into New Africa Deals," *Wall Street Journal,* May 6, 2014. Nicholas Kulish, "Africans Open Fuller Wallets to the Future," *New York Times,* July 21, 2014. "Africa Rising," an advertising placement in the *New York Times* in conjunction with the U.S.-Africa Leaders Summit in Washington, D.C., August 4-6 2014, sponsored by Sonatrach, the Algerian state-owned oil company.

To understand the duality of robust growth and exacerbating poverty read the report, "The African Economic Outlook," produced annually by The UN Economic Commission For Africa, UNECA. John Defterious, "Nigeria: How Violence Threatens Revival," CNN, May 7, 2014. Kamahl Santamaria, "Counting the Cost—Nigeria," Al Jazeera, April 19, 2014. "Economic Outlook for the Nigerian Economy, 2013-2016," National Bureau of Statistics, February 2013. Daniel Magnowski, "Nigerian Economy Overtakes South Africa's On Rebased GDP," Bloomberg, April 7, 2014. "The Nigerian Economy Well Below Par," *Economist,* November 29, 2014. "The Nigerian Economy to Overtake the U.K. Economy in 2050, Experts Say," *Nairaland Forum,* February 13, 2015. "Micro, Small and Medium Businesses Get $500 Million Boost From World Bank and Development Partners," The World Bank, September 25, 2014.

There are numerous articles about the confluence of the oil glut at a time when the Nigerian Oil Minister, Diezani Alison-Madueke, holds the rotating presidency of OPEC. See "OPEC and the Oil Glut. An Oily Mess," *Economist,* February 25, 2015. Uri Friedman, "How Nigeria Became Africa's Largest Economy Overnight," *The Atlantic,* April 7, 2014. "Africa's New Number One," *Economist,* April 12, 2014. "Nigeria's Economic Policy Failing," *Premium Times,* September 13, 2012. Abiodun Alade, "Anyone Disparaging Nigeria's Economic Progress is Living in Denial," *Vanguard,* February 26, 2015. "The Nigerian Government Conscious of the Overdependence on Oil . . . " Economy, The Embassy of the Federal Republic of Nigeria.

After ignoring the famine that gripped Ethiopia from 1983, Western media turned its attention to the plight of these starving people when intrepid BBC field reporter Michael Buerk, in measured cadences, narrated searing images captured by Kenyan cameraman Mohammed Amin. Buerk's description of "the closest place to hell on earth" led rocker Bob Geldof to gather British and Irish rock royalty to form Band Aid in 1984 and record "Do They Know It's Christmas?" which topped charts around the globe and remains one of the highest-selling songs of all time. The following articles provide the details but nothing captures the hellishness like that BBC report.

Nahu Senay, "Improving Food Security in Drought Affected Areas of Ethiopia," International Federation of Red Cross and Red Crescent Societies, November 11, 2011. A dedicated follower of Food Insecurity in Ethiopia is Alemayehu G. Mariam, "A Glimpse of the Creeping Famine In Ethiopia," ECADF, February 10, 2014. Also: "There Is Famine in Ethiopia in 2014, But It Is Known By Other Fancy Names," Ethiomedia, October 27, 2014. And "Ethiopia's 'Silently' Creeping Famine," *Huffington Post,* January 11, 2010. Susan Franks, "Ethiopian Famine: How Landmark, BBC Report Influenced Modern Coverage," *Guardian,* October 22, 2014. Thomas P. Ofcansky and LaVerle Berry, editors, "Ethiopia: A Country Study," GPO for the Library of Congress, 1991. "The Ethiopian Famine," *New York Times* editorial, July 28, 2003. "The Politics of Famine," *Socialist Worker Review,* May 1985. Katherine Manson, "Ethiopia's Middle Class Rises, With Western Diseases in Tow," *Financial Times,* February 27, 2014. Getachew Mequanent, "Is the Rising Middle Class Good For Governance?"

AIGA Forum, September 23, 2011. Asmeret Hailesilasse, "Ethiopia: Emergent Middle Class Brings New Retail Culture in Addis," allafrica .com, September 22, 2013. Yoseph Mennoken, "Ethiopia: Middle Class Housing Registration to Commence This Week," allafrica.com, August 11, 2013. "African Middle Class Triples to more than 310m over Past 30 Years Due to Economic Growth and Rising Job Culture," African Development Bank, October 5, 2011. David Smith, "Ethiopia, 30 Years after the Famine," *The Guardian*, October 22, 2014. Jacques Enaudeau, "In Search of the African Middle Class," *The Guardian,* May 3, 2013. David Berhane,"The Middle Class in African Countries: AfDB Report," Horn Affairs, June 3, 2011. "Illicit Pleasures in Ethiopia. Addled in Addis," *Economist,* March 23, 2013. James Melik, "Africa's Middle Class: Fact or Fiction?," BBC, June 7, 2012. Richard Lough, "Ethiopia Pushes Retail Door Ajar To Foreigners," Reuters, May 26, 2014. Berhanu Fekade, "Report Places Ethiopia among 11 Nations for Prospective Middle Class in Africa," August 23, 2014. Jaco Maritz, "Africa's Middle Class—How Big Is It Really?" howwemadeitin-Africa.com. May 12, 2011. "Ethiopia in Profile," Surya Capital, July 2014.

Chapter Twenty-One: *America's Choice*

Kathy Chu, USA Today, "Yum Brands CEO Takes On The World—A Bite at a Time," *USA Today,* February 27, 2012. Shani Magosky, "Heed the Oracle of Kentucky (AKA Yum! Brands CEO David Novak)," *Huffington Post,* April 18, 2013. David Novak, *Taking People With You* (New York: Portfolio, 2012). Kevin Kruse, "Leadership Secrets from Yum! Brands CEO, David Novak," *Forbes* magazine, June 25, 2014. "David Novak Retiring as Yum! Brands CEO," *Insider Louisville,* May 1, 2014. The CEOTV Show with Robert Reiss, Interview with David Novak, February 8, 2013. Barney Wolf, "David Novak's Global Vision," QSR, May 2012. Adam Bryant, "At Yum Brands, Rewards for Good Work," *New York Times,* July 11, 2009. Christopher Poirier, "Yum! Brands International Product Strategy: How the Double Down Went Global," *Huffington Post,* March 12, 2013. Maggie Lake, The David Novak Interview, CNN, February 11, 2008. Gloria McGonough-Taub, "Leadership Tips From The

Top," CNBC, January 9, 2012. "KFC Named Most Trusted Quick Service Restaurant Brand in India by the Brand Trust Report," franchising.com, March 3, 2015. Shelley DuBois, "Yum Brands Faces Chicken Troubles in China," *Fortune,* May 9, 2013. Charles Riley, "China Trouble Deepens for Yum Brands," CNN, February 4, 2013. Tracey Ryniec, "Problems in China Continue To Plague Yum Brands," *Forbes* magazine, October 21, 2013. "Problems in China Fail to Diminish Yum Brands Long Term Appeal," Seeking Alpha, October 9, 2013. Diksha Dutta, "How Yum! Brands India Expansion is Deviating From Global Strategy," vccircle.com, February 26, 2014. For company background: "Strategy Report For Yum! Brands," Vector Strategy Group, April 14, 2010. "Yum! Brands Harvard Business School Case 712-472," by Jordan Siegel and Christopher Poliquin, revised October 2012. "Yum Brands Realigns Business Divisions To Propel Global Growth," Market Watch, November 20, 2013. "Celebrating 10 Years of Global Growth," *Restaurant News,* October 15, 2007.

"The Tata Group: Out of India," *Economist,* March 3, 2011. Shivani Vola, "India's Tata Group Maps U.S. Expansion," *New York Times,* April 18, 2013. Eva Dou, "Xiaomi Expects Sales To Surge in 2015," *Wall Street Journal,* March 5, 2015. Juro Osawa, Gillian Wong, Rick Carew, "Xiaomi Becomes the World's Most Valuable Tech Start Up," *Wall Street Journal,* December 29, 2014. "Sorry Jack: Alibaba Founder No Longer Tops *Forbes'* China Billionaires List," *Tech In Asia,* March 5, 2015. Also from techinasia.com: "Xiaomi Becomes China's Top Smart Phone Brand For First Time in 2014, Whips Samsung," February 17, 2015. Interbrand, Best Global Brands, 2014 (and prior years). "BOOF!: BOOF with Food Panda," foodeverywhere.com, August 1, 2012. "A World To Conquer," *Economist,* May 31, 2014. Also review the speakers and materials for the *Economist* 5th Annual Health Care in Asia event, March 20, 2014. Bruce Einhorn, "In Asia Public Health Care Gets Less Public," *Bloomberg,* September 9, 2010. Ames Gross and Elaine C. Conavay, "Analysis of Asia's Changing Health Care Delivery Systems," Pacific Bridge Medical, August 5, 1997. "Hospital Companies Prepare to Meet Surging Demand for Health Care in Asia," *Economist,* May 17, 2014. Jason Shafrin, "Healthcare Systems in East Asia," *Healthcare Economist,* April 18, 2007. Stephen Lock, "The State of Healthcare In Southeast Asia," edelman.com, December 20, 2013.

CHAPTER TWENTY-TWO: *MOJO FOUND*

In addition to the many references used to summarize this statement of opportunities facing our middle class, there are a few more places where added color from outside our country can be useful.

Timothy Lane, deputy governor of the Bank of Canada has a great ability to stand above the oil fray and make clear assessments of world price and delivery moves independent of national boundaries. He is a frequent speaker, but I point to his remarks of January 13, 2015, at the Madison International Trade Association in Madison, Wisconsin, as particularly on point given the price slide and the likely impact on world oil reaction.

I also commend the *Economist* coverage of developments in Asia, which they cover extremely well. Their special report "A World to Conquer" gives a great perspective on the ways that Asian business is surging ahead and also where there remain unique opportunities for the Western powers that are motivated to participate in what is unfolding in the East.

INDEX